TRIAL PSYCHOLOGY

Communication and Persuasion in the Courtroom

TRIAL PSYCHOLOGY

Communication and Persuasion in the Courtroom

Margaret C. Roberts, Ph.D., J.D.
Trial Consultants, Inc.

Butterworth Legal Publishers
Austin, Texas

The Butterworth Group of Companies

Butterworths is a worldwide publishing group with companies in Australia, Canada, New Zealand, Singapore, South Africa, the United Kingdom, and the United States. In the U.S. there are legal publishing branches in Austin, Boston, St. Paul, Seattle, and Clearwater, Florida.

Library of Congress Cataloging-in-Publication Data

Roberts, Margaret C.

Trial psychology: communication and persuasion in the courtroom/Margaret C. Roberts.

p. cm.

Includes index.

ISBN 0-409-25105-4 (loose-leaf)

1. Psychology, Forensic. 2. Trial practice—United States. I. Title.

KF8922.R63 1987

347.73'75—dc19

[347.30775]

Printed in the United States of America

ACKNOWLEDGMENTS

I wish to thank my husband, Aubrey L. Roberts, who as an attorney hired me years ago as a trial consultant, for his wisdom and encouragement. His kindness and unselfish giving of his time to this endeavor is gratefully acknowledged. I would like to express my appreciation to Lillian B. Hardwick for research and drafting assistance. Thanks are also extended to Marguerite Rheinberger and the law firm of Moore, Dickson, Roberts, and Ratliff of Sweetwater, Texas. Very special thanks go to David Wyke and Carroll Brown for their patience and never-failing faith in my ability. I would like to express my gratitude to the editor and publisher, A. Michael Beaird, for his guidance and appreciation of the diversified areas of psychology and law.

In conclusion, I would like to dedicate this book to my parents, Bill and Ila Covington; my son, Blake Covington Roberts; and my husband, Aubrey L. Roberts. Their love and support have made this long process possible.

TABLE OF CONTENTS

CHAPTER 1
INTRODUCTION

SYNOPSIS

CHAPTER 1
INTRODUCTION

I. *THE EXPERT ATTORNEY*

Having acquired at least one postgraduate degree, attorneys have every right to feel that a single discipline is enough to master. And with the increasing requirement of continuing legal education, even the formal learning experience does not end with law school graduation. For the trial attorney, filing and drafting pleadings and motions in accordance with federal, state, and local rules, planning and participating in discovery, keeping abreast of changes in relevant laws, and knowing about and understanding past and recent cases are all components of a full-time occupation. Moreover, state and national bar rules at least indirectly speak to all of these tasks by requiring that an attorney be competent.

While competence can mean not missing a filing deadline, being aware of controlling authority, and preparing for trial, what competence means during trial is far less clear. If the attorney writes briefs like Charles Alan Wright, examines witnesses like Racehorse Haynes, and closes like F. Lee Bailey, is he nevertheless competent as a trial attorney when his client is convicted?

> The role of competence in law is rather unique since it is not only an attribute important for its practitioners to possess, but is also part of the very cornerstone on which the adversary system of Anglo-American law is based. This is the principle that if the parties to a dispute are equally represented in a legal forum, the truth will out. . . . It appears that while professional competence remains a central focus of legal policy debates, it has been dealt with almost entirely rhetorically rather than empirically. . . .
>
> The one area of practice that seems to bear the brunt of most criticism is trial advocacy.[1]

While it is easily admitted that law school does not and cannot be expected to develop "all the skills of the competent trial lawyer," it is predicted that either the law school curriculum or undergraduate prerequisites will come to include a deeper study of "other social disciplines."[2]

A. Psychology

A 1984 article suggested a means for determining attorney expertise. The credentials of its authors explain its practical yet scientific orientation: one is a professor of management sciences and psychology; one, a professor of psychology with a law degree; and one, a senior systems engineer at Honeywell, Inc. They observe that "what is needed to assess the validity of many of the criticisms directed toward legal practice and training. . . is a representation or documentation of the structure of expertise in legal practice—especially in trial advocacy since this represents the focus of most complaints."[3]

The authors admit the impossibility of specifying exactly how each of them relates to an ultimate characterization of expertise, but suggest certain propositions of expertise, each of which can be tested. Also, each of the following propositions assumes equal knowledge of the law, equal availability of the case facts, and equal willingness to expend time and effort in preparation:

1. Expert attorneys are better at analyzing legal situations. . . have more complete knowledge for generating action in legal situations. . . . the ability. . . to recognize both legal and people variables. . . .
2. Experts are better at anticipating possible future situations. . . .
3. Experts have more adequate (in the sense of more complete and/or correct) implicit psychological theories. In the last analysis, whatever an attorney does must be assessed against its potential impact on people (client, judge, jury, etc.). If the non-expert has inadequate knowledge, or fails to utilize appropriate knowledge in the case at hand, he runs the risk of an inadequate action, reducing the probability of success, and failing in his obligations to his client.
4. Expert attorneys are most sensitive to the nuances of particular legal contexts.[4]

Certainly the first three of these propositions imply or directly rely on an understanding of psychology. Broadly, psychology is the science of mind and behavior. More particularly, it involves the mental or behavioral characteristics of an individual or group.

Probably no advice as to trial expertise neglects a consideration of the fact finder. A recent volume of an ABA periodical bears a single descriptive word on its cover (apart from the journal title and date)—Persuasion. One of the articles makes the following observation: "The advocate must be a psychologist. He must understand human nature, and he must know how his listeners think, their habits, desires, and emotions."[5]

Another authority begins, "Trial lawyers are to a remarkable degree, professional applied social psychologists."[6] One difference in the professions is that attorneys are interested in empirical results (the strategies that work) while social psychologists focus on creating and testing theories to explain the results.[7] To the extent, however, that social psychology describes human behavior, attorneys can make practical use of the tested theories. The authors present a table containing "[a]ttitude change phenomena relevant to persuasion in the courtroom," admitting that many of these "phenomena" appear to echo common sense. However, sometimes the research "shows which of several competing common senses is correct," and "demonstrates the limits of the obvious." In other words, knowing *why* a particular strategy works allows for the modification of the strategy to accommodate different circumstances. As an example, the authors note the reported tactic used by Clarence Darrow to distract the jury from attending to opposing counsel's closing remarks. He would place a wire inside the cigar he was smoking so that the ash would not fall. According to the story, as the ash grew longer, the jury became more fascinated with it and less attentive to counsel's argument.[8] Given the ban on smoking in modern courtrooms, it would be interesting to discover what devices could have similar effects today, and yet still not be disruptive to the proceedings and/or grounds for a new trial.

Of course, the simplest way to find out the psychology of the fact finder and what will induce attentiveness and belief, is to ask the fact finder. Judge Joe R. Greenhill, former Chief Justice of the Texas Supreme Court, acted as if he had been asked such questions in an article published in 1981, containing suggestions for attorneys presenting cases before him and the other justices.[9] Judge Greenhill advises on procedural matters, such as time limitations on oral argument, as well as practical concerns, such as the provision of an appendix. But he also reveals particularly persuasive techniques, which have psychological bases:

> Distinguish unfavorable cases if you can. If you cannot, and they are crucial, urge the court to overrule them. In any event, be candid with the court. It really helps.
>
> . . . .

> Refer to the court as "the *court*," not: gentlemen, men, buddies, you fellows. . . . It is not a social visit.[10]

Thus, one representative of the court has revealed what will and will not work with them.

Direct questioning does not succeed with jurors for many reasons. While this subject receives greater treatment below, it is enough here to comment on the differences between judges and jurors. Appellate judges are experienced in their task; they know what they are looking for from attorneys. Even if jurors have served on juries before, they cannot generalize from their one or two experiences on techniques that will draw their attention, cause complex facts and issues to make sense to them, or create belief and confidence, regardless of the variables of facts, charges, parties, and counsel. Instead, it may be far more useful to predict juror reactions based on tested theories of human behavior. Still another approach is to analyze jurors as a speaker would analyze an audience and structure presentations accordingly.[11] Even this approach has a basis in psychology.

Thus, this book presents that part of the study of human behavior that has relevance to the trial attorney. Specifically, it examines the importance of order effects—whether who goes first or last really matters—ascertaining whether such effects observable in scientific studies survive in the reality of jury experience. It also explores the importance of fulfilling a juror's expectations on what a trial and its participants will be and look like. Finally, a chapter devoted to juror analysis suggests how an attorney can select and pre-analyze his audience, as well as how jurors' verdicts can be affected by the purely procedural imposition of a particular decision rule (unanimous or some designated majority).

B. *Rhetoric*

Aristotle and Quintilian, authors of *Rhetoric* and *Institutes of Oratory*, respectively, were recently called "geniuses who knew how to make language work. . . . They learned by raw observation of human behavior what makes arguments tell—how to persuade, how to change the minds of biased listeners. . . . Aristotle created the art of rhetoric."[12] Some may be interested to see that the term "rhetoric" is paired with the concept of persuasion. "Rhetoric" is in fact persuasive discourse.[13]

Many believe that "rhetoric" is simply a synonym for flowery language. That misconception may stem in part from the extensive cataloging of formal oratorical devices (figures of speech, such as similes and metaphors) by the classical rhetoricians, an exercise perhaps more indicative of industry than anything else. "Teachers of Greek and Latin rhetoric had such industry; and they amassed so many terms that they had a name for the formal design in practically any expression possible to words."[14] While a rhetorical critic sometimes does no more than list the stylistic devices used by a speaker, such an enumeration reveals nothing about persuasion unless it is related to the speaker's message and intent.[15] "Aristotle suggests use of metaphors because they lend clarity, charm, and distinction to speech, but they must fit comfortably, without stretching. Their relevance must be immediately apparent."[16]

One modern author, reviewing the rhetorical theories of Aristotle, Cicero, Quintilian, and St. Augustine (which spanned 750 years), indicates all of the following as "purely traditional evidences of the rhetorical motive":[17]

a. persuasion
b. exploitation of opinion
c. verbal deception
d. eloquence, ingratiation, for its own sake
e. the art of proving opposites

While Aristotle's definition of "rhetorician" encompassed the speaker's moral purpose,[18] the above list more practically indicates the applications of rhetoric.

The section titled "The Juror as a Unique Subject" lists certain questions that jurors seek to have answered when the attorneys give their opening statements. Among these is, "Who sounds like he thinks like I do?"[19] In other words, the juror seeks identification with the attorney. This is precisely what a persuasive speaker seeks to establish with his audience:

> The key term for the old rhetoric was "persuasion" and its stress was upon deliberate design. The key term for the "new" rhetoric would be "identification," which can include a partially "unconscious" factor in appeal. "Identification" at its simplest is also a deliberate device, as when the politician seeks to identify himself with his audience. In this respect, its equivalents are plentiful in Aristotle's *Rhetoric*.[20]

Of course, before a speaker can sound like he thinks the same way that his audience does, he must first have an understanding of how his audience thinks, which he attempts through audience analysis. For the attorney, such analysis begins with the *voir dire* and the demographic data provided for each of the people in the jury pool. The skillful attorney listens to responses by individual veniremen, attempting to read unstated biases and predispositions into phrasing and word choice. In the same way, such an attorney employs particular language, phrasing, and tone in his opening statement, closing argument, and presentation of evidence, seeking to convince the jurors of a bond between him and them:

> Jurors will feel closer to a lawyer or client who seems to share their own standards, background or life experiences, with whom they can identify and empathize. This causes them to lean more in one direction than another. If they feel that a lawyer is arguing from a shared, basic point of view about life, then, although the opposing arguments in the case can be clear, decisions often revolve around who seems to see truth as they do.[21]

Especially in light of the moral purpose intrinsically associated with classical rhetoric, some may rebel at the suggestion that an attorney may present himself differently for different audiences and different subjects. But every speaker has a multitude of dimensions that are not revealed to any single audience due to dictates of time, practicality, and relevance. Understanding that, for jurors, the opening statement is the beginning of "a very intense personal relationship" between them and counsel, a communications expert advises attorneys that jurors will "begin designing a persona for you, to understand that this is the way you communicate, to predict that this is the way you'll behave and this is what they can expect of you."[22]

"Persona" is a term long used in speech criticism to refer to the group of characteristics describing the speaker. Since everything about a speaker cannot be known from a single presentation, then only his speaking self on that occasion (his persona for that speech) can be described. "Persona," however, is also a psychological term, with its Jungian connection given as part of its definition in some dictionaries. For Jung, the persona was a mask, a "concession to the external world."[23] Therefore, the creation of a persona has a place in the discussion of trial psychology as much as in persuasion.

The rhetorical purist should not long concern himself with the moral propriety of devices used by a speaker, since "pure persuasion" must always remain an ideal—two minds can never perceive the same subject in precisely the same way. While the speaker seeks a certain reaction from his audience, he cannot expect them to respond as he wishes for all of the reasons he gives. He may, by accident or design, select the very words that may trigger the reaction he wants. He may also create the opposite reaction. Additionally, members of the audience may react as he desires, but independently of his persona or argument; in other words, despite the purest of speaker motives (e.g., doing justice), an audience may react for impure reasons (extracting revenge). In the last analysis, a good argument, supported by strong facts, may morally *warrant* presentation by a well-planned (i.e., contrived) persona.

Finally, psychological and rhetorical principles provide categorizations for and analysis of types of argument "proof." The classical terms of ethos, pathos, and logos are the sources of the familiar ethical, emotional, and logical appeals. Ethical appeal is the persuasive ability of the persona alone, measured by the degree of respect he commands and credibility he establishes. Emotional appeal targets the sentiments, and logical appeal, the mind.

Thus, an additional focus of this book is the elements of persuasion. Because most of the trial presentation is verbal (meaning "of words") and most of that is oral (as opposed to written), the emphasis is on verbal components more than nonverbal. However, the effect of certain nonverbal communications on the jury is also examined. Also, while a trial is filled with words, there may be only one place where persuasive discourse as envisioned by Aristotle (i.e., a speech) appears—in the closing arguments. Attorneys are cautioned not to argue the facts in the opening statement, and evidence presentations are exchanges, not speeches. However, the methods of eliciting testimony, the structure and phrasing of questions, and word choice in the opening statement can all produce desired effects in the audience. Therefore, these topics are examined with the ultimate goal of arriving at theoretical guidelines for the trial attorney.

II. *A VALIDATION OF EXPERIMENTAL RESULTS*

Probably any discipline partly justifies its method of operation through criticism of the *modus operandi* of other disciplines. The literary critic understandably has a certain amount of disdain for those of us who read a book once, pausing to reflect over only a couple of phrases or passages, and then set it on a shelf to gather dust. The critic might say that we have missed the fascinating character development, the deft handling of a first-person narrative, and the use of imagery to convey a message apart from the plot. The interesting thing is that even within a discipline, there are operational differences. One critic might explain a book with biographical criticism (i.e., knowing about the author is the only way to understand what he or she has written), while another will say that any written material "means" only what its readers say it means.

Psychologists wage a similar intellectual battle within their own discipline. Predictions of human behavior must be based on descriptions of past behavior and reasons for that behavior. Theoretically, because the subjects are humans, the reasons can be elicited from them. Alternatively, the reasons can be inferred. At least two potential problems exist in the eliciting process. First, people may simply not be honest; if their real reason for doing something would not reflect favorably on them, they may substitute a more socially acceptable reason. Jurors provide an excellent example of this phenomenon: probably no juror would admit it if he determined the guilt of the defendant based on race or ethnicity. A second problem in eliciting reasons for behavior from the subjects is that they may not *know* why they acted as they did. It has been suggested that "the real cause of a juror's decision will be in many instances a factor he himself is only dimly aware of and perhaps unable to articulate."[24] That could probably be said of many of the decisions made by most people, particularly when they concern other people. We should also understand that the kind of reasons elicited for those interested in predicting human behavior is not the kind that we are accustomed to giving. Reasons such as "because I thought I should" or "because I thought that was right" are not informative; what the researcher looks for is *why* we had those thoughts.

Because of the problems with the eliciting process, inference can be more reliable for formulating reasons. As an example, if you are ever in an automobile accident, some written report of that accident (such as that filed by the police or by you, with your insurance company) will probably have a question about the weather (whether it was wet or dry) or the visibility of any traffic signs or signals. The question is not likely to be, "Did you hit the other car because a shrub obscured the stop sign?" Instead, once so many accidents have occurred at a location where an obscured stop sign has been reported, the inference will be that the obscured stop sign is causing accidents. Now, if the reports variously contain information as to wet weather or the competence of one of the drivers (such as driving without a license or under the influence of alcohol), the obscured stop sign may not emerge as a reason or may emerge as only one of several reasons. One way to test the legitimacy of a reason is to eliminate all other possible reasons. This can be done statistically through a determination of how often accidents have occurred at the same location even when the driver was competent and the weather was dry.

Because the mathematics of such a procedure usually lose all but the scientists (and because of the difficulty in formulating bug-free statistical methodology), an acceptable alternative is simulation. That way, competent drivers, unfamiliar with the route, can drive it in dry weather. If they whiz past the obscured stop sign and hit a cardboard replica of another car, it can be inferred that the fact that the stop sign was hidden caused the accident. Naturally, simulation also can have problems. Since the drivers know they are subjects in an experiment about driving, they may drive extra carefully and be more alert than they otherwise would; i.e., they may not behave as non-experimental drivers would. Conversely, knowing they are in an experiment, they may feel free to drive as they never would in real life, being confident that any dangers have been artificially removed. Thus, they may exceed the speed limit and, if they have an accident, thereby indicate still another cause. There is even a remote possibility that some of them may see the stop sign but, knowing that the experiment has probably removed all danger, keep on driving, just to see what will happen.

Literature about juror behavior is particularly concerned about the data-collecting methodology, with each study often beginning with a justification, more than just an explanation, of the method it reflects. It is somewhat ironic that jury simulations receive as much criticism as they do, as if the opportunity existed to record actual deliberations and quiz the jurors then and there as to what they meant by each thing they said and why they "really" decided as they did. In general, the criticism follows the line of a continuum. At one end are people, sometimes college students, often sitting in a classroom, individually answering questions in writing after having read a transcript of a fictitious case. At the other end are people drawn from an actual jury pool, sitting in a courtroom, viewing a videotaped trial, deliberating before a camera, and delivering their verdicts to a real judge, who thanks them and dismisses them. As a researcher, depending on where you are on the continuum, you justify your methodology by noting its superiority over the methods below it, which rely on even less realistic subjects and setting. Following are some of the expressed advantages of (or justifications for) simulations or experiments, realistic or not. Then, responses are offered to some of the more vigorous objections to the experimental approach. Last, a perspective for valuing experimental findings is suggested.

A. *A Justification of Simulation*

"The term 'simulation' is often used to describe any empirical study of legal issues that is not conducted in an actual court setting, and it is tempting to believe that the quality of such a study depends in part on how closely the study simulates or reproduces a court trial."[25] First, every lawyer reading this should understand that "legal issues" is not used in the same way he uses that term daily. The authors, Lind and Walker, are not talking about estoppel or laches; rather, they are referring to legal theory or procedures, and on a grand scale. For example, assuming the validity of the adversary method of presenting evidence (as opposed to the inquisitorial approach), how might a proposed change in welfare hearings or criminal discovery affect adversariness?[26] Whenever a study seeks to test a theory, they argue, it need not closely resemble a court setting, nor need the subjects be like real judges or jurors. The conditions of the test must only be those that will clearly test for the basic statement.[27]

As an example, Lind and Walker describe the proposition that parties to a dispute will be more satisfied with the resolution and will believe the resolution process to be more fair when the adversary (instead of some other) method is used. In the many experiments conducted to test this proposition, they saw no problem in using college students as subjects, since the proposition was not limited to any certain type of party or dispute.[28] Similarly, another experiment tested the idea that, with an adversary method, opposing counsel with relatively equal skill will search more diligently for facts than if they were nonpartisan investigators. Since only the "attorney motive" needed to present in the subjects, and no particular degree of legal skill (just so long as it was about the same in all subjects), the researchers used law students instead of actual trial attorneys.[29] The suggestion is that little information can be gained in the testing of certain propositions by a full-blown trial simulation. In fact, a real or highly realistic simulation could result in a loss of experimental control.

"To be confident that a particular cause is actually producing an observed effect, it is desirable to hold all conditions besides the independent or causal variable constant.[30] That is literally impossible to do with real trials, each having many unique characteristics. But potentially confounding variables can be controlled in a simulation. Also, the personal characteristics of the individual jurors expand the number of variables exponentially. A recorded (stimulus) trial, though, can be shown to many juries, with "multiple replications remov[ing] the potentially confounding effect of individual differences such as social class or gender."[31] Also, with a stimulus trial, shown to different juries, different pieces of evidence can be introduced to test their effects on the verdicts.[32]

The proponents of the highly realistic simulations appear to value such simulations primarily because of what they reveal about jury deliberations, about which we would otherwise have very little empirical evidence.[33] Their motives seem to be to cause the mock jurors to feel so much like real jurors that they will do and say in the jury room exactly what they would do and say if they were judging a real trial. Simon describes an experiment in which the jury was composed of members of a jury pool, instructions were given by a real judge, a recording of a trial was played in a courtroom, deliberations occurred in a jury room, and the verdict was reported to the judge at the end of the day. She admits that, in the opening minutes of the deliberations, the mock jurors seemed to doubt the value of the experiment; "but then something quite dramatic occurred. The jurors became so involved in defending their own interpretation of the case and in convincing others of the correctness of their views that they forgot that their verdicts would have no practical significance."[34]

On the surface, Simon's finding of juror involvement could rebut the frequent observation that "[a] real jury decides the fate of an actual defendant; a mock jury usually knows that its decision will have no such impact."[35] However, the two are not mutually exclusive. What Simon describes looks more like ego involvement than concern for the fate of another human being; also, it should not be forgotten that the mock jurors were being recorded, no matter how unobtrusive the process may have been; such a stage could have induced more of a performance than otherwise. Moreover, one widely supported idea is that most of the jurors have reached their decision before they retire to the jury room; therefore, one inescapable conclusion is that "jurors' talk may often be not very revealing."[36] If even one of these propositions is true, then perhaps the predictable juror behavior that researchers seek to describe need not be inferred from real jurors or even mock jurors in a trial setting. In other words, if the behavior is the same even without the trial trappings, then findings in experiments with no relation to trial could nevertheless be relevant.

Testing for purely behavioral as opposed to "juror behavioral" characteristics also solves another problem faced by simulators—which medium to use. Of course, a recorded trial, regardless of the medium, can be shown to multiple juries and is much easier to present than a live trial. Simon notes that the advantage of a tape recording over a film is primarily cost, with a film being much more expensive. She also suggests that a film might produce an "'audience' reaction" in the jurors, causing them to be passive and less attentive.[37] (If the corollary is that the juror listening to a tape must work harder and be more attentive, lest he miss something, how closely this simulates a real juror experience may be in doubt.)

Hastie, although structuring an experiment with "considerable similarity to the actual criminal jury trials to which its conclusions are to be generalized," notes several differences between the experiment and a real trial. First, researchers and not court officers conducted the procedure. Second, the *voir dire* was unrealistically brief. Third, the experimental trial was videotaped, not live. Fourth, the mock trial was shorter than a comparable live trial would have been. Fifth, mock jurors completed questionnaires indicating verdict preferences before deliberation. Sixth, the mock jurors knew they were being recorded. Seventh, they knew their decisions would not affect the fate of a real defendant.[38] However, he concludes that "[t]he present experimental procedures were carefully designed to match actual trial conditions closely on the major dimensions [being subject, setting, and stimulus material] along which generalization [to real trials] would depend."[39]

Again, the caution seems to concern the purpose of any experiment. If the hypothesis is that jurors in a trial of alleged bank robbers will focus more in deliberations on the details of the getaway car than on the definition of grand theft, then certainly a stimulus of a robbery trial and the act of deliberation would need to be present in the experiment. By extension, if the courtroom environment will more strongly cause mock jurors to believe that they are acting like jurors in deliberation, then even such physical surroundings could be justified. On the other hand, the proposition may be that the sight of a physically attractive person, when it precedes other information about that person, can cause the seer to attribute unwarranted ability to that person. There is no need to place this kind of an experiment in a trial setting, as it concerns general human behavior. For an analysis of the juror, the question becomes whether something about the trial experience negates or otherwise affects otherwise normal behavior.

B. *Responses to Specific Criticisms of Experiments*

Experiments are faulted in two main areas: subjects and settings. Hastie notes that "the vast majority of jury simulations have used students as mock jurors," and that the differences between students and real jurors threaten the validity of jury simulations in the real world. Also, in "highly simplified simulations," mock jurors reportedly have extremely limited involvement,[40] apparently meaning that they do not take their role very seriously.

In response, it should be observed that mock jurors have a much more difficult task than subjects being tested purely for human behavior. The latter subjects are theoretically asked merely, "What would you do if you were confronted with this set of facts?" while the mock jurors are asked, "What would you do if you were confronted with this set of facts *and* you were a juror?" Being a juror is not only another fact; it is a role the subject must play while considering other data. A parallel would be asking a political candidate, "What would you do if you were confronted with this set of facts *and* you were the President of the United States?" Supposedly the candidates report how they, as individuals, view issues; once one is elected President, he is expected to act as he did beforehand, since that is supposedly the basis on which he was elected. The simulations attempt to avoid the additional task of role playing by making the mock juror feel so much like a juror that he does not believe or remember he is playing a role; whether they actually accomplish that is far from clear.

Second, even if a real jury's deliberations were analyzed, the results would not necessarily accurately guide expectations as to other real deliberations. Naturally, this is due to individual differences in the members of the jury. Therefore, although college students are not like real jurors, real jurors in one instance may not be like real jurors in any other instance. In one experiment, in which the mock jurors (who were college students) appeared especially lenient, the researcher explained that (1) they were colledge students (i.e., younger people are generally more empathic) and (2) their campus was physically close to Attica and the experiment was conducted soon after the prison riots there.[41] Conceivably, the riots could have had a similar effect on the juror-aged population in the area, which would mean that an analysis of even a real jury from an actual trial there could not be generalized for trials elsewhere. Similarly, in another experiment, the researchers made an initial observation that their subjects, *actual jurors who were interviewed following the final verdict*, were not representative, in demographic composition, of jurors in that locale or state.[42] In other words, the results of that survey could not be generalized to apply to other trials even in that locale. All of these studies, however, make a contribution to our understanding of human behavior.[43]

Another major criticism of simulations is that they single out an individual stimulus that becomes buried in the complexity of trial; therefore, the reaction to such a stimulus in an experimental setting has little relation to how jurors in a real trial would react to it:

> The variables typically manipulated in laboratory studies of jury decision making (e.g., victim attractiveness or defendant likability) constitute a minute fraction of the total stimulus field to which a real juror is actually exposed in the courtroom. Such truncated experimental settings give undue prominence to factors that are of much less importance when embedded in the more complex courtroom setting.
>
> . . . .
>
> Because of the information vacuum that exists, one would be hard put to find any convincing basis for directly linking the findings of simulation research to the processes and outcomes of real trials.[44]

So how did these researchers proceed to combat the "information vacuum" of experiments? By quizzing real jurors following their trial experiences. Of course, these were the jurors that were found to be not representative of others in their state. Also, no more than seven members of any jury agreed to participate in the interview.[45] While we would find useful any data that describe human behavior, and on that basis alone value the results of this experiment, they do not appear unique. That is, they appear consistent with the findings described by researchers who have conducted or studied jury experiments (e.g., Hastie and Simon), as well as characteristics of human behavior unrelated to the specific jury experience (e.g., personality traits).[46]

C. *A Rationale*

Hamlin, the communications expert who has postulated the needs that a jury seeks to have filled by counsel, gives a layman's explanation of the complicated psychological phenomenon known as first impression:

> It's a familiar and automatic process we all go through unconsciously, whenever we first meet anyone or judge anything—from picking clothes to picking a mate. The judgments are made by instinct—viscerally, not cerebrally. They're based on feelings, not facts. We use our internal library of past experiences, of early conditioning and more recent information, as a reference. We use short cuts—stereotypes and prejudices—to categorize and hasten the process.[47]

People went through this process long before Asch described it in 1946.[48] What Asch did was tell us why and how we did it.

Similarly, no one needs to explain to us what a powerful effect first impressions have, or that, in a competition, the last performance has a position advantage. We "know" these things. What scientists do is tell us how and why we know them. Thus, experiments about human behavior serve to validate intuition and provide guidelines for foreign and as yet unexperienced situations. To the extent that we see conflicting data from various experiments, we step back and try to formulate a new hypothesis, one that will account for both sets of results. The experiments can actually substitute for the experiences that we have yet to have ourselves and help us to predict their outcome once we do live them. The goal of this book, then, is to provide trial attorneys with "more adequate. . . psychological theories" so that they can become "better at anticipating future situations."[49]

NOTES

1. Johnson, Johnson, & Little, *Expertise in Trial Advocacy: Some Considerations for Inquiry into Its Nature and Development,* 7 Campbell L. Rev. 119, 120–21 (1984).
2. McCullough & Underwood, 2 *Civil Trial Manual* 28 (1980).
3. Johnson, *supra* n.1, at 123.
4. *Id.* at 140–42.
5. Hanley, *Brush Up Your Aristotle*, Litigation, Winter 1986, at 39.
6. Saks & Hastie, *Social Psychology in Court* 100 (1978).
7. *Id.* at 101.
8. *Id.* at 102–105.
9. Greenhill, *Advocacy in the Texas Supreme Court,* 44 Tex. B.J. 624 (1981).
10. *Id.* at 626, 628.
11. *See, for example,* Hamlin, *What Makes Juries Listen* (1985).
12. Hanley, *supra* n.5, at 39.
13. I *Quintilian's Institutes of Oratory* 137–47 (J. Watson trans. 1899).
14. Burke, *A Rhetoric of Motives* 589 (1962).
15. Hochmuth [Nichols], *The Criticism of Rhetoric,* III *A History & Criticism of American Public Address* 21 (M. Hochmuth [Nichols] ed. 1955).
16. Hanley, *supra* n.5, at 41.
17. Burke, *supra* n.14, at 588.
18. *The Rhetoric of Aristotle* 7 (L. Cooper trans. 1932).
19. Hamlin, *supra* n.11, at 112.
20. Burke, *Rhetoric—Old and New,* V J. Gen. Educ. 204 (1951).
21. Hamlin, *supra* n.11, at 315.
22. *Id.* at 110.
23. Hochheimer, *The Psychotherapy of C.G. Jung* 36 (1969).
24. Kalven & Zeisel, *The American Jury* 486 (1966).
25. Lind & Walker, *Theory Testing, Theory Development; and Laboratory Research on Legal Issues,* 3 Law & Human Behavior 5 (1979).
26. *Id.* at 6.
27. *Id.* at 10.
28. *Id.* at 14.
29. *Id.* at 12.
30. Hastie, Penrod, & Pennington, *Inside the Jury* 39 (1983).
31. *Id.* at 39–40.
32. Simon, *The Jury and the Defense of Insanity* 34–35 (1967).
33. *Id.* at 42.
34. *Id.* at 38–39.
35. Hastie, et al., *supra* n.30, at 41.
36. Kalven & Zeisel, *supra* n.24, at 486; *also, see* "The Juror as a Unique Subject," section III of Chapter 2, *infra.*

37. Simon, *supra* n.32, at 40.

38. Hastie et al., *supra* n.30, at 42–44.

39. *Id.* at 45.

40. *Id.* at 40–41.

41. Izzett & Leginski, *Group Discussion and the Influence of Defendant Characteristics in a Simulated Jury Setting*, 93 J. Soc. Psychology 277 (1974).

42. Bridgeman & Marlowe, *Jury Decision Making: An Empirical Study Based on Actual Felony Trials*, 64 J. Applied Psychology 91, 93 (1979).

43. See this discussion in "The Juror as a Unique Subject," section III of Chapter 2, *infra*.

44. Bridgeman & Marlowe, *supra* n.42, at 92.

45. *Id.* at 92–93.

46. See this discussion in "The Juror as a Unique Subject, section III of Chapter 2, *infra*.

47. Hamlin, *What Makes Juries Listen* 108–109 (1985).

48. Asch, *Forming Impressions of Personality*, 41 J. Abnormal & Soc. Psychology 258 (1946).

49. Johnson, Johnson, & Little, *Expertise in Trial Advocacy: Some Considerations for Inquiry into Its Nature and Development*, 7 Campbell L. Rev. 140–41 (1984).

CHAPTER 2
ORDERING

SYNOPSIS

CHAPTER 2
ORDERING

S.W. Asch described in 1946 the phenomenal human ability to form an immediate and distinct impression of another person upon first sight.[1] While the focus of Asch's study was the process by which this impression is formed, its prime contribution to psychology is the validation of the term "first impression," along with its common implications.

To say there is a first impression is to allude to a second, a third, and a last, which suggests order. But if the impact of first impression, known as the primacy effect, were absolute, then all prosecutors (or plaintiff's attorneys), who ever gave a persuasive opening argument would always win for that reason alone. The fact that the evidence and opening arguments of defense counsel usually follow those of the prosecution (or plaintiff), when combined with the fact that jurors often decide for the defense, despite an effective prosecutor (or plaintiff's attorney), supports the proposition that he who has the last word has the advantage. That theory is based on the recency effect, or the idea that what one hears last is the most persuasive.

The apparently contradictory notions of primacy and recency, actually reconcilable, suggest legitimate considerations for the litigator. If whoever goes first has the advantage in certain circumstances, what are those circumstances? How does counsel who lacks that advantage counter? If the expected argument and evidence order (prosecution or plaintiff, then defense) is changed, what should the prosecution or plaintiff's attorney do differently to counter the loss of primacy? What should the defense do differently to counter the loss of recency? What do primacy and recency tell us about the most persuasive order of presenting evidence? Will a jury react to order in the same way as the subjects in primacy-recency experiments have reacted?

Being able to answer questions like these should make an attorney a more expert litigator by better enabling him to anticipate possible situations and to assess his words' actions against their potential impact on the judge and jury.[2]

I. THEORY: PRIMACY VS. RECENCY

If this were a book on psychology alone, you would now be presented with a barrage of experiments, results, and conclusions. It is, however, a book on trial psychology. What will follow is a description of enough experimental conclusions to convince you of the truth of the primacy and recency effects. (Actually, intuitively, and through personal experience, you believe in the clichés of "first impression" and "last word"; researchers' results will provide scientific verification while indicating variations of the effects.) Then, because order does not exist in a vacuum, critical elements that can enhance or destroy the advantage or disadvantage of position are examined. Consider, for example, whether the advantage of first place is lost when the prosecutor aesthetically offends the jury, or whether a jury's first view of the defendant at his most unattractive self does irreparable damage. Finally, a convincing reconciliation of primacy and recency is presented. Where appropriate, the relevance to the trial attorney of the proffered conclusions are suggested. Also, the details of experiments show the applicability of the studies to the trial situation.

A. *The Validating Experiments*

When we are given a string of data so great that it exceeds our short-term memory capacity and are later asked to recall or recognize pieces of the data, we are more likely to recall items at the beginning or end of the data string than items in the middle. "This hypothesis has been substantiated so consistently under so many different conditions that it has almost achieved the status of an empirical law."[3] The experiments testing for the primacy and recency effects often use lists of words or numbers and have used visual as well as auditory presentations. After the first list has been presented, the subjects are asked to repeat the words or numbers. Words at the beginning of the list are initially repeated by the subjects; in fact, the primacy effect on the first list is much higher than on later lists. Instead, the recency effect steadily increases with additional lists. Researchers tends to attribute this latter occurrence to a shift in learning process.[4]

A layman's explanation of what happens is that we mentally "rehearse" the first few words that we hear, thereby committing them to long-term memory. When the words continue to come, we must abandon that process, due to sheer data overload. Then we recite the list, knowing we are most deficient in the words at the end. In the second list, we seem to save room in the memory for the later words, which means we slight the rehearsal of the earlier words. Also, if the lists are of the same length, we learn when to anticipate the last words. It is those words that we thrust into short-term memory and then dump out when asked to recite. Since the last-heard words have not been rehearsed, they are not committed to long-term memory and, thus, are not learned well, demonstrated by their not being recalled well if there is some sort of task-filled delay between the end of the list and the recitation.[5]

In testing the validity of primacy and recency, researchers have manipulated the test data and further modified the theories. For example, working from the observation that, prior to "practice" and learning the length of a list, a subject does not demonstrate a recency effect, a 1978 study described a two-stage memory process.[6] In the first stage, the subject notes the first item in the list and then attempts to effect a learning operation, which is usually abandoned as the following items flood in one after another. Also, simply registering the items as the first was registered also fails to succeed, as the items become too numerous. This researcher observed that item position becomes important for identification only when the structure (including length) of the list is known. In a second learning stage, the subject discriminates among the items on the list and commits them to memory according to the most appropriate of various techniques. If all of the words are visually or conceptually related, the subject may fit them into an image or a story. Thus, when the word string is susceptible to this sort of differentiation and classification, primacy and recency begin to fade.[7]

In another experiment, the data were comprised of vacation-type slides, presented in a rapid sequence.[8] The experimenters, Tabachnick and Brotsky, examined the effect of the order of first or last when combined with two other elements: vividness and complexity. First, they found a slight association of high vividness with a recency effect.[9] Perhaps more important, they also discovered that the strength of serial positions decreases as the complexity of the object to be recalled increases. They see this finding to be consistent with the rehearsal theory of memory, which suggests that the early items are rehearsed better in a first list while last items are better rehearsed in later lists. The more complex the object to be recalled, the more difficult it is to reconstruct mentally and review.[10] This conclusion is consistent with the theory that we seek some learning theory apart from order. Notice, however, that the effects of serial position are nevertheless recognized; it is simply that other factors may overcome or supplant those effects. Also, since the recency effect tends to emerge only when a string of information is repeated, which occurs less often in reality than does an unrepeated information string, the primacy effect is likely to be encountered more often.

B. *Effects on Order Principles*

1. *Attractiveness*

As earlier suggested, the primacy effect is viewed as such a consistent finding of social-psychological research that researchers have for some time been testing for effects on primacy.[11] The physical attractiveness stereotype is another consistent finding, according to which, the traits, behaviors, and characteristics of a person who is quite physically attractive are viewed to be more positive than they objectively are. This concept is clearly related to Asch's first impression theory in that all we know about a person that we first set eyes on is what we see. The more pleasant the picture, the more likely we are to form a favorable impression.

A study reported in 1982 sought out the interrelationship between primacy and physical attractiveness.[12] In this experiment the subjects were provided photographs of and cover stories about a group of "stimulus persons" who had reportedly solved a set of problems. The results of this phase of the experiment confirmed the effect of the physically attractive stereotype: regardless of their performance, the attractive stimulus persons were *perceived* to have solved a higher number of problems than they actually did and, thus, more than the unattractive stimulus persons were perceived to have solved. The primacy effect was also confirmed when the subjects were asked to predict how the stimulus persons would perform in the future. Apparently, the first impression of accurate solutions convinced the subjects of the ability of the stimulus persons. Similarly, the first impression of inaccurate solutions could not be erased by later accuracies. The researchers point out that the effects of physical attractiveness seemed to diminish as the stimulus person became more competent.

In a second experiment, half of the subjects were not exposed to the cover story and photograph of the stimulus person until almost all of the problem solutions had been reviewed; the other half saw the attractiveness data beforehand. The subjects were then asked to give their impression of the performance of the stimulus persons. Unattractive persons were judged in accordance with their actual performance, regardless of whether their attractiveness information was seen before or after their performance. Attractive people whose attractiveness information was not seen until after performance were also judged in accordance with their performance.[13]

Overall, the researchers concluded that, when both primacy and physical attractiveness are present, the actual effects of performance are eliminated. However, if one is missing—that is, if the person is unattractive or if his attractiveness is revealed later—he will be judged based on his performance. As an explanation for this, it is suggested that low physical attractiveness does not induce the same initial conclusion as does high physical attractiveness, due to the absence of clear stereotypes associated with low physical attractiveness. Therefore, the perceiver must continue to process information before being able to attribute ability.[14]

To apply these conclusions to a trial situation, they must first be distilled to what *this experiment* showed: attractiveness, when displayed first, causes an audience to perceive general ability or competence. This suggests that a defense attorney having a client accused of medical malpractice will enjoy an advantage if the doctor is attractive *and* is present during the voir dire. If the doctor is not present, then if the plaintiff leads in the voir dire, he can say unattractive things about the doctor that may negate any first impression benefit of the doctor's attractiveness. Similarly, if a plaintiff in a fraud action alleges that he did not understand the effect of a transaction and that the defendant took advantage of the plaintiff's lack of expertise, then, if he is attractive, perhaps the plaintiff should not be present during voir dire. At that time, his attorney can convey the impression that he was incompetent in the subject area, before the jury notes the attractiveness. Finally, if counsel knows something of the expert witness to be called by the other side, comments as to the competence of that witness, prior to his appearance, could remove any positive effect by an attractive expert witness.

2. *Juror Bias*

The discussion in the next section, which reconciles primacy and recency theory, will distinguish the psychological terms "attitude" and "perception." For now, it is enough to know that attitude is more or less the same as judgment and perception is what we think we see. The interrelationship of these terms instantly appears: our judgment about a person must be at least partly based on what we see that person to be. It also appears irrefutable that the first bit of information we obtain about another person significantly affects our impression (perception) of that person. A prospective juror can obtain his first piece of information about a defendant even before coming to the courtroom, through pretrial publicity. If the prospective juror forms a perception about the defendant based on that information and with that perception reaches a conclusion as to the defendant's guilt, then the voir dire ideally discovers that conclusion, which usually results in the venireman's being struck. While that type of bias can be ascertained, it can also escape detection if the venireman is not honest (either with himself or the questioner) and if he wants to serve on the jury.

Another type of bias is even less difficult to ascertain: the prospective juror could resent the length of the defendant's hair, the color of his skin, or even the fact that the defendant is involved in a lawsuit. Because to admit such biases is to admit an unattractive characteristic, they are usually not uncovered in voir dire. These biases, however, may be the purest form of first impression reactions.

A 1972 study concluded that an adversary presentation, as opposed to a straight presentation of the facts, "significantly counteracts decisionmaker bias."[15] The details of the experiment will be reviewed shortly, but the results clearly suggest that the more adversarial a proceeding is, the greater the chance that juror bias will be overcome. A study in 1980, however, flew in the face of that conclusion by indicating that overzealous attorneys risk inducing the jurors to discount all of the evidence presented and causing them to rely upon their original biases.[16] Although the latter study, by Kaplan and Schersching, acknowledges but does not specifically discuss the former, the findings in one are actually consistent with the findings in the other, and both are important for the trial attorney to understand.

In the 1972 study, the subjects were comprised of individuals that were biased against people who behaved unlawfully. They were read a total of fifty facts about a defendant, twenty-five of these facts indicating that a described behavior of the defendant was lawful, and twenty-five indicating that it was unlawful. Although the order of the facts did not change, the experiment called for them to be read in two ways. In one phase, the reading was by two individuals;

a reader labeled as "Prosecution" read the unlawful facts while a reader labeled as "Defense" read the lawful facts. In another phase, one person read all of the facts, acting as if he were an official investigator, in an inquisitorial mode of presentation. In the results, the subjects who were biased toward unlawful decisions (that is, judging that a law had been broken) and who were read the *unlawful* facts in the adversary mode made less extreme judgments than did the subjects who were read the facts in the inquisitorial mode.[17]

The proffered rationale is based on a psychological theory called "reactance," an aversive state created by a threatened loss of the freedom to act or choose. When an individual is threatened in that way, he will act so as to protect his freedom to choose. The researchers explain that someone with a bias may view information in support of his bias as a threat to entertaining an opposing viewpoint; therefore, his protective act is the consideration of that very viewpoint. That reaction does not occur in the inquisitorial mode simply because, due to the neutral appearance of the fact presenter, there is no urging to choose one view over the other.[18]

A parallel explanation concerns the social unacceptableness of certain biases. Knowing his particular bias, the decisionmaker could fear that a decision in accordance with that bias might be viewed as merely an indication of his bias; thus, he more strongly considers opposing information, and his bias is reduced.[19] Notice the two elements at work here: First, for those biased against unlawful behavior, it is the presentation by the *prosecution* (in an appeal to those biases) that makes the decisionmakers conscious of their bias and receptive to making a choice outside their bias. Second, they apparently then use the information supplied by the defense to justify their "new" choices.

The Kaplan and Scherschimg study, reported in 1980, first summarizes biases from theoretical and practical perspectives and concludes that since (1) people cannot avoid having biases, (2) voir dire cannot always detect the various kind of biases, and (3) a purely unbiased jury would mean a jury with no opinions (neither practically possible nor theoretically desirable), then the goal should be to provide jurors with information that will allow them to make decisions apart from their biases.[20] A distinction is also made between perception and judgment; essentially the former is a piece of information that assists in the making of the latter.[21] In addition, the authors coin a phrase for the juror's predisposition about a defendant (or plaintiff) even before they have ever seen him or her: "*initial impression*," or the "response to the judged object in the absence of information."[22] While "first impression" is the effect on perception that the first piece of information about a person has on a perceiver, "initial impression" is what the perceiver believes about the other person, before receiving any (personal) information. For example, an initial impression could be formed about a plaintiff based on a bias against anyone who would sue for damages for pain and suffering. At this point it should be obvious that if no personal information were learned by a juror about someone who was suing for pain and suffering, then the only basis on which he could make a judgment about such a person would be his bias.

This study shows that when the evidence is perceived to be reliable, biases may be abandoned. But when the evidence is unreliable, jurors apparently revert to their biases. Psychology students were used for this study, but only if they were registered voters (and therefore potential jurors), and were selected if they had either harsh or lenient biases. This latter determination was made by test scores that reflected one's tendency to punish lawbreakers.[23] The subjects first read summaries of four cases, in two of which the defendants were obviously guilty and in two of which they were obviously innocent, and then recommended punishment. These recommendations functioned as a control. Then they read other case summaries, half of which mildly favored a defendant's guilt and half of which mildly favored his innocence. For all cases read, the subjects were told either that the case summaries were extremely reliable (with an explanation of who prepared them and the attorneys in the case attesting to their reliability) or unreliable (with the same kind of explanation). There were twenty-four harsh and twenty-four lenient subjects in each reliability condition, and their sexes were equally divided. Subjects were later asked to rate the defendant's guilt (0=definitely innocent and 20=definitely guilty). Justice can best be done to the results by the reproduction below:

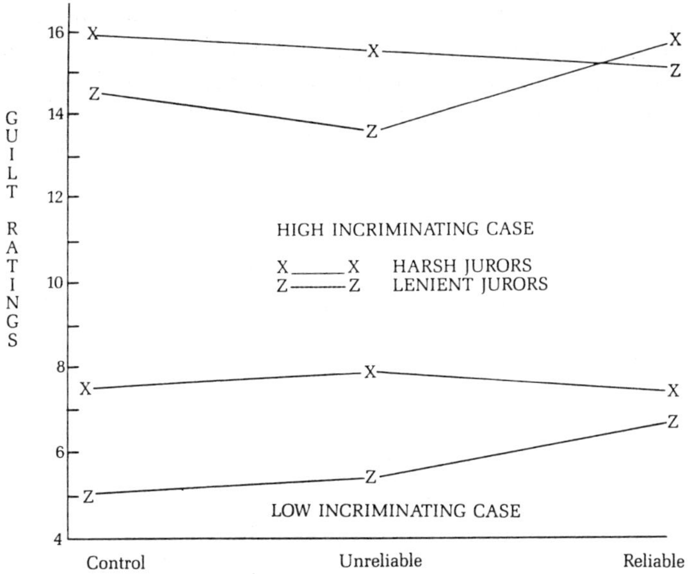

The researchers note that "[r]egardless of whether the evidence gave a predominant appearance of guilt or innocence, both subjects with harsh or lenient prejudgmental biases gave essentially the same response when the evidence was characterized as trustworthy and uncontested. This lack of biasing sharply contrasts with the bias apparent when nothing is said about the evidence, or when evidence is contested and potentially inaccurate."[24] As another indication that bias is returned to when the evidence is lacking, when they later discussed their decisions, lenient subjects cited less incriminating but more exonerating facts when the evidence was contested. However, when the evidence was reportedly reliable, harsh and lenient subjects cited about the same proportion of exonerating facts.[25]

A conclusion at this point would be that, while the adversary mode alone has the propensity to overcome juror bias, for that to occur, attorneys must follow through with what jurors perceive is reliable evidence. Ironically, though, in their zeal to represent their clients and discredit the opposition, effective counsel for both sides can cause the jury to doubt the evidence and revert to a reliance on bias.[26]

In mock trials conducted in situations closely resembling a courtroom,[27] subjects were told that a truncated trial would last only fifteen minutes. That actually occurred with the control group. With the other groups, researchers tested the effect of a situational bias by creating an unpleasant condition. The defense counsel in one trial extended the proceedings to fifty minutes through his obnoxious and argumentative behavior.[28] In other trials, either the judge or the prosecutor caused the delay. As the following shows, the jurors tended to rate the defendant's guilt in accordance with the disruptive behavior:

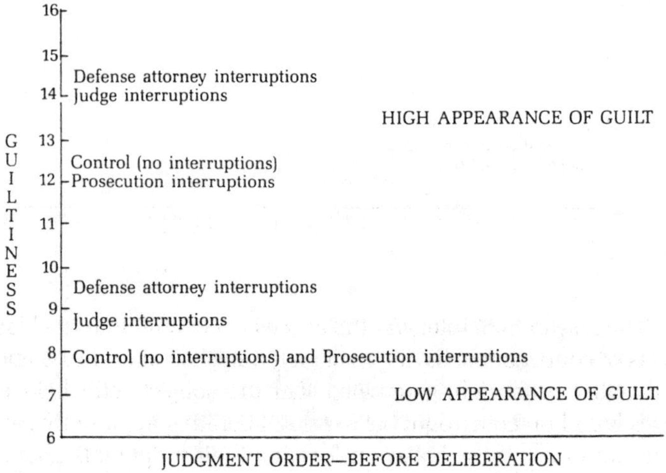

The jurors then deliberated for a brief time, and these deliberations were taped. Although there were very few references to courtroom behavior in these deliberations (which shows that the jurors did not "vent" their feelings about such behavior) and although, in a later debriefing, jurors in all of the delayed trials spontaneously expressed strong feelings about the disruptive behavior (which shows that the jurors had not forgotten that behavior), the post-deliberative guilt ratings changed.[29] The direction of these changes may be surprising:

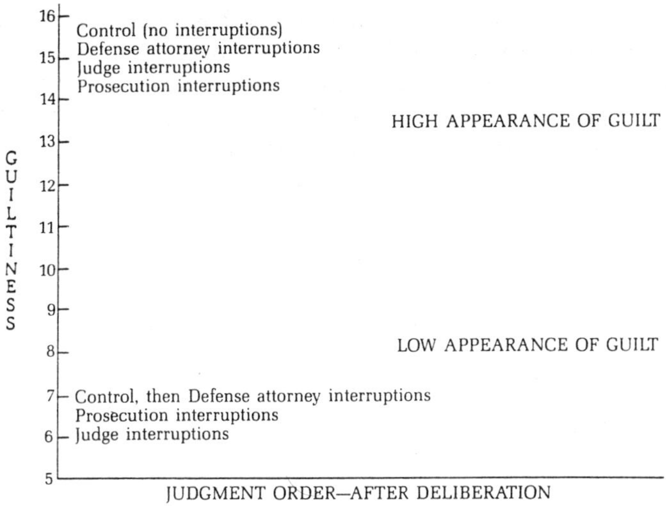

The researchers interpret the above as meaning that the biasing effects of courtroom behavior essentially vanished after deliberation.[30] Although the debriefing revealed that the subjects still held their biases based on courtroom behavior, deliberating apparently caused them not to use those biases in forming their judgments about the defendant. This interpretation must be due to jurors in the control trial giving the harsher guilt rating after deliberation; i.e., this is the guilt rating that would have emerged (and did) with no interruptions at all. The performance of the subjects when the defendant had a low appearance of guilt clearly supports the proposition that disruptive behavior by the defense attorney or the judge induces a guilty judgment, since, once the application of the bias attributable to such behavior is removed, the attitude towards guilt decreases.

However, there are two observations about the results that the researchers do not make. First, across the board, the judgments intensified in their original directions. That is, the guilty-appearing defendant, for all versions of the case, was adjudged more guilty, and the defendant appearing less guilty was determined to be even less guilty, after deliberation. Again, this was true even when there were no interruptions. This polarization of attitudes is explicable by a theory called "choice shifts" and a concomitant body of literature.

Explained further in the section entitled "The Juror as a Unique Subject," choice shift literature suggests that group discussions tend to cause group decisions, as well as individual decisions prior to group discussions, to be more extreme than decisions of individuals after group discussions.[31]

The second observation is that, if the control is the norm, then once the bias towards courtroom behavior is put aside, the assessment of guilt falls *below* what it should have been. With sets of facts that suggested both a high appearance of guilt and a low appearance of guilt, subjects that viewed a disruptive trial—no matter who disrupted it—ultimately rated the defendant less guilty than subjects who viewed a non-disruptive trial. If these subjects were composed of harsh and lenient jurors, then it would appear that they merely reverted to their original biases after discounting the evidence, yet we are not given that information about them. A second, more plausible explanation is that, during deliberation, the subjects realized that part of their assessment of guilt was due to their negative reactions to the courtroom behavior, which they probably recognized as irrational. Therefore, they overcompensated in trying to reduce its effects on their judgments.

Although this is not a conclusion drawn by the researchers, the results and the former experiment suggest that one defense strategy might be to create confusion and annoyance during trial. Then, if the jury is composed of lenient members from the beginning, they are likely to throw out the evidence as being unreliable and depend upon their original biases to assess guilt. In addition, lenient or not, and regardless of whether they discount the evidence, while they might enunciate a harsh judgment if polled immediately after the trial, they may later return a verdict even more favorable for the defense had the trial been without moment.

Kaplan and Schersching also touch on pretrial publicity, considering it to be another effect on a juror's initial impression (attitude or judgment), which can be overcome (like some personal bias) if weight is accorded to the evidence presented. They mention conclusions of others indicating that pretrial publicity *does* affect judgment (both for and against the defendant) before trial but that such effects apparently dissipate when the jurors reach their verdict. Though admitting that this has not been tested for, Kaplan and Schersching suggest that the biases have been overcome prior to deliberation; that is, the evidence has had that effect. Thus, as with the situation of disruptive courtroom behavior, they state the case for a straight presentation of the facts, the inquisitorial approach, to provide jurors with the most unaffected view of the facts.[32]

In their debate over the more preferable mode of evidence presentation from a psychological standpoint—inquisitorial or adversarial—social scientists rely on legal escapes. They remind us, for example, that the court can caution the jury to withhold judgment until all of the evidence has been presented,[33] as if such a warning interrupts the unconscious mental process that seeks conclusions. Despite the logical instruction, a juror attending to the adversary mode feels threatened with a no-choice situation when an appeal is made to a strong bias he has. He therefore automatically becomes more receptive to new, different information. This does not happen when the same information is presented in an inquisitorial fashion.[34]

Moreover, evidence presented in the inquisitorial mode simply may not stand out.[35] On the other hand, in an adversarial mode, evidence may be distorted; this can result from the competitive nature of the mode itself.[36] When experimental subjects were assigned to opposite sides of a case and the evidence was weighted in favor of the defendant and then the plaintiff, and then presented by the subjects acting as attorneys, the fact finders leaned more towards the party that the original evidence distribution did *not* support.[37]

The researchers theorize that the attorneys confronted with unfavorable fact distributions worked harder at uncovering facts and then presented a relatively large number of facts in favor of their clients, essentially overwhelming the number presented by the other side (which actually had the favorable fact distribution). Lind, Thibaut, and Walker then happily conclude that "one important function of the adversary system may be to eliminate chance differences in the distribution of favorable evidence."[38]

Kaplan and Schersching argue that evidence overcomes bias, whether the bias is with the juror when he comes into the courtroom or is formed thereafter. Since one kind of bias can apparently spring from the chance distribution of favorable evidence, then theoretically, an "evidence bias" could be used to counter a juror bias. The degree of bias in a judgment made by a biased juror in reliance on an "evidence bias" boggles the mind. The adversary system, however, evidently through the responsibility it creates in counsel, may work to override biases resulting from chance evidence distributions.

C. *Reconciling Primacy and Recency*

Theoretically, primacy and recency are irreconcilable only if they are viewed as absolutes (e.g., material presented first [or last] is *always* best recalled and therefore most persuasive). If primacy exists under certain conditions and recency under other conditions, reconciliation is possible—and the concepts are practicable—so long as those conditions are generally reliable and can be described. Lind, in a 1982 article entitled "The Psychology of Courtroom Procedure," summarized the existing literature concerning primacy and recency and related it to the usual ordering of evidence and arguments in trials.[39] He notes that *perceptions* are the results of processing information about people; in other words, they are the interpretations of what we "see" when we gain personal (visual and/or auditory) information about someone. The literature suggests that when we are asked to process such information, a primacy effect appears. However, when we are called upon to make judgments, as jurors are, the material presented last is the more persuasive. In a trial, a jury is exposed to various pairs of information, sort of short lists. Usually, the plaintiff's opening argument is followed by the defendant's opening argument; the plaintiff's presentation of direct evidence is followed by the defendant's presentation; the plaintiff's rebuttal precedes the defendant's; and the plaintiff's final argument precedes the defendant's. This pairing fails only at the end, when the plaintiff closes.

There is a parallel between these short lists and the lists of words earlier discussed, where it was concluded that, after the first list ("practice"), the subject begins to focus on the last items, placing them in short-term memory, and dumping them (i.e., not retaining them at all after recitation) when asked to recall. Although evidence and arguments are infinitely more complex than word lists, Lind notes that when attitudes are assessed after the second set of evidence and arguments, it is the materials of the party going last in the second set that most affect the subjects' final attitudes. This recency effect is most pronounced when there is a delay between the first and second sets. In relation to a word list, the delay would give the subject time to reflect on the length of the list and make a change in his learning pattern. Similarly, if there is a delay between the last set of argument and evidence and the making of the judgment, the recency effect decreases. This, too, is consistent with the word list theory; the last-heard words, put into short-term memory, are not learned well.

Admittedly, comparisons between argument and evidence order and word lists cannot be stretched too far. First, what "judgment" along the lines of that made by a juror must be made by a subject recalling words? Second, there are internal orders within each presentation of evidence (e.g., direct, cross-examination, and redirect and possibly recross). How could a juror anticipate the end of each such examination so as to train himself to focus on the evidence last elicited? An attorney could, however, signal the jury to the end of his witness list by indicating the order of testimony in his opening statement and alluding to it later on. The point of comparing word lists with trial simulations is that, in the former, there can be more precise testing for pure ordering effects. If the same results occur under similar conditions (though with more variables), then order effects are real. The less "pure" the test, however, the more examination there must be of the other variables, which might dilute or negate order effects.

Lind also reports an observation that recency effects have experimentally occurred when subjects have made repeated judgments during the course of a trial. During an actual trial, jurors are often repeatedly urged by the court to make no judgment until all of the evidence has been presented. While such an instruction may not prevent mental rehearsals of evidence, that is a far cry from an experiment, when the subject is periodically tested on his recall. Concerning the practical application of the recency effect for trial, Lind suggests that such effects can be expected when the juror is focusing on general issues. However, the attorney can make use of the findings about order effects in structuring his own presentations of evidence and arguments. In addition, the primacy effect is still borne out when the defendant's character or a witness's credibility is a central issue, and his could guide examination. Also, we have seen that attractiveness, when combined with primacy, can affect perceptions as to someone's ability. A third character trait category is opinions, and the effect of order on opinion attribution calls for a more specific reconciliation of the primacy and recency effects.

One explanation of why initial evidence so strongly results in assignment of ability (recall how the descending performers were judged to be more competent than the ascending performers in the attractiveness experiment) is that ability is more or less unchanging in a person. Opinions, or attitudes, that someone might embrace can change with time, education, and experience. If a juror reads that a particular defendant belongs in a certain category or has been quoted as saying something about a particular topic, how will the juror react to an opinion expressed by the defendant in court that conflicts with the category or the supposed quotation? In other words, since the juror may have formed an initial impression of the defendant before the trial, will the defendant's conflicting opinion be disbelieved (a primacy effect)? If the juror knows nothing of a plaintiff before the plaintiff has taken the stand and expressed opinions on a critical issue, what if the defense counsel brings out that the plaintiff belongs to a category of people that would never express such opinions or has made public statements inconsistent with those opinions? Researchers set out to answer questions like these (though not in a courtroom context) in a study reported in 1976.[40]

The experiments concerned clearly expressed opinions about such controversial topics as women's rights and liberalized abortion. Subjects were exposed to one of two types of information about the person: (1) the person was placed in a category (such as deputy sheriff of a small southern town), and (2) a statement was attributed to him or her (such as being overheard as saying " 'If all communities fought busing the way South Boston has we wouldn't be in the mess we're in today' "). The subjects were also told that the person expressed the opinion in question (like " 'I have become convinced that we should pay more attention to equal rights for women in employment and other areas' ").[41] Subjects were exposed first either to a piece of the background information or the expressed opinion; after each exposure, they were asked to rate the person's attitude on the issue. The background information was supposed to induce an expectancy. The results showed no effect of order when the expressed opinion was consistent with the expectancy; in other words, the attitude rating was the same, regardless of whether the opinion or the background information came first.

However, when the expectancy was in conflict with the expressed opinion, the person's attitude was rated lower when the background information followed rather than preceded the opinion. That is clearly a recency effect. The researchers theorize that, when we attribute opinions to group stereotypes, we seldom translate those into attributions to individual members of the group. Therefore, if we first place a person into a group stereotype, we have no details on him. When he says something that seems inconsistent with the group beliefs, we may segregate him into a smaller or unique category of the larger group or totally discount the effect of the group on his thinking. Our original conclusion about his attitudes has been modified. Similarly, when someone first divulges a personal opinion, that is our only information as to how he feels about a topic. If this intimate disclosure is followed by a conflicting group description, our original conclusion about his attitudes is modified.[42] (Recall that we are more likely to believe that changes in opinions, as opposed to ability, are possible.)

The summary of the experimental results is instructive for the attorney whose client must be determined to be a firm believer in his opinions. If a person wants to be understood, he must first disclose those things about himself that are likely to trigger opposing expectations about his beliefs (such as group membership or affiliations) before disclosing his more intimate beliefs and values. If the order is reversed, his personal comments may become assimilated into the group stereotype suggested by the later information.[43]

D. *Conclusions about Primacy and Recency*

While, as descriptions of human behavior, primacy and recency could theoretically be as fluid as the behavior they seek to describe, the following rules can be derived from the foregoing discussion:

General Rules of Primacy and Recency

1. When a single string of information is presented, information at the *beginning* of the string is most clearly remembered.
2. When strings of information of similar length are presented, information at the *end* of the strings past the first string is most clearly remembered. This generally holds true regardless of the complexity of the information, so long as the information is quite vivid.
3. When there is more than one string of information and the information is complex but not very vivid, information at the *beginning* of the strings is most clearly remembered.
4. Information that is recalled from the *beginning* of an information string is better learned than information recalled from the end of a string.
5. Attractive or appealing information about a person learned *first* improves our perception of that person's actual ability.
6. Stereotype information about a person, when learned *after* an opinion expressed by that person that conflicts with the stereotype information, dilutes the validity of the opinion. This

dilution does not occur when stereotype information is learned first.

7. An existing bias is analogous to a well-learned early piece of information. That bias can be temporarily overcome by information *later* learned (but retained for just a short while) only if that later information is believed.

Rules are only as good as their application. The two sections that follow will examine the extent to which the Rules of Primacy and Recency can be applied to a courtroom situation and to the receivers of information in a courtroom—the jury.

II. *PRESENTATION OF EVIDENCE AND ARGUMENTS*

At this point, you might conclude that the Rules of Primacy and Recency provided above could enable you to manipulate, or at least to predict with certainty, the outcome of every trial henceforth. This is a plausible conclusion, given that order effects do exist and that courtroom procedure is marked by a definite order. That, however, is just about where the generalities end, as no two trials and no two juries are the same. As we have seen, variables, such as information complexity and vividness, can affect the impact of serial order; and variables like these are inherent in unique fact situations, parties, attorneys, judges, and jurors. If the Rules of Primacy and Recency are to serve as tools for the trial attorney, he must know when he can rely upon them. Thus, he should be able to recognize the conditions under which serial order effects may appear in the courtroom.

The following examination of courtroom "order" begins with traditional, practical notions of the effects of first and last statements and is only tangentially tied to psychological study. Rationales then appear for the *invalidation* of primacy and recency in the courtroom context. This section is presented, first, so as not to slight a body of research and second, because conclusions reported there are actually support for the final section. The last section contains a discussion of theories of primacy and recency that make sense of the invalidation objections and actually reflect the intuitive, practical notions first discussed.

A. *The Traditional Approach*

"In cases involving issues of fact, counsel for the parties are of right entitled to make an opening statement to the jury outlining the facts intended to be proved."[44] It is the party who shoulders the burden of proof on the issues of fact, usually the plaintiff, who has the right to open and close.[45] While statutes can vary this order, the plaintiff's opening argument is usually followed by the defendant's, the plaintiff begins the presentation of both direct and rebuttal evidence, and the plaintiff begins and closes the final argument, with the defendant's closing argument coming between the plaintiff's first and closing arguments.[46]

It has been suggested that in allowing the prosecution to close in criminal trials, the law has attempted to balance the heavy burden of proof (beyond all reasonable doubt) thrust on a prosecutor. Thus, "the law has always assumed that the last word to the jury is the best word." The rationale has been not only that the last speaker has the opportunity to refute the prior argument, but that his words will be most clearly recalled at the time of deliberation (a recency effect).[47] By the same token, in allowing the one with the burden of proof to open, the law has sought to provide that party with another balancing advantage: first place.

Despite the fact that an opening statement is the first of only two real speeches (as opposed to exchanges) an attorney may present in a trial, attorneys often underestimate its importance. This attitude may be due to the limitations placed on an opening statement. Specifically, it is not the place to argue the facts, to discuss applicable law, or to detail upcoming testimony.[48] However, John A. Appleman notes that, according to studies made by the University of Chicago, 65% of jurors form unchanging beliefs about cases immediately after the opening statements. (The author's research has determined that the majority of jurors do make their decisions early in the litigation forum. Approximately seventy percent of the jurors have reached a verdict by the conclusion of the *voir dire* [in those states that allow a full *voir dire* examination] and only rarely change this opinion. More than eighty percent of the jurors have decided the case by the conclusion of the opening statement. Obviously, these jurors are not determining the case on the facts alone. The juror's predisposition, which allows a selective perception of the merits of the case, is the major variable in the decision. Therefore, trial counsel must structure the *voir dire* and opening statement to ensure that the jurors will formulate a favorable impression of the case, client, and attorney.)

In isolation, this statistic seems to belong in a section that clearly supports the psychology of primacy. But the context in which this statistic is applied to the opening statement is far more practical and intuitive than scientific. Immediately after citing the 65% figure, Appleman says,

> This does not mean, of necessity, that the opening statement alone has done the job. It is more likely that the attorney who has prepared his case with such care as to select the jury intelligently, and to discuss the nature of the case comprehensively, probably is the type of lawyer who, and who has the type of case which, should and will win.[49]

Notice that without mentioning in psychological terms the topics of juror bias, first and initial impressions, complexity of information, and the adversarial mode, Appleman has acknowledged them all. With what authority, then, does Appleman speak? The preface to his book describes him as the epitome of the "country lawyer" (which you recognize as an appellation attorneys frequently adopt today), literally appropriate since his office and residence were four miles from the nearest town, which then had a population of 35,000. Born in 1912, by the time his book was published in 1967, he had "probably tried as many jury cases as any lawyer who [had] ever lived. . . and with phenomenal success."[50]

Attorneys who seek to instruct colleagues in trial excellence have the following to say about opening statements:

> The plaintiff's lawyer, who usually speaks first, has a distinct advantage. . . . He can get the jury to think with him about the facts of the case and to view them in the light he wishes. . . . to motivate the jury in his direction.
>
> . . . .
>
> The opening statement can technically be waived by either party, but this is generally an unwise procedure.
>
> . . . .
>
> Waiving one's opportunity to open to the jury with a favorable presentation of the client's case is tactical suicide.[51]

These same attorneys have similar comments about closing arguments: "Counsel's closing argument. . . is the culmination of his efforts to persuade the jury. As such, its importance cannot be overstated. . . . The jury expects and looks forward to the closing argument."[52] While the foregoing comments could simultaneously support both primacy and recency effects, their authors apparently feel no compulsion to explain why they give such high ratings to both the beginning and ending of the trial. Their unscientific conclusions will ultimately provide a practical lens for viewing primacy and recency findings.

The opening and closing statements of a trial, along with the overall presentation of evidence and the closing arguments, are part of what is called the trial's gross order. Internal order refers to the order in which evidence and testimony are presented by each side.[53] Internal order must also exist within the examination of each witness. (Technically, even an opening and closing argument could have an internal order.) Researchers (and attorneys) who conclude that a climactic internal order (weak-to-strong evidence), suggestive of recency, is more effective do not clearly account for the evidentiary building-blocks requirement; that is, conclusions from witnesses must often spring from a predicate. For example, a scientist cannot opine that a particular transmission line facility emits life-threatening radiation until he has first established his credentials and his familiarity with the particular facility. Despite the evidentiary requirement, as information recipients we are more likely to believe information that builds to a conclusion (which is not the same thing as preceding strong evidence with weak evidence) than a conclusion that is followed by the rationale. To the extent that a party's entire trial presentation may be based on a building-blocks theory, a climactic ordering of weak-to-strong evidence is an inaccurate description if "strong evidence" turns out to be the conclusion. Therefore, while internal order may be contained in gross order, they do not appear to be susceptible to the same kind of statements about order effects.

In addition, first and last positions in the internal ordering of witness examination can quickly become blurred. Although the plaintiff may examine a witness, he can be interrupted many times by opposing counsel. Indeed, the defense may lodge a lengthy objection to the witness before plaintiff's counsel has asked a single question and may take the witness on *voir dire* many times thereafter. With the potential of cross-examination, redirect, and re-cross, ordering per se may be less important than the final position on some issue elicited from the witness—and probably because of the culmination of the building-blocks approach rather than a recency effect.

When attorneys consider examples of internal ordering at trial, they tend to focus on methods of examining witnesses that will best elicit the supporting facts. They advise that the first witness should be one who can basically give a narrative of the facts outlined by the attorney in his opening argument because "[t]he jury will usually retain its first impression of the case, and the stronger this first witness is, the stronger the case is."[54] Notice that such a witness serves to verify what the attorney has already said. Although this witness, who is usually the client, is potentially the strongest witness with the strongest evidence, he cannot be reserved for last place. First, his testimony may well need to precede that of other witnesses. Second, since what the attorney has said in his opening statement is not testimony, his delineation of the facts cannot be relied upon by the jurors. The client's narrative, though, will be under oath, and the client will have knowledge of the events he describes. As later witnesses fill out parts of the client's story, the jury can plug in evidence where it belongs. Without the client's narrative, the jury is forced to use a building-blocks approach with no blueprint. Thus, if the initial witness has a critical primacy effect, that witness is more likely reinforcing (or validating) the primacy effect in the attorney's opening statement.

As a practical matter then, when preparing and presenting their cases attorneys are concerned with both the opening statements and closing arguments and with inducing the jury to piece together a set of facts suggesting a certain conclusion. For logical purposes alone, the presentation of evidence must often follow a chronological or building-blocks approach; and whether evidence at the end of such a sequence is strong per se may be more coincidental than planned. The following sections examine the justification for greater attention by litigators to ordering effects.

B. *Theories for Invalidating Primacy and Recency Effects in the Courtroom*

Two particular schools of thought suggest that psychological findings of primacy and recency are of little use in the courtroom. One author plainly states that such findings "have less to offer attorneys planning trial strategies than they do to courts and legislatures designing trial procedures."[55] He reviewed the great body of literature concerning the order of trial presentation, which initially described a primacy effect but later detected a recency effect. He accurately concludes that "[s]ometimes primacy is found to operate; sometimes recency."[56]

Based on one approach, primacy and recency are not helpful in the courtroom because of a "wash" theory; i.e., they cancel out each other. First, this view suggests that primacy effects are dramatically reduced because the information recipients, the jurors, now that information presented first will be refuted. Thus, "first inpressions are not so strong that later information will be discounted."[57] In fact, it is argued that due to the "heightened receptivity" to information presented second, along with "the sharpened recall of the more recently presented evidence," the party going second may have the advantage.[58] This would be a gross order advantage.

Concerning internal order, the authors conclude that a climactic order (weak-to-strong evidence) is more effective than an anticlimactic order (strong-to-weak evidence), especially in second positions in the gross order.[59] Thus, the gross order advantage that the defense has in usually going second, is offset by the climactic order advantage given to the plaintiff or prosecution (as the last words are best recalled), which also usually has the last closing argument. The researchers argue that as long as both sides employ a climactic order in their respective presentations, the traditional gross order of trial "appears remarkably well arranged to neutralize the effects of order and thus maintain the fact-finding process relatively free of this powerful yet legally irrelevant influence."[60]

A second invalidating approach questions the courtroom applicability of primacy and recency based on the nature of the experiments that have detected these phenomena. Specifically, researchers have actually described two *kinds* of primacy. One is primacy in serial learning: items appearing early in a string of information are better remembered than items appearing late. The other is primacy of *persuasion*, meaning that the side of an issue presented first will have a greater effect on the listeners than the side presented second.[61] In the section on Primacy and Recency, the difficulty in comparing simple word lists with serial presentations of ideas or testimony was noted. Thus, a differentiation between order effects in serial learning and persuasion, being much more complex, makes sense. Researchers, however, do not generally appear to make the distinction when structuring their experiments. Instead, they seem to view presentation of ideas as merely a more complex serial learning event, not a totally different occurrence. Therefore, when the expected findings of primacy and recency are upset, the results are attributed to the greater complexity of the learning task and/or other effects (e.g., vividness of information).

That is a perfectly plausible explanation. Another explanation is that primacy of persuasion, as a unique province, has not yet been established. A Law of Primacy in Persuasion was enunciated in 1925 by a researcher named Lund. The underlying experiments involved an instructor who first polled his students as to their opinion on a subject, spoke on one side of the subject, polled the students again, spoke on the other side of the subject, and polled the students once more. He found that the opinion change resulting from the first communication was greater than from the second communication, ergo, the Law of Primacy in Persuasion.[62]

Over 20 years later, two researchers essentially duplicated Lund's experiments but could find no significant primacy (or recency) effects.[63] A difference in the experiments suggests a problem with Lund's approach. Lund had the teacher take both sides of the issue; the later experimenters used someone from outside the school. They theorize that, with Lund, the students seemed to believe the teacher's first position because they were in a classroom situation and motivated to learn; basically, they believed what their teacher told them. When he reversed his position, they were suspicious both of his shift in view and of their role—i.e., they may have realized that they were being used in an experiment.[64] The later researchers then conclude that "primacy is not an easily reproducible phenomenon but may occur only under a certain set of conditions. Hence it is probably premature to postulate a universal law of primacy."[65]

In a summary of the various studies of both sides of an issue presented in succession appears the statement that "[t]he public is not necessarily permanently swayed by the view to which it first lends an ear, or biased by the man who first captures its attention."[66] In fact, there are only certain conditions under which the side of an issue presented first may disproportionately affect opinion: (1) when it is unclear that incompatibly different items are being presented;[67] (2) when the same communicator presents both sides of the issue; (3) when the recipients of the information take some action that commits them to the first viewpoint before hearing the second (such as expressing an opinion); (4) when the issue is unfamiliar to them; or (5) when the recipients have a low cognitive need (as opposed to, say, a high emotional need, which might be met by the lead speaker). In certain situations when primacy effects have been considered dangerous, such as trials or political debates, these conditions are unlikely to occur, since the issues are clearly controversial and different speakers represent different viewpoints.[68]

To the extent, therefore, that a courtroom presentation is viewed as an exercise in persuasion, there may as yet be no set rules of primacy and recency. Moreover, if there are—that is, if they are the same as the rules that apply to serial learning—the "wash" theory suggests that such phenomena cancel out each other by virtue of the gross order imposed by statute or courts.

C. *A Realistic Application of Primacy and Recency to the Courtroom*

Everyone assumes that a trial is a purely persuasive experience. Books are written on how to persuade a jury, and the word "persuasion" evokes images of debates and orators. However, these concepts totally conflict with the restrictions placed on counsel in opening arguments (no drawing of inferences), the court not allowing counsel to arrive at conclusions while eliciting testimony, and the court's repeated admonitions to the jury *not* to reach conclusions before the evidence has all been presented.

> Upon completion of this part of the proceedings, however, a radical change occurs in the general character of the communications received by the jury. The art of advocacy comes into play as both sides seek to present their position as forcefully as possible. No longer are the communications factual and informative. Instead they are argumentative and persuasive, as the lawyers are permitted to draw all "reasonable" inferences from the evidence in attempting to maximize the probability that the jury will accept their position.[69]

Two critically relevant points for the litigator can be made here. First, if primacy and recency seem not to apply to persuasive discourse, in failing to signal which presentation (the first or last) has the advantage, then probably by definition, it is only the closing arguments that are *not* susceptible to primacy and recency effects. Simply, no other part of the trial qualifies as "persuasive discourse." Second, if closing arguments are so unique a form of presenting information that they are immune to effects of serial order, then their effectiveness with the jury must derive from other criteria. It is this author's opinion that a trial's closing arguments can be viewed as persuasive speaking. The same kind of analysis performed on speeches of the stylistic elements of word choice, pauses, inflection, accent, as well as the selection of persona (the role played by the attorney) and the structure of argument, can suggest the elements of successful closing arguments.

The structure of an argument can vary with the point to be made. For example, if proposals are being compared and contrasted, all points of comparison could first be presented, and then all points of contrast; or, on each topic, a point of comparison and a point of contrast could be made. If a solution to a problem is sought, one way to win support for a certain solution is to suggest other possible solutions but then to indicate why each of those would fail, ultimately arriving at the preferred solution. All of these structures could be said to have order, but one particular argument structure relevant to a litigator may more clearly reflect a serial effect. In the closing argument, an attorney may want to say something about the opposition's position. Not doing so, or pretending that there is no opposing view, may appear to be exactly that—pretense. A clever orator, though, can actually suggest to his listeners what his opponent may say. Even if the opponent says something slightly different, the listeners may *think* it sounds like what they have already heard. Then, if the original speaker has persuaded them how to feel about his viewpoint, they may dismiss it. Practically, this approach could also work for the second speaker in a sequence, as he summarizes what the earlier speaker has said and gives the audience reason to disregard it.

Researchers have examined whether, in using this method, a speaker should present his arguments or his opponent's arguments first. In concluding that the speaker should begin with his own arguments, researchers have recognized a primacy effect. However, this does not seem at odds with the proposition that order effects do not clearly emerge in persuasion; the primacy effect here seems to relate purely to the ordering of information in a string. Such a conclusion is certainly useful in persuasive speaking.

Although the researchers state that whatever arguments are presented first will exercise the greater influence,[70] the term "arguments" is probably a misnomer for information. The experiment (conducted some thirty years ago) used a pamphlet urging high school students to volunteer in their local Civil Defense Organization. The pamphlet began by stating the government's need for civil defense volunteers. Then, in one form of the pamphlet, seven paragraphs indicated positive results of volunteering (such as saving lives through early warning systems) and then seven indicated negative results (such as tedious, all-night vigils). In a second form of the pamphlet, the seven negative results preceded the positive. An explicit plea for volunteers was at the end of both pamphlets.[71] The researchers then tested for attitude towards the communicator's point of view and found that it received considerably greater acceptance by subjects who had read the positive information first.[72]

The researchers suggest that, because of the powerful stimulation from the earlier information, an audience will ignore or discount the negative information, though it may clearly contradict the communicator's position. This occurs when the source of the information is prestigious and the audience is unfamiliar with or unconcerned about the negative data.[73] Notice that the limitations on this conclusion paraphrase the realization that serial ordering effects with information lists are primitive learning tools, relied upon only when more sophisticated reasons for recalling items of ideas are absent. If the recipients had been familiar with the negative information or had somehow "cared" about it, then there might have been no serial effect at all. Similarly, had they embraced positive views about civil defense work before reading the pamphlet (unlikely, since these were high school students), then seeing the negative information first would not have changed their receptivity to the communicator's position.

Although the presentation of evidence in a trial is not per se persuasive and must be conducted without advocacy,[74] primacy and recency cannot consistently apply there because of (1) constant interruptions in information strings (the tennis match effect of cross-examination and witness *voir dire*), (2) non-repeated information strings (recall that recency shows up after "practice" with strings of similar length), (3) and interference from other variables, such as the vividness and complexity of the testimony or the evidence. However, it is those very interferences with serial ordering effects that can cue the attorney to recall tools. If vividness sharpens recall, that suggests the use of demonstrative evidence. If complexity dulls recall, that guides the direct examination of an expert witness.

An analysis of the particular words of attorneys and witnesses appears in a later chapter, but the technique of demonstrative evidence warrants attention here, since it can enhance recall when order effects are smothered. To demonstrate is to show. Do not overlook the most basic showing of ideas to the jury. In a recent condemnation proceeding (*Houston Lighting & Power Co. v. Klein Independent School District*, No. 393,755 (County Ct. Law—Houston,

Texas, argued November 18, 1985)), an expert witness employed a deceptively simply but highly effective use of demonstrative evidence. A scientist, he opined as to the effects of radiation on children from a high-powered transmission line facility recently built near their school. Since any health effects on the children would not be detectable for some time, his conclusions could only have been speculative. However, his phraseology and method of presentation undoubtedly caused the jury to believe them without question. On his own, he had caused his conclusions to be printed on poster boards for the jury. The beginning words on his first poster were "An experiment is now in progress." Their chilling implication of possibly negative "experimental" results apparently struck the jury like a lightning bolt.

Demonstrative evidence includes anything that can help to convey a first-hand impression to a juror or judge as opposed to a second-hand impression, such as would be conveyed by someone's spoken words.[75] While some argue that the probative value of demonstrative evidence may be outweighed by its emotional effect, the response is that the information added by such evidence may be more significant than any sympathies produced.[76] An experiment reported in 1980 tested for the difference in awards made to a plaintiff who had lost his leg, when the artificial limb he would have to wear was just described orally and when it was physically passed around to the jurors. Subjects listened to tapes of speeches by the attorneys and instructions by the judge. With one group of subjects, though, the recorder was shut off about two-thirds of the way through the plaintiff's attorney's speech and an artificial leg was removed from a plastic bag and white sheet. The experimenter described it as the type of leg the plaintiff would have to wear from then on, and passed it around to the mock-jurors.[77] After the presentation, the subjects individually awarded sums to the plaintiff. The average dollar amount for those who had not seen the artificial limb was $62,500, as contrasted with $73,257 for those who had. Following deliberation, the figures rose to $68,333 and $75,833, respectively.[78] While this will be discussed further in the chapter on the juror, the researchers noted that the group, referring to the deliberations of the jurors as opposed to individual assessment, "did have a distinct role to play in enhancing the impact of demonstrative evidence."[79]

Starting from the closing arguments at the end of the trial, we have come forward, testing the applicability of primacy and recency effects. A consideration of the opening statements should be prefaced by a return to the wisdom of the famous country lawyer:

> From the time a lawyer steps into the courtroom, the jury forms an impression of him. Indeed, in smaller communities, impressions are formed long before that. . . . [the lawyer] should be the same man outside of the courtroom who seeks to win a case in the arena. Jurors are extremely conscientious and want to do that which is right. They want to accomplish substantial justice. But the fact that they like the laywer makes it easier for them to believe that he would not be on the wrong side of a case, and to give greater credence to his utterances.[80]

This passage from Appleman encompasses not only Asch's concept of first impression but also the idea of initial impression, or the pre-courtroom impression that a juror may have (bias).

If the suggested effect of the lawyer as a person (or a *persona*—the image he projects in trial) seems to have an unjustified effect on the jury, consider what it is a lawyer attempts to do. He must change the attitude of the jury or judge from neutrality or hostility to supportiveness. That is not unlike the task of the salesman, who must change the inactivity of his audience to the act of purchasing. While ideally it is the accumulated evidence that creates the desired change in the fact finder, the confusion created by different views of the evidence or a strong dislike of a witness may not suggest a resolution for the juror. However, "[c]ounsel alone may be so acceptable to the jury that his words alone can give to a juryman the support necessary to reduce his conflict and change his attitude."[81] The implication is that, if a juror must have some reason to make a choice, his or her opinion of the attorneys may be the only clear basis.

Without repeating the information in the section on primacy and recency, the following conclusions about the opening statements seem logical:

1. Primacy and recency seem not to apply to persuasive discourse. Since opening statements are supposed to be factual presentations, then primacy and recency effects are not excluded.

2. Since opening statements are factual, they are similar to information strings. However, as each attorney will present his client's version of the facts, the information strings are not repeated information strings. If each string is unique, then the primacy effect

should result *for each string*, if all other things are equal; that is, what each attorney syas first is likely to be best recalled.

3. Since the jury will see both attorneys at about the same time, first impressions will begin to form almost simultaneously. The attorney who first addresses them, however, will naturally have the opportunity to complete his impression (or induce the jury to complete their impression of him). This process can result in a positive or a negative impression, depending on how and how well the attorney presents himself, his client, and his client's position.

4. Since the jurors know that a second attorney will follow, they expect to have the opportunity to compare their first impressions of both attorneys. The second attorney does not necessarily have an advantage, but rather a standard, to meet or beat. Very likely, by the end of the opening statements, each juror knows which attorney he prefers.

And precisely how scrutinizing are jurors in assessing the attorneys? Appleman tells a story about the wife of an attorney friend of his. She sat on a federal jury, and Appleman and her husband quizzed her as to her and the other jurors' reactions to the case. He reports:

> Do you know the things she mentioned? The fact that one of the attorneys did not have his shoes shined, that his left shirt sleeve was frayed, and that he needed a haircut. "Why," she said, "we couldn't go along with a laywer like that!"
>
> This was the wife of an attorney. . . . You and I form immediate impressions of each person whom we meet based upon his dress, his poise and conduct, his speech, and his mannerisms. A jury does the same thing.[82]

As discussed in the section on primacy and recency, impressions formed before a juror comes into a courtroom are based on non-personal information about the parties. After finding no clear evidence of a law of primacy (in persuasion), Hovland concedes that "it may be that when no prior knowledge of the topic is involved, a law of primacy does operate." He then concludes that, "the nearer one comes to achieving primacy in the sense of first presentation of unfamiliar material, the more apt one is to obtain primacy effects."[83] This serves as additional explanation for the absence of primacy in closing arguments. Following the presentation of the evidence, the jury is now informed.[84]

As to the beginning of trial, one author posits the idealistic suggestion that true primacy exists only at the beginning of the trial, before the jury has any information about the issues to be decided.[85] This situation is realistic only if there has been little enough pre-trial publicity for a jury of specifically uninformed persons to be selected. Moreover, it is probable that many of the selected jurors have opinions about the kinds of issues involved. Finally, it is possible that some will have undetected biases against general characteristics of the parties and/or their claims. Instead of saying that a primacy effect may result if the jurors have no information about the trial subjects, it is more accurate to say that, in many potential jurors, a primacy effect may have already occurred and an initial impression has been formed. The juror brings that effect into trial in the form of a bias.

Because subtle or concealed biases can escape even the most careful *voir dire*, an attorney can never assume that he is starting with a clean slate with his audience. If he is, his job should certainly be easier. If he is not, he should give them every reason to resolve any conflict they may feel in his favor. And while primacy may not then operate in its purest form in his opening statement, he can personally attempt to make a strong first impression.

D. *Surviving Rules of Primacy and Recency*

The Rules of Primacy and Recency suggested at the end of the first section of this chapter follow, along with comments on how well they will survive in the context of the courtroom:

General Rules of Primacy and Recency

1. When a single string of information is presented, information at the *beginning* of the string is most clearly remembered.

This rule survives with the opening statements. What each attorney says first will probably be best remembered from each opening statement.

2. When strings of information of similar length are presented, information at the *end* of the strings past the first string is most clearly remembered. This generally holds true regardless of the complexity of the information, so long as the information is quite vivid.

This rule has no applicability to the opening statement, the overall presentation of evidence, or the closing arguments.

Hypothetically, it could apply to some types of testimony, if the witness were describing repeated processes of similar length. An example could be a witness explaining how various offshore oil properties were valued and, for the record, detailing the process with each property.

3. When there is more than one string of information and the information is complex but not very vivid, information at the *beginning* of the strings is most clearly remembered.

This rule has no applicability to the opening statement, the overall presentation of evidence, or the closing arguments. Hypothetically, it could apply to some types of testimony. Although the building-blocks approach is probably best suited to inducing belief in a listener, if a witness's methodology for arriving at a conclusion is quite complex, the attorney may have the witness first state his conclusion and then proceed to support it.

4. Information that is recalled from the *beginning* of an information string is better learned than information recalled from the end of a string.

This rule survives with the opening statements. What each attorney says first will probably be best remembered from each opening statement. Moreover, as the opening statements are supposed to be factual, they could be considered the beginning of the entire information string that includes all of the evidence presented at trial. An attorney could capitalize on this rule by presenting a clear, logically ordered summary of his client's position and then having this summary immediately verified by his client or another witness who could give a narrative presentation of the facts.

5. Attractive or appealing information about a person learned *first* improves our perception of that person's actual ability.

This rule survives with the opening statements with regard to the attorneys. Moreover, it will apply to each witness, as well as the parties.

6. Stereotype information about a person, when learned *after* an opinion expressed by that person that conflicts with the stereotype information, dilutes the validity of the opinion. This dilution does not occur when stereotype information is learned first.

This rule applies to the attorneys as well as to the parties and witnesses.

7. An existing bias is analogous to a well-learned early piece of information. That bias can be temporarily overcome by

information *later* learned (but retained for just a short while) only if that later information is believed.

This rule applies to the opening statements and could persist throughout the trial if the attorneys are unable to provide the jurors with a reason to forgo any bias.

Naturally, some of the above rules will be modified still further in their applicability when viewed in relationship to the juror, in the next section.

III. *THE JUROR AS A UNIQUE SUBJECT*

A tiny subset of data concerning primacy and recency involves subjects in the field of counseling. "The Primacy and Recency Effect in Counselor Response," published by Tyson and Kramer in 1981, directly addresses earlier reported experimental results. These results indicated that when a counselor is presented with alternative communications, he or she responds to the most recent of the communications. Since recency is generally thought to appear only after information strings are repeated, which would probably not occur when information is conveyed to a counselor, this finding was especially interesting and seemed correlated to the counseling field. Recognizing the importance of a response by a counselor (whose words could soothe or trigger unstable emotions of the person on the other end of a telephone line or across a desk) and the need for a counselor to respond to the "right" message, Tyson and Kramer tested for serial ordering with counselors.

The subjects, counselors with at least a year's experience, were given twelve statements, each containing two sequentially distinct communications, and then responded.[86] Their responses were classified as being either to the first communication, the second, or both (or unclear). The researchers observed that

> frequency of primacy, recency, and both responses varies from one statement to the next, which seems to indicate that the [subjects] were responding more to the content of the messages rather than the position of the message in a statement. This, of course, is what one would hope for in a counseling situation.[87]

In other words, responsible counselors are so attentive to content in message streams that they are immune to base ordering effects. Either by instinct or training, they know not to ascribe undue weight to a message merely because it appears first, or last.

The juror is as unique a subject as a counselor. They both have a degree of responsibility that sets them apart from college students attempting to recall a list of words or mock jurors deciding the fate of a make-believe defendant. And as he must judge, the task of the juror may be more difficult than that of the counselor. Moreover, while both the counselor and the juror act individually in performing their tasks, the juror is thought to act in concert with eleven others. After he was withheld expressing any opinion as to the evidence he has heard, but undoubtedly committed much of it to memory, in the form in which he recalled it, the juror must then match his version and his interpretation of it against those of others.

But despite his role as a member of a conscientious group, the juror is first and foremost an individual. Descriptions of his thought processes and behavioral patterns will probably be the same both before and after he has become a juror. If, as many have observed, the jury's "*real decision is often made before the deliberation begins*,"[88] then it may be twelve (or less) individuals that must be convinced and *not* one twelfth of a group. Therefore, studies that detail the effects on individual perception and recall of ordering in information strings, the vividness and complexity of information, and personal attractiveness are useful in analyzing the juror. The question is, to what extent do the unique characteristics of jury service modify individual, non-juror behavior? Answering this question will involve examination of "juror personality" traits and the deliberation process and its effects. Woven throughout this discussion are observations of ordering effects. Then follows a treatment of the reaction by a juror to the specific primacy effect of physical attractiveness, as well as vividness of information, which is known to overpower a purely ordering effect.[89]

A. *Individual Juror Traits*

Although the subject is covered in depth in a later chapter, attorneys often exclude or accept potential jurors on the bases of education, sex, race, occupation, and geographic background. Each of these characteristics concerns the juror as an individual, and the validity of such an examination is rooted in the individual (as opposed to group) decision theory. Moreover, a kind of primacy effect is relied upon by the attorney who selects jurors having a background similar to his client's; that is, the attorney is assuming that such jurors have an initial (and initially favorable) impression of the client.

However, this kind of data tells us little about how jurors will interact with each other in the deliberation process. And to the extent that this process overcomes individual decisions, clues on how jurors may assess guilt and punishment and can persuade each other to accept these assessments are as potentially valuable as those indicating a favorable or unfavorable bias towards the client.

A 1980 study had as its main purpose the investigation of "the effects of personality dynamics on jury decision making in terms of actual decisions rendered as well as individual jurors' perceptions of the deliberation process."[90] The researchers mailed questionnaires to 226 males and 324 females randomly selected from persons who had served on Baltimore city juries for a six-month period; 80 males and 117 females responded. Though the response rate was only 40%, a comparison of demographic characteristics (obtained through court records) indicated those who responded to be representative of the general and the jury population.[91]

Concerning the effect of the deliberation, the jurors answered questions that inquired about their personal decision in the case and asked whether they acted as foreman, changed the decisions of other jurors, made their personal decision with ease, were now satisfied with the decision reached, and believed that *some* decision was preferable, even though they might not have been certain of the decision. They also provided information that allowed the researchers to describe the existence of three personality characteristics: socialization, empathy, and autonomy. The reasoning was that very socialized people should be predisposed to follow social rules ("an orientation to obey the letter of the law rather than the spirit"), to reach, therefore, more guilty verdicts, and to arrive at their decisions relatively easily, due to a clear understanding of their duty to society. Highly empathic individuals, though, because they would be more inclined to consider a defendant's intentions, would be more likely to render not guilty verdicts. Also, such people would possess the traits of poise and charm, which could enable them to influence others. Finally, very autonomous people, being independent and decisive, could withstand group pressure, make decisions rather easily, and glean satisfaction from their decisions.[92]

The results of the questionnaire and personality data were correlated with other personal data, such as sex, age, and education. As suspected, individuals with high socialization ratings produced more guilty verdicts, but only if they were males; females with high socialization ratings produced more not guilty verdicts. Higher socialization scores increased with age. Empathy levels increased with education but decreased with age, and were associated with more not guilty verdicts. The hypothesized effect of empathic persons in persuading others was observed only in males. Autonomy also increased with education but had no relationship to age; for both sexes, high autonomy scores were correlated more with not guilty verdicts than with guilty.[93]

Although the researchers do not do so to the following extent, several conclusions about the verdict predisposition of jurors—based solely on their personalities—could be drawn from the above findings:

a. A highly socialized (more rule-oriented) and educated (more autonomous) female, regardless of her age (and degree of empathy) may be expected to deliver a not guilty verdict. However, she will not likely influence other of the jurors to render the same verdict she does.

b. A highly socialized (more rule-oriented), older (less empathic), educated (more autonomous) male may be expected to deliver a guilty verdict. Although he may not be likely to influence the other jurors, he will probably be resistant to influence himself.

c. An under socialized (less rule-oriented), younger (more empathic), educated (more autonomous) male may be expected to deliver a not guilty verdict. Also, he may be able to influence other jurors.

d. A less educated (less autonomous), younger (more empathic) male or female, regardless of their socialization (which would not be as great as if they were older), may not be able to arrive at a verdict with ease. Therefore, they may be susceptible to influence by others on the jury. Also, this influence need not be purposeful; an uncertain juror may as easily be influenced by the sheer superiority of education and maturity in other jurors.

Another field of research posits that experienced jurors become more rule-oriented or socialized; that is, they tend to convict more. Theoretically, as service increases, jurors are exposed to more and more of the same kinds of crimes, alibis, and legal arguments and "grow weary . . . and irritated with those who apparently commit crimes."[94] However, in one mock juror study, the subjects were asked to detail their prior jury service; their reported experiences bore no strong relation to any other measured individual differences among the jurors. Perhaps more important, experienced jurors demonstrated no better recall of relevant evidence at the end of the trial or the legal definitions provided. Finally, prior jury service was unrelated to contributions during deliberations.[95]

Studies in this field of research are faulted for their lack of comparability. For example, kinds of cases, terms of jury service, and number of jury experiences in total and in sequence (some jurors may sit on more than one case in response to a single call) have not been constant. Also, it is possible that the nature of the first case a juror sits on could affect his decision the second time he serves (e.g., a vandalism case followed by a rape case as opposed to a rape case followed by a vandalism case). One author safely concludes that "it seems probable that guilt-preferences are at least partly moulded by the kind and order of prior experiences." He then suggests a reduction of jury service to a single trial (as opposed to a set number of days of service, and possibly multiple trials), which has been the practice in Texas state courts for over ten years.[96]

B. *Effects of the Deliberation Process*

With many estimations as to the time jurors reach a verdict ranging from the end of *voir dire* or opening statements to the close of the evidence, the critical question may be, "whatever it is, what does deliberation accomplish?" Kalven and Zeisel analogize deliberation to film developing: "it brings out the picture, but the outcome is pre-determined."[97] In other words, deliberation produces consensus, not a decision. Researchers in this area have been especially conscious of the need to describe realistic jury deliberations. Realistic is the closest possible to reality, as described by Kalven and Zeisel in their introduction to *The American Jury*. They attempted in the early 1950s to record actual jury deliberations, with the consent of the trial judge and counsel but without the jury's knowledge. When their effort became known in 1955, it was followed by "public censure by the Attorney General of the United States, a special hearing before the Sub-Committee on Internal Security of the Senate Judiciary Committee, [and] the enactment of statutes in some thirty-odd jurisdictions prohibiting jury-tapping."[98]

Thus, experiments are often designed to simulate relevant elements of the jury experience. Researchers who reported in 1978 the effects on jurors of the type of decision and the number of alternatives given, incorporated into their experiment an element missing from an earlier study: deliberation. They credit Vidmar with findings indicating a correlation between not guilty verdicts and the severity of the least severe guilty alternative (i.e., there would be more not guilty verdicts when the least severe alternative was second degree murder than when it was manslaughter). However, they note the omission in Vidmar's study of deliberation, "which usually includes exposure to different viewpoints, peer pressure, and interpersonal conflict."[99] Verdicts were taken from the subjects, who were college psychology students, both before and after deliberation. The independent variable was the severity of the charge (and accompanying punishment), being first or second degree murder. The results confirmed Vidmar's findings; before deliberation, there were "significantly more" not guilty verdicts for first than second degree murder.[100] However, the number of not guilty verdicts for both charges increased following deliberation; and "[m]ore subjects in the first degree condition changed their verdicts to not guilty than did those in the second degree condition."[101] The researchers hypothesize that mock jurors may be biased towards not guilty verdicts because they are supposed to find guilt only if the evidence indicates it beyond a reasonable doubt (as if that were an uncommon instruction for a real jury). Second, they suggest that opposing viewpoints expressed in deliberation may have caused those with guilty verdicts to doubt their decisions (as if those with guilty verdicts did not have the same persuasive power over the others).[102] More plausible explanations exist for a shift in verdicts following deliberation.

While the unique province of the jury has induced a precise focus, some believe it is instructional to widen the parameters and view these twelve (or fewer) individuals as a small group. Group discussion literature contains a subset called choice shift literature; it indicates that group discussion "serves to polarize attitudes causing group discussions, and individual decisions after group discussion to be more extreme than decisions of individuals prior to group discussion." Another subset concerns group problem solving and contrasts the performance of a group with that of an individual when both are confronted by a eureka task (having an obvious correct answer) or a human relations task (having no one obvious answer but many alternatives, which must be weighed for relative adequacy). Groups usually perform better than individuals with the eureka task, the data being "to problematic" with the human relations task.[103] With the choice shift literature as support, one could explain the leniency shift described in the above paragraph: the decision of the members of the group, most of whom apparently favored a less harsh verdict, became more extreme (even less harsh). The concept is not difficult to visualize; individuals who decide in a minority see that they are in a minority, hear the reasons of the majority, doubt the reasons for their initial choice, and shift. In that way, the group has become more extreme because more of its members now embrace the view that the majority originally did. It is conceivable that members of the original majority, due to anything they might say in support of their position or even by the fact that they are in the majority, become even more convinced of the soundness of their position and advance it more sincerely. Thus, they appear more extreme in their decision.

Although choice shift literature seems to be malleable to the results of this experiment, the fit is less than perfect. The experiment described earlier reflected twenty-three total verdict changes (i.e., for both first and second degree verdicts), of which ten were to guilty.[104] If those ten could be viewed as marginal—almost guilty—before the deliberation, wouldn't the polarization have resulted in a decision of even less than almost guilty instead of guilty? Also, what is the definition of a "more extreme" post-discussion decision? Obviously, a shift in the seriousness of a charge toward that originally indicated by the majority would be an example. Also, if eight jurors say not guilty before deliberating and eleven say not guilty after deliberating, that clearly seems an emphasis of the group's original inclination. But what if, in one case, eight jurors say ten years, four say five years, and then all twelve agree on eight years; and in another case, eight jurors say five years, four say ten, and then all twelve agree on eight years? Since the resulting punishment is the same, was the first jury originally lenient and became more lenient? If so, was the second jury originally harsh and became harsher?

Two studies of university students were undertaken at Purdue to test whether individual sentencing judgments would shift systematically after group discussion and whether any shifts would reflect a polarization.[105] The first study involved groups of three subjects who were given a written summary of an alleged negligent homicide incident; half of the groups received information that described the defendant positively (warm, sincere, friendly, etc.) and half that described him negatively (cold, insincere, impolite, etc.). The subjects individually selected a prison sentence of one to twenty years and recorded their impressions of the defendant on thirteen bipolar adjectives. Then, each group engaged in a discussion to reach a unanimous decision concerning the defendant. Before deliberation, the subjects rated the positive defendant more favorably, and gave the negative defendant a longer sentence. After deliberation, female subjects became more lenient in their sentences if the defendant had been described positively; the highest initial sentences were given by females to negative defendants. Males became more lenient regardless of the defendant. The average sentence for both type of defendant fell from 7.44 years before deliberation to 6.53 years afterwards.[106]

In the second study, five-person, same-sexed groups were given positive or negative information about the defendant ("defendant salient groups") *or* about the victim ("victim salient groups"). While subjects in the victim salient groups were more punitive than subjects in the defendant salient group, both groups shifted toward leniency after deliberation (7.34 years to 6.18 years). Females doled out substantially harsher penalties than males before deliberation, regardless of the salience level, shifted only slightly towards leniency in the defendant salient groups, and shifted sharply toward leniency in the victim salient groups. Males were initially more punitive in the victim salient groups than the defendant salient groups; after deliberation, they had virtually no shift in the victim salient groups but shifted substantially towards leniency in the defendant salient groups.[107]

The researchers thus conclude, "[a]s with previous studies of [subject] penalty judgments, results failed to conform to those predicted on the basis of the polarization hypothesis."[108] In other words, they interpreted the leniency shifts as not being in accord with the groups' initial tendency. Evidently, with a sentence range of one to twenty years, the researchers viewed the 7.44 and 7.34 years as harsh; therefore, only by giving longer sentences could the groups have demonstrated polarization.[109] Alternatively, the researchers may have interpreted more extreme decisions as meaning harsher penalties, which is as baffling as the other possible explanation, since "more extreme" should mean further in the original direction of the group.

The difficulty in applying choice shift analysis to jury decisions may lie in the wide range of choices available to jurors, with possible sentences varying with the crime, and extenuating circumstances mitigating the punishment. Concerning the applicability of group-task discussion literature to jury deliberations, even to the extent that a jury is asked, "Is the defendant guilty?" it is not clearly confronted with a eureka task. An example of such a task might be a group of employees trying to decide how to convince their boss to let them have off Friday instead of Monday of a long weekend.

The group members would seek and share information, truly working together to arrive at a single solution. When, however, a jury is asked to weigh alternatives (assess the importance of evidence, judge the credibility of witnesses, determine whether all elements of a crime have been proven, etc.), it may be assigned more of a human relations task, less susceptible to traditional aspects of group discussion. Those are judgments that responsible (socialized), confident (autonomous), and competent (educated) people do not trust to others; however, those who are less autonomous and competent may be swayed by the opinion (verdict) of other jurors. If that is the case, then we return to an earlier suggestion that counsel address twelve individuals, who will behave like individuals and arrive at individual decisions.

The theoretical difficulty of applying choice shift to jury decisions may exist mainly with some of the definitions (or lack thereof). Whatever the label, there is usually a shift between the initial ballots of juries and the final verdicts. Post-trial interviews of juries following 225 trials revealed that, after the first ballot, the jury was unanimous for acquittal in 12% of the cases and unanimous for conviction in 19% of the cases; the jury hung in only 5% of the cases.[110] Therefore, some change occurred from the first ballot to the final, unanimous verdict in at least 64% of the cases. A study reported in the section called Theory: Primacy vs. Recency may offer the greatest support for choice shift, yet that was not the point of the experiment (therefore, the results may be unreliable for that conclusion). Two sets of subjects were given data indicating either that a defendant was guilty or that he was not. Then, in three groups of each of those two larger sets of subjects, either the defense attorney, the judge, or the prosecution offensively interrupted the trial many times; the fourth group served as the control, having no interruptions. Next, the subjects assessed the guilt of the defendants, both before and after deliberation. Although the interruptions affected the guilt assessments both before and after deliberations, for all versions of the trial (that is, regardless of who interrupted or whether there were no interruptions), the guilty-appearing defendant was adjudged more guilty after the deliberations, and the innocent-appearing defendant was adjudged less guilty.[111] Thus, these findings support choice shift, or both a leniency shift and a tendency toward harsher verdicts.

Instead of describing a leniency shift or a harshness shift for jurors, others have made comments that reflect the range of personalities and values that a jury encompasses:

> The jury, in the guise of resolving doubts about issues of fact, gives reign to its sense of values. It will not often be doing this consciously; as the equities of the case press, the jury may, as one judge put it, "hunt for doubts." . . .
>
> [W]e suspect there is little or no intrinsic directionality in the jury's response. It is not fundamentally defendant-prone, rather it is non-rule minded; it will move where the equities are.
>
> . . . .
>
> Thus while the jury is often moved to leniency by adding a distinction the law does not make, it is at times moved to be more severe than the judge because it wishes to override a distinction the law does make.[112]

Another way of saying that the jury is "non-rule minded" is saying that it is composed of twelve individuals, each of whom is likely to be guided by his or her own set of rules.

Moreover, if observations about decision shifts are to describe a jury convincingly, they should account for the variations in decision rules. In one extensive mock jury study that used subjects from jury pools, three verdicts were possible: manslaughter, second degree murder, and first degree murder. Subjects were divided into juries with three decision rules: twelve-out-of-twelve, ten-out-of-twelve, and eight-out-of-twelve. Under all decision rules, the most popular initial verdict was manslaughter; the most popular choice by the end of deliberations, though, was second degree murder. The researcher resisted the temptation to conclude that this meant juries were prone to come to harsher verdicts after deliberation, as the verdicts concerned only a single stimulus case. Additionally, he studied the likelihood of verdict shift as correlated with the decision rule. Although verdicts of not guilty and first degree murder were the most unpopular for initial decisions, the results indicated that jurors under a twelve-out-of-twelve decision rule are unlikely to stay with these decisions. Jurors under a non-unanimous decision rule, however, are much more prone to maintain their original, though unpopular, positions.[113] (And why not? If two-four minority positions are reserved anyway, where is the pressure to change?) The effects of decision rules will be given more consideration in a later chapter; the point here is that juries are not necessarily harsh or lenient, before or after deliberation. Much depends upon the combination of personalities, to what extent the decision rule will require forgoing an originally expressed verdict, the nature of the particular case and the parties, as well as "where the equities are at any given time [which] will depend on both the state of the law and the climate of public opinion."[114]

C. *Content of Jury Deliberation*

What then, goes on when the jury deliberates? And what does that tell us about the effect of deliberation? "To begin with, we suspect that the jurors' talk may often be not very revealing. . . . the real cause of a juror's decision will be in many instances a factor he himself is only dimly aware of and perhaps unable to articulate. . . .yielding to sentiment in the guise of evaluating factual doubt."[115] In examining "juror's talk" and armed with the idea that deliberation is a persuasive exercise, we might logically begin with the assumption that the foreman of the jury will probably be the most persuasive individual and that his selection will be a careful one. After a credible defense of experimental juries, Rita James Simon describes that a particular recorded trial was presented repeatedly to various mock jurors, all of whom had been drawn from local jury pools.[116] In particular, she examined the jury's reactions to criminal cases involving the insanity defense,[117] but her analysis included influence within the jury. Concerning the selection of the foreman, she observed that the foreman is "[a]lmost always. . . selected very quickly, and usually without a formal vote."[118] Coincidentally, both she and Kalven and Zeisel excerpted the foreman selection portion from the same experimental jury.[119] One juror, a male white-collar employee, nominated another juror, a female clerical worker, as foreman, since she was "sitting in the head chair." She batted the nomination back to him, since she understood he had served on a jury before and she had not. After a bit of reluctance on his part, she urged, "Go on, you act as foreman." And the matter was settled.

Simon notes another interesting finding about the foreman: although male jurors that "hold important positions in the larger society" talk more during deliberations and are more likely to become foreman, "they do not appear to wield more influence."[120] If their positions are indicative of their socialization and maturity and their willingness to talk suggestive of their education and independence, such individuals could be lacking in empathy. According to the earlier discussion of juror personality traits, these people would not be expected to be influential with others.

In one study, the goal was to discover "what actually goes on in the jury room during deliberation." The researchers, Bridgeman and Marlowe, interviewed sixty-five actual jurors following the completion of ten felony trials, via a questionnaire. The researchers were unable to persuade more than seven jurors from any single trial to participate in the interview.[121] Because they can be compared with the juror "personality traits" discussed earlier in this chapter, similar characteristics of these jurors are depicted below:

EDUCATION		24 grade or high school		41 college
OCCUPATIONS	8 blue-collar 6 students	12 housewives 3 retired	28 white-collar	8 professional
POLITICAL ORIENTATION	1 radical 1 extremely conservative	21 liberal	32 moderate	9 conservative
CHURCH ATTENDANCE	9 weekly	3 every 2 weeks	26 monthly	39 never

The researchers observe that the above conflicts with the stereotype of jurors in this area (a small California county), consisting of older, politically conservative, and relatively poorly educated individuals. They theorize that the presence of a college campus in town could be the cause for difference and that those jurors who did not participate in the survey may have conformed more to the norm. In any event, they do not view these jurors as representative of California or even Santa Cruz jurors in general.[122] In the terms of the juror personality traits earlier discussed, those jurors with a college education would be expected to be more autonomous; the majority, being younger than the norm for that area, would be expected to have more empathy; and the moderate political leanings would suggest less rule-orientation (socialization).

The eleven defendants in the ten trials were found guilty on eight counts and not guilty on three counts; only two defendants were found not guilty. This 82% conviction rate contrasted with the overall

90% conviction rate for felony trials in Santa Cruz County. This difference, indicating a slight leaning towards not guility, could be due to the personality traits of the jurors noted in the previous paragraph. In the first ballot, forty-two of the jurors voted guilty, nineteen voted innocent, and four voted undecided. Not in any case did the final outcome of the trial differ from the original ballot vote.

As to the effect of deliberation, only fifteen jurors mentioned deliberation in response to a question as to the main reasons they eventually voted the way they did; eleven jurors said that the opinions of other jurors most influenced them; and no one felt that his or her vote was determined by the foreman.[123] The foreman was not selected in a consistent manner; "the most commonly used practice was for someone to spontaneously nominate a foreperson and for the others to quickly agree."[124]

When asked when they first became convinced of the defendant's guilt or innocence, twenty-three jurors said near the beginning or the middle of trial, thirty-one said by the end of trial but before deliberations, and only eleven said that they were undecided at the end of trial.[125]

The jurors' answers clearly revealed their sense of responsibility and desire for justice, and they often made comments indicating that the experience was the most important event of their lives. As to their willingness to serve again, two said they would never want to, ten said they would serve again but reluctantly, and fifty-three said they would willingly serve again.[126] As to prior service, fourteen had served before, but this was the first trial for fifty-one of them.[127]

Based on admissions of when the jurors formed their verdicts, Bridgeman and Marlowe conclude that decisions are largely made on the basis of evidence and testimony; and, as earlier indicated, these decisions were made for 70% of the jurors before the deliberations began. When asked what they relied on or attended to during deliberations, 59% of the jurors said that the most influential post-trial factor was the chance to engage in a "review of the evidence."[128] Bridgeman and Marlowe offer an explanation for this comment, which is peculiar in light of 70% of the jurors already having made a decision based on the evidence: during deliberation, "the juror seeks consensual validation for his or her judgment by learning the verdicts and arguments of the other jurors.[129] Similarly, researchers in another study concluded that

> jurors are not seeking opinions or attempted answers from their fellow jurors, but instead are seeking positive reactions and agreement with their own position, *i.e.*, attempting to manipulate other jurors toward agreement with their own opinions. . . . jurors are more intent on obtaining agreement and support than on debating and discussing the issues.[130]

This observation is consistent with the rationale of Bridgeman and Marlowe, which suggests a focus on the integrity of the *individual decision*. Such a comment would not characterize discussions in a group seeking a common goal. If jurors independently (that is, without discussion) come to their own decisions, decisions with which they are quite comfortable, and primarily seek further validation of those decisions during deliberation, then the earlier consideration of individual personality traits and related degrees of persuasiveness seems warranted. But persuasive skills can probably *not* be determined by questions to the jurors. Hastie tried this with his experimental juries and found a "clear. . . tendency to rate one's own persuasive influence and open-mindedness as higher than average ratings for other jurors."[131] Certainly, some jurors are more susceptible to influence than others. One communications expert, examining the trial experience from the perspective of the jury, says very practically that "[m]ost people are followers. . . just not willing to be exposed and vulnerable to the attack of the majority." Jurors who "knuckle under" may simply run out of arguments after one or two statements or feel that the others are smarter than they are (which, in juror trait analysis, is one reason more educated people are likely to be more autonomous and to withstand group pressure). Even though they take their responsibility as jurors quite seriously, "they are, after all, only people." Unless those in a minority can add new arguments to their position or get support from at least one other juror, "most dissenters will fold."[132]

Based on his findings, Hastie hypothesizes that "the deliberation process is largely a recapitulation at the group discussion level of processes that occur in the mind of each individual juror before deliberation."[133] Concerning the experimental trial with the defense of insanity, Simon notes "surprise at how freely the jurors shared with each other some extremely personal and revealing accounts of their experiences with mentally ill relatives and friends. These experiences probably influenced a juror's verdict as much as his exposure to the particular details surrounding the defendant's behavior."[134] Again, this sharing of experience was undoubtedly done as a rationale for a juror's decision; it may even have served as a basis for another juror shifting his verdict, though it clearly was not evidence.

One marked characteristic of the deliberation process, however, is collective recall. Testing for individual recall, prior to deliberation, Hastie found only about 60% accuracy for information directly stated in the testimony and less than 30% accuracy for material directly stated in the final charge. In contrast, group recall, indicated by the mention of a fact by any juror, was over 90% correct for evidentiary matters and 80% accurate for information in the charge.[135] As we have already seen, most jurors begin deliberations having already made a decision. Since it is supposed that their decisions are based on the presented evidence, then they already have an idea of "what happened." They apparently share their ideas during deliberation. But as Hastie observes, "once jurors' constructions of the evidence, their stories of what happened, were formed and stabilized, these stories were relatively resistant to persuasive argumentation from other jurors."[136] Therefore, collective recall for the evidence could be 100%, which would simply mean that every piece of evidence was recalled by some juror and fit into his or her story of what happened. That conclusion does not mean that all jurors considered all relevant evidence. The suggestion is that only those jurors who are undecided (that is, their stories of what happened are incomplete) will be truly "persuaded" during deliberations. Others, who forsake their original verdicts, may be overpowered by stronger personalities.

Hastie, however, suggests one other way in which verdicts may change during deliberation, even when jurors believe they know "what happened":

> Given the difficulty of comprehending and applying the instructions, many of the successful persuasive efforts to change verdicts during jury deliberation appeared to occur when the persuader focused on legal rather than evidentiary issues. Jurors seemed much more willing to admit that they were confused or even incorrect concerning legal issues than to admit that they misunderstood the evidence, misjudged the credibility of a witness, or put together their stories in an implausible fashion.
>
> . . . .
>
> [V]irtually every dramatic shift in juror verdict preferences, such as the reversal of a majority faction by a smaller faction, occurred because of changes in opinion about the law or jury procedures.[137]

Despite the improved collective recall of the court's instructions over that of the individual jurors, Hastie nevertheless concludes that problems in understanding, recalling, and applying the instructions "are major obstacles to proper jury performance." In comparing the errors made by the jurors in their comments regarding evidence with those made as to the instructions, Hastie found fact errors occurring about half as often as instruction errors.[138] Most recall errors concerned definitions of manslaughter and self-defense; the most accurate juror on each jury recalled only half of the elements or conditions of these verdict categories.[139] Some jurors persisted in their own definitions, despite reinstruction from the court. For example, some jurors generalized that manslaughter applies only when a death results from a traffic accident or from a weapon that is not obviously deadly.[140]

Another observed problem stems from the *order* of multiple charges, similar to the concern about jurors sitting on a case involving a felony being harsher in their verdicts on the next case, though it may involve a misdemeanor. Though the term is not used, a primacy effect is being suggested here, in that the first experience causes a predisposition towards later similar events. It may be the recollection of the first event that causes the jurors to be harsher in the second. In one experiment, nearly 500 mock jurors were presented with a video-taped trial in which the defendant was charged with reckless homicide (RH), aggravated battery (AB), and criminal damage (CD) to property. The charges were "dramatically and logically independent," though they were derived from events that occurred at approximately the same time and place. The order of the charges was varied, with the testing being specifically for differences in a descending order of seriousness—RH, AB, CD—or an ascending order—CD, AB, RH. If order had no effect, then the defendant should have been found guilty of AB with equal frequency for each charge. However, there were significantly more guilty AB verdicts for the descending than the ascending charge. What is more shocking is that, even when the verdict was not guilty on both the RH and CD charge (that is, the first charge in the sequence), there were significantly more guilty verdicts on the AB charge when it followed the RH charge. The researchers conclude that, even when separate charges are ostensibly unrelated, jurors do not decide them separately and independently.[141]

The court's charge to the jury is often the joint effort of both counsel and the jury himself and reflects statutory requirements, as well as models formulated by experts who are thought to have given such models a great deal of thought. Thus, the proper forming of a charge is beyond the scope of this material and is the focus of existing treatises. However, the court's instructions as to the law and verdict categories are the boundaries into which each juror fits his version of "what happened." The means of conveying information to facilitate the formation of these versions *is* within the realm of this book. Thus, the focus now turns to how counsel may proceed to convey a certain structure of the facts to the individual jurors, based on suppositions as to how the jurors will receive these communications. An examination of the actual words and arguments used will appear in a later chapter; here, the concerns are ordering effects and devices that override such effects.

D. *The Juror's Processing of Information*

The previous section presents the idea that the traditional effect of primacy is muted or perhaps even altered into a recency effect because of the unique perspective of the jury. Since its members know that the first position will be refuted, first impressions will be less influential than otherwise and may even create a heightened receptivity to the second position.[142] In conjunction with the University of Chicago finding that 65% of jurors form unchanging beliefs about cases immediately after the opening statements and the author's research that approximately 70% of jurors have made a decision at the conclusion of the *voir dire* and over 80% at the completion of the opening statements, the explanation could be that jurors form a first impression of the plaintiff, which they then compare with a first impression of the defense, which leads them to a first impression of the case. Since no evidence has yet been presented, this first impression of the case must be based on something within the juror. In turn, this first impression may well shape the weight he gives to evidence as it unfolds, the credibility he assigns to witnesses. According to the earlier referenced study by Bridgeman and Marlowe, 35% of actual jurors interviewed after trials indicated that they became certain of the defendant's guilt or innocence before all of the evidence had been presented.[143] In other words, they may have selectively excluded any evidence after the point of their decision that conflicted with their impression of the case.

Bridgeman and Marlowe also determined that the jurors' first view of the defendant was "emotionally toned," with jurors reporting an initial hesitance to make eye contact with the defendant. When asked, after they first saw the defendant, what they believed about his guilt or innocence, almost 20% said they believed he was probably guilty, 77% said they were not sure, and the remainder said he was probably innocent (the legal presumption). The researchers basically discount these reported first impressions, saying that only 6% of the jurors claimed to have arrived at a fairly certain verdict at the beginning of the trial and that the majority reported "keeping an open mind" during trial and admitting to having formed only a tentative hypothesis at first.[144] This may be a prime example of the superiority of experimental juries for determining actual thought processes. Real jurors, even if they were promised that their comments would be kept in confidence, would undoubtedly be reluctant to admit that they had defied the court's instructions to withhold judgment, especially after professing such a sense of justice and responsibility. What real juror would reveal deciding a case for an emotional (i.e., nonevidentiary) reason? As earlier noted, Kalven and Zeisel suggest that jurors may not even know why they decide as they do, but hypothesize that they are more likely "yielding to sentiment in the guise of evaluating factual doubt."[145]

Attorneys, accustomed to courtrooms, often never know how uncomfortable jurors may be in that environment and how inadequate they may feel to perform the role into which they have been thrust. Hamlin compares jurors to new patients in a doctor's waiting room, disoriented and unable to predict exactly what will happen next.[146] She says that from the beginning, jurors look to counsel for a leader, teacher, helper, and guide. Her description of questions that a juror seeks to have answered in the opening statement indicates how a lasting first impression can be formed and how that formation is the result of comparison of counsel:

> Who is the teller?
> Who's bringing the message?
> What does he or she know?
> Is it enough?
> In which of these two guides will I place more confidence?
> Who sounds like he thinks like I do? Whom can I believe in and trust?
> Who is telling me "This is wrong and this is right?"

She adds that "the one thing [jurors] want to know most of all is what's going to happen," in the form of a blueprint, so that "they can follow the story."[147] Remember Hastie's finding: once jurors piece together "what happened" in their own minds, their versions of the facts are impervious to change.[148]

How do jurors form their stories? Practically, this is a process that begins before the juror enters the courtroom. Ideally, it is a process that continues at least until the end of trial. Hastie explains that a juror first uses " 'factual' knowledge of the social and physical world that appears relevant to the case." In other words, he relies on what he believes—whether true in the absolute sense or not—about the accuracy of eyewitness testimony, how alcohol might affect someone's motor coordination, what another's motives might be, how another person might act in a particular circumstance, etc. Then, he employs certain information strategies, probably unique to him, to organize the data, filtered first through his "factual" knowledge, into a mental "product" which he then transforms into a decision. His first task in the courtroom may be encoding the trial contents. Although the idealized juror is "a relatively passive record-keeper. . .who encodes the events of the trial verbatim," selective recall, forgetfulness, reorganization, and inferential embellishment make the actual juror less than perfect. Throughout the trial, the court will instruct the jury that certain events, though occurring in the jury's presence, are not evidence, such as comments of counsel and inadmissible material. In trying to make a story of what happened, the juror must compare each item of evidence for admissibility; if admitted, it must then be evaluated for credibility and any implications within each context that refers to it. Finally, jurors must evaluate the fit of their final versions of the story into each of the possible verdict categories in the charge. Based on empirical evidence, the "stories jurors tell are. . .related to the verdicts they choose."[149]

As observed in the previous chapter, beyond the opening statements, a trial can become so unsequenced that, except perhaps for the very first witness, pure ordering effects are smothered. That is, the first words out of later witnesses' mouths (even the first words from the first witness) have no assurance of being recalled by the jury simply because they were first. Although collectively jurors may state during deliberation the great majority of all important as well as irrelevant facts, by that point many of them will already have formed their stories. One goal, therefore, should be to ensure that jurors lock into memory certain facts while they are piecing together their stories. Information in a string of data will stand out if it is vivid. Before examining the effects of vividness on jurors' recall of information, though, the degree of influence of even earlier data should be examined, the attractiveness of the parties.

E. *The Effect of Attractiveness on Jurors*

Bridgeman and Marlowe believe that defendant attractiveness, like pure ordering effects, has "undue prominence" in experimental settings and becomes much less important when "embedded in the more complex courtroom setting," in which such a factor comprises only "a fraction of the total stimulus field."[150] The counter-argument, of course, is that it is precisely in an experimental setting that variables can be manipulated so that their effects can be isolated and described with certainty. Also, we have seen that although the real juror may be unique in the sense of responsibility he feels, he is not likely to call up a brand new set of "factual" data (i.e., his frame of reference, with which he will interpret the evidence he hears in court) or adopt different cognitive processes. For example, in the section on primacy and recency it was pointed out that the adversary method of presenting evidence triggers an *unconscious* response to an existing bias. When one feels that his bias is overtly being appealed to, he rebels, sensing that he is being denied the option to choose contrary to his bias. Therefore, using data presented by the opposing side, he exercises his freedom to choose (to be different) and, in effect, overcomes his bias.[151] Although one could argue that the increased sense of responsibility may enhance this effect, the result is no different—either way, the bias is overcome. The point here is that, even if they do not describe the behavior of actual jurors or even mock jurors, findings as to human reactions to attractiveness in others are valid descriptions of human behavior.

In a study reported in 1978, ninety-one undergraduate students acted as nondeliberating jurors in an automobile negligence trial. Although the use of slides and an audiotape caused the introduction of various other stimuli such as those presented in an actual trial, physical attractiveness affected both the direction of the verdict (whether for plaintiff or defendant) and the size of the damage award to the plaintiff. The researchers conclude that society tends to "value physically attractive persons more highly than those who are physically unattractive."[152] They suggest, however, that varying the legally relevant factors of the case may show that physical attractiveness influences decisions only when the evidence is ambiguous or weak.[153] (This sounds much like the observation of

Appleman and others that the personal appeal of the attorney may be the only basis for a jury to make a decision, when the evidence is confusing or contradictory.[154]) And since physical attractiveness is often the first information we receive about someone, the foregoing means that the effect of physical attractiveness may control a juror's decision if the evidence turns out to be unreliable or confusing.

Between May 1975 and May 1977, ten subjects visited criminal trials in certain counties in Pennsylvania whenever possible and observed seventy-four defendants. After watching the defendants for a half hour, the observers rated the defendants on nine bipolar scales. Attractiveness was one of the measures; but, based on periodic checks, the subjects were unaware of the relative importance of the attractiveness measure. The observers also indicated, as best they could, the defendants' age, sex, race, alleged offense, and, if it was announced, the verdict. Verdict and sentencing data were also obtained later from the clerk's office. Complete information was obtained for seventy-three of the seventy-four defendants.[155] The findings indicated that (1) attractiveness affected (lessened) the sentencing, although not the conviction/acquittal occurrence, but (2) while an asset for some crimes, actually seemed a liability for more serious crimes, such as murder, as indicated by the six physically attractive defendants who received sentences of ninety-nine years or more.[156] The implication is that, while we may value physically attractive people more, we may also expect more from them. (An experiment reported in the primacy and recency chapter indicates that attractive people are presumed to be more competent than unattractive people). Therefore, we may tend to punish them for the very act of wasting their presumed talent when they commit crimes so serious as to indicate that the perpetrators will never lead useful lives.

Izzett and Leginski sought to discover whether defendants' personal characteristics would continue to influence sentences after jurors had been given the opportunity to discuss the case.[157] The results of their experiment (in which the defendant was attractive for half of the subjects and unattractive for the other half), prior to deliberation, confirmed the finding of other studies, that unattractive defendants receive harsher sentences than attractive defendants.[158] The researchers had hypothesized that once the jurors began to discuss their verdicts and their reasons, the bias against unattractiveness would emerge (or at least be recognized by those holding it) and then be expelled. The result was that the subjects exposed to an unattractive defendant shifted significantly towards leniency. However, there was *no change* in the sentence for the attractive defendant, although the hypothesis also supposed that the bias in favor of the attractive defendant would emerge and be ousted. The researchers provide additional information about the subjects, which is interesting in light of the juror personality traits discussed earlier. These were college students (recall that empathy and thus not guilty verdicts are more associated with younger people) at a campus not far from the Attica prison riots when those riots were still in the news. Thus, the researchers believe that these subjects might have had a special disposition towards leniency, which might explain why they did not increase the sentence for the attractive defendant.[159] Another explanation, detailed below, is that the appreciation of attractiveness is an innate value, not recognizable as a bias.[160]

Kalven and Zeisel's *The American Jury* is really a study of why judges and juries disagree. The data are derived from judge's reports of actual jury trials, along with their assessment of the reason for any disagreement. Then the authors, based on information supplied by the judges, as well as some information stemming from an experimental jury study, offer their own explanations for why the jury has decided as it has. They note two broad kinds of individual defendant characteristics, those that affect credibility and those that affect sympathy. Then they provide another classification of whether a defendant is sympathetic, average, or unattractive.[161] Notice that with this classification, physical attractiveness is a sympathetic trait. The comments of the judges as they described the defendants in their reports of the cases suggest a pairing of physical attractiveness with other sympathetic traits (such as youth or goodness), which implies a connection between outer and inner beauty:[162]

> An attractive young lady. . . .
> Blonde, young bride. . . .
> [N]ice looking, has two small children, [she] cried. . . .
> Well dressed and spoken; presented an overall good appearance. . . .
> [Y]oung good looking defendant. . . .
> Defendant was very handsome, personable man of 36 years of age. . . .

Of course, other characteristics trigger sympathy, such as physical disabilities, old age, and crying. But it is interesting that Kalven and Zeisel, admitting a wide range of characteristics that can move the jury, include physical attractiveness as having as innate an effect on our sympathies as qualities having or indicating more substance:

> [T]he capturing of this human variety by the summary terms must blunt the delicacy of the sentiments that may be evoked as the jury's empathy moves from the widow to the beautiful girl to the cripple to the veteran. We obviously confront here a deep response to other humans.[163]

F. *The Effect of Vividness on Recall*

Hastie, who points out how important jurors' stories of "what happened" are for their resulting verdicts, observes that "[t]he clarity or detail in a juror's mental conception of an event or episode described in testimony was a major determinant of the perceived validity and significance of the event." He describes one poignant example of this, when mock juries were deliberating on a robbery case, in which the central issue was the accuracy of an eyewitness identification. Because many details of the crime seemed irrelevant, the attorneys failed to mention them or elicit them in testimony. The jurors nevertheless spent a considerable amount of time trying to complete the picture of the crime with details having marginal relevance, such as how much money was stolen. *"Failure to supply such details in testimony resulted in the devaluation of relevant evidence."*[164]

In the section on primacy and recency, we examined certain recall techniques. If bland information was given in a single, unrepeated string (like word lists), subjects tended to recall items at the first of the list. If such lists were repeated, words at the end of the list were best recalled. If information became more interesting, however, or personally meaningful to the subject, its order in the string appeared to have no relationship to its being recalled. Judgments can be based only on relevant facts available in memory. Therefore, such judgments should logically "be disproportionately influenced by facts easily recalled and relatively uninfluenced by facts impossible or difficult to recall at the time the judgment is made." That means that the better a detail is recalled, the greater contribution it will make to a judgment. The authors explain that those details that are recalled are those that are "available in memory." While availability in memory might be affected by any variable that influences the "memorability or retrievability" of data, one such variable is the concreteness or vividness of the information.[165]

The researchers with the availability hypothesis conducted an experiment in which fifty-four students at Stanford University participated in two thirty-minute sessions conducted forty-eight hours apart. They all read descriptions of a trial involving drunk driving. Some of the subjects received a description of the defendant as a "good guy" and some, as a "bad guy." Then they read, at their own pace, eighteen arguments, each having a single evidentiary idea and being about twenty-two words long; half of these arguments implied that the defendant was guilty and half that he was not guilty. Each argument, though, had a vivid as well as a pallid version. Great care was taken not to change the probative value of the evidence or to make it so dramatic that it would have an immediate subjective effect. The changes were therefore very slight. For example, one argument suggesting that the defendant was drunk when he left a party had the following as its pallid version: " 'On his way out the door, Sanders [the defendant] staggered against a serving table, knocking a bowl to the floor.' " The vivid version said, " 'On his way out the door, Sanders staggered against a serving table, knocking a bowl of guacamole dip to the floor and splattering guacamole on the white shag carpet.' " The subjects then rated the probative value of each argument.[166]

Next, they were asked three questions about the defendant, and given an eleven-point scale for answering. They were asked how drunk they thought Sanders was at the time of the accident; what their personal opinion was as to his innocence or guilt; and, assuming they were members of a jury with the requirement of beyond all reasonable doubt, what verdict should be rendered. After giving the verdict, they were dismissed but returned forty-eight hours later. At that time, they were asked to describe in writing as many of the arguments as they could recall and then to answer the same three questions again, as if for the first time.[167]

Concerning the initial judgments, the researchers anticipated that neither the vividness of the arguments nor the favorableness of the defendant would have any effect, since almost all of the arguments should have been recalled at that point (recall that the session lasted only thirty minutes). Subjects with vivid arguments for the prosecution rated Sanders as guilty as subjects with vivid arguments for the defense. Also, the subjects with "good guy" descriptions judged the defendant as guilty as those with "bad guy" descriptions.[168] Based on the probative value ratings, the researchers conclude that the evidentiary weight of arguments was the same, whether they were vivid or pallid versions, whether they referred to good guys or bad guys, and whether they were evaluated at the first or second session.[169]

In the second session. subjects recalled 73% of the eighteen arguments, regardless of the good or bad description of the defendant and the vivid or pallid versions. However, "subjects disproportionately recalled the vivid arguments" and remembered slightly more damaging than exonerating evidence about the favorable defendant. Moreover, the first argument recalled by 75% of the subjects with a good guy description was a prosecution argument; 48% of the subjects with a bad buy description first recalled a prosecution argument. The results "indicate that vividness, and to a limited extent the defendant's favorableness, had a significantly greater effect on delayed than on immediate judgments."[170] Although the less vivid forms of the arguments had the same probative weight, they faded from memory, making them unavailable to assist with the second judgment. In addition, the fact that subjects more often recalled incongruent information about the defendant (such as more condemning information about the good defendant) caused this information to be disproportionately used in the later judgments.[171] Apparently, the incongruence alone made this information more vivid.

The researchers then examined the relative evidentiary strengths of arguments in light of their recallability, which are independent factors. They conclude that "[r]ecallable arguments that are unimportant will have as little impact as important arguments that are unrecallable."[172] However, although the presumption is that the unimportant but recalled arguments will not be relied upon,

> the availability heuristic can be "fooled" when memorability is unrelated or inversely related to the diagnostic value of the evidence. Then flashy, dramatic facts can flood the mind of the decision-maker, outweighing by their insistence alone the more pallid truths of the case.[173]

In other words, dramatic facts can remind the jurors of certain arguments; unavailable facts associated with other arguments will cause those arguments also to be unavailable. This analysis has special meaning for the jurors trying to construct their versions of what happened, particularly if the trial lasts for days or weeks. If the critical facts have been presented in a vivid fashion, the jurors are likely to incorporate them into their stories. Otherwise, as suggested by Hastie, the jury may search for any facts that will help them complete the story, which may mean that the resulting story does not contain all of the critical facts.

There is some evidence that the effect of vivid evidence, if combined with an emotional topic, is enhanced by the deliberation process. An experiment is described in the previous section in which two versions of a trial are presented for subjects. In one version, the subjects hear a tape recording of the attorneys' arguments. In another, at the point when the plaintiff's attorney is discussing the artificial leg that the plaintiff will have to wear due to the accident that spawned the trial, the tape is stopped, and an artificial leg is unwrapped from a sheet and passed around to the jurors. As indicated in that chapter, the jurors who saw the limb, as opposed to just hearing it described, awarded the defendant a greater sum of money ($73,257 vs. $62,500). However, after deliberation, the award by the jury that saw the limb increased to $75,833. The researchers believe that when the individual jurors pooled their emotional reactions to the limb, the result was " 'objective' evidence necessary to support a suitable enlarged verdict."[174] In this instance, the dramatic effect of the evidence, which the researchers in the "availability" experiment sought to avoid, is emphasized. However, that effect should have occurred at the individual level, when the jurors made their pre-deliberation judgments. When they later discussed the case, and then again made individual judgments, the effect had intensified; i.e., the vivid evidence was more "available" than before the discussion.

The distinction should be made between vivid evidence and one extreme form of it, which might be called drama. A dramatic event stands out because of its comparison with other events. Making a fact vivid is providing life-like details; it is precisely because a photograph contains so many details that a picture is worth a thousand words. A dramatic event is like the use of a unique word in an essay or the use of profanity to make a point. If the word is used more than once, it is no longer unique, and even its original effect is diminished. Similarly, someone given to profanity cannot rely upon it for embellishment, as it is a part of his or her normal language. Therefore, if every piece of evidence is dramatically presented, there is no relief; it is all on the same plane, much as if it were *all* non-dramatic.

G. *Surviving Rules of Primacy and Recency*

Below are the original rules of primacy and recency posited at the end of the first section in this trilogy, as modified at the end of the second section, with observations as to their survival in the realm of the jury:

General Rules of Primacy and Recency

1. When a single string of information is presented, information at the *beginning* of the string is most clearly remembered.

This rule survives with the opening statements. What each attorney says first will probably be best remembered from each opening statement. Moreover, the jury is receptive to a side preference, which would be based on a comparison of the two attorneys, as well as their presentations. The jury seeks at this point an outline for the factual story that they will later fill in with evidence.

2. When strings of information of similar length are presented, information at the *end* of the strings past the first string is most clearly remembered. This generally holds true regardless of the complexity of the information, so long as the information is quite vivid.

This rule has no applicability to the opening statement, the overall presentation of evidence, or the closing arguments. Hypothetically, it could apply to some types of testimony, if the witness were describing repeated processes of similar length. An example could be a witness explaining how various offshore oil properties were valued and, for the record, detailing the process with each property.

Since most jurors will have formed their versions of what happened and probably their verdicts by the end of trial, the last statements of the attorneys will not likely alter any opinions. However, for the jurors who are at that point undecided, persuasion in the closing arguments could assist them in making their verdicts; and a summary of the evidence could help them to complete their stories of the case.

3. When there is more than one string of information and the information is complex but not very vivid, information at the *beginning* of the strings is most clearly remembered.

This rule has no applicability to the opening statement, the overall presentation of evidence, or the closing arguments. Hypothetically, it could apply to some types of testimony. Although the building-blocks approach is probably best suited to inducing belief in a listener, if a witness's methodology for arriving at a conclusion is quite complex, the attorney may have the witness first state his conclusion and then proceed to support it.

4. Information that is recalled from the *beginning* of an information string is better learned than information recalled from the end of a string.

This rule survives with the opening statements. What each attorney says first will probably be best remembered from each opening statement. Moreover, as the opening statements are supposed to be factual, they could be considered the beginning of the entire information string that includes all of the evidence presented at trial. An attorney could capitalize on this rule by presenting a clear, logically ordered summary of his client's position and then having this summary immediately verified by his client or another witness who could give a narrative presentation of the facts. This rule is particularly applicable in light of the jury's need to form a story of the events and their desire to have the foundation of that story provided as soon as possible.

5. Attractive or appealing information about a person learned *first* improves our perception of that person's actual ability.

This rule survives with the opening statements with regard to the attorneys. Moreover, it will apply to each witness, as well as the parties. Concerning convictions, physical attractiveness will not turn jurors' heads, but it can determine the size of awards to plaintiffs, as well as the severity of the punishment. Attractive defendants will receive less punishment, however, only for the less severe crimes, and may receive even longer sentences than their unattractive counterparts for more serious crimes.

6. Stereotype information about a person, when learned *after* an opinion expressed by that person that conflicts with the stereotype information, dilutes the validity of the opinion. This dilution does not occur when stereotype information is learned first.

This rule applies to the attorneys as well as to the parties and witnesses. This rule more concerns the credibility of a witness and the presentation of testimony, which will be discussed in a later section.

7. An existing bias is analogous to a well-learned early piece of information. That bias can be temporarily overcome by information *later* learned (but retained for just a short while) only if that later information is believed.

This rule applies to the opening statements and could persist throughout the trial if the attorneys are unable to provide the jurors with a reason to forgo any bias. Prior experience by the juror, such as the kind of trial he may have recently been a juror for, may determine how he may decide a later trial. Existing biases are best ascertained (if at all) during the *voir dire* (in which section below they will receive further discussion).

H. *Modification of the Theory*

The author, when first employed as a jury and trial consultant some ten years ago, was influenced by the studies in existence at that period of time. I looked for support of these studies in my actual practice; for example, the jury functions as twelve individuals who arrive at reasonable conclusions based on the evidence. Many people believe this to be the case. Many experienced trial lawyers operate in the courtroom as if this were true. My experiences and studies have led me to modify this basic premise and identify an additional factor that controls in jury deliberations. The most important modification that I have made is that the jury's decision is really a function of *three* or *four* strong jurors—not twelve individuals. During the twelve-person jury's discussion, there will emerge at least one leader who will have three or four supporters; and more than likely, there will be another leader who will have three or four followers. The remaining jurors will be passive and decide in favor of the position of the dominant or "in control" group.

The most important aspect of this, as applied to trial counsel, is that during *voir dire* these strong personalities must be identified. This sometimes requires artful *voir dire* questioning to discover a latent jury leader. The assertive and verbal juror will be easy to identify. But often this person disqualifies himself or herself by advocacy or claims to know more about the lawsuit than he does or expresses an opinion on punishment or damages that eliminates him. Here, it is interesting to point out that the skillful trial attorney can take the verbal juror who is opposed to his position and allow him to take such a stance that it is clear to that juror that he has a bias or prejudice or "leaning." The lawyer can then invite the juror to ask the "reasonable" trial judge to be excused because of his preconceived beliefs. Then, the trial attorney does not have to strike him—you gave him an out! What is more difficult to do is find a potential leader for your side. You want to discover enough to satisfy yourself that this juror should or would be likely to follow your side, but not allow the other side to eliminate him (that is, disarm the other side so this juror is acceptable to opposing counsel).

The presiding juror is most important to identify, so try to choose him. Professionals, school teachers, males who are more educated, wealthier individuals, or more verbal persons are likely to be the presiding juror. This juror has the court's charge in his hands and reads it to the jury. He supplies the inflections in his voice and the emphases. He writes the notes to the judge and reads the responses. He decides on the coffee breaks and the times to vote and recess. He is looked upon to lead the other jurors. Depending on his skill in this area, the presiding juror can and often does control the jury.

The most important factor in predicting how a juror will decide a case is whether the decision he makes as a juror in this case will be well-received by the people with whom he comes into daily contact, such as his employer, co-workers, family, and friends. The trial lawyer must convince the juror that this decision will be heralded by his peers as a noble and acceptable act.

There is, however, a limitation on this principle. As a trial attorney, you have identified the personality of the juror (from the information that you have received from and about him through pretrial investigations and *voir dire*) as a person who will most likely be predisposed to one side or the other. You have gotten along well with the juror or he seems friendly or maybe, even a friend of yours. However, it is almost guaranteed that in a close contest and hard fought trial, this juror will throw your friendship or his good feelings aside and return a verdict consistent with his predisposition. This means that it is unlikely in the experience of the jury that a juror will vote in a way different from his conscience and background, life experiences, attitudes, beliefs, and biases.

Practically, as a jury and trial consultant, the author advises plaintiff's attorneys to maximize on the effects of primacy. Defense counsel should capitalize on the theory of recency. The plaintiff, without a doubt, has an advantage in a short trial of one week or less. Therefore, defense attorneys must do something to decrease the effects of primacy. Defense counsel should structure as lengthy a trial as possible to decrease the impressions of what was first presented. Defense counsel should present as many witnesses, fact and character, as possible. (Of course, the witnesses must not be repetitious or irrelevant). The number of witnesses can help to erode the memory of the initial presentation. Also, defense attorneys should obtain a commitment from each prospective juror on *voir dire* that he or she will not leap to a conclusion, having only heard one version of the facts. This psychological technique attempts to counteract what in reality often does happen and also to make jurors less susceptible to group pressure. Psychological research has demonstrated that if individuals are required to make a public commitment to a position, then they are less likely to conform with the group's contrary decision. Deutsch and Gerald in an experiment found that six percent of those subjects who stated an opinion publicly yielded to the group's decision. However, twenty-five percent of those subjects who made no prior commitment conformed to the group's decision.[175]

Litigators should realize that emotionally toned material is recalled longer and more vividly than factual communication. For maximum impact emotional testimony should be presented initially (for a primacy effect). Expert testimony, which is factual, should be presented at the end of the trial for maximum recall (for a recency effect). The least important testimony should be presented in the middle of the trial since this testimony will have the least retention.

Unique or novel events, facts, or themes will be remembered. In the psychological field of learning, motivation, and memory (concerning the serial-position curve), if one item is made distinctive from other items, the clearly distinct item will be learned faster. This concept is referred to as the Von Restorff effect.[176] The litigator can achieve this effect in the courtroom by pacing his questions and varying his voice tone prior to asking a critical question. He can also utilize the powerful tools of demonstrative aides. The standard cliches, "a picture is worth a thousand words" and "seeing is believing" are most truthful statements because of the Von Restorff effect. The attorney should create the anchor or red flag that the jury will hear something unique or novel. Psychological studies demonstrate that if participants are informed that a communication which they will hear is unique or novel, then they are more influenced by the communication than the exact communication without the notice of novelty or uniqueness.[177]

The trial attorneys should consider the rules of primacy and recency in structuring each day of trial. Each day should begin with a "good" witness for the effects of primacy. The jury's attention is the most intense in the morning. Also, each day should end with a "good" witness for recency effects. The uneventful witnesses should be presented in the middle of each trial day, when the jury is bored, fatigued, asleep, or daydreaming and consequently has a decreased attentional span. Successful litigators must be psychological strategists, either instinctively or from academic study.

NOTES

1. Asch, *Forming Impressions of Personality*, 41 J. Abnormal & Soc. Psychology 258 (1946).

2. Johnson, Johnson, & Little, *Expertise in Trial Advocacy: Some Considerations for Inquiry into Its Nature and Development*, 7 Campbell L. Rev. 119, 141 (1984).

3. Tabachnick & Brotsky, *Free Recall and Complexity of Pictorial Stimuli*, 4 Memory & Cognition 466 (1976).

4. Goodwin, *Changes in Primacy and Recency with Practice in Single-Trial Free Recall*, 15 J. Verbal Learning & Verbal Behavior 119 (1976).

5. *Id.*

6. Helstrup, *Presence and Absence of Serial Position Effects in Short-Term Memory*, 19 Scandinavian J. Psychology 301, 306 (1978).

7. *Id.* at 301, 306.

8. Tabachnick & Brotsky, *supra* n.3, at 466.

9. *Id.* at 469.

10. *Id.* at 460.

11. Benassi, *Effects of Order of Presentation, Primacy, and Physical Attractiveness on Attributions of Ability*, 43 J. Personality & Soc. Psychology 48 (1982).

12. *Id.*

13. *Id.* at 53–56.

14. *Id.* at 57.

15. Thibaut, Walker, & Lind, *Adversary Representation and Bias in Legal Decisionmaking*, 86 Harv. L. Rev. 386, 397 (1972).

16. Kaplan & Scherschung, *Reducing Juror Bias: An Experimental Approach, New Directions in Psycholegal Research* 149 (P. Lipsitt & B. Sales ed. 1980).

17. Thibaut et al., *supra* n.15, at 399.

18. *Id.* at 399–400.

19. *Id.*

20. Kaplan & Scherching, *supra* n.16, at 151–52.

21. *Id.* at 150.

22. *Id.* at 152.

23. *Id.* at 153.

24. *Id.* at 155–56.

25. *Id.* at 156.

26. *Id.* at 159.

27. *Id.* at 160.

28. *Id.* at 161.

29. *Id.* at 163. Kaplan and Scherschiing place findings for judgment order before and after deliberation on a single graph.

30. *Id.*

31. Izzett & Leginski, *Group Discussion and the Influence of Defendant Characteristics in a Simulated Jury Setting,* 93 J. Soc. Psychology 271, 272 (1974).

32. Kaplan & Scherschiing, *supra* n.16, at 165.

33. *Id.* at 159.

34. Thibaut et al., *supra* n.15, at 399–401.

35. Kaplan & Scherschiing, *supra* n.16, at 159.

36. Lind, Thibaut, & Walker, *Discovery and Presentation of Evidence,* 71 Mich. L. Rev. 1129, 1143 (1973).

37. *Id.* at 1142.

38. *Id.* at 1143.

39. Lind, *The Psychology of Courtroom Procedure, The Psychology of the Courtroom* 14, 24–26 (N. Kerr & R. Bray ed. 1982).

40. Jones & Berglas, *A Recency Effect in Attitude Attribution,* 44 J. Personality 433, 433–35 (1976).

41. *Id.* at 436.

42. *Id.* at 444–47.

43. *Id.* at 446.

44. 75 Am. Jur. 2d *Trial* § 202 (1974).

45. 75 Am. Jur. 2d *Trial* § 213 (1974).

46. Lind, *The Psychology of Courtroom Procedure, The Psychology of the Courtroom* 14, 24–25 (N. Kerr & R. Bray ed. 1982).

47. Lawson, *The Law of Primacy in the Criminal Courtroom,* 77 J. Soc. Psychology 121, 125–26 (1969).

48. 75 Am. Jur. 2d *Trial* § 204 (1974).

49. Appleman, *Preparation & Trial* 189 (1967).

50. *Id.* at v.

51. McCullough & Underwood, 2 *Civil Trial Manual* 576–78 (1980).

52. *Id.* at 647–48.

53. Walker, Thibault, & Andreoli, *Order of Presentation at Trial,* 82 Yale L.J. 216 (1972).

54. McCullough & Underwood, *supra* n.51, at 591.

55. Saks & Hastie, *Social Psychology in Court* 107 (1978).

56. *Id.* at 105–106.

57. Walker et al., *supra* n.53, at 223.

58. *Id.* at 224.

59. *Id.*

60. *Id.* at 226.

61. Hovland, *Introduction, The Order of Presentation in Persuasion* 1 (C. Hovland ed. 1957).

62. Lund, *The Psychology of Belief. IV. The Law of Primacy in Persuasion,* 20 J. Abnormal & Soc. Psychology 183 (1925).

63. Hovland & Mandell, *Is There a "Law of Primacy in Persuasion"?*, *The Order of Presentation in Persuasion* 13 (C. Hovland ed. 1957).

64. Id. at 20.

65. Id. at 21–22.

66. Hovland, *Summary and Implications*, *The Order of Presentation in Persuasion* 154 (C. Hovland ed. 1957).

67. As the previous chapter on primacy and recency indicates, this is a rationale for the adversarial approach instead of the inquisitorial method of presenting evidence.

68. Hovland, *Summary and Implications*, *supra* n.66, 154–55.

69. Lawson, *supra* n.47, at 125.

70. Janis & Feierabend, *Effects of Alternative Ways of Ordering Pro and Con Arguments in Persuasive Communications*, *The Order of Presentation in Persuasion* 117 (C. Hovland ed. 1957).

71. Id. at 118–20.

72. Id. at 125.

73. Id. at 127–28.

74. Devitt & Blackmar, 1 *Federal Jury Practice & Instructions* 119 (1977).

75. Wasserman & Robinson, *Extra-Legal Influences, Group Processes, and Jury Decision-Making: A Psychological Perspective*, 12 N.C. Central L.J. 96, 136 (1980).

76. Id. at 136–37.

77. Id. at 140–43.

78. Id. at 147.

79. Id. at 150.

80. Appleman, *supra* n.49, at 721.

81. Marshall, *Law and Psychology in Conflict* 84 (1966).

82. Appleman, *supra* n.49, at 721.

83. Hovland, *Summary and Implications*, *supra* n.66, at 139.

84. Lawson *supra* n.47, at 128.

85. Id.

86. Tyson & Kramer, *The Primacy-Recency Effect in Counselor Response*, 37 J. Clinical Psychology, 88–90 (1981).

87. Id. at 90.

88. Kalven & Zeisel, *The American Jury* 488 (1966).

89. See "Theory: Primacy vs. Recency," section I in this chapter.

90. Mills & Bohannon, *Character Structure and Jury Behavior: Conceptual and Applied Implications*, 38 J. Personality & Soc. Psychology 662, 663 (1980).

91. Id. at 664.

92. Id. at 663.

93. Id. at 665–66.

94. Hastie, Penrod, & Pennington, *Inside the Jury* 143 (1983).

95. Id. at 144.

96. Davis, *Order in the Courtroom, Psychology and Law* 254–56 (D. Muller, D. Blackman, A. Chapman ed. 1984).

97. Kalven & Zeisel, *supra* n.88, at 489.

98. *Id.* at vii.

99. Roberts, Hoffman, & Johnson, *Effects of Jury Deliberation on the Verdicts and Social Perceptions of Simulated Jurors: Vidmar Revisited*, 47 Perceptual & Motor Skills 119 (1978).

100. *Id.* at 120–21.

101. *Id.* at 122–23.

102. *Id.* at 123.

103. Izzett & Leginski, *Group Discussion and the Infuence of Defendant Characteristics in a Simulated Jury Setting*, 93 J. Soc. Psychology 271, 272 (1974).

104. Roberts et al., *supra* n.99 at 121.

105. Rumsey, Allgeier, & Castore, *Group Discussion, Sentencing Judgments, and the Leniency Shift*, 105 J. Soc. Psychology 249 (1978).

106. *Id.* at 251–53.

107. *Id.* at 253–55.

108. *Id.* at 255.

109. Rumsey et al. explain that, if the subjects could be assumed to have equated a midpoint on the sentencing scale with neutrality (i.e., less than ten years would have been lenient), then the results were consistent with polarization. *Id.* at 255. The concept of "neutrality" being equated by a juror with half of the possible punishment still seems to miss the point.

110. Kalven & Zeisel, *supra* n.88, at 487–88.

111. Kaplan & Scherscing, *Reducing Juror Bias: An Experimental Approach, New Directions in Psycholegal Research* 163 (P. Lipsett & B. Sales ed. 1980).

112. Kalven & Zeisel, *supra* n.88, at 494–95.

113. Hastie et al., *supra* n.94, at 100.

114. Kalven & Zeisel, *supra* n.88, at 495.

115. *Id.* at 486.

116. Simon, *The Jury and the Defense of Insanity* 34–36 (1967).

117. *Id.* at 3.

118. *Id.* at 113.

119. *Id.* at 223; Kalven & Zeisel, *supra* n.88, at 483.

120. Simon, *supra* n.116, at 119.

121. Bridgeman & Marlowe, *Jury Decision Making: An Empirical Study Based on Actual Felony Trials*, 64 J. Applied Psychology 91, 92 (1979).

122. *Id.* at 93.

123. *Id.* at 94.

124. *Id.* at 95.

125. *Id.* at 94.

126. *Id.* at 97.

127. *Id.* at 93.

128. *Id.* at 94.
129. *Id.* at 95.
130. Goldman, Freundlich, & Casey, *Jury Emotional Response and Deliberation Style*, 11 J. Psychiatry & L. 332 (1983).
131. Hastie et al., *supra* n.94, at 80.
132. Hamlin, *What Makes Juries Listen* 316–18 (1985).
133. Hastie et al., *supra* n.94, at 169.
134. Simon, *supra* n.116, at 178.
135. Hastie et al., *supra* n.94, at 80–81.
136. *Id.* at 169.
137. *Id.* at 169–70.
138. *Id.* at 88.
139. *Id.* at 81.
140. *Id.* at 170.
141. Davis, *supra* n.96, at 258–60.
142. See "Presentation of Evidence and Arguments," section II of this chapter.
143. Bridgeman & Marlowe, *supra* n.121, at 94.
144. *Id.* at 95–96.
145. Kalven & Zeisel, *supra* n.88, at 486.
146. Hamlin, *supra* n.132, at 105.
147. *Id.* at 111–13.
148. Hastie et al., *supra* n.94, at 169.
149. *Id.* at 18–23.
150. Bridgeman & Marlowe, *supra* n.121, at 91–92.
151. See section I of this chapter, "Theory: Primacy vs. Recency."
152. Kulka & Kessler, *Is Justice Really Blind?—The Influence of Litigant Physical Attractiveness on Juridicial Judgment*, 8 J. Applied Soc. Psychology 366, 374–75 (1978).
153. *Id.* at 376.
154. See section II of this chapter, "Presentation of Evidence and Arguments."
155. Stewart, *Defendant's Attractiveness as a Factor in the Outcome of Criminal Trials: An Observational Study*, 10 J. Applied Soc. Psychology 348, 351 (1980).
156. *Id.* at 359.
157. Izzett & Leginski, *supra* n.103, at 272.
158. *Id.* at 277.
159. *Id.* at 273, 277.
160. Kalven & Zeisel, *supra* n.88, at 193–94.
161. *Id.* at 194–95.
162. *Id.* at 202–203.
163. *Id.* at 217–18.
164. Hastie et al., *supra* n.94, at 170 (emphasis added).

165. Reyes, Thompson, & Bower, *Judgmental Biases Resulting from Differing Availabilities of Arguments*, 39 J. Personality & Soc. Psychology 2–3 (1980).

166. *Id.* at 4.

167. *Id.* at 4–5.

168. *Id.* at 6.

169. *Id.* at 7.

170. *Id.* at 5–7.

171. *Id.* at 9.

172. *Id.* at 10.

173. *Id.* at 11.

174. Wasserman & Robinson, *Extra-Legal Influences, Group Processes, and Jury Decision-Making: A Psychological Perspective*, 12 N.C. Central L.J. 96, 143, 147, 150 (1980).

175. Deutsch & Gerald, *A Study of Normative and Informational Social Influences upon Individual Judgment*, 51 J. Abnormal Soc. Psychology 629–36 (1955).

176. *Woodworth & Schlosberg's Experimental Psychology*, Vol. II, Third Edition, (J. W. Kling & L. A. Riggs ed. 1971) 1016.

177. Sears & Freedman, *Effects of Expected Familiarity of Arguments upon Opinion Change and Selective Exposure*, 2 J. Personality & Soc. Psychology 420–25 (1965).

CHAPTER 3
THE DRAMATIC BASIS OF TRIALS

SYNOPSIS

CHAPTER 3
THE DRAMATIC BASIS OF TRIALS

Ling Lee Blume was a divorce attorney's dream of the helpless, battered wife.[1] She was Oriental, brought to this country with little knowledge of the language and none of the culture by an overbearing American who met her overseas and married her. She was the constant victim of both his physical and mental abuse. As an ultimate punishment, her husband announced that they were going to give up their child for adoption. He had her accompany him to the local adoption agency, where the social worker observed Ling Lee's black eye, bruised face, and abject passivity. The social worker called in a representative of the women's shelter, who arranged for placement of Ling Lee and her baby. While she was at the shelter, she requested help in obtaining a divorce, and Legal Services Corporation provided counsel.

Ling Lee's attorney was a woman who had handled over 800 divorces, many of which had been contested and many of which had been sought on the grounds of physical cruelty. She had not, however, handled a divorce before a jury or against a pro se opponent. Mr. Blume, you see, represented himself, contested the divorce, and requested a jury trial.

Ling Lee's counsel was most concerned about racial prejudice towards her client and biases against divorce. Her concern was unwisely placed. During trial, she was accompanied by her female assistant and flanked by a veritable cheering section composed of four female law students working at Legal Services and attending the trial for the experience. In view of such apparent feminist pressure, the jury rushed to the defense of the underdog, Mr. Blume, by unanimously denying the divorce decree. (The dazed Ling Lee exited for parts unknown.)

While all due regard for the older male attorney, it is suggested that Ling Lee's attorney should have had such a companion at the counsel table, "a 'dummy'. . . to consult with during the trial . . . [and] help legitimize the role of the female attorney for the jury." The author explains:

> A trial lawyer must be able to anticipate and meet the expectations of a jury. All too often, these expectations are formulated by prime time television. And, a lawyer should be able to replicate as far as possible the television drama. . . . If this seems like a contrived show or a cop-out we dispute the notion. Once in a trial

there is no excuse for not playing the game skillfully.[2]

The idea of constructing a realistic scene with believable characters for a certain audience does no more than provide a unifying concept for the elements of a trial that have already been discussed. The trial attorney does not present every facet of himself to the jury; he adopts a persona, which may well be an exaggeration of an existing aspect of his character and personality. The persona, though, is not the totality of the attorney; it is the *role* he plays when he is in the courtroom. In addition, jurors expect a story and attempt from the beginning to piece together that story themselves.

The "drama" of the courtroom, however, is perhaps best understood as a mere example of behavior in a social context. Thus, "performing" in that arena becomes subject to no more criticism than does reacting towards another individual. Put simply, in the presence of society (which can be even one person), we act differently than we do when we are alone. It also follows that personal appearance would be a deference to society (e.g., how much grooming would we do were there no one around?). Since clothing is a primary contribution to first impression, that first impression can be determined in part by clothing. As the costuming in plays indicates, clothing in fact assists in defining the characters and establishing their credibility.

I. DRAMA

On its face, the term "drama" often has repugnant connotations when controlled and honest people consider it in relation to themselves. That reputation is undeserved. The first definition of "drama" in a popular dictionary is that it is a "composition in verse or prose *intended to portray life or character* or to tell a story." The last definition refers to dramatic quality and gives an example: the drama of courtroom proceedings.[3]

As Kenneth Burke, famed scholar of the drama of human relations, explains,

> drama proper is the symbolizing or imitating of action, whereas the "dramatistic" is a critical or essayistic analysis of language, and thence human relations generally, by the use of terms derived from the contemplation of drama.[4]

Burke therefore devised a critical pentad (five interrelated elements of every social interaction)—act, agency, agent, scene, and purpose—

with which to describe (and explain) human behavior.[5]

"All the world is not, of course, a stage, but the crucial ways in which it isn't are not easy to specify."[6] The universality of a dramatistic approach to human behavior (i.e., using terms from the theater) is clear from even the title of one book concerning individual action: *The Presentation of Self in Everyday Life.* Therein, the author uses "the term 'performance' to refer to all the activity of an individual which occurs during a period marked by his continuous presence before a particular set of observers and which has some influence on the observers."[7] This description could certainly apply to a speech, as well as to an entire trial. Even the purely "legal" instructional manuals incorporate theater language:

> The advocate's role is to lead the minds of the jury and the judge to his client's point of view. He has set the stage in the opening statement, in which he has placed his client as the principal actor. The last act will be his closing argument before the jury.[8]

James Herman, a practicing trial attorney, has no doubt about the applicability of theater principles (let alone terminology) to the courtroom: "Trial work is a performing art. . . .Yet we lawyers pay little attention to even the most rudimentary principles of performance." He believes that the formal setting of a courtroom and assemblage of jurors makes even more demands than the daily interactions we have with others. The jury audience is composed of "sophisticated entertainment consumers, having been exposed to countless hours of television, movies, plays, radio and public speeches. They take a professional performance for granted. They do not tolerate a poor performance."[9]

Some trial attorneys blanch at the idea of a "dramatic" quality to litigation work. But even the sober instructive manuals cannot avoid recommending a bit of embellishment: "Counsel should let his imagination revolve about the facts and the law and particularly about the way he presents his case in court. If the presentation could be imaginative, it would certainly be more interesting and more likely to capture the attention of the jury."[10] John A. Appleman, the "country lawyer" introduced in an earlier chapter, has this to say about the role of a trial attorney:

> Jurors come, in part, to be entertained. They are entitled to be not cheated in this respect. But let me caution any embryonic trial lawyer against "hamminess," because artifices of any type will cause an instant reaction against the attorney and the cause which

> he represents so that he falls into the "villain" role. When he does, he loses his case.[11]

Appleman also admits to having a "slight flair for the dramatic" himself.[12]

Probably no trial attorney would object to the analysis of courtroom presentations as communication. One interesting comment on the interrelationship of the "disciplines" of trials, theater, and communication is the observed "real need" for "theater scholars to develop a sound orientation to communication theory" and "communication scholars to develop an active concern for artistic communication."[13] Until recently, the theater scholars have not seen the relevance of communication theory, nor have the communication scholars seen the relevance of theatrical communication. Theatrical activity, however, can be reformulated into a communication framework. Though the translation of "symbolic gestures, make-up, and movement," into "transformation of event-data into information" is less than perfect for both the theater scholar and the communication scholar, the parallel is clear.[14]

Moreover, notice the shared elements in the following descriptions of an advocate and an experienced actor. The kind of actor specifically described below is that found in Asian theater, which tends to be director-free.

> [A]dvocacy is habitually spoken of as an "art," not a science. Advocates are the product of experience and considerable self-discipline.... They are shrewd enough to observe others with more expertise and to adopt the best of what they see. Advocates are created from lawyers...who train themselves rigorously to battle effectively in a courtroom.[15]
>
> [E]ach performer seeks to shape his artistic behavior by doing what has been handed down to him from past generations....The actor wastes no time on gaining insights and polishing techniques that are part of what he has already brought to the role many times before....The performer's focus is much less on what to do than on doing it as well as possible.[16]

A. *The Courtroom Situation*

In behavior analysis terms, the courtroom context provides a setting in which the trial attorney enacts his role: "A setting tends to stay put, geographically speaking, so that those who would use a particular setting as part of their performance cannot begin their act until they have brought themselves to the appropriate place and must terminate their performance when they leave it."[17] Herman emphasizes the importance of setting by urging attorneys to rehearse their closing arguments in the actual courtroom. He advises that clients and witnesses also benefit from rehearsals, thereby becoming more comfortable in the foreign context of a courtroom.[18] Given the caution that trial attorneys should fulfill the jury's expectations, it is interesting to see the mirror image of that in an instruction to attorneys in another guide: "Teach Witnesses How to Conduct Themselves and *What to Expect*." Particularly with inexperienced witnesses, "[i]t is good practice to take the witnesses into the courtroom before the trial begins or at recess and literally show them where they will sit."[19]

Thoughts of a conventional courtroom would yield ready assent to the effect of environment on a communication situation, with regard to the message to be conveyed, the role of witnesses and attorneys, and the expected behavior of all concerned. Ceilings of courtrooms are usually higher than those of offices, and the judge is usually elevated, with both suggesting loftiness and requiring a certain solemnity. There is usually a stark symmetry to the positions of the counsel tables and the rows of public seating; the witness box may even be balanced on the other end of the bench by a seat for the judge's courtroom clerk. Everything connotes a serious, formal occasion.

But there is something other than the physical environment that dictates behavior in the courtroom. Imagine, if you can, a small partitioned room in the Wilmington Opera House, sectioned off from a huge room used for gatherings of opera fans and supporters at intermissions and other social occasions. The small, rectangular room contains three long folding tables, two positioned in front of the third. A single chair sits behind the third; several metal folding chairs surround each of the other two tables. A podium is centered between the two tables with chairs, and boxes and file cabinets flank those tables. This was the site of a seven-week trial, known as an appraisal hearing, in the Court of Chancery; the case was tried to an Appraiser, who sat at the table with the lone chair. The date was 1981; and the Opera House was used because of a shortage of space in the courthouse, not because of the insignificance of the claim, which was nearly $10,000,000. Despite the informality of the physical surroundings, for almost two months, up to a dozen people, every business day, filed into the "courtroom," professional in attire, attitude, and demeanor, and argued a case.

Studying the ways in which humans interact with their environment is not the exclusive domain of the psychologist or even the sociologist. One view of rhetoric (with "rhetoric" being variously defined as persuasive discourse or "functional, pragmatic communication"), is that it is "a critical mode of functional interaction" between people and their environment.[20] This "situational view of rhetoric" describes four main components. There is (1) the "rhetor," who perceives (2) a problem with the environment, as well as (3) a solution to the problem, and attempts to induce (4) an audience to accept and implement his solution.[21] Notice how closely the role of the rhetor tracks that of the advocate:

> The winning trial lawyer. . . believes in the efficacy of his client's claim. . . .The advocate's role is to lead the minds of the jury and the judge to his client's point of view. . . . His effectiveness, in good part, will depend upon his ability to think as the jurors think and to heighten, through his argument, their favorable reaction to his side.[22]

Although the rhetorical analysis of attorneys' arguments will be the focus of a later chapter, it is appropriate to observe here that speakers can misperceive the rhetorical situation based on mistakes they make about the audience, the problem, or constraints (such as rules or regulations). For example, a trial attorney could assume that his audience is fairly religious and begin his closing argument by relating the story of Cain and Abel. But if the jury is composed of sophisticated New York residents and the case concerns churning in the stock market, religious allusions may miss their mark. Two quite well-known examples of inaccurate situational analysis are the speeches that Richard M. Nixon made when he resigned, one to the nation and the other to the White House staff:

> Both situations invited fitting responses, but he misconceived them. His most important error was this: he mistakenly thought that the central exigence was his own suffering of what he regarded to be unmerited punishment. . . .The basic flaw in Mr. Nixon's perception of his "resignation situation" was his failure to recognize, or his refusal to admit. . . that his fitting response must blame himself or praise the very persons and institutions responsible for his fall.[23]

While, when speech critics refer to situation, they usually mean the reason for a speech (such as an occasion) as well as the actual surroundings, physical trappings do more than create an expectation in the audience of behavior of the speaker; they can also cause the audience to impute intent to the speaker. This alone demonstrates the effect of physical environment (why else would the creation of sets in theaters be a profession in itself?).

> If you are sitting in an audience facing a platform on which stands a microphone with a table bearing a few glasses and a pitcher of water nearby, and I arise to approach the microphone, you expect me to speak; the context gives the cues to my intentions. If in such a set of circumstances I should jump onto the table and tap-dance, the audience would probably greet me with laughter even though I danced well and even though tap dancing on tables is a common occurrence.[24]

The reason for such an audience response would be that, given the context (which is suggested by the physical surroundings), only if the performer intended to be funny would he dance in such a situation. This is another way of saying that the situation creates certain expectations in the audience.

Herman, beginning with the expectations of a jury, gives advice to trial attorneys as if he were directing a play. That is, he does not prescribe a script as much as he suggests how to enact or enliven any script. He has three primary rules for "better communication" to a jury. The first is

> be larger than life. The size of the courtroom and the distance between the lawyer and the jury make a conversational performance appear lackluster and flat. *Don't be afraid you are overacting.* Audiences adjust automatically to the bigger movement, gesture and voice *required by the circumstances.*[25]

If you have trouble seeing the rationale here, recall a movie or television show you have seen that used a non-actor, such as a popular sports figure, for a minor part. He knew his lines, and you supposed that he had been through many rehearsals, but in comparison to the actors that surrounded him, he sounded as if his vocal chords were in a vise, he had no vocal range, and he moved as if he had rigor mortis. You probably observed that something was "wrong" with him. However, when the former professional athlete turns professional actor, like Don Meredith, we simply do not see anything objectionable; we focus on the performance, to the extent of believing the character.

Herman's second rule is "get rid of clutter," referring to verbal tics, which, though unnoticed and/or accepted in conversation, glare before an audience.[26] One of the worst offenders here is the phrase, "you know"; it can literally begin, end, or interrupt any—and every—sentence in a conversation. The reality is that an audience can become so attuned to such a tic that they listen for it and filter out anything around it, keeping a mental count of how often it appears. Reportedly, a pet shop owner in Madison, Wisconsin follows every sentence with "on there"; to realize how distracting a verbal tic can be, simply imagine someone tacking that on to every sentence.

The third rule is "make artistic decisions in selecting voice, movement and gesture. Variety is a guiding principle."[27] Citing the physical dimensions of a courtroom, Herman notes that conversational volume will make the jury strain to hear. Of course, at times, that may be a goal, since "the shout and the whisper juxtaposed can be most dramatic of all."[28] If you were on the debate team throughout high school and college, you may have perfected an incredible speed of speech with nonetheless optimum enunciation. Bear in mind that the audience and other circumstances of the courtroom no longer call for you to be the fastest tongue in the West. For the most part, you are not being timed when you speak in the courtroom, and your audience will not consist of professional debate judges. Use variety in speed for dramatic interest.

"Movement and gesture command attention." Therefore, Herman advises that movements and gestures be planned, judiciously used, and coordinated with the text (i.e., motivated by something that was said).[29] Two of Houston's most noted trial attorneys, each with some twenty years' experience, opposed each other in a suit a few years ago. The plaintiff's attorney was tall and broad-shouldered; he wore a rather full-cut coat and, of course, left his coat unbuttoned while he was seated. Whenever the defendant's attorney delved into a particular area, the plaintiff's attorney would leap from his seat, arms flailing, and make an objection; his open coat would fly out around him, adding to his dramatic image. Not to be upstaged, the defense attorney prefaced his next inquiry into the sensitive area with, "Now, your Honor, I know my friend Mr. ____________ is going to jump up like a flock of turkeys when I say this." From that point on, the plaintiff's attorney could not resort to his former objection technique without reminding all present of "a flock of turkeys."

Herman has also diagrammed a typical courtroom, as if it were a set stage, and suggested relative strengths of twelve positions during summation.[30] For example, he observes that the podium is a good place to being a summation if a formal tone is used. However, since it is a physical barrier between the attorney and the jury, it causes him to become a "'talking head.'" Herman says that position one, centered directly in front of the jury box, is the strongest, since the attorney is then the closest person to the jury. Also, in fully facing the jury, the attorney then uses the strongest body position.[31] When using this position, however, attorneys should be careful about intruding on the personal space of the jurors in the first row. An attorney who leans on the jury box may risk offending the jurors right in front of him; if they are pressed against the backs of their seats and pulling their heads back, they are literally trying to put more space between him and themselves.

Position nine is where the client sits, and the defendant and his counsel are assumed to be at the table (or the end of a table shared by both parties) furthest from the jury. Herman advises using this position when the desire is to draw the client into the summation. Since, however, the prosecutor is in the jury's line of vision, Herman warns the defense attorney to "keep an eye" on him, as the prosecutor is then in an excellent position to upstage. The opposition's expert witness can be upstaged by strategic positioning of the examining attorney. The witness, perhaps a professional expert, will undoubtedly try to look directly at the jury. If the examining attorney moves upstage, to the other side of the bench from the jury, the witness must either look away from the jury to answer the questions, or incongruously look at the jury when the question has come from another direction. As a final comment concerning positions in the courtroom, Herman says that changes in positions should correlate in some way to the text of the argument and recommends that "courtroom choreography" be planned when other parts of the summation are being composed.[32]

In any given courtroom position, Herman notes that an attorney can assume one of a variety of body positions. He advises that, instead of offering a profile to the jury, which masks facial expressions and makes gestures difficult to interpret, attorneys and witnesses should "cheat out" so that they face the jury with a three-quarter front. In this way, they still appear to be talking to each other but are basically facing the jury. He advises that an attorney should never turn his back on a jury unless it is for dramatic effect.[33] Of course, one other time an attorney should turn his back is when he makes a face that he does not want the jury to see.

B. *The Concept of Role*

Returning to the idea of setting or situation as comprising more than the physical environment, consider the task of a person who suddenly finds himself in a new situation; for example,

> [w]hen the individual [moves] into a new position in society and obtains a new part to perform, he is not likely to be told in full detail how to conduct himself, nor will the facts of his new situation press sufficiently on him from the start to determine his conduct without his further giving thought to it. Ordinarily he will be given only a few cues, hints, and stage directions, and it will be assumed that he already has in his repertoire a large number of bits and pieces of performances that will be required in the new setting.[34]

Perhaps the greatest demand placed on the individual is the expectation by others of "some coherence among setting, appearance, and manner,"[35] or the appropriate role for the circumstance. Regardless of what he does when he is alone, when he is with others, a person tends to emphasize characteristics that confirm his role. One clear example is that of a baseball umpire, who is compelled to convey the impression that he is sure of his judgment; the instantaneousness of his decision contributes significantly to his appearance of certainty.[36]

In the drama of the courtroom, every person present plays some role for the jury. The attorney, however, can potentially exercise control only over the roles of himself, his client, and the witnesses he calls. While advice as to the preferred role or manner for an attorney may seem to stem from a desire to avoid offending any jury member, the hope is that it instead springs from insight into the function of the legal profession:

> The lawyer must be positive in his attitude, confident in his approach to the problem, and ready both physically and mentally to go to trial. He must be confident without being overconfident.[37]
>
> The winning trial lawyer is not a facade. He is a sincere man. . .and his battle is partly won when the jury realizes that he is sincere and not posturing.[38]
>
> A lawyer should walk with shoulders back, chin up, radiating confidence but not cockiness, with a smile of genuine liking for his fellow human beings upon his lips. Courtesy should so

> permeate his mannerisms that it is instinctive, not a cloak donned for the occasion. This will reflect itself in the way in which he greets the jurors, the court, the court attendants, and his opponents.[39]

Appleman says that the competent trial attorney wants his mannerisms and conduct to make him a hero, not a villain. He reports that one of his friends claims his secret to success in the courtroom is that he always tries to be "the nicest guy." When he is the defense counsel, the jury does not want to see him hurt; when he is the plaintiff's attorney, the jury wants him to win. "The advocate, accordingly, does not permit anything to occur during the trial which will place his opponent in a more sympathetic position than himself." Appleman suggests that excessive verdicts are usually the result of jurors' taking a dislike to a defendant or defense counsel.

> The hardest type of defendant to defeat is what I would call the "collapsible defendant." The plaintiff's attorney can flail out in all directions, but he encounters no great resistance from the mild and gentle person on the other side. That man only wants to do what is right, and wants the jury to do what is right. Rarely does he get hurt.[40]

There is more than the suggestion that the trial attorney must exercise careful control over his role. Appleman appears to have the solution: "[An attorney] should be the same man outside of the courtroom who seeks to win a case in the arena."[41] In other words, the attorney should simply be himself. Recall Appleman's background; his office and residence were four miles from the nearest town, which, in about 1967, had a population of 35,000.[42] Everyone in and around town undoubtedly knew Appleman; his reputation, personality, and character must have preceded him in every courtroom appearance, and had he acted differently in any single "performance," his audience would have known that.

In contrast, the average attorney who walks into a courthouse in the downtown area of a large city is only one of a multitude. When they first set eyes on him, the jurors do not know that he is a good husband, brilliant scholar, wonderful father, competent attorney, and all-around fine fellow; he must convey all relevant attributes through his current words and actions. Performers, aware that their audience is constructing a composite of who they are, try to ensure that as many minor events as possible in a performance will occur so as to convey either no impression or an impression that is consistent with the overall effect that is being conveyed.

> When the audience is known to be secretly skeptical of the reality that is being impressed upon them, we have been ready to appreciate their tendency to pounce on trifling flaws as a sign that the whole show is false; but as students of social life we have been less ready to appreciate that even sympathetic audiences can be momentarily disturbed, shocked, and weakened in their faith by the discovery of a picayune discrepancy in the impressions presented to them [such as] the dissonance created by a misspelled word, or by a slip that is not quite concealed by a skirt.[43]

Laughter is one way to treat inadvertent disruptions in the conveyance of impressions; if participated in by both the performer and his audience, laughter indicates that they both recognize the disruption and acknowledge that it is not to be taken seriously.[44]

There is a pleasing congruence between the recommendation of sincerity in the trial attorney and Herman's assessment that trial work calls for performances. Herman plainly says that you cannot trick the jury into believing your client's version of the facts when "you are thinking what a scumbag and liar" he is; your thoughts and feelings will be apparent, regardless of your words. Instead, he tells you how to believe what you say, with an approach adapted from the way actors learn a role. First, decide what you *should* be thinking and feeling when you are saying certain things. For example, if your words note the district attorney's failure to produce certain available evidence, then you should feel anger that an innocent man may be railroaded. Second, try to actually conjure up a feeling that is appropriate for a part of the text, perhaps by recalling the last time you had that feeling yourself. Third, if you cannot think or feel what your words say you should, change your text. Finally, try to express what you think and feel by not using words at all.[45] Notice that the focus here is external signs and the consistency among those signs:

> Whether an honest performer wishes to convey the truth or whether a dishonest performer wishes to convey a falsehood, both must take care to enliven their performance with appropriate expressions, exclude from their performances expressions that might discredit the impression being fostered, and take care lest the audience impute unintended meanings.[46]

Besides his own, the other role in the courtroom upon which the attorney can hope to have an effect is that of his client. Moreover, the attorney can also seek to bring the client more into action by having him assist with props or large exhibits in the summation. As Herman points out, "[t]he star of the innocent man show is, after all, the client." Of course, he quickly adds that the advice to bring the client more into view presumes he is personable, "that is, unarmed, *sans* tattoos, without metal things stuck thorugh various parts of his body and not possessed of an unnerving stare."[47]

Precisely because the record of a trial never indicates how a client looked to or acted before a jury (unless the behavior is the basis for a motion for mistrial), it is suggested that an attorney owes a duty to his client to advise him "in no uncertain terms" of suitable courtroom behavior. Detailed prohibitions include rocking back and forth in his chair, smoking in front of the jury (such as during a recess or before or after court), talking loudly in the courtroom or halls, anything that might distract the jury from the witness who is testifying, and excessive movement. In short, "[t]he client must be told that if the jury does not like him, then in almost every instance his case will be either damaged or lost."[48]

Appleman emphasizes how important it is for the jury to come to know the client. Particularly when the opposition is trying to prove contributory negligence or ordinary negligence, counsel wants the jury not to judge his client by an unrealistic standard of perfection. Instead, the client is the ordinary person contemplated by the law, susceptible to frailties, "just an average guy."[49]

It should be kept in mind that often, instead of simply depicting the role of the defendant as that of an attractive or morally fit person, the attorney also has the obligation of making the jury understand the role of the client in the events that sparked the lawsuit. Sometimes this involves educating the jury as to the lifestyle of the client and normal, expected behavior of a person living that lifestyle. In other words, the jury must be made to believe the motives attributed to the performer in the described situation. As an example of how difficult this task can be, consider the criminal cases of women who have fought back against men who have battered or raped them. While most people adopt the concept that killing in self-defense is justified, "it is difficult for jurors to apply that concept to a particular set of facts which necessarily include a dead person and issues of fact concerning the events surrounding the killing."[50] It is naturally important that the jury believe the defendant's account of the facts, as well as her fear for her life when the killing occurred. But it is unlikely that the jury will identify with or even understand the defendant's lifestyle and background, which may include staying with a battering husband, welfare fraud, and prostitution. The defense counsel who tries to present the defendant to be someone she is not risks the jury's detection of an attempt to hide something. While she should be presented in the most favorable light, hiding what counsel believes to be irrelevant facts can undermine the credibility of the defense. One thing the attorney can do is acknowledge that offending facts may come out but remind the jurors that the defendant is not on trial for offenses related to some of these facts (such as drug-related crimes) and that these facts should not enter into the deliberations.[51]

Humanizing the client is particularly critical when it is a corporate defendant. "A corporation is much more anonymous and impersonal than an individual; the responsibility for payment of the award does not lie with one individual, but is diffused through great numbers of people." Thus, juries consistently award larger sums of money when the defendant is a corporation. Especially in personal injury cases, when the defendant is a corporation, demonstrative evidence of the plaintiff's injury could raise legal, ethical, and psychological issues.[52]

In an experiment that tested for both the effect of the corporate status of a defendant and the use of demonstrative evidence, mock jurors were presented with different versions of a trial. In one version, the defendant was a corporation; in the other, an individual. Also in one version, midway thorugh the argument of plaintiff's counsel, when he was describing the artificial limb his client would have to wear for the rest of his life, the tape recorder was stopped and an artificial limb was unwrapped from a sheet and passed around to the jurors. In the other version, there was no demonstrative evidence. The jurors individually decided awards before deliberating and then again after deliberating. Prior to deliberating, the mean award to the plaintiff against the corporate defendant was almost twice the award against the individual defendant, when the demonstrative evidence was used ($114,310 vs. $73,257). When the evidence was verbal only, the corporate defendant still was assessed higher damages, though not in the same proportion as for demonstrative evidence ($83,666 vs. $62,500). Moreover, "[s]ubjects perceived the plaintiff's attorney's presentation of evidence as more emotionally arousing when the defendant was a corporation, regardless of whether the evidence was demonstrative or verbal."[53]

When the client is a corporation, institution, or government agency, a representative sitting at the counsel table can give the jury a person with whom to associate the entity. Ideally, this person should be pleasant, outgoing, otherwise attractive, and not too highly placed in the corporation. For example, a sales manager of a corporation would help counteract the jury's impression of a corporation as being big, impersonal, and uncaring.[54]

An attorney should personalize almost any witness that he puts on the stand. Asking preliminary questions about background will make the witness more of a real person to the jury and make them more receptive to the witness.[55] Talking about his background also usually makes a witness more comfortable, since he is talking about a subject with which he is familiar; in turn, his ease makes him more conversational and interesting.[56]

This concern about the comfort of the witness leads to consideration of another role. The jury observes the role played by a witness (as well as those played by counsel, the judge, and courtroom officials), and, to this point, the focus has been on (1) the appropriateness of the role for the message to be conveyed in the particular environment and (2) the consistency in the portrayal of the role. It should be recalled that most witnesses have never played that role before. This is a prime reason that rehearsal is so recommended for witnesses. The attorney should never forget that he is much more comfortable in his role than is the witness in his. Therefore, especially because of the threat of cross-examination by opposing counsel, who sees part of his responsibility as attacking the witness's portrayal, an attorney should consider the plight of the neophyte witness and do everything possible to put him at ease.

Look at this from the witness's point of view: before he takes the stand, you and he are on a first-name basis and feel that you are working together on the case. If you open the examination with a cold request that he state his name for the jury, he may be put off by the formal interrogator in you. Not only could that make him nervous (if you have abandoned him, who is going to protect him from opposing counsel?), but he could well convey this discomfort to a jury, who might misunderstand its sources. Greet the witness—"Good morning"—and more casually indicate that you like to have him state his name so that the jury can begin to get to know him.[57]

The jury will also be very attuned to the relationship portrayed by the attorney and the witness. First, they *want* to believe that the witness is hearing and answering the questions for the first time.

But "the impression of reality fostered by a performance is a delicate, fragile thing that can be shattered by very minor mishaps."[58] Thus, if the attorney asks a question and then looks down at his notes to find his next question, he loses "the sense of a real conversation" with the witness. Moreover, he appears rude and uninterested in what the witness has to say; that signals to the jury either that a canned answer is on its way or that they, too, have no reason to be interested in what the witness is saying. The attorney who is well-prepared knows the material so thoroughly that he rarely needs to rely on a list of written questions; by listening to the witness's answers, the attorney can elicit the desired testimony in a way that appears natural:

> Let the end of each answer trigger your next question. See the process as a tennis game in which you keep feeding your opponent easy shots for him to hit back. You swing when his ball lands. If you do not listen, you may very well miss a key point or a graceful lead-in to the next question.[59]

Handling older witnesses may present a special challenge. If the person has been a relative recluse for a time, then the experience of testifying may cause even more anxiety than for a younger witness. However, the opposite may be true. "In our youth-blinded culture, older people often live lives of loneliness and experience feelings of irrelevance. Being singled out and put in the spotlight on the witness stand can be a unique experience to them." With this opportunity to be important, they may talk excessively or become disorganized, which could nullify the potential benefit of their testimony.[60] When the infamous line of Westec cases came to an end in 1979, one of the defendants in that trial was a seventy-year-old gentleman who was basically a self-made millionaire. As a young man, he had probably been regarded as brash and headstrong, but remarkably bright and successful. As an older man, he was most cantankerous. To make matters worse, his hearing was going bad. Literally the only one in the courtroom who could control him on the stand was his attorney, an imposing man in his own right, though thirty-five years younger. Speaking very loudly and calling him "sir" with almost every sentence, the attorney would, from time to time, sternly but with the greatest respect, advise the witness to answer only the question asked him but to answer the question asked. In no way did the attorney seem inconsiderate; in fact, he even appeared heroic, successful in harnessing his feisty, thundering client—and for his own good.

C. *Conclusion*

> Those who conduct face to face interactions on a theater's stage must meet the key requirement of real situations; they must expressively sustain a definition of the situation; but this they do in circumstances that have facilitated their developing an apt terminology for the interactional tastks that all of us share.[61]

The fate of the trial attorney who fails to "sustain a definition of the situation," to portray the role required by the context of trials in the setting of the courtroom, is suggested by a personal experience relayed by Herman. It was his first summation; the jurors looked confused, and his client made disparaging comments about him in Spanish. As Herman finished his remarks, he then heard the sound of snoring. The district attorney announced his taking "judicial notice" that one of the jurors was asleep. Herman reports that the judge replied, "Well, perhaps the lawyer who put him to sleep should be in charge of waking him up."[62]

It has been my experience as a jury and trial consultant that while the type of juror selected is most important, the courtroom stage can be used to maintain and shape jurors' feelings. Jurors often determine the case on how they feel about the main "actors." These feelings are established and crystallized by the communications, both verbal and nonverbal, that are transmitted within the courtroom stage. In fact, it has been stated that "no more than 30% to 35% of the social meaning of a conversation or an interaction is carried by the words."[63] Another researcher in perception estimated that 93% of a message is determined by nonverbal factors.[64] The communication interchange within the courtroom stage involves the perceiver (the juror) reacting to the total gestalt of the speaker (attorney, client, or witness), not simply the spoken words. For example, the author has observed that attorneys often fail to familiarize the client (or witness) with the courtroom environment. Prospective jurors are watching the attorney, client, and other members of the litigation team from the beginning of the *voir dire.* These first observations are most important in the formulation of an opinion regarding the attorney, client, and, consequently, his cause of action. The potential jurors often interpret the natural and to-be-expected nervousness of the client as an indicator of untruthful behavior. Therefore, the client should be exposed to the courtroom setting in advance of the *voir dire* phase of the trial. I recommend taking the client to the courtroom prior to the trial date, letting him sit at counsel table, and then explaining to him in detail, exactly what will transpire at trial in order to habituate him to the courtroom setting. The attorney would be wise to instruct the client as to proper behavior during *voir dire* (and the trial). The client should be instructed to look at the jurors and establish and maintain brief eye contact. Jurors will evaluate this behavior as positive, sincere, and friendly. Also, interest can be connoted by the client's leaning forward and nodding in agreement with the prospective juror's response to an inquiry. It is crucial to create a positive initial impression for both the attorney and client. The social psychology research has consistently documented that positive impressions create a "halo" effect and that negative impressions are very difficult to erase as people tend to ignore information that contradicts the first impression.[65] Attorneys should make every effort to be perceived as the most credible, sincere, trustworthy, confident, and well-prepared person in the courtroom.

In conclusion, the majority of trial attorneys do not appreciate the power of the courtroom stage and only a limited few know how to perform on it. The law school curriculum does not require formal training in the theatrical arts. The author has suggested to several litigators that they enroll in a theatrical arts course at the nearby university or volunteer for a role in the local community drama production. Advocates should have the discipline and motivation to learn about the important forum presented by the courtroom stage and most importantly, how to make effective use of it.

II. *DRESS AND APPEARANCE*

"One's appearance commands the gaze of an audience. An eyebrow is lifted. There is a smile or a frown, an approach or withdrawal. One blushes with shame for the shamelessness of the other's appearance or with embarrassment at one's own."[66] A psychological examination of appearance is more rooted in practical considerations of an attorney than might initially be supposed. First, psychological experiments confirm what anthropologists have long noted, that appearance is a legitimate "dimension of communication." In fact, it is suggested that every exchange between people has two main components: actual discourse and appearance.[67] Therefore, unless he is blind, a juror cannot segregate the words of counsel from the visual image of the speaker before him. The attorney can work towards achieving a consistency between the image he presents and the position he takes; he can also assist his client (and certain witnesses) in the projection of images compatible with their testimony (and can use clothing cues as a kind of non-verbal *voir dire*). Judgments concerning the speaker can be correlated to the physical appearance of the speaker. The conclusion that physical attractiveness can cause a viewer to attribute greater ability than otherwise to another is explained in an earlier chapter.[68] The addition to that conclusion that will appear in this chapter is that clothing can determine the assessment of physical attractiveness.

Second, appearance is an integral part of the conception of self.[69] Thus, being in costume is thought to help actors "get into character." The attorney who practices his closing argument in his bathrobe before a bedroom mirror is not likely to sound the same as when he practices it in an empty courtroom in his suit.

Third, the rhetorical notion of persuasion via identification with the audience seems to encompass the first and second points above: "identification *with* one another. . .cannot be made without identification *of* one another."[70] In other words, before the speaker can identify with his audience (or they with him), he must first determine *who* they are. This he manages, in great part, by appearance. Similarly, they must determine who he is before they can decide whether he is one of them. The attorney who believes in the role he presents the jury—a role selected because of his judgments about the individual members of the jury, as well as the nature of the case and client—can also induce the jury to believe in him.

A. *What and How Clothes "Mean"*

"[W]hen one's dress calls out in others the 'same' identifications of the wearer as it calls out in the wearer, we may speak of the appearance as meaningful."[71] For example, policemen wear uniforms to announce their role in society; their appearance is validated when the public sees the uniform and places the wearer in the role of protector and law enforcer. The term "identity" is distinct from "self;" "identity establishes *what* and *where* the person is in social terms."[72] Therefore, the *what* established by the uniform causes guests concern when a policeman appears at a party; that is not *where* he is supposed to be unless there is a problem. Notice, then, that "identity" seems synonymous with "role," as being a unified combination of characteristics selected for their congruence with setting and with an expectation of their effect upon the audience.

Part of the effect of appearance is that it enables an audience (or, simply, the perceivers) to "very quickly and confidently form judgments about . . . religious, political and ethnic background and make snap decisions regarding . . . social, professional or sexual desirability." While such first impressions may be contrary to the truth, they tend to persist.[73] In fact, when perceivers believe they know about an individual's background, if he expresses an opinion that is inconsistent with that background, they are likely to discount the validity of the opinion.[74] Therefore, if appearance is an initial clue as to background, an expert witness could, by his appearance, seem to be the wrong person to be expressing the opinions he will express. In other words, he will lack credibility.

From one perspective, it makes perfect sense that appearance cues perceivers to one's background. Appearance is a substitute for past and present action and suggests to the perceiver how one will act next. That appearance and clothing represent "action" further demonstrates that applicability of the concepts of role and setting: "this can be clearly seen in the doffing of dress, signaling that an act is done (and another act about to begin) the donning of dress, signaling the initiation of a new act, and the wearing of dress, signaling that action is going on."[75]

"Appearance" is also described as providing information as to the performer's social statuses, as well as to his "temporary ritual state," i.e., whether he is working, playing, socializing, etc.[76] Clothing is the "most salient public aspect of a person's appearance." Thus, it naturally follows that clothing signals social status. The more subtle observation is that the social status of the observer determines the value placed on the social status signaled by the clothing.[77] In an experiment demonstrating this, subjects were selected because of their presumed values and social standings: teacher trainees, agricultural students, business students, and behavioral science students. The stimulus materials consisted of photographs showing a person of the same sex and age as the subjects. The photographs differed only in the dress of the person, which ranged from a business suit to a costume of shorts, thongs, and a T-shirt and to "hippie" garb.[78] The experiment was designed so that each subject saw photographs of a person dressed as the subject would dress, along with photographs showing other attire.[79]

Although the photographs all depicted an academic setting, which would suggest more casual clothing than an office, the business students responded postively towards the suit. Similarly, each group of subjects responded most favorably to the clothing that reflected their presumed values. It is interesting that, across the samples, the short, thongs, and T-shirt met with common acceptance. Most subjects described the person in those clothes as "an average person, with a balanced interest in study and sport, conscientious yet easy going, enjoying the freedom of youth yet prepared to conform to the social order when required."[80]

The experimenters arrive at three conclusions about the meaning of clothing. First, since all samples viewed the suit and slacks as "polite, conservative," then interpretation occurs at a general level of cultural consensus. Second, meaning occurs at the level of the social community, defined here by the source of each sample and demonstrated by the preferred dress, according to the sample. Third, clothing is subject to individual interpretation. Here, the researchers found that the type of dress worn by each individual in a group, as compared with dress worn by others in the group, affected the individual's response to a photograph, "over and above the main effects of sample and type of photograph."[81]

Stereotyping is a generalized effect of appearance on most perceivers. The results of one experiment suggest that stereotyping emanates from wearing apparel instead of facial characteristics, since the models in the test photographs wore blank expressions and had similar physiques and coloring. Both subjects, but especially the males, found the models wearing makeup, bright colors, and short skirts to be sophisticated, immoral, and physically attractive. Both sexes also rated the models wearing glasses as shy and unimaginative but intelligent. The faces of the models wearing glasses were deemed less attractive than those of models without glasses.[82]

Another experiment focused purely on the effects of the physical dimensions of women's clothing on perceivers. As might be expected, less clothing (as in tank tops and short skirts) communicated youthfulness and vivaciousness. Long skirts were associated with sophistication and arrogance and wide skirts, with friendliness.[83]

As earlier suggested, we dress partly for ourselves, to establish to ourselves who we are. "As the self is dressed, it is simultaneously addressed, for, whenever we clothe ourselves, we dress 'toward' or address some audience whose validating responses are essential to the establishment of our self."[84] In other words, unless we get that validating response, we cannot be sure that we have dressed so as to appear as we want to appear. Understanding how this cycle works can truly be an asset to the amateur psychologist and interpreter of clothing. Consider the possible client of the criminal attorney that Herman describes: tattooed, with "metal things stuck through various parts of his body."[85] It is precisely because he *knows* how people will react to him that such a person causes himself to have such an appearance. Whenever he walks down the street, reactions from more conventionally attired people convince him of the characteristics he is projecting. Therefore, to such a client who refuses to change his attire because it is "him," the following speech could be warranted: "You may be communicating to the vast majority of people—people like those that will be on the jury—that you are cruel and perverse and resent their way of life and that, if it's possible with those traits to have any friends, your friends are the same way. How could you possibly expect to generate believability and induce compassion by conveying such information about yourself to these people?"

Trying out roles (for fit?) is something that begins early in individual development. The child acts out two general kinds of roles. In one, he anticipates socialization and pretends he is a plausible character, such as a parent, a storekeeper, or a customer. In the other, he acts out a role that he could never realistically fill, such as a past or futuristic character. There is great emphasis in either role on costuming (or "dressing out"), though it might be only donning the larger clothes of a parent. Apart from this choice about clothing, children usually have little to say about what they wear until they reach a certain age or maturity. Many adults recall that when they were given this choice as children, they selected clothing of their peer group, the identifying "uniform."[86]

> While the costume of play may be construed as any apparent misrepresentation of the self, permitting the wearer to become another, the uniform is precisely any apparent representation of the self, at once reminding the wearer and others of an *appropriate* identity, a *real* identity. The team-player is uniformed; the play-actor is costumed.[87]

In other words, the uniformed individual can look at others dressed as he is, note their characteristics, and be confident that those characteristics are also imputed to him; the others' acceptance of him confirms that imputation, making their acceptance the reaction he desires. The individual with "metal things stuck through various parts of his body" also receives the reaction he desires; and, though its permutations may boggle the average mind, he may also receive acceptance from others that dress as he does.

While the idea of clothing as an aid to "getting into character" will be further explored later, another personal effect of clothing is its therapeutic value:

> Many people can relate instances in which the clothing they wore changed the way they felt about themselves, or the way they behaved. Clothing can be used to alter mood; indeed, some therapists . . . recommend the purchase of new clothing to certain depressed clients.[88]

The evolution of dress in individual development allows the following comment on the above observations. Dissatisfied with their current identity, people can revert to the childhood practice of play-acting, adopting a temporary fantastic new identity, or perhaps permanently changing their social circles, as well as their real identity. "Life must be viewed as a continuous socialization, a series of careers, in which old identities are sacrificed as new identities are appropriated, in which old relations are left behind as new relations are joined. Each critical turning point of life is marked by a change of dress."[89]

Clothing, therefore, tells others what the wearer hopes to tell them about himself. This telling may be imperfect, however, if the perceiver does not interpret clothing in the same way the wearer does. For example, if the woman who dons a pastel polyester suit intends to convey that she is a serious busines woman, she will fail to do so if her audience is wearing gray wool suits. But the attorney during the *voir dire* can turn this knowledge to advantage. The pastel polyester suit tells him that the woman considers herself as taking the potential jury task seriously; it may also tell him that she could admire his female client wearing a gray wool suit.

A communications expert says that, during *voir dire*, "[o]bserving clothing is a great way to collect information on who's casual or an indulger, who's a perfectionist, a narcissist, a conformist, a combatant or an individualist."[90] She goes on to indicate certain manifestations of these character traits in clothing. If "[e]verything matches," the wearer is probably a fussy perfectionist who may not overlook errors or social transgressions (i.e., breaking the law). Running shoes or other sports-oriented clothing suggests health consciousness, inner direction, and discipline. Showy, flashy clothes are worn to draw attention to a self-involved person; such a person may not be able to attend to others and may therefore be incapable of empathy and bored with ordinary, lower-class people. Very casual dress is indicative of less rule-orientation; but if age and dress are incongruent (e.g., jeans and sneakers for an older man), certain psychological problems may be suggested, such as an inability to accept aging. Anti-social clothing, like that of the punk rockers, signals hostility to current institutions, which is particularly acute when worn in defiance of the somber environment of the courtroom.

Since fashion caters to women, they probably have more clothing options available than men. The flamboyantly dressed woman is trying to get ahead and be noticed and is probably somewhat independent. Expensive clothing signals self-interest; "frilly feminine things" suggest the traditional woman—nurturing and non-violent; and a classic suit conveys independence and worldliness. The attorney is also advised to notice the size and shape of purses carried by women, as well as how the women carry them; a purse clutched tightly under an arm may convey distrust of others and a history of living in unsafe neighborhoods. In addition, one could make various inferences about people's values and social status based on the type and quality of shoes they wear.[91]

If people dress to convey information about themselves to others, then one piece of information that probably everyone hopes to convey is attractiveness (the conscious exception here could be the metal-things-stuck-through-the-body type, but others of his ilk may even find that attractive). An experiment described earlier used photographs of women with the same coloring and similar expressions; the results suggested that wearing apparel, particularly glasses, caused some of these women to be judged less physically attractive. In an experiment reported in 1983, the same model was used for all photographs. Her facial expression and posture were the same for all photographs, with only her clothing changing. Participants in the experiment were divided into judges and subjects, all of whom were female undergraduate students. The model was twenty-one years old, and the clothing she wore for the photographs was borrowed from the campus clothing store and from students that did not participate in the experiment.[92]

The first step in the experiment was to establish which photographs showed an attractive model (it was, of course, the same model in all photographs). Participants called judges selected four attractive, three neutral, and four unattractive photographs. Then, the seventy-two subjects in the experiments ranked the photographs selected by the judges on a continuum from exceptionally attractive to exceptionally unattractive.[93] The amazing result was that, while the judges agreed among themselves as to attractive/unattractive photographs, the subjects often radically disagreed with the judges.

The researchers offer two explanations for the differences. First, they point out that previous experiments have relied on extreme variations in attractiveness, suggesting that reasonable people might usually agree under those conditions. When the variations are less extreme (and how extreme can they get when the model does not change?), standards of physical attractiveness may vary from one individual to the next. Especially since the clothing changed, the attractiveness assessment could have been related to the same aspects of identification that emerged in the experiment with the man in the academic setting wearing four different outfits. Second, when the judges made their evaluations, they were looking at and comparing sixty-nine photographs. Each subject saw only one photograph. "A photograph may be judged attractive when compared to others but quite differently when considered on its own."[94] If the differences between the subjects' and the judges' assessments here indicate a valid trend, it is that the comparison exercised by the judges resulted in more assessments of attractiveness. In other words, *relative* attractiveness is more readily recognized than absolute, unless the absolute is extreme (such as movie star caliber).

The practical implications for the trial attorney of the comparison basis of attractiveness could emerge with multiple defendants. If one defendant were (or could be made to be) attractive in comparison with the others, he could benefit by the comparison. While it is not clear that the other defendants would necessarily be damaged by the comparison, an attorney would probably construct a different defense for the attractive defendant than for the others, which states the need for separate counsel.

B. *Clothing Strategy*

Because people are begining to understand that clothing communicates, "the reason for being interested in clothing has changed from concern about esthetics to strategy," though this shift is "more likely to be made by people who see themselves as actors on life's stage." Based on responses to a questionnaire seeking college students' awareness of themselves as social entities and their interest in clothes, students who saw themselves as taking an active role in their social relationships were also concerned about the appropriate clothing for those roles.[95]

Clothing strategy encompasses not only the effect of apparel on others, but also the effect on self. If "getting into character" is unacceptable terminology, then view the appropriate clothing as providing confidence "when one must engage in stressful situations, ranging from first dates and courtroom appearances to job interviews." Such confidence emerged in an experiment when subjects participated in mock job interviews, thinking they were real. The researcher purposefully scheduled the interviews so that some of the students would have to come directly from class, with no opportunity to change. The students were questioned after the interview to determine how well they thought they had done. Those who had worn a jacket and tie not only felt that the interviewer had a higher opinion of their abilities than students dressed otherwise, but also requested a starting salary of an average of $4000 more than the other students.[96]

Unless the individual is alone, almost any explanation of the connection of clothing to self-concept depends upon perceiver feedback: (1) People may learn through trial and error that certain clothing evokes certain responses in others and are reinforced by the rewards and costs of such responses. (Here, one can almost imagine a rat in a Skinner cage; but instead of running a particular route to get to the food, he must pop on a certain hat.) (2) "[C]lothing affects the way we are perceived as individuals by others." (3) By identifying an individual's membership in certain groups, clothing "will determine others' behavior toward the wearer and often generate a self-fulfilling behavioral prophecy." It follows, then, that beliefs about the strategic importance of clothing should be related to the individual trait of public self-consciousness, and demonstrating this was the object of an experiment.[97]

Subjects consisting of an equal number of males and females completed questionnaires designed to measure public self-consciousness (concern about impressions made on others), private self-consciousness, and social anxiety. These measures were correlated with the subjects' clothing attitudes.[98] As the researchers had expected, the relationship between public self-consciousness and clothing measures was "especially powerful."[99] This relationship, however, was stronger for men than for women, even though women indicated a superior interest in and awareness of clothes. The experimenters conclude that women's interest in clothing is inbred while men's is more utilitarian or strategic, bent on "increasing the value of the self as a social commodity on the interpersonal marketplace."[100]

In another experiment, researchers sought the relationship between dress and personality for males and females. Responses to the clothing questionnaire identified clothing consciousness (the extent to which a person is concerned with clothes), exhibitionism (one's desire to wear revealing clothing), practicality in clothing choices (as opposed to the aesthetic value of clothes), and designer tendency (the degree to which a person would like to be involved in clothing as a vocation). The subjects were also measured with four personality/behavioral tests.[101]

While gender differences in personality traits with each clothing measure always appeared, the personality traits of both sexes were quite similar for two clothing measures and radically different for two. The chart of these traits and measures is produced below.[102]

Summary of Clothing and Personality Relationships

	Clothing consciousness	*Exhibitionism*
High males	Conforming; not valuing beauty; believe people are easily manipulated	Aggressive; confident; unsympathetic; low family self-concepts; moody
Low males	Aggressive; independent; do not believe people are easily manipulated	Guarded; believe people are easily manipulated
High females	Inhibited; conforming; loyal	Radical; detached in relationships; high moral-ethical self-concepts
Low females	Forceful; independent; low motivation for heterosexual relationships	Timid; feelings of inferiority; low motivation for heterosexual relationships
	Practicality	*Designer*
High males	Inhibited; not leadership oriented; rebellious; not motivated toward friendship relationships	Cooperative; warm; impulsive; irritable; conforming
Low males	Success oriented; forceful; self- and other-analytical	Adventurous; egotistic; independent; anxious

	Practicality	*Designer*
High females	Clever; enthusiastic; guarded; not leadership oriented	Irrational; confused; ebullient
Low females	Self-centered; not motivated toward friendship relationships; independent	Efficient; believe people are not easily manipulated; pessimistic about future jobs

The chart above could be helpful to the attorney during *voir dire*, if he is first able to assess the clothing dimension into which each of the potential jurors falls. Certain guidelines for this kind of assessment have already been given. For example, if a mature male appears to have little regard for the effect of clothing on others (i.e., he seems to dress only for himself—low in clothes consciousness) but is wearing the appropriate clothing for the time of year and the kind of work he does (practicality), he will make up his own mind about the facts in a case and is unlikely to be swayed by more conventional individuals on the jury. Although he may not have leadership qualities by nature, his unwavering stand may well attract weaker personalities on the jury. Similarly, the female who appears to have dressed with the sole purpose of covering all exposed flesh and in the drabbest of colors and fabric (scoring low on the exhibitionism measure) may feel inadequate even to come to a decision at the close of trial and be content to be swept along by the majority.

Another use of this chart is as a guide to what jurors may think of clients and witnesses who betray these clothing predispositions. Recall that as a projection of self, clothing elicits from others the validations of the signals we send about ourselves. Therefore, jurors could well articulate the very personality traits they see reflected in the clothing habits of others. (While we do not know enough about coverage of the metal-things-stuck-through-the-body ensemble to be certain, its wearer would appear to fall into the exhibitionism category. With the concomitant personality traits for that category, the earlier suggested speech by counsel seems justified.)

One limitation of the chart is the incompleteness of the personality traits in depicting a complete individual and how he may behave. That is, the temptation to apply the characteristics absolutely must be avoided; instead, one should attempt to construct an entire personality that will account both for the traits that appear in the chart and for other attributes of an individual who may fall into one of the categories. For example, a female who believes that others always notice what she wears (i.e., having clothing consciousness) is indicated as being inhibited, conforming, and loyal. The consciousness concerning clothing could describe a woman wearing a gray wool suit in a business environment in which her peers are men who are also wearing dark business suits. The adjectives "inhibited" and "conforming" seem, at first glance, at odds with the earlier description of a woman in a business suit being independent and worldly. The descriptions are actually compatible. Women did not define the business suit as a work uniform; men did. Thus, to the extent that a woman in a traditionally male field opts to wear the clothing of her peers, she is a conformist (by the same token, all of the males wearing suits have also conformed). However, the fact that she is in a traditionally male field indicates her independence.

In the business world, clothing strategy has been gaining in popularity for several years, with many people believing that "the business suit. . .can function as a magic amulet that protects the wearer during the rite of passage to a new role as an 'executive.' "[103] Although women have persistently been edging their way into traditionally male professions, business clothing strategy for women has been slow to catch on, seemingly regarded almost as a fad. Probably the primary cause of this has been the strict dichotomy between "dressing correctly" and "fashion." "Whereas fashion has always meant personal expression, esthetics and, above all, constant change, the new emphasis upon strategic business clothing emphasizes conformity, rigidity and continuity."[104]

The strategic dresser appears to be aware of, and even seeking, the results of conformity, rigidity, and continuity. One subject, asked whether he would prefer to wear a greater or smaller variety of clothes at work, replied, "A smaller variety so you will look the same every day. So people will identify you. They look for the same old landmark." Another subject, who had just opened a small business, gave this answer to the same question: "A smaller variety for both sales and shop. I think if a person dresses about the same continually, people will get to know you. Even if they don't know your name, you're easier to describe."[105] Simply, the daily change of dress that most women reflect (dress one day, blazer the next, and slacks another day) "projects inconsistency. Consistency is important in business. In business the consistent mode of dress is a suit."[106] Even when a woman wears a suit one day, when she follows it with a clinging dress and, later, with a sweater, skirt, and boots, she is saying that the suit was merely a fashion item to her.

Molloy made waves with his *Dress for Success* books for men and women. While much of his advice in the women's book is equally applicable to professional men as well as professional women, men are generally aware of the need to dress appropriately for business and what such dressing entails. A survey of American men conducted for the Celanese Corporation asked what they wanted their clothes to say about them. Most men replied " 'confident,' " instead of sophisticated, sexy, or stylish.[107] Therefore, this discussion of professional women's clothing strategy is primarily for the female attorney. However, Molloy actually tested for the effects of styles and colors of clothing; therefore, his comments are useful for the male attorney, too. Finally, his findings as to the colors that tested best for conveying authority and believability, for example, would assist any attorney in advising his client and witnesses as to dress.

Molloy claims that women dress for failure in allowing the fashion industry to influence their choice of business clothes, in continuing to view themselves primarily as sex objects, and in letting their socioeconomic background influence their clothing choices.[108] Holsey, a clothing consultant, tailor, and lecturer on quality clothing, explains why women have trouble dressing for business:

> [T]hey have not had mentors to guide them. When our brothers graduated from college, father took them aside and bought them suits. When most women graduate from college, mother buys them some new dresses. Non-working mothers usually do not know much about the corporate world. Consequently, most women enter [an] interview and their first job unaware of their position. They wear the prevailing style, which is usually inappropriate for business.[109]

In 1984, readers of a magazine for female executives were surveyed. The more than 8,000 responses indicated that these women, aged twenty-five to thirty-five, with good education and income, were in an ideal position to set fashion trends. However, they reported little interest in fashion, far more involved with "the tactical properties of clothing."[110]

The phrase "dress for success suit" may well be founded on Molloy's basic test for the ideal outfit for the "typical efficient executive." Five groups of subjects—male executives, female executives, male office workers, female office workers, and the general public—

were asked to visualize a male executive. Then they were asked to select his picture from a stack of twenty-five; the almost unanimous choice showed a man in an upper middle-class suit and tie. Next, the subjects were asked to visualize a woman executive and then to select her picture from a stack of twenty-five. The results of over 1000 interviews showed that the total response of all groups was that the navy suit and the highly tailored navy pantsuit were the most efficient garments, but the "male executives overwhelmingly chose the woman wearing a gray suit as the typical efficient executive."[111] The suit, that is, a skirt and jacket of the same color and fabric, ranked above a skirt with a blazer. Holsey explains this is because "[s]eparates communicate not enough money to afford suits."[112]

Molloy found that solid colors tested best (followed by tweed and then by the kind of plaid that is only one or two degrees stronger than the plaid in men's business suits), and that wool and linen were the preferred fabrics. The colors that tested best in solid-colored wool or linen suits were the average gray of a man's suit and the average blue of a man's suit. Other colors that tested well included navy, other shades of gray, camel, black, dark brown, deep maroon, and deep rust. Molloy advises against suits in pastels or any bright colors. Blouses that tested successfully had a wider range of acceptable colors (including orange and maroon), but for the most part were the lighter shades generally seen with men's suits. As with suits though, solid colors tested best, and the white blouse resulted in high authority and high status ratings.[113]

Molloy then ascertained the color combinations that would most successfully convey authority, presence, and believability. The solid gray suit with a white, white-on-white (a pattern of the same color), or a pink blouse (in a corporation in which the men would wear pink shirts) tested highest for authority. The gray suit with a white, rust, pink, maroon, or black blouse tested highest for presence. A medium-blue suit with a white blouse topped the list for believability.[114]

Dress for attorneys, regardless of their sex, receives at least a mention in many guides to litigation and appellate argument. While some of the advice seems correlated to the effect of an attorney's dress on the jurors, other suggestions imply that the very profession requires a certain mode of dress. Also, although Molloy-like testing results do not appear alongside these recommendations, one can detect the consistency. Appleman, in a section entitled "Even minor details may affect jury reaction," has this to say about clothing:

> When the attorney enters the courtroom. . . he should not be overdressed. He should wear no flashy jewelry. The same rules apply to him as to the male witnesses to whom he would give instructions. A white shirt, simple dark tie, plain dark suit, clean shoes, no lodge emblems which will antagonize any particular juror, and no diamond rings.[115]

The Civil Trial Manual argues that the "dignity of the profession" commands a certain clothing response by attorneys: "The lawyer historically has not dressed in conservative clothes merely because such an attitude of dress necessarily appealed to him. Rather, this form of dress has been an attempt to enhance the prestige and dignity of the profession."[116]

A treatise originally published in 1961 notes that, in most appellate courts, business suits are the customary dress; and, when that is the case, "it would be a mistake to appear in more formal attire." The author describes that some years earlier, counsel arguing before the United States Supreme Court would not be recognized unless wearing a long coat, three of which (small, medium, and large) were kept on hand for "practitioners hailing from the forks of the creek." Although government attorneys and leaders of the bar in large cities began wearing "cutaways," the author nevertheless observes that "any private practitioner would be well advised, on any of his appearances before the Supreme Court to wear formal dress—even if he has to go out and rent it."[117] A publication appearing some twenty years later advises that

> [d]ress in appellate courts no longer need be formal, even in the United States Supreme Court. Conservative—which means reasonably dark, or at least not too light—business suits for men and the equivalent for women are the most satisfactory, though many lawyers seem to consider any combination of coat and trousers adequate without suffering any dire consequences.[118]

C. *The "Amphibious" Suit*

Even if law firms do not publish dress codes for their attorneys, new associates somehow know to come to the office in a dark suit, and every courthouse in every major city is filled with people wearing suits, usually in the acknowledged business colors. What is the explanation, then, for the attorney with twenty years of practice under his belt, a stable of racehorses, and a vacation home in the mountains, who shows up for trial in a wrinkled suit, probably seersucker (the wash-and-wear variety), when his opponent is decked out in his best dark wool? Where has he been that all of this talk of appropriate and conforming dress has passed him by?

The seersucker suit first drew attention when the head of the company who tailored and manufactured it, Joseph Haspel, waded into the Atlantic Ocean "up to the peaked label of his seersucker suit." He then turned around, came ashore, and set off for a business meeting later that day in a suit that had "drip-dried into presentable shape." Before air conditioning, Haspel's lightweight suit became a welcomed alternative to the scratchy, dark mohair suits that most men had been wearing.

> True, it rumpled easily, but it quickly became the summertime uniform of wealthy landowners and businessmen in the torrid South. Their Northern counterparts, with less compelling reasons to adopt the wrinkled garb, opted for a sharp crease over short-term comfort. They sometimes looked down their noses at the inexpensive suits—which retailed for $10—and thought of seersucker as the poor man's fabric.[119]

In the 1930s, the seersucker suit had snob appeal among Ivy Leaguers, but by the 1940s it was so associated with the lower classes that it became almost a badge of poverty. After Haspel's famous walk in the Atlantic in the new, "crisp, washable fabric that would hold a crease," some of the objections to the suit fell away; but the unique weaving of the threads nevertheless produced a crinkled texture. Priced at a reasonable $39.95 in the 1950s, the 100% cotton seersucker suit now sells for $280. The fabric has fallen into the hands of designers like Jeffrey Banks and Alexander Julian, and now "Brooks Brothers sell status-suit wrinkles." The fashion-minded seersucker wearer of today is "a picky guy who wants to project a casual or don't-care image."[120]

But the experienced trial attorney who dons a seersucker suit projects a different image, perhaps that suggested by "Gregory Peck, playing a shrewd country lawyer [and sporting] a Haspel in the 1962 film *To Kill a Mockingbird*."[121] It may be that he is counting on the middle-aged jurors associating certain values with the suit, viewing him as down-to-earth and modest, and believing him when he presents his client's version of the facts. It may also be that, in wearing the seersucker suit, he causes himself to believe that those associations are warranted. "One's clothes impart value to the wearer, both in the wearer's own eyes and in the eyes of others."[122]

The "amphibious" suit is, of course, merely an example of a deviation from a set rule. The attorney who can make such deviations without reproach or other undesirable consequences is usually preceded by his reputation, such that the normal uniform is not needed to place him in his profession. His experience also makes it unnecessary for him to conform in order to feel at ease. "People, it turns out, are most reliant upon the symbolism of clothing during the process of transition from a familiar role to an unfamiliar one."[123] Insofar as the effect on the jury is concerned, to the extent that the attorney is discovered to be impersonating someone of a lower status than he really is, such a revelation may not defeat his cause.

> When a disclosure shows that we have been participating with a performer who has a higher status than he led us to believe, there is good Christian precedent for our reacting with wonderment and chagrin rather than with hostility. Mythology and our popular magazines, in fact, are full of romantic stories in which the villain and the hero both make fraudulent claims that are discredited in the last chapter, the villain proving not to have a high status, the hero proving not to have a low one.[124]

D. *Conclusions*

The dress of the client and the attorney should be considered carefully. The author has studied the effect of suit color on surrogate jurors' perception with regard to honesty, trustworthiness, and power. It was discovered that the light grays, dark grays, dark blues, and the pinstripes are the preferred colors for projecting an honest, trustworthy, and powerful image. The fabric of the suit should be 100% wool. It was also determined that attorneys should wear a white shirt for the maximum effect. Let your opponent be the one who wears the browns, tans, and greens and is perceived as "one of the fellows." When in the courtroom the litigator should be perceived as an officer of the court, and the solemn "uniform" portrays the official look. This uniform is especially important in criminal defense litigation. The criminal defense attorney must not let the prosecutor create the impression that it is *his* court as opposed to the jury's court and the litigant's court. The attorney who represents the citizens accused is as much an officer of the court as the prosecutor is. In civil litigation, the attorney should make a special effort to ensure that his expert witness will arrive at the courthouse in his power uniform of gray or dark blue, with a white shirt, instead of his usual campus attire of earth tone tweeds.

The client must be carefully dressed to produce the desired reaction by the jury. The desired visual impact of the client on the jury must be maximized. The client should be dressed in a manner that is consistent with the theme of the case. For example, in a medical malpractice case in which the plaintiff was a female, the author created the impression of a frail and helpless victim through oversized clothing and a hair style that caused the plaintiff to look despondent. The plaintiff wore three different outfits, with minimum accessories, in a two-week trial. The new hairstyle and clothing were worn by the client several weeks prior to the trial date so that she would feel normal and comfortable. Major revisions in appearance must be accomplished in time to allow the subject to feel good about herself or himself.

The attractiveness of the client and attorney should be taken into consideration in trial preparation. It is a well-known fact that attractive people do better in courtroom proceedings. Research has demonstrated that attractive people are more persuasive[125] and are perceived to be more credible,[126] intelligent, competent, warm,[127] and successful in careers and marriages.[128] In general, juries are more lenient with attractive defendants and award more damages to an attractive plaintiff than an unattractive plaintiff. Two confounding variables must be evaluated in view of the above general statement. Juries are influenced in their decision by the attractiveness of the victim, and juries are influenced negatively against a "too attractive" female client. Juries may also be affected negatively by a "too attractive" female attorney. Perhaps male jurors are threatened by the attractive female and the female jurors may be jealous of her.

It was not surprising to learn in interviewing several jury members in a well-publicized murder trial that the jury disregarded the testimony of several eyewitnesses in acquitting the accused citizen. Many of them believed that wealthy, handsome men (like the accused) do not commit the crime of murder and do not act in the manner the accused was alleged to have behaved.

In jury selection, the trial attorney should also consider the dress and appearance of the juror.

> By a man's fingernails, by his coat sleeve, by his boots, by his trouser knees, by the callosities of his forefinger and thumb, by his expression, by his short cuff—by each of these things a man's calling is plainly revealed. That all united should fail to enlighten the competent inquiror in any case is almost inconceivable.[129]

The author makes note of the fact that a prospective juror considered the occasion solemn enough to wear a suit. The style of the shoes and quality of the leather should be evaluated. The reader may enjoy reading about how shoes portray psychosexual messages and the basic classifications of men's and women's footwear in the witty book *The Sex Life of the Foot and Shoe*.[130] I like also to look for items that prospective jurors carry, such as keys on their belt loops (perhaps, a badge of authority), pens or pencils in the pocket, reading materials, quality of the leather of the handbag, and whether the shoes and handbag are coordinated. Space or territory is correlated with power. Leaders claim more space by, for example, putting feet in the aisle, extending an arm on the back of the next seat, or placing a coat in front or beside. Therefore, the amount of territory or space possessed should be considered.

Whether there is a correlation between color preference in clothing and personality is a matter of dispute. However, there may be a broad connection between the colors chosen for clothing and personality. Keep in mind that jurors do not wear only one color consistently; however, they do tend to follow certain color patterns. People who select warmer colors (yellow, orange, and red) tend, in general, to be more social, extroverted, and active than those who select cool colors (violet, blue, and green), who tend to be more introverted, reserved, and detached. Based on my experience, specific colors are correlated with the following personality traits:

a. Blue is associated with tradition, order, reservedness, and quietness.
b. Green is associated with being conventional, materialistic, and sociable.
c. Off-white (beige) is associated with being conservative, sophisticated, and secure.
d. Orange is associated with cheerfulness, sympathy, and good naturedness.
e. Pink is associated with indulgence and overprotectiveness.
f. Purple is associated with sensitivity and creativity.
g. Red is associated with being impulsive, competitive, sexy and dramatic.
h. Yellow is associated with intelligence and high ideals.

As an example of decoding color messages, I have observed that prospective female jurors who dress in strong contrasting colors tend to be emotional and not afraid of being judged negatively by others. Females who blend colors tend to be more fearful of taking risks and are more conventional. As a jury and trial consultant, I am always interested in whether the jury will take the same seats each day of trial and if so, how long it will be before they decide on "their" seat. It is usually the more independent person (for example, the female who dresses in a dramatic color combination such as green and red) who selects different seats for the duration of the trial.

Some jurors do plan and consciously choose their clothing for the selection of the jury. An excellent illustration of this fact is provided by the foreperson of the Angela Davis jury:

> What should I wear?...
>
> At work I wore pant-suits almost exclusively. Would pantsuits at a time like this really represent the "true" me? Even though that was what I usually wore, I really felt that I was more a conservative-suit-and-low-heels type. I didn't want to go into court on Monday morning and have the attorneys look at me and mis-categorize me.
>
> What was my category anyhow? I tried to think of what role I fit into in today's society.
>
> I had a job, a husband and three children.... Politically, I had been a Democrat since the summer of 1952.... In recent years, as my distress over the war in Southeast Asia increased, I found I was aligning myself with the liberal wing of the Democrat Party.
>
> Socially and morally, I was pretty conservative—by the standards of the day. I had been raised strictly in a middle-class, small-town environment—a Catholic—and I accepted the mores of that time and place. I like people on a one-to-one basis, I do not like organizations and clubs, I am not a "joiner." I was just becoming aware of the Women's Movement.... So, in an effort to stereotype myself, I decided the night before on a tailored cashmere suit and flat walking shoes.[131]

Personality indicators such as dress, appearance, and color should be considered in jury selection. However, the attitudes and beliefs of the prospective jurors should be weighed more heavily in the decision to accept or reject a particular venire-person than the above-mentioned correlates.

In summary, the jury's attention is focused primarily on the lawyer and his client and his witnesses in the courtroom. The impression that is desired must be a consideration in trial preparation. Dress of the main characters must not be left to chance. Dress and appearance are factors that should be considered by the trial attorney to be as important as the actual words from the witnesses' mouths.

NOTES

1. Dierking, *How to Lose a Court Case*, 4 Social Action & the L. 58–59 (1978).

2. *Id.* at 59.

3. *Webster's New Collegiate Dictionary* 345 (1974) (emphasis added).

4. Burke, *Linguistic Approaches to Problems of Education*, I *Modern Philosophies of Education: The Fifty-fourth Yearbook of the National Society for the Study of Education* 263–64 (Henry ed. 1955).

5. Burke, *A Grammar of Motives* (1962).

6. Goffman, *The Presentation of Self in Everyday Life* 72 (1973).

7. *Id.* at 22.

8. McCullough & Underwood, 2 *Civil Trial Manual*, 540 (1980).

9. Herman, *The Theatre of Summation: Acting, Directing and Playwriting for the Criminal Defense Lawyer*, Forum, June-July-Aug. 1984, at 20.

10. McCullough & Underwood, *supra* n.8, at 541.

11. Appleman, *Preparation and Trial* 724 (1967); *also see* "Presentation of Evidence and Arguments," section II of Chapter 2.

12. *Id.* at 723.

13. Cobin, *Communication Theory and Theater: An Exercise in Relationship, Rhetoric and Communication* 126 (J. Blankenship & H. Stelzner ed. 1976).

14. *Id.* at 120.

15. McCullough & Underwood, *supra* n.8, at 535.

16. Cobin, *supra* n.13, at 124–25.

17. Goffman, *supra* n.6, at 22.

18. Herman, *supra* n.9, at 28.

19. Cone & Lawyer, *The Art of Persuasion in Litigation* 96 (1966).

20. Bitzer, *Functional Communication: A Situational Perspective, Rhetoric in Transition: Studies in the Nature and Uses of Rhetoric* 21 (E. White ed. 1980).

21. *Id.* at 23.

22. McCullough & Underwood, *supra* n.8, at 535–41.

23. Bitzer, *supra* n.20, at 37–38.

24. Scott, *Intentionality in the Rhetorical Process, Rhetoric in Transition: Studies in the Nature and Uses of Rhetoric* 53 (E. White ed. 1980).

25. Herman, *supra* n.9, at 20 (emphasis added).

26. *Id.*

27. *Id.*

28. *Id.* at 21.

29. *Id.* at 22.

30. Herman, *The Theatre of Summation: Acting, Directing and Playwriting for the Criminal Defense Lawyer, Part II*, Forum, Nov.-Dec. 1984,

at 20–28 (hereinafter cited as "Herman, Part II").

31. *Id.* at 22.

32. *Id.* at 23–25.

33. Herman, *supra* n.9, at 24.

34. Goffman, *supra* n.6, at 72–73.

35. *Id.* at 25.

36. *Id.* at 30.

37. Cone & Lawyer, *supra* n.19, at 98.

38. McCullough & Underwood, *supra* n.8, at 535.

39. Appleman, *supra* n.11, at 722.

40. *Id.*

41. *Id.* at 721.

42. *Id.* at v.

43. Goffman, *supra* n.6, at 51 and 55.

44. *Id.* at 53.

45. Herman, *supra* n.9, at 28.

46. Goffman, *supra* n.6, at 66.

47. Herman, Part II, *supra* n.30, at 21.

48. Cone & Lawyer, *supra* n.19, at 97–98.

49. Appleman, *supra* n.11, at 722–23.

50. Ridolfi & Arguedas, *Women's Self-Defense Cases: Jury Work and Legal Strategy, Jurywork: Systematic Techniques* 223–24 (B. Bonora & E. Krauss ed. 1979).

51. *Id.* at 232–33.

52. Wasserman & Robinson, *Extra-Legal Influences, Group Processes, and Jury Decision-Making: A Psychological Perspective,* 12 N.C. Central L.J. 96, 136, 138 (1980).

53. *Id.* at 143, 147–49.

54. Carlson, *Successful Techniques for Civil Trials* 195 (1983).

55. *Id.*

56. Hamlin, *Effective Direct Examination*, Litigation, Winter 1986, at 15, 17 (1986).

57. *Id.*

58. Goffman, *supra* n.6, at 56.

59. Hamlin, *supra* n.56, at 17.

60. *Id.* at 66.

61. Goffman, *supra* n.6, at 255.

62. Herman, Part II, *supra* n.30, at 20.

63. Birdwhistell, *Kinesics and Context* 158 (1970).

64. Mehrabian, *Communication Without Words*, 2 Psychology Today 52 (Sept. 1968).

65. Linz & Penrod, *Increasing Attorney Persuasiveness in the Courtroom*, 8 Law & Psychology Rev. 11 (1984).

66. Stone, *Appearance and the Self, Dress, Adornment, and the Social Order*, 216, 221 (M. Roach & J. Eicher ed. 1965).

67. *Id.* at 217.
68. See Chapter 2, section I, "Theory: Primacy vs. Recency."
69. Stone, *supra* n.66, at 217.
70. *Id.* at 219.
71. *Id.* at 230.
72. *Id.* at 233.
73. Solomon, *Dress for Effect*, Psychology Today, Apr. 1986, 20–21.
74. See Chapter 2, section I, "Theory: Primacy vs. Recency."
75. Stone, *supra* n.66, at 229.
76. Goffman, *supra* n.6, at 24.
77. Noesjirwan & Crawford, *Variations in Perception of Clothing as a Function of Dress Form and Viewers' Social Community*, 54 Perceptual & Motor Skills 155 (1982).
78. If "hippie attire" seems dated even for 1982, it should be noted that the experiments are from Australia, which may lag behind the United States in political college garb. Also, it is unclear when this experiment occurred.
79. Noesjirwan & Crawford, *supra* n.77, at 156–57.
80. *Id.* at 161.
81. *Id.* at 160–63.
82. Hamid, *Style of Dress as a Perceptual Cue in Impression Formation*, 26 Perceptual & Motor Skills 904, 904–905 (1968).
83. Gibbins & Coney, *Meaning of Physical Dimensions of Women's Clothes*, 53 Perceptual & Motor Skills 702–22 (1981).
84. Stone, *supra* n.66, at 230.
85. Herman, Part II, *supra* n.30, at 20, 21.
86. Stone, *supra* n.66, at 236–41.
87. *Id.* at 241.
88. Solomon, *supra* n.73, at 27.
89. Stone, *supra* n.66, at 243.
90. Hamlin, *What Makes Juries Listen* 72 (1985).
91. *Id.* at 72–73.
92. Buckley, *Perceptions of Physical Attractiveness as Manipulated by Dress: Subjects* Versus *Independent Judges*, 4 J. Psychology 243, 244 (1983).
93. *Id.* at 245.
94. *Id.* at 246–47.
95. Solomon, *supra* n.73, at 26–27.
96. *Id.* at 27.
97. Solomon & Schopler, *Self-Consciousness and Clothing*, 8 Personality & Soc. Psychology Bull. 508, 509 (1982).
98. *Id.* at 510.
99. *Id.* at 511.
100. *Id.* at 513–14.
101. Rosenfeld & Plax, *Clothing as Communication*, 27 J. Communication 24, 25–26 (1977).

102. *Id.* at 28–31.
103. Solomon, *supra* n.73, at 27.
104. *Id.* at 28.
105. Stone, *supra* n.66, at 224.
106. Keltner & Holsey, *The Success Image* 2 (1982).
107. Solomon, *supra* n.73, at 28.
108. Molloy, *The Woman's Dress for Success Book* 15–16 (1977).
109. Keltner & Holsey, *supra* n.106, at 3–4.
110. Solomon, *supra* n.73, at 28.
111. Molloy, *supra* n.108, at 42–43.
112. Keltner & Holsey, *supra* n.106, at 19.
113. Molloy, *supra* n.108, at 52–56.
114. *Id.* at 57–60. Molloy does not make clear that the authority, presence, and believability outfits are ranked in order of their testing success, but this assumption is made based on other such rankings in the book.
115. Appleman, *Preparation and Trial* 721–22 (1967).
116. McCullough & Underwood, 2 *Civil Trial Manual* 57 (1980).
117. Wiener, *Briefing and Arguing Federal Appeals* 338–39 (1967).
118. Stern, *Appellate Practice in the United States* 400 (1981).
119. Pennington, *Rumpled Aplomb*, Continental, June 1986, at 19–20.
120. *Id.* at 20–21.
121. *Id.* at 20.
122. Stone, *supra* n.66, at 222.
123. Solomon, *supra* n.73, at 27.
124. Goffman, *supra* n.6, at 60.
125. Mills & Aronson, *Opinion Change as a Function of the Communicator's Attractiveness and Desire to Influence*, 1 J. Personality & Soc. Psychology 173 (1965).
126. Wilson, *Perceptual Distortion of Height as a Function of Ascribed Academic Status*, 74 J. Soc. Psychology 97, 102 (1968).
127. Cash, Begley, McCown & Weise, *When Counselors Are Heard But Not Seen: Initial Impact of Physical Attractiveness*, 22 J. Counseling Psychology 273 (1975).
128. Dion, Berscheid & Walster, *What Is Beautiful Is Good*, 24 J. Personality & Soc. Psychology 285 (1972).
129. Holmes, Sherlock, *quoted in* unpublished paper *The Effects of Physical Appearance in the Courtroom*, Professor K. Bryon McCoy, Director of Continuing Legal Education, University of Houston Law Center.
130. Russi, *The Sex Life of the Foot and Shoe* (1976).
131. Timothy, *Jury Woman* 9–10 (1974).

CHAPTER 4
JUROR ANALYSIS

SYNOPSIS

CHAPTER 4
JUROR ANALYSIS

The juror as a psychological specimen is examined in an earlier chapter, essentially in answer to the question, "Does a juror respond any differently than anyone else when confronted with certain stimuli?" The answer is, in general, no; we are probably all predictable as a genus of social animals (or at least our responses to and in social situations are detectable and describable, within norms), even though the variety of species may be great. Another chapter discloses that the setting of a courtroom does cause a jury to be an audience (and with great demands), but that is not a unique transformation, since other settings make for other audiences.

With the conclusion that jurors do act like other people, such that what may be said about others may also be said about jurors, one may wonder at the philosophical basis for three more sections devoted to the jury as opposed to human behavior in general. The explanation is that prospective jurors and jurors metamorphose—through no act of their own—such that their behavior (and the behavior of others toward them) warrants examination throughout the course of trial.

Members of a venire, having responded to a jury duty call, sit in a large pool of prospective jurors until a number of them are segregated for consideration in a particular trial. At this point, they are somewhat like fraternity or sorority pledges. If the judge conducts the *voir dire*, they may be aware that all eyes are sweeping them, and are not directed towards the bench. If the attorneys ask the questions, and especially if they conduct individual interviews, the prospective jurors are being hurried through a personal evaluation that takes weeks to months for fraternities and sororities. In a relatively brief amount of time, the attorney tries to make friends, lay traps for enemies, ferret out innermost secrets, and determine intellectual strengths and weaknesses. Unlike the fraternity or sorority, though, once he has determined the unsuitability of a "pledge," he must guard against revealing his dissatisfaction, fearful of alienating other of the pledges (whom he might find acceptable) and, perhaps, of not being successful in a challenge for cause (i.e., being stuck with the unsuitable one). Thus, at this stage of a trial, prospective jurors are simultaneously probed and courted, with the result of being axed or retained. The limits to which attorneys can and should be able to probe the venire are examined in the first section below.

Once impaneled, the jury is an audience, certainly still to be courted, but safe from further probing. Counsel become like actors in an improvised play, rushing backstage after each scene to consult with the director, who has been observing the audience through a hole in the curtains. Did the audience like the one-liners? Well, then, let's have more of them! Within the general guidelines of presenting the necessary and promised evidence, attorneys can modify their technique throughout trial so as to comply with their audience's perceived requirements. Methods for gauging the jury as trial progresses are discussed in the second section below.

The jury as a deliberating group is also discussed earlier, where reference is made to the potential effects of changing the size of the group (such as to six members) and altering the decision rule (to a specified majority instead of unanimity). Literature suggests that these modifications create still other changes to the jury, which are explored in the third section below.

I. *VOIR DIRE*

In the last decade, *voir dire* has become an impassioned topic, with attorneys arguing as follows:

> We are committed to the adversary system as the best means of arriving at the truth. *Voir dire* by the attorneys is an essential part of that system. . . .The trial bar must act quickly. Protest is not enough. We urge the American Bar Association to draft and submit to the Congress a bill making it mandatory that trial counsel be given the right of *voir dire* of prospective jurors.[1]

Judges respond with similar persuasiveness:

> I believe strongly in the jury system. It is such an integral part of our judicial procedure that we must, in the selection process, place primary emphasis on the main object of jury assignment—the rendering of a fair and impartial verdict based solely on the evidence and the law. If the initial orientation of the prospective jurors is centered on this goal, the system has been served. I suggest that the conduct of the *voir dire* by the court is the better means of achieving this objective.[2]

Now, view this debate through the lens of contributions made by social scientists who assist the trial attorney in identifying those jurors who are negatively predisposed to counsel's character, cause, and client. These negative predispositions cannot be identified during *voir dire* alone.[3]

A. Voir Dire—*Functions and Options*

Two attorneys, in their 1966 book on persuasion in litigation, explain in a section on jury selection that *voir dire* has four functions. It is interesting that only the first of these functions is clearly equated with the idea of *jury selection*: ascertaining and removing those persons "who might be unperceptive, unintelligent, or unresponsive to [the] client's cause," and retaining, "if possible, the more intelligent members of the panel, as well as those who by reason of temperament or experience might tend to favor [the] client's version of the controversy." In determining the relative responsiveness of a potential juror, one must search out emotional susceptibility (since "emotion precedes thought in almost all decisions") and prejudices.[4] As indicated in Chapter 2, section I, "Theory: Primacy vs. Recency," a bias concerning a particular cause of action or an individual who would be involved with that cause of action exists prior to the receipt of specific information about the individual and his grounds for the cause of action.[5] While it is clear that "[j]urors do not come to the box with minds like blank pages,"[6] before an attorney can test the depth of a bias and feel that he can overcome it, he must first be able to detect it, and this is a part of the first function of *voir dire.*

Voir dire also enables an attorney to uncover and eliminate the unpredictable juror, or the individual who might not behave as others in his situation could be expected to behave. Examples would be a social misfit and an iconoclast. It would be difficult in a closing argument to appeal to the values of these individuals while also trying to succeed with the other members of the jury. In addition, determining the values of unpredictable individuals may pose an insurmountable challenge.[7]

A second function of *voir dire* "is to ascertain the background of specific jurors in order to determine which lines of reasoning or argument a given juror would be most receptive to."[8] In speech criticism terms, this is pre-speech audience analysis. Certainly a speaker attempts to ascertain details about his audience so that he can couch his message in terms that he believes will be well received by the audience. Without knowing who comprises his audience, any attempts by the speaker at identifying with them can be no more than haphazard. Usually, speakers have little information about their audiences beyond the standard demographic data and do not have the opportunity to talk to their audiences, which is often afforded attorneys during *voir dire*. Thus, if audience analysis is a goal, one might argue that attorneys enjoy an advantage beyond that of speakers. But the occasion for a speech tells a great deal about those who attend it; prospective jurors do not "attend" the trial of their choice, nor is their "attendance" at jury duty voluntary (it is in response to a call or notice). How can one systematically seek to persuade without knowing his audience? Also, do questions asked by judges result in the kind of information that will allow attorneys to perform audience analysis? Those who would prevent attorney questioning might respond that the attorney makes no speeches prior to closing argument, by which time he should have come to know his audience by watching their reactions throughout trial. Whether or not it is a "legitimate" function of *voir dire*, the astute attorney will attempt to analyze any juror responses from the standpoint of his potential persuasiveness.

A third function "is to predispose the jurors to certain ideas and positions."[9] Judicial purists object to the suggestion that merely in the jury selection process, counsel can begin to determine the verdict, prior to the presentation of any evidence or even a summary of the facts. Perhaps a more widely accepted wording of this function would be "eliminating the juror's bias,"[10] for it would help to make a juror more neutral than otherwise. There is a psychological basis for confronting a juror with his bias as soon as possible; once he is aware of it, he more than feels free to act in opposition to his bias; he is almost compelled to do so.[11]

A final function of *voir dire* is "to impart information,"[12] which some believe is more suited to the opening statement. The authors admit that "attempting to use *voir dire* extensively for this purpose is inadvisable" but suggest that "if opportunities are seized, information or ideas may be legitimately imparted." One of the examples provided implies that what the authors had in mind here was information that may cause prospective jurors to seek to be excused or to admit some prejudice. The anticipated length of a trial may pose such hardships on someone that he would harbor great resentment for the plaintiff (the one responsible for the trial); thus, trial length could be mentioned during the questioning.[13]

Concerning the above four functions of *voir dire*, one belief is that educating potential jurors as to certain issues and establishing a rapport with them are only side effects of a thorough *voir dire*, the main function of which is to determine prejudices and their potential effects.[14] Even the most conscientious attempts to detect bias, however, can fail due to certain behavioral characteristics of the venire. First, potential jurors tend not to speak out when addressed questions as a group, because they are surrounded by strangers, they are unaccustomed to being in (much less saying anything in) a courtroom, and they are likely to be confused by what is happening. Judges and even attorneys assume that no response is a negative answer, when it may be no answer at all. Second, to the extent that questions seek to uncover prejudices, unless they are phrased most delicately, no one could answer affirmatively without professing to having a socially undesirable trait. And if the questions are too carefully phrased, jurors may not understand what they are being asked. Third, jurors may lie, either failing to disclose a bias due to social pressure or consciously attempting to be selected for a trial:

> Conscious attempts to be selected for a jury are not limited to highly publicized cases. In Detroit Recorder's Court, jurors serve for a month. In most cases, defense attorneys will use a peremptory challenge on those jurors who have been victims of a crime similar to that charged or who have close relatives or friends who are police officers. Jurors, who were interviewed in the Detroit study, reported that they noticed that by the second week of jury service some potential jurors in their jury box, who had previously mentioned that they were victims of a crime or had a friend or relative on the police force and had thereafter been excused from a jury, had stopped volunteering that information when asked those questions.[15]

It is argued that, because of the above limitations, attorneys should be able to obtain as much information as possible about each prospective juror. Also, questioning individual jurors appears to result in more honesty; and questioning them outside the presence of other jurors prevents their adopting what they may conclude have been acceptable answers by other jurors. While *voir dire* conducted by attorneys is thought to establish rapport with the jurors, one justification may be that with such rapport, the attorneys can better determine whether a juror has an unshakable bias.[16] That is, the attorney may well have a sensitivity to the facts and issues of the case that the judge cannot be expected to share; and, to the extent that the attorney is able to promote an exchange with a juror, the attorney may be better prepared to uncover prejudice or animosity.

In federal court, *voir dire* can be conducted by the judge or counsel (or the defendant, in criminal cases), in the discretion of the court.[17] A similar rule governs ten states, in ten states only the judge may ask questions, in about twenty-two states the judge and counsel may ask questions, and in the remaining states, attorneys must ask the questions.[18] When counsel cannot ask questions, each side is allowed to request the judge to ask certain questions of the prospective jurors, which many courts require to be written prior to trial. Since attorneys may well read prejudice into expressions or other behavior of venire members, they will undoubtedly think of particular questions at the time of *voir dire*. One suggested tactic is for the attorney to request orally that the court ask a question of a particular juror, while looking all the while at that juror. The implication is that, even if the court refuses, the attorney may have received sufficient information in the juror's nonverbal response on which to base a challenge.[19]

While topic areas suitable for *voir dire* would understandably depend upon the case, a review of various state and federal court decisions results in the following list of areas in which specific *voir dire* is necessary:

1. race or nationality;
2. religion;
3. political perspectives and attitudes;
4. attitudes toward women's roles and sex prejudices;
5. social or economic prejudice;
6. credibility of police testimony;
7. attitudes toward youth;
8. pre-trial publicity;
9. other areas:
   (a) a party's notoriety;
   (b) jury experience with crime;
   (c) willingness to give commensurate damages in a civil case;
   (d) past relationships with a party, or attorney, or potential witnesses;
   (e) past or present government employment of potential jurors or their families.[20]

The list indicates two sources for cause challenges to prospective jurors: (1) specific facts, such as relationship with a party, but mostly (2) indications of a state of mind that, by interpretation, makes a juror biased.[21]

A general *voir dire* usually seeks the following information:

1. residence;
2. occupation;
3. family composition;
4. acquaintance with plaintiff or defendant;
5. acquaintance with attorneys or their firms;
6. acquaintance with witnesses;
7. prior jury service;
8. prior witness experience;
9. prior litigation experience.

Beyond this, depending on the particular facts and issues, jurors might be asked whether they or family members have ever been involved in an automobile accident, are in any way connected with an insurance company, have negative feelings about corporations, etc.[22] Based on responses to these questions (as well as information provided prior to the *voir dire*, on juror information cards or sheets), attorneys then often generalize about what kind of jurors certain types of people make:

> Plaintiffs in personal injury cases frequently try to select bartenders, barmaids, waiters, waitresses, artists, musicians, salesmen, carpenters, and mechanics. New jurors, those without prior jury experience, are often preferred by veteran plaintiff's attorneys. Defendants in injury damage litigation frequently try to include accountants, statisticians, bankers, insurance employees, and utility company personnel. Jurors who have previously served on personal injury cases are often preferred, unless it is found that the juror was on a jury which returned a very substantial plaintiff's verdict in a prior case.[23]

On the surface, these generalizations about the types of jurors people will make appear to be connected purely to objective data, such as occupations and prior jury service. However, the underlying assumption concerning occupations, for example, is that people who are prone to act a certain way or have certain predispositions are likely to seek certain occupations. Thus, consciously or not, attorneys rely on occupations and other objective data as personality cues. Personal injury attorneys really do not want "bartenders, barmaids, waitresses" as jurors; they want empathic people, people who like other people. It is simply that people who like other people tend to take people-oriented jobs. A prosecutor may say that he prefers mature business executives because they are more likely to deliver a guilty verdict; what he means is that he prefers a juror who is rule-oriented, autonomous, and not very empathic.[24] "[T]he ideal result is to have a jury without personal experience causing them to be inherently hostile to your side of the case, and, if possible, a jury with a psychological tendency to favor your cause."[25] Therefore, whether or not they have the credentials, trial attorneys are called upon to utilize the skills of the sociologist and psychologist.

B. *The "Ideal Juror" Continuum*

What makes up the ideal juror? It should come as no surprise that the answer depends on who is asking the question. Theoretically, the attorney should answer, "someone who is not against me/my client/his cause of action/etc." (for easy reference, this answer will be referred to as "someone who is not against me"). The problem is that not everyone agrees on the meaning of "someone who is not against me." Judges tend to believe in only the apparent meaning of those words. However, if someone is not against you, then he is *for* you, right? Therefore, an attorney could be within the definition by seeking jurors in favor of him/his client/his cause of action in addition to (or even to the exclusion of) "someone who is *not against* me."

If, as we have concluded, determining who is for or against you requires a certain amount of psychological analysis, then the attorney who is better at such analysis will more likely select jurors who are for him than will other attorneys. By extension, if there are experts who are better at such analysis than even proficient attorneys, it would follow that such experts should be hired to assist with jury selection. It then follows that the side of a case best equipped with psychological analysis personnel could select a more favorable jury than the other side. In fact, the verdict could be predicted with a certainty that increases proportionately with the expertise of the psychological analysis experts. Thus, a continuum emerges, correlated with respective *voir dire* techniques:

"Ideal Juror" Continuum

expert guidance	expansive attorney questioning	questioning by judge
probable verdict	"someone who is for me"	"someone who is not against me"

Following is an explanation of the position of many judges, a description of the methods of juror selection borrowed from (if not implemented by) the social scientists, and a review of the prediction of the result of unbridled *voir dire.*

1. *Judge-conducted* Voir Dire

A United States District Judge for the Southern District of Florida, with thirty years in private practice and nine on the bench, writes, "The use of challenges is a right to reject, not to select." This is over the admission that while he was an attorney, he believed in the right of an attorney to conduct *voir dire.* His argument is that when attorneys conduct the questioning, there is inevitably advocacy. He also postulates a definition for the ideal *jury* that combines "someone who is for me" with "someone who is against me": "Complete neutrality is admittedly impossible. The most that can be expected is a jury with random biases which will tend to balance each other." Given that goal, and the advocacy nature of counsel, he concludes that the judge is the most likely choice to make the determination as to the jury, since his impartiality is clear. He realizes that many attorneys see purposes of *voir dire* beyond "the intelligent exercise of peremptory challenges or challenges for cause": establishing juror rapport, preconditioning the jury, and orienting them. He discounts the first of these as being incongruous with the professed reason for *voir dire*; moreover, that goal should be reserved for after the jury has been sworn and trial has begun (i.e., once the jurors have become an audience). Juror preconditioning and orientation, he argues, are valid only insofar as they assist in the determination of a fair and impartial jury.[26]

It is said that "[t]he most frequently mentioned justification for court-conducted *voir dire* is to save the time of the court, the jurors, the parties, and the attorneys."[27] The presumption is that though attorneys may take longer to question the panel, the time is well spent. That does not always appear to be the case. Perhaps because of the adversarial positions of counsel, when one "injects elements not properly within the ambit of a fair *voir dire* examination, he opens the door for his opponent to retaliate. When the opponent attempts to retaliate, the court must intervene." One might wonder what impression this kind of scene makes on the venire, particularly if it becomes animated. The district judge referenced above notes that essentially each time he allowed attorneys to conduct the questioning, there were many objections, and "the tendency of counsel to argue their cases or to seek an advantage or to engage in tedium" required many interruptions by the court. Also, he describes the last case in which he allowed the attorneys to conduct the questioning, after he had conducted a preliminary *voir dire*. Though he requested that counsel not inquire into areas that he had already covered, they asked repetitious questions of each juror in areas already included in the court's questioning.[28]

Judge Wiseman, Chief Judge of the United States District Court for the Middle District of Tennessee, presents an argument falling more towards the middle of the "Ideal Juror" Continuum. First, he notes that the discretion afforded judges in allowing attorneys to conduct the questioning is seldom exercised: "Had the judiciary truly exercised the discretion conferred by the existing rules, I doubt that the controversy would exist." He suggests that Rule 47(a) should be revised to require that, if the court conducts an initial *voir dire*, counsel be permitted to supplement with oral questions. Any excessive time consumption, repetition, and argument by counsel could be controlled through the court's exercise of discretion, which would be reviewable by the circuit courts. As to the concern over advocacy emerging during the questioning, he suggests that this is a way to get at the truth and uncover juror bias. He accepts as purposes of *voir dire* the establishment of juror rapport and preconditioning the jury, since everything an attorney does is designed to accomplish these goals. However, he is not blind to the possibility of "obsequious fawning" and simply being argumentative; such action, he contends, can be recognized and halted by the judge.[29]

Judge Will, Senior United States District Judge for the Northern District of Illinois, responds directly to Judge Wiseman. The basis of Judge Will's position is the acknowledgment that despite the degree of preparation or strength of facts, cases are won and lost depending on which attorney is better at *voir dire* and jury selection. In other words, even without recognizing the potential contribution of expert social scientists, he believes that attorneys who are proficient in selecting juries are more likely to pick "someone who is for me" than other attorneys. This means, of course, that the verdict is based on something other than the evidence adduced at trial and, indeed, is virtually determined before trial even begins.[30]

Thus, Judge Will developed a questioning procedure that he believes "almost all counsel who have appeared before me agree selects fair and impartial juries, even though I know some would have preferred to practice their jury-picking skills and to conduct the *voir dire*." First, he begins with the premise that time is *not* of the essence, though he does not think that a complicated or highly publicized case should require jury selection to last for days. Second, he attempts to instill impartiality in jurors, or ferret out bias, by impressing upon them their responsibility to the litigants, as well as to themselves. Third, he allows counsel to suggest questions at pretrial and during *voir dire*. Fourth, believing that both counsel and the court should be given the opportunity to observe the jurors, he has each panelist give a brief personal history. He follows up with questions he believes necessary, based on the juror's statements, and usually asks whatever additional questions counsel suggest. Finally, whenever he detects someone who expresses honest doubt about being fair or impartial, if counsel consent, he usually excuses that person, which means that counsel can reserve their peremptory challenges for their own reasons. Judge Will concludes that "[t]he selection of a fair and impartial jury is so essential to justice that it should not be used by advocates as a first step toward winning a case. . . .The time to win a case is after a fair and impartial jury has been selected, not before."[31]

2. *Expansive Attorney Questioning*

Notice that the goal of finding "someone who is for me" says, in itself, that with this degree of questioning, the attorney is exercising audience analysis, as well as using persuasiveness. If he detects that the juror is like he is, then the attorney has identified with the juror, and identification is the first step of, if not synonymous with, persuasion.[32] To determine whether he *can* identify with a juror and vice versa, the attorney must elicit certain information about him; that is, in a very short period of time, the attorney must come to know the juror.

Advice as to whether to seek a jury trial reveals that audience analysis should precede that decision. The first suggestion is to "wait until you know who the trial judge will be before making your decision," at which time as much information as possible should be gathered about him. If he is a federal judge, his profile will appear in the *Almanac of the Federal Judges*, which will indicate his education, publications, noteworthy rulings, and the like. Lexis and other index systems can be consulted for newspaper and journal articles about him. Even with all of this background information, "there is no substitute for direct observation." Thus, assuming the name of the judge is known long enough before trial to allow for a "pre-speech" audience analysis, attorneys usually have a far greater opportunity to perform this kind of analysis with judges than with prospective jurors. The point, however, is that the analysis is the same, regardless of the audience, apparent in the sort of idiosyncrasies in judges (biases?) that one should look for: reluctance to award punitive damages; failure to pay attention to unique facts in a common cause of action; distaste for long trials; preference for the little guy over big companies.[33]

As indicated earlier, even the most apparently objective *voir dire* provides information that leads to conclusions about the personalities and characters of the prospective jurors. Prior service on more than one jury could indicate any side preference (such as plaintiff or defendant); also, how the juror may have fared in any case in which he was a party could suggest a predisposition or a revenge motive. While the observation was earlier made that people gravitate toward the occupations to which their personalities are best suited, another opinion is that "[p]eople who pursue a particular occupation for a long time often develop ingrained habits of thought that may affect their conduct as jurors." Thus, an accountant is assumed to be prone to check and recheck matters. Though occupation may be an initial personality clue, it should be recalled that some people simply do not like their jobs and feel trapped in them. Thus, a positive correlation might be drawn between personality and occupation only after a determination of the individual's job (or personal) satisfaction. Income associated with particular occupations is also a guide as to a damage award that jurors might believe to be adequate, since people with little or no opportunity to save money may not be able to envision estimating the cost of living for a disabled person for the rest of his life.[34]

For obvious reasons, a juror with poor sight or hearing might miss testimony and demonstrative evidence, and other health problems, such as those requiring frequent medication, could cause a trial to run less smoothly than otherwise. Because health problems comprise such a delicate issue, attorneys should avoid asking about them outright since, if the individual winds up on the jury, he could feel resentment against the prying attorney. Visual cues, such as how a person moves or whether he wears thick eyeglasses, should be relied upon, as well as any investigation conducted prior to the actual *voir dire*, if juror information is available then.[35]

Juror age, sex, and ethnicity are usually indicated either in the information provided to counsel or are fairly determinable on sight. Since those comprise "audience" data, attorneys attempt to draw conclusions about personality from them, but the conclusions are as varied as the attorneys who state them.[36] Probably one reason for this is that the attorneys never or rarely conduct any experiments per se to determine correlations between these data and juror decisions. Nor should they; that is rightly the province of the professional social scientist, who has the time and background to devise experiments and interpret the results. Attorneys might naturally receive the verdict, reflect on the composition of the jury, and mentally assign a motive to each juror. Rarely if ever can the validity of the motives be tested. Moreover, it is difficult for anyone to ignore preconceived views (instilled by society) about how a person of a certain age and sex will behave; such views create an expectation that may cause *any* act by the individual to be interpreted as a result purely of the age and sex. Finally, it may be impossible to base assumptions about behavior on any piece of data in isolation, and to the extent that combinations of data are required, the question then becomes, when is the combination sufficiently complete? This is not to say that some attorneys are not as proficient at reading people as the most expert social scientists; the probability of proficiency is merely less, and the accomplished attorneys are likely to be unable (or unwilling) to communicate the secrets of their success.

Even the purely "psychological methods" for jury selection are still in an experimental stage and those in the field recommend "more empirical research." However, there are several psychological techniques which can be used in jury selection to enhance the attorney's already developed selection skills. A psychologist or similar professional assisting in juror selection could provide a "clinical opinion" based on one or more of the following: nonverbal communication, associational image factors, and personality and demographic attributes. Appearance, mannerisms, and gestures during *voir dire* form the basis for a clinician's inference as to how the individual will likely respond to general issues. Associational image factors refer to the physical descriptions of items and people with which the individual surrounds himself; since these would include the juror's house, front yard, car, and business associates, investigation beyond the *voir dire* would be necessary. Age, occupation, sex, height, weight, personal experience (such as prior trial experience), and the like are the demographic attributes used for placing the juror in certain groups. "The assumption is made that certain groups will identify and sympathize with your client more readily than other groups and that this identification will color their judgment—particularly concerning ambiguous issues." Personality attributes include personality type, personality structure, and the needs and values of the individual; and the clinician makes inferences as to these attributes based on his study of the other factors (nonverbal communication, associational image factors, and demographic data), as well as his own intuition.[37]

The thoroughness of the above procedure, along with the required ability to integrate the various data, suggests that professional assistance in jury selection could become an industry of its own. Other skills of the psychologist or sociologist are called upon for psychographic surveys, which facilitate a correlation of community attitudes toward social and legal issues with actual data about the venire. Then, "[s]tatistical weighting techniques are used to develop a psychological profile of the most and least desirable types of juror." Still another method attempts to integrate the "commonsense methods used for years by attorneys with technical methods used by psychologists." Composite Personal Psychological Profile (C3P) studies produce "multivariate profiles" using demographic, nonverbal, and associational data, along with rating scales completed by a pool of attorneys. If the location is a small community, one or more of the attorneys usually know certain of the venire, and the subjective evaluations are included. Finally, in recognition of attorneys' confidence in their own juror selections, intuition/observation training seeks to instill or sharpen non-professional psychological skills:

> I/O training is individual and small group coaching of the attorney to improve behavioral observational skills and to increase the validity of conclusions based upon these observations. This approach has great intuitive appeal to those attorneys who are going to trust their own judgment anyway, regardless of an expert's recommendations, because the expert's skills are added to the attorney's own armamentarium.[38]

An earlier chapter discusses the supposed effects on jurors of the personality traits of socialization, empathy, and autonomy.[39] Two other personality types are thought to be directly related to jury decision-making. The authoritarian type, first described in the 1950s, displays "a tendency to adhere to conventional, middle class values;

submit to authority figures; punish violators of norms; adhere to stereotypes; identify with power figures; be sexually repressed; and project one's own feelings and attitudes on others." While decisions of juries, when correlated with this type of personality, reveal that authoritarians are harsher as jurors than nonauthoritarians, it has also appeared that when the defendant is similar to the authoritarian, he is less certain of guilt than other jurors. Also, the high authoritarian tends to recall more information about a defendant's character, while a low authoritarian recalls more situational evidence.[40]

In general, the authoritarian is thought to be particularly poor for the defense in criminal defense litigation and in civil litigation where punitive damages are requested. The author has made observations for authoritarianism in both criminal (including those in which the state sought the ultimate penalty) and civil litigation.[41] Defense counsel must be especially cautious with the authoritarian personality or his client will not receive a "fair trial." By fair trial is meant one in which the authoritarian will assume the citizen accused innocent *unless* proven guilty beyond a reasonable doubt.[42]

In one trial in which the author assisted the trial team, a comparison of the demographic characteristics of the jury panel and a random sample of registered voters was made for purposes of requesting a new panel. For example, the demographic characteristics of people in the jury panel were obtained. These traits were compared with a random sample of registered voters; had the panel been like the actual voters, then the groups would have been statistically similar. From the most recent list of registered voters, names were drawn as subjects for telephone interviews. Interviewers completed the telephone calls, inquiring about demographic data as well as relevant attitudinal issues. Results of the interviews showed that the jury panel was older than the random sample, and partly for this reason, the panel was shuffled before jury selection began.

Then, researchers conducted personal interviews with certain members of the sample in the individuals' homes. Of the total that had been called, only a small number were interviewed. The questions asked of these individuals were designed to detect authoritarian personalities. Certain questions sought this information in an unobvious way, dealing with the ages and activities of children, religious attitudes, leisure activities, organizational memberships, and supervisory positions at work, etc. The interviewees were also asked about the extent of their agreement with, for example, statements that countered public with private rights; about their degree of trust in the government; about political philosophy and orientation; about planning a vacation or taking a spontaneous vacation, etc.[43]

The sample revealed a high trust in the government and a high respect for law and order. Thus, defense counsel were advised to assess the jurors' trust in government and respect for law and order. Although the judge himself in this particular case met many of the defense's criteria for an undesirable juror, he gave the defense great latitude in selection, permitting the attorneys to ask their own questions and to direct them to the prospective jurors. Based on answers received during the interviews, the picture of the "ideal juror" was formed. Since women were revealed to be slightly more liberal on several questions, the desired juror was a middle-aged female, who had a blue-collar job but was not in a supervisory position.[44] (Notice that the attitudes were first assessed and then correlated with occupations; that is, the attitudes were not assumed to exist because of the occupations.)

Another personality type concerns responsibility for one's acts, with "externals" believing that outcomes are determined by factors beyond individual control, such as fate, and "internals" thinking that we have at least some control over what happens. Naturally, "internals" are going to be harsher in their attributions of responsibility for a crime to the defendant, as well as in their punishments.[45] While seeking out the authoritarian personality may be the goal for trials in which the government is a party, determining juror internal-external locus of control may have more applicability in other litigation, especially personal liability cases.

A statistical modeling approach to jury selection, in which profiles of potential jurors are developed based on demographic and social-psychological traits that can be used to predict behavior, relies on two basic assumptions. First, "not only will people vary from one another in their opinions, but people with different opinions will vary in terms of what type of characteristics they have." Second, if critical characteristics can be isolated, they can be used to predict the behavior of prospective jurors. Data are collected through interviews of a sample. How the data are analyzed, however, can vary. One approach, using "contingency table analyses and correlations," facilitates a determination of whether an association exists (and, if so, to what degree) between a particular demographic characteristic and certain beliefs or attitudes, such as a relationship between income level or occupation and a conviction orientation.[46]

However, statistical modeling techniques can take into account *several* demographic characteristics and beliefs. The difference between this and simply an association between a particular characteristic and certain attitudes is that people with the same attitudes could have different demographic traits. Therefore, eliminating potential jurors merely on the basis of demographic characteristics could result in striking people who have desirable attitudes. The procedure involves dividing the sample into subgroups with relatively homogeneous opinions and then further analyzing these subgroups to determine which characteristics were additionally important. "Through the combination of [both steps] the predicted likelihood that a potential juror believed in guilt or innocence of the defendant was established using both demographic and social-psychological characteristics." A major advantage cited for this approach is that attitudes (such as believing in guilt in the presence of racial prejudice) can be assessed without attitudinal questions being asked directly in *voir dire*. When attorneys are allowed to ask their own questions, apparently innocuous inquiries concerning demographics are more likely to be allowed than attitudinal questions. In addition, when preliminary demographic information is known about the jury pool,

> one can establish probabilities of the presence of certain types of jurors in the jury pool. Therefore, peremptory challenges can be exercised in a manner that maximizes efficiency; initial minimally acceptable jurors may be excused based upon the knowledge that more favorable jurors are likely to be still available.[47]

Another reported advantage of mathematical modeling is that it enables one to estimate sensitive beliefs that jurors may tend to misreport.[48] In fact, given that members of a jury panel are in unaccustomed surroundings and amid strangers, inducing them to disclose any information about themselves beyond statistical data may be an insurmountable challenge. Setting aside the question of who is better able to do this, the judge or counsel, if an actual information exchange is established with venire members, they will be more likely to reveal personal information.

> Self-disclosure may be defined as that which occurs when A knowingly communicates to B information about A which is not generally known and is not otherwise available to B. Since such information may be seen as typically disclosed only to friends,

> it indicates to the recipient that he is liked and trusted by the discloser. Hence, such a self-disclosure may be assumed to be a reward or positive outcome for B.[49]

An experiment that tested for self-disclosure involved procedures that could be likened to individual questioning in *voir dire*. Subjects comprised groups of four unmarried female undergraduates (who did not know each other before the experiment). When they arrived at the laboratory, they were given ten minutes to get to know each other. Afterwards, each girl rated her degree of liking for each other girl. Then, they were seated around a table that had a wooden partition separating them. Communicating by written notes, they would ask each other questions that had been pre-rated for intimacy levels, and then respond to each other in writing. The results indicated that (1) the more one girl liked another, the greater the amount of self-disclosure and (2) higher self-disclosures were made to those from whom each girl had received high self-disclosure (the norm of reciprocity). The experimenters had hypothesized that high authoritarians would disclose less than low authoritarians, but the results did *not* support this hypothesis.[50]

In theory, a questioning attorney should be able to induce prospective jurors into self-disclosure if they like him and if he also reveals something personal. The bind is that, before he decides the exact nature of the persona to present to his audience (which will ideally be one with which the jury can identify), he must know who his audience is. If he presumes that he knows his audience, based on the information gained before *voir dire*, presents a persona based on that assumption, and has assumed wrongly, then he has gotten off to a bad start (perhaps irreparable, if we recall the lasting effects of first impressions). Moreover, he is no closer to eliciting the personal information he wants. The attorney who can induce an exchange, however, should have a definite advantage. Hamlin, the communications expert, advises through example that counsel can use visual clues as guidelines. If a prospective juror is wearing running shoes and the attorney wants to know why he runs (which may result in information suggesting that the individual is merely health conscious or that he is body-conscious to the point of being narcissistic), the attorney might ask about the shoes, saying he has a pair like them himself.[51] From the response, the attorney could then volunteer the extent of running he does, and follow it with a question as to the juror's reasons for running. In a similar vein, Richard "Racehorse" Haynes has prefaced his question as to whether the prospective jurors had any feelings about him, with the following:

> Let me say this. I have to be green as grass to know, to think that everyone who has ever heard of me, for example, would have an opinion and they would like to have me come to dinner with them on Sunday evening. I get some mail that indicates to me that some people would not like me to come to dinner. I know that. . . . If you, I would like to think I'm a grown man, and if you have something to say, I can handle it. I might cry and suck my thumb later on about it, but I can handle it.[52]

The goal of attorney *voir dire* is to elicit responses from the prospective jurors. Of course, it would be ideal if the content of the responses were to clearly convey the attitude for which counsel is searching. But since the ideal is rarely met, the attorney or social scientist must take whatever response is given and *interpret* it. An article that appeared in 1978 described a "new method" for evaluating potential jurors based solely on their behavior during the questioning. It suggests that communicative behavior can be divided into verbal, paralinguistic, and kinesic. Verbal refers to the words and their order. Paralinguistic, referring to how something is said, includes pauses, pitch, tone, and speech disturbances. Kinesic behavior, also known as body language, encompasses not only body movement and gestures but also eye contact and facial expressions. While attorneys, based on their training, are probably adept at analyzing verbal communication, they are generally not accustomed to noticing and interpreting paralinguistic and kinesic behavior. "This omission is unfortunate because, for the purposes of voir dire, the nonverbal cues may be the most important part of a prospective juror's behaviors."[53]

An experiment reported in 1966 confirms the ability of paralinguistic behavior to reveal accurate information about the speaker's personality.[54] The same experiment, though, demonstrated that listeners do not have a uniform ability to interpret paralinguistic behavior accurately. This has to do in part with the individual listener; apparently, either you can detect personality from speech alone or you can't. In addition, certain traits are more difficult than others to identify by speech. The following table indicates which personality traits tend to defy detection in the absence of other clues, such as the content of response and/or demographic data.[55] Thus, the attorney who feels confident that he can select sensitive, religious jurors purely by the way they talk has almost a 50% chance of being wrong unless he just happens to be an extraordinary judge of people.

Order of Difficulty for the Eighteen Scales

Scale	*Percentage of Judges Who Made Mistakes*
Forceful–Gentle	13.4
Assertive–Reserved	15.4
Realistic–Idealistic	16.0
Bold–Cautious	18.6
Quiet–Talkative	20.5
Youthful–Mature	23.1
Sensual–Intellectual	27.6
Critical–Supporting	28.2
Gregarious–Detached	30.8
Patient–Impatient	32.6
Emotional–Unemotional	34.6
Religious–Nonreligious	38.5
Simple–Complex	41.3
Thick-skinned–Sensitive	43.0
Competitive–Cooperative	46.1
Serious–Humorous	48.6
Orderly–Casual	51.9
Agile–Slow	74.4

Another experiment concerned the ability to convey attitudes vocally and through facial expressions. Subjects therefore participated in two sessions, an encoding phase and, one week later, a decoding phase.[56]

Several conclusions emerged from the results. First, "whereas the face is generally superior to the voice for communicating variations in attitude, this is more true for certain individuals than for others." Moreover, in the decoding process, facial communications are given more weight than vocal communications. Both were found to be true for males as well as females.

A second conclusion, which does indicate a difference between the sexes, is that women are better at encoding negative feelings than are men. The suggested reason for this is that our culture discourages the explicit verbalization of negative attitudes, and men have greater latitude in such explicit expressions. Women were so much better at encoding negative attitudes that, even though men were better at encoding positive attitudes, women were better at encoding overall. Women were also superior in detecting variations in attitudes communicated by others.

A related third conclusion is that those individuals seeking social approval conform to the social expectations of not expressing negative attitudes, even through nonverbal methods. Despite these *encoding* differences, "high and low social approval-seeking subjects did not differ in their ability to decode positive or negative attitude."[57]

Since, above all, the attorney or social scientist wants to determine attitude during *voir dire*, then such a determination must rely on the prospective juror's ability to convey a certain attitude, as well as the perceiver's ability to interpret that attitude. The following brief statements are drawn from the above conclusions and are designed to assist the attorney who relies on nonverbal cues to determine attitudes:

1. Males are better than females at expressing positive attitudes.
2. Females are far better than males at expressing negative attitudes.
3. Facial cues are more reliable than vocal cues in expressing attitudes.
4. High and low social approval-seeking individuals interpret positive and negative attitudes equally well.
5. Low social approval-seeking individuals do not express positive attitudes as well as high social approval-seeking individuals.
6. High social approval-seeking individuals do not express negative attitudes as well as low social approval-seeking individuals.
7. Females are better than males at detecting variations in attitudes of others.

In the experiment described above, tone would have been the most significant vocal cue (since only single words were judged, pauses would not have been used). In an experiment designed to test the independent effects of tone and content on judgments of attitudes in the speaker, single words were also used. The first important finding was that listeners *can* attend only to tone or content in judging attitude. In addition, although subjects asked to attend to tone only were somewhat influenced by variations in content, their "responses indicated a stronger and more consistent set of effects due to tone than due to content."[58]

One suggestion for the trial attorney who may have assistance at the counsel table is to have one person focus solely on the content of the prospective jurors' responses while having another attend only to tone. This is based on the experimenters' conclusion that, when the subjects were asked to attend to the total message (content and tone) and the tone and content were inconsistent, the tonal component made a "disproportionately greater contribution to the interpretation of the total message than . . . the verbal component."[59] The suggestion is that we can disregard what people say based purely on how they say it. But how people express themselves, including the tone they might use, depends not only on what they might be feeling at the time but also on regional and cultural differences. The greater weight of tone than content, however, could cause a listener who is not segregating the two to form an impression of attitude based more on tone than content. To the extent that tone is due to regional or cultural differences, and not legitimate attitudes, the listener who relies more on tone could be mistaken. If one listener were focusing on content, however, he could at least point out the attitude based on content, for possible reconciliation with the attitude inferred by the listener who would attend only to tone.

The experimenters explain why nonverbal communication can supplant actual words, suggesting that the implicit communication is the more legitimate indicator of attitude.[60] However, people may use facial expressions and tone to soften otherwise harsh words. During the *voir dire*, counsel hopes that prospective jurors will be honest enough to admit to certain biases, even if such biases are socially unacceptable. If one felt he were being totally candid in his words, he might attempt to blunt their thrust (as well as save face) with a pleasant tone and a smile. Because he was honest in his words, he could then feel that he had discharged his duty. If the attorney fails to strike him because of his nonverbal behavior, the client could be the one to suffer.

"[I]f a person wished to disguise his true emotions, he could fairly easily display false emotions on his face. Body postures and movements are not as easily controlled, however, and also should be watched for signs of emotion." In general, the more "immediate a person's body orientation to another," the more positively he regards that person. Immediacy includes eye contact, leaning forward (toward the other person), the distance between the individuals, and the extent to which one faces another squarely. Also, the more relaxed the body position of a person is during interaction with another, the more positively he regards the other. But while a slight recline in body position is associated with relaxation, an extreme reclining angle indicates a hostile or negative attitude (a recoiling). Eye contact is thought to indicate not only honesty but also positive feelings toward, as well as expectation of approval from, another. Since a prospective juror usually knows no one in the courtroom, his eye contact with the respective attorneys can indicate "from whom he *expects* approval and a positive relationship. It is reasonable to assume that such an expectation of approval from an attorney representing a particular side is indicative of bias in favor of that side."[61]

3. *Expert Guidance*

There are attorneys who will dispute the following two statements. "Since the attorney who is actually conducting the *voir dire* must attend to his or her own performance, it will be next to impossible for him or her to make a systematic evaluation of the jurors' nonverbal behavior. Therefore, it will be necessary for the lead attorney to use other observers to make the evaluations."[62] As we will later see, the flip side to scientific jury selection depends upon nonscientific intuition and commonsense evaluation by a single questioner. However, when counsel does make the decision to use additional evaluators during *voir dire*—even if they are simply other members of the law firm—he may be only one step away from bringing in the professionals, to the extent his client's budget can afford it. (Costs of implementing expert assistance may range from a minimum of $2,500.00 for consultation, without surveys and investigations, to $100,000, which would include a community attitudinal survey, mathematical model mock trial, focus group, shadow jury, and other facets of the psychological techniques.[63])

There are two major potential differences between the analysis of prospective jurors by laymen and that by sociologists and psychologists. The first is that the layman's predictions of attitude and behavior are likely to be affected by prejudices of some kind. The second is that for the most part, the layman's observations are neither systematic nor thorough. It is a fact that the attorney who is not a psychologist or sociologist simply has not been formally trained to detect and interpret the assorted behavioral cues that people have at their disposal. When a litigant does have the opportunity to avail himself of the guidance of experts in jury selection, he appears to have a better chance of obtaining a jury that is not negatively predisposed to the attorney's character, client, and cause of action.

Pretrial jury research and simulations have evolved within the last ten years. These techniques have been successfully utilized in both the more notable cases and in the not so notable cases. A look at the outcome tends to indicate that these techniques do have great value (in both civil and criminal defense litigation).[64]

As the percentage rate of success of professional guidance increases, two issues of concern to the legal community emerge. First, "by promulgating these [jury selection] systems are we in effect really guaranteeing an impartial jury, or are we not in essence 'stacking the deck' and obtaining an 'acquittal-prone' jury?" A second issue, which stems from an affirmative answer to the first, is that with investigation and psychological research and analysis costing $20,000 and upwards, only two classes of people will be able to take advantage of the expert guidance: the rich and the "notorious minority." If the average defendant cannot pay for such research and analysis, the claim is not that he is being denied equal protection of the law: "the real crux is—is he being *afforded* equal protection of the law?" The suggestion of unfairness becomes particularly acute in light of the probability that the prosecution will be unable to match the psychological research and investigative efforts of the rich or notorious client (for whom a defense fund may be established).[65]

While the following response does not rise to the level of a solution to the perceived problems of inequity and the futility of certain trials, it may help to place in perspective expert guidance in jury selection. Arguments similar to the above have either long been possible, or already made, with regard to attorney trial competence. Resigned clucking is common when the rich or notorious minority obtains the representation of the likes of F. Lee Bailey or Racehorse Haynes. Renowned success of attorneys is generally chalked up to expertise. If they achieve such success sans expert guidance, do they have an advantage over less proficient counsel that warrants remedying? And what if the successful attorneys have within themselves expertise beyond that of even proficient counsel? That is, does the medical malpractice attorney who is also a doctor have an unfair advantage over opposing counsel who is not? Should the attorney who is also a sociologist or psychologist by education and/or training be barred from trial work?

"The response to a question, the quickness to grasp its meaning, the play of expression upon a juror's face, the attempt to court counsel's favor (or vice versa), and the matter in which an answer is given rather than the words spoken—all of these are important in selecting a qualified jury."[66] The preceding could have been written by a psychologist, but it was not. It could have been followed by a description of a procedure used by experts to select jurors, but it was followed instead by the detailed *voir dire* methodology of a "country lawyer." While this rebuts the presumption that the analytical processes used by laymen in assessing jurors is non-systematic, the organization and thoroughness required to produce a system may simply be signs of expertise. And while accurately assessing and interpreting the behavior of others requires recognizing and setting aside one's own prejudices, that is not necessarily a task that can be accomplished only by professional psychologists. At this point it is appropriate to recall an earlier expressed proposition concerning expert trial attorneys: "Experts have more adequate (in the sense of more complete and/or correct) implicit psychological theories. In the last analysis, whatever an attorney does must be assessed against its potential impact on people (client, judge, jury, etc.)."[67]

4. "*Do-It-Yourself* Voir Dire"[68]

The jury selection methodology of the "country lawyer" is discussed below; this preface is based on the article whose borrowed title serves as the heading of this section. There, Judge McGarry, of the Sixth Judicial District, expresses doubts that *voir dire* plays a significant role in the outcome of any case and suggests this is true for three reasons. (The author adamantly disagrees with Judge McGarry as to the significance of *voir dire*, but in a sense of fairness, has presented his viewpoint for the reader's consideration). First, it is "almost always . . . true . . . that good cases win and bad cases lose." (For a correct assessment of the merits of a case, he advises consulting only someone who has nothing to gain or lose by the outcome of the case.) Second, "juries almost always do the right thing." Third, verdict mutations, which are verdicts that should not have occurred, do occur. "There is no rational explanation. There is no basic understanding. They just happen."[69]

Advising the acceptance of the fact that nothing can be done about mutations, Judge McGarry suggests how each attorney can select the best jurors for *him*. And while he recommends reading texts on *voir dire* "boilerplates and badinage," Judge McGarry believes the best way to pick a jury is unique to each individual attorney:

> Now, buried down in each of us is a set of standards that we use in measuring up a person as a friend, foe, inferior, superior, or what have you. And for each of us the standards are different. So there *are* no packaged or canned questions that will work for everyone in all cases. A juror who might do just fine for one lawyer might be a poor choice for another. As near as I can figure it, you will do best with a juror who you feel comfortable with—who you could strike up a friendship with—or who you admire.

Above all, he suggests that the attorney ask the kind of questions that will make prospective jurors talk (raw data for the psychologist) and will allow the attorney to get to know them. Usually these are personal questions, concerning hobbies, exercise, pets, and positions on controversial issues. The responses should provide sufficient information on which to base challenges. Simply, Judge McGarry advises striking "[t]hose you instantly despise . . . . You simply must rely on that gut instinct. If you don't like him . . . he doesn't like you. Rely on it. Bet on it." His brief guidelines for selection follow:

1. You like them? Keep them.
2. You tolerate them? Keep them.
3. Your opponent likes them and you like them? Keep them.
4. Your opponent likes them and you tolerate them? Keep them.
5. You despise or mistrust them? Challenge them.[70]

It is probably more than coincidental that the advice above echoes that of John Appleman, a renowned "country lawyer," which appeared eighteen years earlier:

> The simplest of all rules for the selection of jurors is: "Do you like the guy?" If you do, and if you feel that the juror likes you, he will probably be a good juror. . . .
>
> [O]n the other hand, no matter how highly a juror has been recommended to you, if there is something about him which causes you to bristle, the chances are that his reaction to you is precisely the same. Don't take him![71]

The *voir dire* procedure that Appleman describes (only a sampling of which is presented here) is quite similar to that undertaken by the professional psychologist; they both essentially try to get to know the prospective juror. And like the sociologist, Appleman recommends investigating the background of the juror and making assumptions based on group associations (such as precinct information). Certain of the recommended data sources follow (some are more likely to be helpful with small communities rather than large cities, and some are not available in all areas): professional jury services, city directory (which provides information as to home ownership and occupation), politicians and public officials, salesmen who travel regularly in the area, local attorneys, and the family physician.[72]

Appleman suggests how to evaluate the appearance of jurors, indicating dimensions that social scientists may not uniformly recognize. First, he believes that after the age of forty, one's face betrays character, disposition, and temperment. Evidence of unhappiness or bitterness implies a lack of sympathy for others. "Usually it is the person who is happy, contented, and relaxed who makes a good juror for the plaintiff." Next, he matches personality types with body structure. The mesomorph, who is muscular and heavy-boned, is thought to be logical. The endomorph, who is often overweight and jolly, can be good for the plaintiff if the jolliness is legitimate. The male ectomorph, thin and small-boned, may be vindictive and selfish or an idealist, in search of perfect justice. "This applies to men only, however; never take a skinny woman for the plaintiff."[73]

Concerning demographic traits, Appleman likes representatives of minority groups, as they have "known what it means to be deprived of justice and . . . want to see that others are not so deprived." He is also partial to Jewish people and people whose ancestors came from the Mediterranean because they are very sympathetic and have strong family ties. As to the sexes, he advises that "[w]omen are inordinately cruel to each other. In fact, men ordinarily are better jurors for plaintiffs in almost any situation than are women, unless possibly it is a question whether a woman driver was negligent." But if the plaintiff is a young, handsome male, he recommends women of any age.[74]

Appleman's rules for asking questions display a remarkable understanding of human behavior. First, he says you should try to memorize the names of the jurors while the court or the opposition is questioning them. Then, call each by his or her name when you ask questions, and be sure that you pronounce it correctly; if you fear you cannot, ask the juror for help. (The author always recommends to trial counsel that he call each juror by name from memory. My experience is that the jurors will be impressed with the attorney's intellect and sincerity—both important factors for positive regard and liking by the jurors. This will also create a nice contrast from opposing counsel who will not have memorized each juror's name.) Never correct a juror's pronunciation of a word or do or say anything else to embarrass him. When you refer to the occupation of each juror, do so with a dignified term, such as "maintenance engineer" for "janitor." If the opportunity arises, you can flatter the juror by revealing your knowledge of information that has not been revealed in the *voir dire* but that you have uncovered in your investigation:

> For example, one moment you are very businesslike; then the next moment, "You aren't, by any chance, the wife of Jim Evans, who works for Railway Express, are you?" She says "yes" and you then nod as if satisfied, which you were all along—and immediately move to another juror. The impact often will remain.

Concerning the atmosphere during the questioning, Appleman disagrees with the many attorneys who remain "unnaturally solemn." He notes that the jurors are uncomfortable and tense, which makes it difficult to establish any rapport with them. Thus, he believes that "[w]ithout becoming cute . . . it pays to kid around a little with them," especially at the beginning, to break the ice.[75]

The final touch that Appleman recommends is that, after you have finished interrogating the prospective jurors, turn around and quietly talk to your client. Even if you talk about the weather, give the impression of "bring[ing] the client into the general picture, before you exercise any challenges."[76] Although the last step in the *voir dire*, this is one of the first steps in inducing the jury to identify with the client (as opposed to the attorney). After the case has concluded and the jury has begun to deliberate, Appleman instructs his client (plaintiff or defendant) to sit outside the courtroom, alone, awaiting their return. He wants the jury to see his client there when they leave for a meal or to retire for the evening, as well as when they return, and identify with him or her individually, and not the entourage that could include counsel and any assistants and well-wishers.[77] (The author recommends to a client that he also go to the cafeteria where jurors lunch, go to the snack bar during court recesses, etc. throughout the duration of the trial so the jurors will see the client as a "person" similar to the jurors themselves and not just as "plaintiff" or "defendant." Of course, this assumes a client will conduct himself properly and that this is an appropriate tactic. For example, in a personal injury case, the attorney may want the jury to have limited exposure to the injured party so as not to habituate to the injury.)

C. *Goal: Knowledge of People*

"The advocate must be a psychologist. He must understand human nature, and he must know how his listeners think, their habits, desires, and emotions."[78] Whatever the technique, or whoever applies it, the goal is knowing people. Appleman summarizes that

> [t]he difficulty with the average trial lawyer is that subconsciously he fears and distrusts jurors. He conceives of a jury as a type of wild animal which is going to bite and rend and claw him if he gets sufficiently close to the bars. As a result, much superstitious nonsense has grown up as to how to select jurors.[79]

The "superstitious nonsense" may well have spawned the systematic thoroughness of the social scientists in the field of jury selection. "Some lawyers have such enormous talent and charisma that they can make a fried egg look like a T-bone steak. These people are themselves mutations, and if you are one, pay no attention to me. Do your own thing."[80] Nevertheless, the trial attorney should be aware of the techniques used during *voir dire* and the trial itself and acquainted with the innovative procedures and methods that are now available to help him know people, and obtain the best result possible from a jury trial. Attorneys are like professional golfers. Who wins and who loses can be determined by the difference of one stroke. Some win more and some less! The innovative psychological concepts such as interpretations of nonverbal communication, submittal of questions worded to elicit maximum response and maximum information, trial simulations, etc. can be that difference of one stroke.

D. *Helpful* Voir Dire *Hints*

If all the world is a stage and we are merely players, then project the courtroom as the potential setting for a drama. The attorneys and clients, the judge and court personnel are the players, actors if you will. Consider the audience, the jury, twelve men and women there for only one purpose—to watch, critique, and finally judge the upcoming production and the quality of the performances. Each will in fact perceive the events of the next several hours or days or perhaps weeks with a different background, a different manner, a different moral attitude, and a different personal history. Because all people come to be prospective jurors and function with preconceived notions, prejudices, feelings, beliefs, biases, and attitudes, there are astronomical personality variable combinations possible in each person to complicate the guesswork in determining whether a juror will be favorable to any particular aspect or issue of the case. It would be tough enough to anticipate with any constancy the selection of a few who would judge the performances and tender the verdict one sought if facts were undisputed and the laws were "Black letter!" But because by definition this is not the case of a trial, since there must be disputed issues to give the court jurisdiction even to hear a case, selecting jurors who all possess human qualities, frailties, and individual differences becomes an even more complex technique. This is a process, vastly underrated by the legal community, that needs more attention and focus from educators and practitioners alike, for no other one aspect of the trial can more determine the attorney's success than choosing wisely the twelve or six people who will ultimately decide the fate of his efforts. It is in a drama such as this that the final scene, the verdict, is all important. After all, in this one circumstance what is important is not how you play the game but whether you win or lose!

To predict the verdict more reliably and more carefully develop the strategy of one's efforts in presentment of evidence and witnesses, careful selection of jurors is mandatory. Every successful trial lawyer knows the most important people in the courtroom are the jurors. After all, they are the ones deciding the verdict. Therefore, experienced litigators agree that the jury selection process is the single most important aspect of the trial proceedings. Because different interpretations of the same evidence can influence the final verdict, most, if not all seasoned trial attorneys, are aware of the vast importance that a person's occupation, religious beliefs, educational background, race, sex, or personal history have in the biasing of one's opinions. It is the author's opinion that once the last person on the jury is seated, the trial is essentially won or lost. There are no neutral, unbiased jurors in reality. Jurors appear at the courthouse with biases and predispositions that determine how they selectively perceive the evidence and, consequently, the outcome of the case. Most jurors make a determination immediately and then perceive the evidence in a manner to support their decision and resulting rationalization. Jurors function with baises, prejudices, feelings, and attitudes that are consistent with their backgrounds. They were children, brothers and sisters, mothers and fathers before being selected as jurors. The *voir dire* process offers little opportunity to ferret out the effects of a prospective juror's life experiences. The biases and predispositions of the prospective jurors remain unidentified. The litigator's position may be compromised by jurors' preconceived biases, attitudes, and notions. In the past, trial counsel selected jurors based on instinct, hunches, and educated guesswork. More predictable results may be obtained by application of information and principles from the social sciences.

Yet few give the time and effort that this aspect of the proceedings, jury selection, or more appropriately termed "juror elimination," warrants. If we consider the age-old maxim that all is fair in war—and certainly trials are intellectual and highly technical wars—then every attorney worth his license had better be as prepared as possible, as ready as practicable, and more intuitive than his opponent in perceiving these details. The overall strategy then is to develop a panel of jurors who agree so solidly with your convictions, identify so totally with your conclusions, and are so overwhelmed by your logic that it does not even occur to any one of them that you ought not win the war from the beginning. It is at the moment that the jury announces its verdict that we are furnished both the end of the story and how well the attorney's intuitive powers have worked at casting the fate of the verdict.

Many lawyers believe that they can convince an impartial jury. However, there are no impartial jurors, since jurors bring to the courtroom biases and predispositions that largely determine the outcome of the case. Therefore, the strategy of assuring the verdict begins much earlier. How then do we launch our aspirations to achieve this goal? Through careful selection of "ideal" jurors who are partial, prejudiced, and predetermined. "Partial!" you say. "Prejudiced!" you say. "Predetermined!" you exclaim. Yes! Of ocurse, all litigators realize that the dominant jurors must be aligned with the attorney's particular point of view at the verdict stage of the trial if the attorney is to win the decision. And they know that if they can select jurors who are already on their side at *voir dire*, then their work is basically done. It is important to realize that truly the only person in the courtroom who really would like for each and every juror to be without bias, prejudice, or opinion is the judge, who must himself remain "neutral" in his efforts to tackle the tough job of directing the cast of characters through the play. Each attorney wants to win; therefore, each attorney wants to lure as many jurors to his side as possible. To achieve adequate, if not ultimate, juror selection or "elimination," insightful preparation takes place before as well as during *voir dire*. No one can emphasize the importance of maximizing every effort and every means available to select a jury that is as receptive to your methods, theme, logic, client, and counsel as possible. It is during *voir dire* that a skilled professional can determine the partiality of prospective jurors, their qualifications for jury service, their knowledge of the parties and the case, and their attitudes toward issues and thus, intelligently begin to select his or minimize his opponent's human support group.

The trial attorney must master the art of jury selection. My research confirms the conclusion indicated in another section that prospective jurors make a decision about the case and litigators within a few minutes of exposure to the participants; and most have reached a decision before the *voir dire* is completed and certainly, by the conclusion of the opening statement. Most important is the fact that these opinions rarely change.

To understand the nuts and bolts of the jury selection process is a well taught concept in procedure classes throughout law school. Using challenges for cause to strike disqualified or problem jurors is the basic premise of *voir dire*, or so one is taught. But to understand what types of jurors counsel wants to exclude and include in the jury box on any particular case is highly specific to that case, client, and even that particular litigator. There are endless variables to consider and little time and opportunity to acquaint jurors and counsel. This puts an extreme importance on first impressions. Seasoned trial attorneys know all too well that decisions concerning whether to keep or strike a potential juror are typically made, from the perception of the attorney, from the limited questioning and visible observations possible before and during *voir dire*. On the opposite side of the jury box are prospective participants in the judgment process of the case whose first impressions of both client and advocate will be both lasting and most difficult to change. In this particular situation, the mere appearance of disfavorable or favorable traits may be as important to the juror as the actual traits themselves.

While it is most helpful to observe the jury panel in their unguarded moments (for example, prior to the beginning of *voir dire*, during recesses, in the hallways, and at lunch), it is wise to realize that they too are calculating, observing, and forming impressions of the client's guilt or innocence or cause of action and the attorney's competency, confidence, and general demeanor. The skilled attorney should be aware of who talks to whom; who is nervous; who is friendly; what people are reading; and how they dress, wear their hair, and gesture. That same attorney should be cognizant of these identical impressions being presented by himself and his client. This relationship between law and psychology is not addressed in law school and thus requires years of trial and error experience, knowledge of psychology's role in juror selection, or some carefully guided thought as to the dynamics of this group. The goal in jury selection is to obtain as much objective information as possible. This information will serve to reinforce the attorney's intuition or cause him to hesitate about his decision and re-evaluate a prospective juror. Noted criminal defense attorney Richard "Racehorse" Haynes, has expressed his opinion on the role of information and intuition in jury selection:

> The bottom line as I see it is that in jury selection you have to use as many advantages as possible, and social science and statistics in the courtroom are just the latest or our ever more sophisticated techniques. That does not mean that I would ever permit a social scientist to preempt my opinion to make the seat-of-the pants, back-of-the neck judgment based on everything I've learned and read in my career. Jury selection is still guesswork right down to the wire. The difference is that now jury selection is a little more intelligent guesswork.[81]

The essence of jury selection is that experience and intuition are essential, but the added bonus of psychological skills and education in making decisions, strategies, and developing tactics will often make the difference in the end result. As an example, take a highly publicized criminal case pending in 1979 against an accused multimillionaire. A pretrial poll conducted ascertained that over 90% of the community where the trial was pending was aware of the case and that over 80% of those answering the poll believed pretrial that the citizen accused was guilty! Working in coordination with the defense firm, the author developed a lengthy questionnaire seeking information from potential jurors about such issues deemed important to the defense as jurors' pretrial knowledge of the case and their attitudes toward law enforcement, politics, religion, divorce, etc. The defense team looked for people who could understand the complicated issues that the defense planned to raise. It was astutely realized that this was no ordinary criminal case and thus required an out of the ordinary jury. The pretrial questioning period was utilized in yet another way—to educate and attempt to sway the jurors before they were even chosen to serve on the panel! It proved to be an effort well spent when much to the prosecution's surprise, the jury brought in a "NOT GUILTY." Pretrial questioning of jurors and planned strategic jury selection probably led ultimately to the acquittal.

Speaking to the jurors' initial impression of counsel, it must be taken into account that there is yet another hurdle for the legal profession to overcome in every trial by each lawyer representing a client. Most of the public at large has been somehow involved in a legal matter. Each individual will view the profession depending on his or her experiences, good or bad. An attorney's role as an advocate has been blamed for everything from the erosion of moral values to court congestion. It is a definite public relations problem. To best represent his client, the advocate must be aware of how the jury will observe him and his role (including his concern for his client's affairs). He is after all the spokesman, the representative. There is a story to be told and he will want the jury to agree with its every premise; but to allow the jury to hear the story, he must overcome the public perception that the entire judicial system is crooked, inadequate, and a mockery of basic American ideals such as innocent until proven guilty, justice for all, and punishment for the offender. Making certain that prospective jurors are comfortable with their surroundings, their role in the trial, and their belief in the role of the court and advocates in the finding of justice are as important and basic to having a receptive audience as allowing jurors adequate breaks, speaking directly TO and not AT the panel, and affording all courtesies ethical. This not only enhances the attorney's status as a caring and honest advocate but also posits the jurors in the honored position that the judicial system of this country has accorded them. Because of this status, the court personnel will treat jurors with great respect and thus align the jurors with the court. If an attorney is obviously in disfavor with the court due to attitude or aloofness, this alignment of jurors and court will work against that advocate. Often the respect afforded the jurors is misinterpreted as a desire of the court to be "friends" with them and sometimes leads them to want to "repay" the court for being so nice. This can be a major problem for the defense attorney in a criminal case.

In small communities trial circumstances are much different from those in large communities. In the small community all parties and court personnel are generally known by everyone, including the lawyers, judge, and jury. This creates a friendly atmosphere. The scene is substantially different in larger city areas where juries are most often unfamiliar with plaintiff or defendant, lawyers, witnesses, and even other jurors. "Demeanor of the parties to the suit, principals and witnesses, manner of presentation of the evidence, and psychology of courtroom procedure take an important place in the trial."[82] You must realize that jurors feel disoriented because they do not frequent courts and, in fact, may be in the courtroom for the first time. In a situation where initial impressions are all important, it must be pointed out that those same impressions can interfere with objectivity. Why not utilize this psychological premise to an advantage and give the jurors an initial image of stability, honesty, and self-confidence that begins the initial relationship between advocate, client, and juror? Dress, act, and think the part of a skilled professional who knows his case, the law, and most important, the merits of his client's position.

The client, too, must give the jury a good impression throughout the case. He must appear worthy of their time and consideration and happy to have them hold his potential fate in their hands. Every person experiences life with the three primary perception systems: sight, sound, and tactile sense. Yet it has been noted that 93% of the variance in impressions about other people can be attributed to impressions given through nonverbal information. Nowhere more acutely can this form of communication be seen than in the case of the observant juror who arrives at his verdict based on what he perceives. Take, for example, the case of the defendant accused of murdering his wife in California some years ago. The prosecutor had motive and masses of evidence clearly pointing to the defendant. The one thing missing was the body of the victim. The defense attorney made sure to select a jury that could understand that if no body was found, then there existed no proof that a crime had been committed. He called no witnesses and even held little cross-examination of the prosecution's witnesses. The verdict seemed clearly to be for acquittal, though, as the defense attorney in closing argument spellbound the jury. He began by arguing the merit of refusing to convict one of murder where no body existed. He pled the defense well and at his conclusion remarked, "Ladies and Gentlemen, this defendant did not kill his wife. In fact, she just walked into the courtroom!" When everyone turned to look at the courtroom door, there was, of course, no wife. However, that everyone was unsure enough of her death to look was enough to scream reasonable doubt, and acquittal was absolutely assured. Imagine the surprise when the jury returned a "GUILTY" verdict. The defense attorney naturally wanted to know how the jury could have possibly reached such a decision after what seemed to be a brilliant ploy on the part of the defense counsel. Approaching jurors after the trial was over he asked, "How could you have convicted him? Didn't everyone turn to look for the victim?" One juror enlightening the bewildered defense counsel replied, "Everyone except the defendant!" The defendant's attorney failed to have his client react with innocence, and a very perceptive juror observed the discrepancy between the attorney's evidence and the defendant's reaction. The game, the war was lost by one nonverbal omission.

Once an attorney has been careful to provide the right setting for the drama and adequately prepare the cast of players, he must begin to consider his audience. What type of juror does the lawyer need to obtain his verdict on this particular case? Obviously the factors vary depending on criminal versus civil litigation, individual versus corporate participants, type of suit, size of damages sought, and parties' personalities. But there are generalizations about people that prove helpful in making quick, though hopefully well reasoned and educated, decisions about who will best serve your client's needs.

The legal process by which the jury is selected is limited in time and opportunity to determine the effect of an individual's life experiences; therefore, a juror's biases and predispositions remain unknown variables. Add to the limitations on time, a reluctance by most potential jurors to really open up and be honest in their answers and the lack of candor and possible naivete on the part of jurors concerning their own biases and this presents yet another challenge to attorneys in ferreting out the choices for qualified jurors. In everyday life, ideas are pretested or preexamined for content by techniques such as marketing research and theatre dress rehearsals. The prosecutor has had the benefit of pretesting his case before a grand jury. However, in spite of the limited availability for pretesting ideas by the defense, or by both sides in civil litigation, more predictable results in trial may be obtained by the use of information and principles learned from social scientists. What social scientists know about human behavior can be tailored for use on the jury system and advantageously applied in the trial court. Receiving a reversal on appeal is great, getting a new trial is wonderful, but receiving a favorable jury verdict is better than anything else. It is winning!

One specialized study of physiognomy believes that people with particular physical attributes tend to have the same characteristic responses. Imagine how easy it would be to choose "your" jurors if all fat people truly were jovial and less likely to vote for harsh punishment, whereas people with distinctive and sharp features proved to be opinionated and stubborn in conviction. Albert S. Osborn studied this phenomenon and reported his empirical data in "The Mind of the Juror," suggesting the mouth to be a primary and easily visible way to determine one's sensibilities and propensities. As he reported, a small, puckered mouth is unsympathetic and obviously not a wise choice for the criminal defendant. He also notes that men who have mouths that contrarily turn up at the corners are not to be trusted. While these studies and ones like them may be fun to view, they are not the type of data that most psychologists and attorneys will find to be standard and absent of deviation enough to utilize in casting the jury box.

There are, however, some generalizations that do tend to show sensibly a bias or trend and help to make preliminary determinations possible. An important principle in jury selection, in both civil and criminal trials, is to find out who the prospective jurors are and what they think about themselves. A basic rule of human behavior is that if one thinks negatively about himself, he is unlikely to think positively of the client. Research indicates that a person's perception of his growing years affects his attitudes about life. These developed attitudes are like a second skin and acompany the juror into the jury box. It is helpful to inquire about where a person grew up and note emotional reaction to revealing this information. Eye contact, facial expressions, posture, and basic body movements, nervousness, or tension can all be the visual cues to psychological responses and if carefully analyzed may reveal much about a juror's basic feelings about himself.

Psychological and sociological techniques can afford an advantage in *voir dire*. The jury consultant can assist the trial attorney in designing questions for *voir dire* to elicit the maximum response for evaluation and also to condition the prospective jurors to his theme or theory of the case.

An effective *voir dire* should include five basic types of questions. These categories are analogy, educational, commitment, correlational, and selectional.[83] Open-ended questions may be prefaced with "How do you feel about" or "What are your thoughts on" or "Why." The attorney in *voir dire* should focus on what he or she feels is critical to the case and artfully educate and commit the prospective jurors to these critical issues.

Psychological research indicates that the first attorney who presents his or her theme is more strongly believed (concept of primacy). Therefore, a simple and concise theme or theory of the case must be presented well in *voir dire* by a series of conditioning inquiries and open-ended questions.

During *voir dire* a jury and trial consultant evaluate verbal, nonverbal, and group behavior. Since some persons will misstate the truth during *voir dire* examination,[84] the verbal content cannot be strictly relied upon. Keys to the truthfulness of answers are (1) choice of words, (2) immediacy of response, (3) maintaining of eye contact, and similar action. Comparing the response of the juror to the defendant's attorney, to the court and to the plaintiff's attorney gives insight into the juror's personality and true feelings. The juror's response to basic background questioning will provide a baseline for comparison to his or her responses on more critical or case-related inquiries. Anxiety may be exhibited by unfinished sentences, deep breathing, blocked or disjointed thoughts. Loudness of voice may indicate dominancy. The overall gestalt of the prospective juror, rather than one gesture or one response, should be used for evaluation purposes. A detailed discussion of communicative behavior is provided in an article by Suggs and Sales.[85] The trial attorney can also benefit from expert assistance in jury selection by his own biases (which could cause him to misjudge individuals during the stress of trial) being minimized.[86]

While the Juror Information Card provides noteworthy general background details, it can also be helpful in formulating preliminary questions with which to further detail a juror's life. Often, the simple facts hurriedly answered on these cards are only partial, incomplete answers. Further questioning shows more evidence of a juror's background, such as the fact that he has two families, two jobs, or owns a second residence. This more enlightened view of the juror can form the framework for more extensive questioning into these areas; ask him to explain job responsibilities and spousal employment, for example. Taking this aspect of a juror's background one step further and thus becoming familiar with the part of the community that he is from, trial counsel should first know which sections of town comprise ghetto or "silk stocking" areas. Placing a pin on each prospective juror's home on a map and identifying neighborhoods and circumstances of his residence, counsel can further determine whether jurors live near each other, or perhaps the client, and whether there exist the same or similar economic situations. Drive-by observations and photographs of the prospective juror's homes can produce useful data. Bumper stickers, burglar bars, neatly trimmed lawns, and other significant information can be of great assistance to the trial attorney when properly evaluated by a behavioral scientist. For example, people who post crime-watch stickers on their homes or fences, or who have elaborate burglar-alarm systems, are more aware of crime and more predisposed to convict. In a personal injury suit involving children, the bumper sticker "Have you hugged a child today?" proved to be an indicator of a favorably predisposed juror.

Basic information about prospective jurors may be obtained from public records such as property records, credit agencies, voter registration records, and police accident records. If time and financial resources permit, an extensive investigation of prospective jurors is recommended. Investigators talk with community leaders and persons representative of the community about a prospective juror's experiences, attitudes, activities, and reputation (referred to as community network analysis).

A Juror Questionnaire should be developed for use on the day of trial. Such questionnaire requires approval of opposing counsel and the court. This questionnaire is designed to elicit more detailed and relevant information than the typical Juror Qualification or Information Card completed in most jurisdictions. An extensive questionnaire was completed by jurors on the day of jury selection of the *State of Texas v. T. Cullen Davis* case. A lengthy questionnaire was mailed to prospective jurors for completion prior to the first day of jury selection in the *United States v. John DeLorean* case.

When comparing the socio-economic background of the jurors and the client, one must realize another very basic premise of psychology, that of interaction. Everyone realizes that persons working as a group will develop leaders and followers, some will work well together, others may not. But little is ever articulated, much less taught to attorneys, about the important role group dynamics can have in predicting the group's reaction to the evidence presented in a case. These twelve people do not work as independently of each other as most attorneys would like to think. Often they form two groups of six each, or three groups of four each, or any other combination, each with its own leader, its own dominant and passive players. They come to a verdict often after much time, frustration, and discussion or argument. The way each person relates to the next varies depending upon the two personalities. The more subgroups, the less discussion seems to take place. Women discuss more varied issues than men; men talk more, in general, than women; and upper-socio-economic status individuals deliberate more than their lower-socio-economic counterparts. Keeping these, and other aspects of the group dynamics in mind, one can better prepare to select the perfect balance of personalities. However, in actuality, jury selection is "juror elimination" and "damage control." That is, prospective jurors are eliminated from the panel or "deselected" and for example, given a choice between two less than "ideal" individuals, when the attorney should make a determination as to which person will be most persuasive and influential in the group. This person has a higher detrimental potential because of his likely effect on the group and its decision.

Do remember that group behavior or dynamics are important in jury selection. Dominant members of a jury determine or direct the decision-making process. The leaders, followers, and indecisives should be identified so that the proper subgroup formation can be anticipated. Also, the prospective cohesive bonds of the subgroups should be considered. For example, in a negligence case involving a defendant hospital and plaintiff child, three strong prospective groups for the plaintiff are readily apparent: mothers with children, those who feel they have been inappropriately treated by a health care provider, and those who are sympathetic to the theme of the defenseless vs. the powerful institution. Those individuals with similar experiences and attitudes will tend to cluster together.

Practitioners with experience have found generalizations documented by social scientists to be both standard and accurate. Examples of these generalizations are offered with the disclaimer that they are just that, general statements, not hard and fast rules. Illustrative of this premise is the population segment of wealthy people who are cognizant of their wealth, property, and efforts to gain and maintain their assets. It would stand to reason that they, as jurors, will be respectful of the rights of others in protecting their property. The poor, however, believe in laws for the rich and as jurors tend to help others who are poor. Older jurors are usually more conservative and less likely to identify with a younger client. Elderly people, fearful of crime due to their more helpless nature as years go on, are quick to be won by the prosecution, whereas younger jurors tend to exhibit less respect for authority and are less emotional than other jurors. Women tend to be lenient on punishment and understand pain and suffering but are more critical of other women as witnesses and acquit defendants in rape cases. Women too, do not think in terms of large money judgments. Middle-aged men take a hard, traditional view of the male/female relationship and are readily tough on conviction of rape defendants and other crimes committed against women. Religion tends to bias views: atheists and agnostics are considered non-traditional and possess the propensity to be different from the norm and hence are often found to be very liberal jurors.

Each attorney should also master the technique of what works individually for him. Obviously, some audiences will be more or less receptive to his particular age, sex, physical traits, demeanor, and methods. One plaintiff's medical malpractice attorney, who is himself Baptist, finds Baptist jurors especially easy to reason with and generous in damage awards to his clients. His reasoning is that they live by the theory that the world is full of evil and corruption and they want to help right the injustices. It has been found that an attractive, young female attorney will be given less consideration by young, female jurors than her male counterpart. Knowing that an underlying jealously factor may exist, she would be wise to avoid choosing that population segment for any trial she will litigate as lead counsel. Older, more established men project too stern and traditional a demeanor to work well with younger, more liberal, and sometimes more rebellious and less establishment-oriented men as jurors. Thus, the attorney's persona can create both restrictions and alliances with jurors.

Considering all of the aforementioned factors, how can a reasonably seasoned attorney utilize the methods available to him? Social scientists as trial consultants have devised innovative concepts to aid the litigator in successful prediction of jury verdicts through well planned, strategic jury selection or "elimination." One way that has been developed is the use of focus groups, composed of three to nine participants chosen to represent the characteristics of people in the community likely to be chosen as jurors. Group discussion is conducted by the group leader and monitored by the trial team via closed circuit television. The jury and trial consultant is the group leader. The important facts and issues of the case are presented without the use of witnesses or attorneys. The leader must artfully identify the issues and generate discussions in order to obtain meaningful feedback. Feelings, impressions, reactions, and opinions of the participants are determined. While the discussions concerning these issues may last from several hours to days depending on the complexity of the case, the goal is to provide feedback for the litigator at a less expensive price than the more reliable mock trial or mirror jury. The added advantage to a focus group is that specific facts may be pointedly set out for the group to scrutinize, unlike the mock jury situation where jurors may consider only what they deem important. The focus group can provide valuable insight into the problems the actual jury will face.

If a more realistic view of testing the case is favored, mock or mini trials can be set up. This simulation of an actual trial uses a mock courtroom complete with witnesses and evidence. (The author has conducted several mock juries in a room within an office. However, I prefer to do such in the courtroom studio of Dr. Robert Gordon. Mock jurors in the studio courtroom environment seem to assume a more vested interest in the outcome—as if they were transformed into actual jurors.) Twelve or six "jurors" are chosen once again to represent the community in judging the presentation of opening statements, examination of witnesses, and closing arguments. The case is presented to this mock jury in a simplified fashion. The number of witnesses and issues is limited to the three or four critical to the case. The attorney who will try the case presents the direct examination. The cross-examination is conducted by an associate who role plays the opposing attorney. Photographs, charts, and other demonstrative evidence can be presented and viewed by the panel. Condensed arguments for both sides and a jury charge are given. The jury is then allowed to deliberate and answer issues, including the assessing of damages in a civil action. A video tape is made and transcribed and categorized for important points and issues. Even experienced lawyers, who believe they instinctively know which theories will work best with the jury, are surprised as they watch the videotape of this jury working its way through the evidence to a verdict. An attorney noted that "because practice and rehearsal comprise a large part of trial preparation, it makes sense to practice the impact of a potential trial strategy on a mock jury."[87] The trial team can observe the reactions of this simulated jury to the issues and theories presented in the case. This procedure is probably most valuable in helping the experienced trial lawyer accurately evaluate the jury's acceptance of the witnesses' testimony and demeanor. The technique is invaluable for preparation and testing of a trial strategy. Discussing the mock jury's impressions, opinions, and reactions after the verdict produces a better understanding of the case and its potential impact on the actual jury.

During jury selection for the actual trial and throughout the trial, reference should be made to information gained from the mock trial for guidance in the presentation of the case. The profile of the "ideal" juror can be influenced by the facts learned from the test jurors. During *voir dire* a potential juror's attitudes and opinions may be compared with those of the mock jury, and thereby a more predictable verdict is possible. The strengths and weaknesses of the case may be more accurately evaluated. The information obtained also may be used in settlement negotiations. A brochure that contains a videotape of selected parts of the mock jury's deliberations, including the damages awarded, can be a powerful tool for settlement. The mock jury techniques allow for a determination of the probable outcome of a case and can give insight into the reason for such a result.

Prior to the *voir dire*, trial counsel should have identified the type of juror desired. The author refers to this as the profile of the "ideal" juror. Such profile may be derived from knowledge and experience or, more accurately, from data obtained in a community attitudinal analysis.

The community attitudinal analysis is conducted under the direction of the jury and trial consultant, usually a Ph.D. in psychology, who prepares questions calculated to elicit specific attitudes about the client, the issues, and the damages. This analysis can be conducted in person or by telephone and is typically done by a market research team using random or stratified sampling.

From this data the jury consultant develops the profile of the "ideal" juror. Although never encountered, this "ideal" profile can serve as a measuring device for ranking prospective jurors. Those jurors possessing more of the characteristics of the "ideal" juror will be highest on the scale, and those with fewer of the desired characteristics will be the first eliminated. This survey by the author was used in the murder trials of Texas multi-millionaire T. Cullen Davis to determine the profile of the "ideal" juror.[88]

No method can absolutely predict a prospective juror's response in a given situation; however, the analysis makes a correlation between observed characteristics and known attitudes to predict how a prospective juror is likely to react in a given situation.

A Dallas personal injury case provides an illustration of an effective use of the community attitudinal analysis concept.[89] The attorney representing the injured plaintiff in an accident involving an amusement ride at the State Fair of Texas in October, 1983 wanted to know what punitive damages he could expect from a Dallas County jury. Subjects in a telephone interview were asked questions about their awareness of the alleged facts and their attiutdes about awarding punishment damages in addition to basic background information. A profile of the "ideal" juror was derived with independent predictor variables; of equal importance was the discovery of the converse or "worse" juror profile. Of particular importance was the average amount of punitive damages likely to be awarded by the residents of Dallas County. The results of the research verified the trial team's subjective judgment as to the punishment orientation of Dallas County people. The results of the analysis were presented by videotape to the defendants at a settlement conference. Even though the case settled for many million dollars following this conference, the mathematical function and data obtained in the research would have classified prospective jurors into either "pro" or "con" groups. This grouping could have been used by the attorney during *voir dire* to aid him in determining which jurors would be favorably disposed to award punitive damages.

Startling accuracy has been obtained by the use of a simulated jury during the actual trial. The simulated jury also has been designated a "mirror" or "shadow" jury. Attorneys may evaluate the reactions of the jury to the evidence, witnesses, and trial counsel by the use of a simulated, shadow, or mirror jury. Although the discussion here is what to do before trial, it is not inappropriate to discuss the use of the shadow or mirror jury during trial. All pretrial jury work should result in trial counsel's identifying the characteristics and personality constructs of the most favorably predisposed juror possible. This is important when one talks about the utilization of a mirror jury because you now want to make arrangements to hire a pool of people in advance of trial, from which can be selected a group of six, nine, or more to serve as a mirror jury. This group of six to twelve people should match as closely as possible the demographic characteristics and background of the actual jury panel. These persons are then employed to observe the trial, leaving the courtroom when the actual jury does, and only discussing the case during the interview with the jury and trial consultant at the end of each day. The mirror jury deliberates each evening, and the information, both positive and negative, is analyzed and interpreted by the trial consultant for use by the trial attorney. This method has the advantage of permitting the trial attorney to have objective and unbiased feedback as to the status of the case on a daily basis at a time when the attorney still has the opportunity to correct misimpressions or to clarify an important point by calling additional witnesses or presenting other evidence. The daily feedback from the mirror jurors assures the attorneys that the correct impressions are being created by the trial.

This concept was recently employed by the author in a Texarkana, Texas medical malpractice case.[90] A comprehensive jury selection was accomplished and a six-member mirror jury with characteristics similar to the real jury was organized to monitor the month-long trial (in the Texarkana medical malpractice case, a community attitudinal analysis was conducted, the profile of the "ideal" juror derived, drive-by photographs of prospective jurors homes taken and analyzed, in-court assessment of prospective jurors made, and a mirror jury monitored).

These selected simulated jurors sat in the courtroom, listened to the evidence, and observed only what the actual jury did. This mirror jury was debriefed each evening as to their understanding of the evidence and reaction to the witnesses, attorneys, demonstrative evidence, and general feelings and impressions about the case. After the close of the evidence the mirror jury reached a verdict identical to that of the actual jury on the liability issues and was within 7% of the 3.11 million dollars awarded by the actual jury.

The feedback from the mirror jury was especially helpful in evaluating the understanding and comprehension of technical and medical information. Their comments were utilized to present the testimony in a more understandable way and shaped the final argument. Information from these observers allowed the compilation of a list of additional evidence that needed to be presented to satisfy them of the negligence of the defendant hospital and doctors. The mirror jury was also given the charge and examined for comprehension of terminology and responses.

While many jury reactions and verdicts are unpredictable, the use of the mirror jury reduces considerably the unpredictability of juries. There is no substitute for the information obtained from this "mirror" jury, which attends the real trial on a daily basis. One commentator has noted that "the shadow becomes an on-the-spot lay advisor for the trial laywer."[91]

If the author could convey one message to anyone who is going to select a jury, it would be to identify the weaknesses of the case and to talk about them with the prospective jurors. For example, assume you have a criminal case in which the victim was brutally disfigured but survived, your client cannot be connected with the crime, but for circumstantial evidence, and he does not intend to testify. The problem in this situation is that the victim's condition could so overwhelm the jury that they would want to convict someone, just because the victim was so horribly treated, and consequently, may well overlook any reasonable doubt which may exist. Trial counsel must discuss with the prospective jury members the horrible disfigurement of the victim and acknowledge that all will be sick to their stomachs. Ask if anyone will convict *(name)* of this act just because it occurred and *(name)* is the only one available. In a civil suit, for example, assume you are worried by the fact that the plaintiff was an alcoholic, but this did not play a part in the liability. It is important on *voir dire* that you enter into a discussion about the fact that your client was an alcoholic. You must reveal this fact to the jury. Admit to the panel that you have fears and doubts. "I'm afraid that you will not find for *(name)* because he was an alcoholic, but *(name)* was a father, husband, the breadwinner and did not deserve to die at the hands of the defendant. Will you discount his value because he was an alcoholic?" After the jury closes the door and begins deliberating, you will not be able to talk about the problems of the case. The jurors will discuss the alcoholism in the jury room. Therefore, you had better discuss it with the jury.

A second important point to remember is not to proselytize the juror or try to convert him or her to your view. You want to discover the juror's true feelings, since he will not change or vote against his conscience and predisposition.

Third, after you have discovered how a juror feels, never take a juror, if there is any way to eliminate him, where the vote he has to cast for your client will run contrary to personality traits. The strongest motive to a juror in any case is that, when he goes home or back to work and associates with the people that he sees on a regular basis, his verdict must find favor with them and be explainable. A skillful attorney will provide, in closing argument, a reason why the juror can decide the case in favor of the client and be proud of his decision.

Another important factor is to listen to the jury. Try to understand what the juror is really telling you. Pay close attention and get the true message. If the juror cannot sit on the jury because of the length of the trial, listen to him. You don't want anyone on the jury who doesn't want to be there!

Also, don't ask meaningless questions such as "Can you be fair?" "Can you be impartial?" Phrase your questions to be open-ended. For example, "How do you feel about jury service?"

Remember that you and your client are in the spotlight from the very beginning to the very end. Twelve pairs of eyes will observe and evaluate *all* that transpires in the courtroom.

Don't be fawning or obsequious to the jury. It is important that jurors like your client and the lead counsel in the case. Lead counsel has to be perceived as sincere, trustworthy, well-prepared, and in control of the courtroom. The jurors are actually totally confused by the facts, issues, and evidence. They are afraid that they will miss something. Therefore, they will choose one person that they can trust and that is how they decide the case. On *voir dire* the attorney must establish his credibility.

The jurors should be able to identify with the client and secondly, the attorney, especially if the client is unacceptable or defective. Jurors must like the attorney and client. Attorneys and clients whom jurors like win cases! (Avoid anyone whom you can identify as not liking you or your client.) Remember to humanize or personalize the client.

The case must have a simple and concise theme, which should be established in *voir dire* and referred to numerous times: "This is the case of the missing nurse. Had she been where she should have, the baby would have survived"; "This is the case of Amway doctors."

The attorney should anticipate what will be in the court's charge and prepare the jury for the charge. For example, the author recommends writing a definition (which will be in the charge) on a poster and asking a juror if he can accept the definition. (As an aside, but most important, at the end of closing arguments, if possible, you should attempt to hand the charge to one of your jurors. This may help to get him selected presiding jury, simply because he is holding the charge.)

Jury selection is the focus of this chapter, but it should be noted that only ten percent of all cases filed are ever presented to a jury. There is room for social scientists in the negotiation and settlement of cases, too, but that is subject matter for another book. In litigation it is the trial attorney who wisely seeks as much information and assistance from all possible sources (including social scientists with available techniques including community attitudinal surveys, in-depth *voir dire* preparation, focus groups, mock or mini trials, and shadow or mirror juries) who gives his client the state-of-the-art representation, for it is in the cases where systematic jury selections have been utilized that results have been consistently favorable. Perhaps a fitting summary for this section might be the position expressed by trial attorney Aubrey Roberts "Since the life, liberty, or property of a client will rest in the hands of an ordinary human being, the more one can learn about him and how he functions, the better job can be done for the client."[92]

E. *Selected Questions from an Actual* Voir Dire

The author has selected portions of the *voir dire* of criminal defense attorney Richard "Racehorse" Haynes from the solicitation of capital murder trial of Texas multi-millionaire T. Cullen Davis as an illustration of an excellent *voir dire*. Mr. Haynes was assisted in the defense of T. Cullen Davis by Mr. Phil Burleson, Mr. Mike Gibson, and Mr. Steve Sumner of Dallas, Texas. I was associated with the defense team for the jury selection and other psychological, computerized and compilation aspects of the trial.

The following introductory remarks were obtained from Mr. Haynes. It is my understanding that the introductory remarks were taken from the transcript of the *voir dire* of the Davis trial and were spoken to the entire panel of prospective jurors.

> May it please the Court, ladies and gentlemen, as His Honor has told you, my name is Richard Haynes and I am a practicing attorney here in Houston, Texas, representing Mr. Thomas Cullen Davis, who is the citizen accused here today. You are now involved and understand how we go through this business of selecting jurors; the effort, as those of you who are in the sciences can now perceive, is indeed not a very scientific one at all. It really is more a matter of an educated guesswork on the part of the lawyers who are entrusted with the responsibility of endeavoring to select from fifty people, twelve people who are qualified to serve on this jury and from my point of view to sit in judgment on Thomas Cullen Davis.
>
> We have rules that have been handed to us by older lawyers, whether they are accurate or not, I am not certain. We are told to take in things such as occupation and don't take this one because he is too tall, and don't take that one because he is too fat or don't take that one because he has

long hair or short hair or a mustache or no mustache.

When you get right down to it, it is not very scientific. What we are really relegated to and what you as citizens are relegated to because you are part of the system, is total reliance upon your candor in the responses that you make. Absolute total reliance. All of the lawyers, the prosecution and the defense, alike, are members of the system. We are part of the system. We are officers of this court. We are endeavoring, both sides, to ask these questions. We are permitted, by law, to impose upon you and your time and to trespass upon your time with these questions.

As the Court has told you, it is no lawyer's desire to intrude into an area that is private. That is unto you yourself. Here, perhaps, is the last vestige of voluntary service to the community that a citizen can provide, now that they have the abolition of the draft, and you have answered the summons to be here and give us your time and be away from your work and your families and to participate in the system.

Without you it does not work and the lawyers on both sides recognize that we trespass on your time, but I can assure you, as you must certainly know, it is so vital and so important that we get twelve citizens who are qualified to serve on this jury. It may be that a citizen is qualified in every way to serve either in any other kind of case or any case, but for some reason known to that person, they are not qualified to serve on this jury and I am confident that each of you will agree with me that we will have no system at all—we would have no jury system if the citizens who came up to serve on this jury had some preconceived notion that dictated a little bit to that citizen, the end result that is sought by this system.

If we have any citizen at all serving on this jury that has some preconceived notion, some bias, however slight it may be, that would keep them from being totally fair and impartial, then I am sure you will agree with me that we'd need to know about it.

Now, likewise, there is no lawyer in the system on either side of this docket who would not champion your right to have an opinion or the right to have an opinion of anything that you wanted to. As citizens you are entitled to an opinion about anything. Likewise, if you have an opinion about any aspect of this lawsuit, then the litigants on both sides are entitled to know something about that opinion.

Now, let me say this to you right at the very beginning. There is no right or wrong answer to these questions asked of you. The only requirement is as much candor as you can muster, and there is another step because as Judge Moore told you earlier, no citizen forgoes the right to privacy and you and each of you will not be required to answer any question if you think even for an instant that I am infringing upon your right to privacy and if I decided to ask you a question and I can assure it will not be in an effort to pry into some area of your life, that ought to be private to you, but if I ask you a question and you feel that that question impinges upon your right of privacy, please call it to my attention and we will ask the Court's permission to go before the Court and ask the question again to the Court and the Court will make a decision as to whether you are obliged to answer that question or not or whether I am entitled to ask it or not.

So you are protected in that regard and you do not have to give any answers to any questions that you don't feel right about in your own mind, and that you could give without impinging upon your right to privacy, even to the slightest extent, and I want to assure you of this.

Let me just first, some of the fundamentals that are related to the trial of a criminal case, and that is what this is. Those of you who have before served know these things, and those of you who do know it, I apologize in advance for the repetition, but it is vitally important that we have some understanding right up front about the fundamentals.

His Honor has told you that the burden of proof is upon the prosecution which you know and have known since time one, since we were grade school children. We learned that all persons are presumed innocent until their guilt is established by legal and by competent evidence beyond a reasonable doubt.

And, one of the few times in the course of a trial that I will agree with the prosecution, I do agree that the Court will not charge this jury or instruct this jury on what reasonable doubt means, but will leave it to you and each one of you to decide in your minds, after having heard all of the evidence, what reasonable doubt means. It has been defined as being that doubt which would cause a reasonably prudent person to hesitate—in the conduct of his or her own most important personal business. I like that definition.

Now, because it is not defined and because it's incumbent upon each of you if selected to serve on this jury and from my vantage point it's important if you sit in judgment on Thomas Cullen Davis, it's important, it's vitally important that you and each of those, those of you who are finally selected, start off in neutral with no preconceived notions that would keep you from being totally fair and impartial.

I want you to think, if you will, about how you feel. For example, isn't the prospect of sitting in judgment on another human being where a serious criminal accusation, the sort of four-pronged accusation—first, the prosecution will endeavor to prove solicitation of capital murder. If they do not prove that, alternatively, they will prove attempt—they will endeavor to prove attempted solicitation of capital murder and failing to do that, they will attempt to prove it is a different date and finally, if there is no proof the prosecution will endeavor to demonstrate by proof, to conspiracy to commit the offense, and His Honor has told you that the—even though the prosecution has pled it in the alternative facts and we cause this or we have that and that and then we have four accusations.

But, it is pled in that fact and you would be permitted as jurors to take it with you back into the jury room when you commence your deliberations, the indictment in the lawsuit to read along with the Charge on the law that will be given to you by His Honor.

No juror is expected to remember those observations or comments made by the lawyer or about the law at this juncture because the truth of it is what we say about the law now, while it may be the law and it is the only law that applies to a lawsuit and that is the law that the Judge gives you when you finally go back to the jury deliberation room and you take it back with you and read it. That is the only law that is applied in terms of the law of this State.

I would like to ask you to think about this so that I can talk to you a little bit further when I come to you individually. How you would feel about sitting in judgment on a person in this serious offense—a person of immense wealth and that may seem at first blush facetious, but I can assure you, you examine your thoughts you will recognize and know that many times an intelligent sensitive person or people are feeling things against those of great wealth.

If one has a feeling, however slight it might be against a person of great wealth, one would be entitled to that feeling. You have a right to any feeling that you have. You have a right to feel any way that you want to feel, but if, indeed, you do feel something in your mind and in your heart, however slight, against a person of great wealth and I can tell you that the evidence will determine straight out that Mr. Davis is a person of immense wealth, but if that preempts your ability to be a fair and impartial juror, however slight it may be, then you need to let me know about it and more importantly, you need to let Thomas Cullen Davis know about it, and I will talk to you, with your permission, a little more about it personally when it comes time to talk to you individually.

I would like to ask you to reflect upon this. There are a number of lawyers representing the prosecution and a number of lawyers, three at the table, and Mr. Sumner will be here, I expect, at the end of the week, or the first of next week. The number of lawyers that appear in a litigation should not, in and of itself, be a fact that would cause any citizen to have a feeling prejudicial or some preconceived notion against the citizen on trial, and yet, if one reads the papers and from the juror cards that you citizens sent back to us, that information sheet, we know on both sides that you read the newspapers and we know that lawyers for the most part are classed, at least unfortunately are not held in great repute, and may be caught as a consequence of the long and hard venture.

We enhance our problem or maybe it is more difficult for us, but one should not see it as any admission of guilt as far as Thomas Cullen Davis is concerned, because he has three lawyers and will have four, than you should draw a similar finding that the prosecution has four lawyers representing the prosecution.

Likewise, as you know, in the course of a trial lawyers on either side will make whatever objections they deem are proper. You have seen some brief examples of this during this period of time and we have been discussing your prospect as jurors as to your serving on this jury, to sit in judgment of Thomas Cullen Davis.

When a lawyer makes an objection that they deem proper on both sides, His Honor will make a ruling. Sometimes the objection of the lawyer has a way of irritating the citizens who serve on juries because objections do interrupt. But, I want to caution you this and question of you this, that you are not permitted any aggravation you have with reference to the lawyer to prevent you from being fair — a totally fair person, and if indeed you have had the experience and have had some aggravation towards lawyers for the objections that they air at the time that they deem proper, you are entitled to feel that way, but please permit the aggravation to extend only to the lawyer, not to the citizen accused.

His Honor has told you that in this litigation there has been an application for probation made. Whether you were told, and this is repetitious, but so vitally important, that the law required those who are eligible to make that eligibility known to the Court and to the prosecution in advance of the trial before the trial commences. Each of you, myself, and all of you who are eligible, and that is because we have never before been convicted in this or any other state of a felony, are eligible to make an application, myself, you, any one of you who are on trial would be eligible to make that known to the jury. You have got to make that application in advance, under oath. You have to swear to this Court, to the clerk of this Court, you have never been convicted of a felony in this state or any other state of the United States.

Now, this puts the prosecution on notice, if indeed one should make such an oath to God that they have never been before convicted of a felony in this or any other state, and the prosecution had evidence to the contrary, that certainly would be demonstrated to the jury because a person who has before been convicted of a felony in this or any other state is not eligible.

Now, what concerns the lawyers, what concerns me and my colleagues representing Thomas Cullen Davis is that because of the paradox of having to make this application in advance and the paradox is one comes into the court and enters a plea of not guilty, and I tell you now that the plea of Thomas Cullen Davis in this case will be not guilty, and we will persist in that plea throughout this trial, but a citizen comes into court and enters a plea of not guilty in response to the questions asked by the Court. "Not guilty, Your Honor." And at any time concerning this filing of this application for probation says in the event that you find me guilty, I ask that you please consider probation; and I would not want, nor should you want, as a member of the system, any citizen who would think that following the law to make that eligibility known is any sort of concession. Nor should you want, nor do we want, any citizen who would say at the conclusion of a trial because, as you know, that is how we have these trials.

The concern by the jury is to determine whether or not the citizen accused is guilty or not guilty. If they find that the State has not met its burden of proof, if they have a reasonable doubt after considering all of the evidence that has been presented and after considering what was not presented, the omission on the part of the prosecutorial teams, anything that is before them properly that is logically inferred, they can draw from what is presented to them, and after considering all of this there remains in the mind of a juror, reasonable doubt, they are obliged by their oaths as jurors and by the law to find this citizen not guilty.

So they simply say not guilty, in which case the trial is over but in the event, in a case where a jury considering all of the evidence is persuaded beyond a reasonable doubt that the citizen on trial is guilty, then they are obliged to decide what punishment is proper under the facts and circumstances. Under the law adult probation, as we call it, which is the application to this court, it is sort of a case and you need to search your minds and hearts so that when I talk to you individually you can tell me how you feel about the law of probation.

Remember this, you have a right as citizens, to disagree with any part of the law. You can do it now. If you have a disagreement with the law, you can simply say: "Lawyer, I disagree with the law," and we can talk about it. And if you have a disagreement on the law, perhaps, it is that you should not serve on this jury; because part of the law that would be involved, even though it is no concession, that the law of probation is involved, we have the right to know how you feel about that the same way as the prosecution has a right and did ask how you felt about the maximum punishment. You need to ask yourselves in your own minds and in your own hearts how you feel about the law so that when I talk to you individually, you can tell me how you feel and what concerns you may have.

I would want, and that is what you should want — no citizen who has ever gone to trial imposed upon him or her a jury who would dodge that first obligation, that first obligation to insist that the prosecution prove to you beyond a reasonable doubt guilt as accused.

I get a recurring nightmare of those who are in the system, and a citizen having heard evidence, of course, you don't hear evidence in criminal cases without there being what could be called some smoke and we have all known that story that "where there's smoke, there's fire", but the law is more sophisticated than that and you don't convict people on smoke. They must prove the allegations.

But, suppose you had — just suppose for a moment, for the purpose of a juror, who, after having heard all of the evidence, still has that reasonable doubt in his mind, but thought, I know this citizen made an application for probation and so, well, I still have a doubt and I know I ought to find this person not guilty but I will go ahead and find him guilty because I would not want a guilty person to be around, but then when it comes time to deliberate on punishment, you would put him on probation.

That would be hedging and the system does not need or want nor should you as a citizen, and you should insist on full compliance with the law.

So, I ask you, yourselves, how you feel about the law of probation in your minds and in your hearts as to what it is and when it comes my turn to talk to you individually, we can talk about that for a moment.

I do not intend to ask you about your political affiliations. That is private to you and the sanctity of the ballot box and I am the champion of the law on both sides, but I would like to ask you individually whether you have been active in politics, other than at the ballot box, or have you participated in grass roots politics or been present or active in campaigns for the candidate of your choice.

I will ask you when I get to you individually about your outside interests and hobbies, and I will ask you individually if you have any prior union affiliations and if so, whether or not you have been active in the union and you are entitled, if you think that my questions are transcending out of the bounds of propriety in that area, to call it to my attention so that we can petition the Court.

The juror's function, those of you who have served would know this, is to be the judges of the facts presented. You get all the law from the Court but, as jurors, those of you who are ultimately selected to serve on this jury, to sit in judgment of Thomas Cullen Davis, will be the exclusive judges of the facts, the credibility of the witnesses, and the weight to be given their testimony and essentially what that means is this: As a juror you know, those of you who served, have a right to believe all of what a witness says or part of what a witness says or none of what a witness says. That is your prerogative and your obligation as jurors.

You judge the credibility of the witnesses and curiously enough, for the most part, the law does not give to jurors criteria by which they may judge credibility of a particular witness in a case.

The law gives no special credibility to any particular witness. No one gets special credibility at time one. The theory is, I am confident you will all agree, I want you to think about it, because some people disagree. Witnesses are under oath and the mere fact that a witness is a police officer or a deputy sheriff or an FBI agent, a law enforcement agent of any kind, does not give that witness special credibility at time one.

But there are those, and I know people who feel this way, and I'm confident either some here do or may know people who are intelligent, sensitive people, literate people, concerned people, and they feel in their own minds and hearts that a police officer or an FBI agent ought to be entitled to special credibility because of their jobs and their profession of law enforcement and they honestly feel that way.

Well, if you honestly feel that way about it, you are entitled to it. You are entitled to the way you feel. What I would like to know, what the system requires and what Cullen Davis desperately needs as a citizen and is entitled to, are citizens who will tell us that candidly, if you feel in any way, however slight it may be, that a police officer is to be believed, his testimony is to be believed before the testimony of some other citizen, simply because he is a police officer and for no other reason, if you really feel that way, I want to know about that and please tell me when I talk to you individually. There are those who feel that way.

But no witness is entitled under the law to special credibility simply because of their position in life. The fact they wear a uniform or are in law enforcement, or any other, such as lawyers, judges, nobody gets special credibility under the law.

You judge credibility of each witness exactly like you do every other witness. Of course, you could take into consideration all of the factors that are permitted by the Court's rulings to be demonstrated for you.

There is another factor with reference to this case that I think important to talk to you about now. I know it directly affects several of the citizens who are here assembled on a commission basis. I cannot represent to you as a lawyer representing—one of the lawyers representing Thomas Cullen Davis how long the lawsuit will last. Because the truth of it is the lawyers don't know. Lawyers for both sides, the prosecution and the defense, have represented to the Court, who was interested because of the scheduling problems and so forth and in obtaining this courtroom in how long this case would last, and the suggestions from both sides were to the effect that four weeks, five weeks, something in that area and that's not a guarantee, that any lawyer on either side can give you. Those were the representations made on both sides.

Now, the reason I say that to you is this: If in fact a perfectly qualified citizen, qualified to serve not only on other jury cases but on this jury case, is in a situation where a protracted trial works a financial hardship, and it will if you are on commission or if your source of income is curtailed to a being—by your being at this courthouse from nine to five, if it works a financial hardship, we all regret that part. Here is the key and here is what I want you to think about and only you know if it is indeed a personal concern, because we are all concerned about our families and our obligations and our jobs and so forth, if a personal concern about the deprivation that occurs, financial deprivation, such that it would be keeping you from being the same sort of fair and impartial judge you would want to be, you have only one opportunity to talk about it and that is now. The lawyers on either side as you have already seen demonstrated and will take into consideration those things and present the same to the Court and the ultimate ruling will be from the Court because everybody knows that jury service does work hardships on all persons who serve.

But, if it were to keep you, the preoccupation concern about the deprivation would keep you from being the same fair and impartial juror you would otherwise be, then it would be time now, now is the time to talk about it. Again, I am not representing to you the case will last that long. It may last less or it could conceivably go longer. I don't know. You think about it and let the lawyers now know and more importantly, you let the Court know.

Now, as you know, those of you who have before served, perhaps all of you know, that in a lawsuit, the prosecution, because it has the burden of proof, goes first, pretty much the same as they were permitted to first inquire of the prospective jurors, they likewise, are permitted first to put on evidence because they have the burden of proof. They get to make the last argument because they, the prosecution, have the burden of proof. What we ask those conscientious people who are ultimately selected to sit in judgment on Thomas Cullen Davis, that you not finalize in your conclusions until such time as or in your opinion until such time as you have heard all of the case and all of the evidence and it is submitted to you by the Court.

Now, everyone realizes that as we go along people tend to form opinions about things as the prosecution mentioned to you yesterday. You are obliged as you sit as jurors to listen to fellow jurors. You are obliged as jurors to exchange ideas and concepts with fellow jurors, but the ultimate obligation on the part of the jurors, is to vote his or her own personal

> conscience as to the jury function and that must be unanimous, but it requires individual judgment of each person who serves on the jury, taking into consideration what everyone else has to say, and the jury experience as those of you who have before served know that it is a unique experience.
>
> You come to this courtroom, strangers to each other. Those of you who are selected to serve on this jury will be instructed by the Court that at the time you are not actually in the courtroom together as a group, you are not to discuss the case even with each other. You don't deliberate on the case until such time as you have heard all of the case; you have been given all of the law that applies; and you go back in the jury room and what that does is that it permits the jurors, because we can't talk about the case, to talk to each other and you are traditionally learning something about the backgrounds of some of the jurors and their homes and their ideas and their dreams and their trips and their children and all of those things that human beings talk about as jurors because they can't talk about the case.
>
> As a consequence, jurors traditionally find that of twelve people selected, they're a cross-section community. They will find members of the jury for whom they have the greatest respect possible in selecting character and integrity and personal habits and traits and fast friendships live long. Friendships can be accomplished in the course of jury duty.
>
> When you get down to voting as jurors, despite the fact that you have formed a friendship with some juror; despite the fact that you have fellow jurors, you have great confidence in the integrity and intellect of a fellow juror; you must vote your own conscience, how you personally feel after a fair consideration of all the evidence.
>
> As to a fair consideration of what fellow jurors have to say, it is the personal obligation of each juror to vote his or her own conviction. I am sure all of you know that.

The individual questioning of the prospective jurors was lengthy and exhaustive. It took approximately six weeks to select twelve jurors to sit in judgment of Mr. T. Cullen Davis.

The author has chosen several relevant topics to illustrate an effective *voir dire*. Mr. Haynes asked the following representative *voir dire* questions individually.

1. *Establish Tone*

The trial attorney should establish a warm conversational atmosphere before questioning the prospective juror about critical issues. The attorney should let the juror respond.

Q. All right. I take it that the—the—that you have over the years supported your husband in his chosen profession, that is, of firefighting and now arson investigation. That is, you have not encouraged him to get back with General Dynamics or Bell or some other form of activity?

Q. And I gather that you take some personal pride in the fact he is happy in his work and that he—and the type of work that he does, that is, as a civic function in serving the community?

Q. All right. And that understandably would cause you to have some, likewise, pride and general good feeling about other people similarly situated, that is, other men who serve the community either as police officers or firefighters in activities of that sort; is that true?

Q. Which leads me to this, (name): You have a—I expect in this particular litigation that we will have the testimony of a number of Fort Worth City Police. They will testify—I would suspect they will be called to testify by the Prosecution. You have a profound regard for the profession of law enforcement, do you not? I mean, you think of it highly?

Q. Well, that's what I was getting to. If a police officer, for example, or some perosn wearing the uniform of a police officer testified to a specific thing, like, "The light was green," then a non-police officer, that is, just a citizen, testified that, "The light was red," do you have any feeling that because of your regard for those who serve the community in law enforcement capacities, that you might be inclined to believe the police officer more than you would the citizen simply because he is a police officer and for no other reason?

Q. Court says you can answer that, (name)—you see what I'm getting at? Because of a regard for people who engage in the service to the community, that is, in law enforcement, that you have some feeling that you would give greater credibility to the testimony of a police officer than you would to someone who is not a police officer just because he was a police officer and for no other reason.

Q. Would you do that in any way? You can see my concern as a—as a lawyer since you are married to a—an arson investigator and I am representing the citizen who's on trial . . . .

Q. For an example, if you were the wife of a lawyer who represented citizens who were accused of crimes, the Prosecution would understandably and legitimately be concerned perhaps you might tend in such a role to identify more with—with the Defense than you would with the Prosecution. Does that not . . . .

Q. Well, I understand that, but the question is whether there might be some natural tendency to just think in terms of leaning towards, just a slight leaning toward the Prosecution simply because your own husband is engaged in a form of law enforcement?

Q. You could sit on a criminal case and—and find the citizen who is accused not guilty and it would not be uncomfortable for you when you came home and discussed the events with your husband who is in law enforcement —

Q. See what I am getting at, (name)? I'm not talking about this case, but in a criminal case where you served as a juror and you found that the accused citizen was not guilty, the question is would it be uncomfortable for you when you went home to discuss the event, which would be legitimate. There's no prohibition against wives talking to their husbands and that's understandable and natural. Would it be uncomfortable for you when you went home to say, "I sat on a jury in a criminal case and after hearing the evidence I found the Defendant not guilty"? Would it create any lack of harmony there in your own home at all?

Q. And—and this is—you're the only one that can answer this question: In the event you were selected to serve on a criminal jury, sit in judgment on a citizen accused of a criminal offense, because your husband is—let's make it in the area of—of murder, a murder case. Because your husband is in law enforcement, do you have any feeling at all, however slight, that you might have any leaning toward the Prosecution simply because your own life is, in effect, involved with law enforcement? You see what I am saying?

Q. Wouldn't bother you in the slightest?

Q. You could be just as fair as you would—could if your husband was involved in the defense of citizens who are accused of crime?

Q. What is your personal feeling, (name), about lawyers who represent citizens accused of crime? How do you feel about that?

Q. Yes. What is your feeling about lawyers who represent citizens or who are accused of crime, lawyers who practice criminal law, represent people who are accused of a crime?

Q. All right. Don't have any special feeling that perhaps there is anything distasteful about the role chosen by a lawyer who does in fact elect to represent citizens accused of crime?

Q. Okay. Have you heard of any of the lawyers representing the Prosecution?

Q. Has anything you have heard about them in any way create any feeling in your mind or your heart that would cause you to tend to lean toward the Prosecution?

Q. Have you heard anything about the lawyers representing the citizen on trial, Thomas Cullen Davis?

* * *

Q. All right.

I will ask you a few questions. They are not designed to invade privacy. If you think for a moment that they do, just let me know and we will take them up with the Court.

Q. Fair?

Likewise, if any question I ask of you is less than artful—it's ambiguous, vague—just let me know and I will rephrase it—

Q. —so that at the conclusion of our interview we can know with certainty that the question was understood and that the response given by you was the response you want to make—as your accurate, careful response.

Have you ever been active in—in the Union there at your place of employment, sir?

Q. May I ask, please, (name), your age?

Q. And where did you obtain your education, sir, and to what extent?

Q. And have you had any academic training after that time—in any institution or anything?

Q. The—where you work at—the General Motors in Arlington, have they had at any time any seminars or workshops or programs designed to permit the employees to know more about what they are doing and how they are doing it and so forth?

Q. And, (name), where is she from initially, please, sir?

Q. And were ya'll married before you came to the—what you designate as the HEB area?

Q. And did she likewise attend school there in Arkansas?

Q. Are you active in your church other than by attendance? By that I mean do you hold office or teach?

Q. And have you held any other office in your church other than the office—that office?

Q. At some prior church you had perhaps you held some other office?

Q. What other office did you hold?

Q. Was that here in the Fort Worth—

Q. —Tarrant County area? Alright.

And does (name) at this time hold any office in the church or is she active other than by attendance?

Q. Children's church?

Q. (Name), do you know if your church has announced any position on the issue of capital punishment, either as a church being in favor of it or as a church being against it?

Q. Yesterday I think Counsel for the Prosecution indicated something to you about Mr. Cullen Davis's wealth and said something to the effect that he's a millionaire or something like that, and I'll just tell you right out front that I—that I am confident that the evidence will show that he is—that he is indeed a man of great wealth and I'm sure you would agree with me that that fact in and of itself should not create any atmosphere or attitude that would deprive one of—of a fair trial?

Q. Do you agree?

And you indicated that that fact in and of itself was not a factor that would tend to influence you in your thinking, just in and of itself influence you in your thinking, to the point where you couldn't render fair and impartial consideration of the rest of the evidence?

Q. Right? All right.

And is that—likewise would be true, I take it, if the evidence shows it's immense wealth, it's incredible, almost rude and vulgar, so wealthy. You see what I'm saying?

Q. Would—that fact in and of itself should not close the mind, stampede the judgment in any way, but I can conceive of a situation in the minds of some people where it might and in that same theme, does it offend you to the slightest or create any feeling in your mind or your heart against Thomas Cullen Davis that he has several lawyers seated here at the table?

Q. Including, I think—I don't think he was here yesterday—Senator Bill Meier, a State—a State Senator, but that fact in and of itself would not tend to create any feeling in your mind as against Mr. Davis, would it, sir?

Q. Okay. If he had 30 lawyers or 50 lawyers or however many?

Q. All right.

Now, if it developed during the course of the trial, (name), that Thomas Cullen Davis, citizen on trial, was in the process of divorce—well, I'll just tell you now that I'm—the facts will show that as between a woman by the name of Priscilla Davis and a—this many, Thomas Cullen Davis, a divorce was in process. Suit had been filed for divorce.

Some people have such a strong feeling about divorce—and they are entitled to feel that way if they want—that the mere fact of divorce in and of itself is enough to close the mind, stampede the judgment.

Do you have any such feeling about the institution of divorce that would keep you from being fair and impartial in this case?

Q. Do you have any feeling about the private ownership of handguns?

Q. Not offended by private ownership of handguns by—by citizens?

Q. Okay. Would you create or pass a law if you could outlawing private ownership of handguns?

Q. Do you know any other citizens who are prospective jurors in this particular case?

Q. We have a (name), who's already been—(name) who's already been accepted, and (name) who's already been accepted, and a (name) who's already been accepted.

Q. And the people behind you, who are out there in the jury room or the witness room now waiting to be called to go through this—this situation, do you know any of those people other than casually since you have been here in attendance on the Court?

Q. Okay. Have you ever before served as a member of any Grand Jury Commission?

Q. Have you ever before served as a member of any Grand Jury?

Q. Have you ever before made application to be a member of any law enforcement agency?

Q. It—let me say this to you, (name): That the—that under the law, the taking—intentional taking of the life of another by a person is murder—capital murder under these specific circumstances—without regard—without without regard to the age of the deceased. It is just as against the law and just as much murder to take the life of a week old child as it is to take the life of an 85-year-old lawyer or Judge or some other citizen. Age under the law is not recognized in that way. In other words, the law doesn't say if a person deceased is under 15, it's this kind of offense. If it's over 15 and before 30, it's this kind, and so forth. Murder is murder, and yet it is a factor. Age of the deceased is a factor. Would be—it would be hard for it not to be a factor for juries' consideration; correct?

Q. You know, if you had a person of very old age as against a robust assailant, who in fact you believed beyond a reasonable doubt took the life of that older person, that would be a factor. Couldn't avoid that, and on the other end of the spectrum if the age of the deceased is tender, tender age—12 years old—that's a factor, but the question is while I'm not saying to any prospective juror, "Ignore that," because you can't ignore that. You are not supposed to ignore that. Would that fact in and of itself, just the tender age of a deceased, in and of itself without consideration for any other factor be—be such a factor that it would cause you to close your mind to a fair and impartial consideration of all the rest of the evidence?

Q. Okay. Can you see why I would ask the question?

Q. You have—you have children of tender ages. It would be difficult for a juror with children of tender ages not to, to some extent in a particular case, relate to or identify with the tender age of a deceased in a murder case, at least for awhile—

In the case I—I expect to—to—that the Prosecution will have testimony from people who are members of the Fort Worth Police Department, maybe even Fort Worth Sheriff's Department. I'm not sure, but at least from the Police Department. Police officers. Law enforcement officers in some capacity.

Under the law a man's or person's job occupation, title, does not entitle that person to greater credibility just because of the job, and yet there are some people who think if it is a police officer, that automatically they are entitled to greater credibility.

Now, if that's the way they feel, fine. They are entitled to feel that way, but what I'm entitled to know about it, more importantly, Thomas Cullen Davis would be entitled to know about it: Do you have any feeling that the testimony of a police officer ought to be given greater credibility than the testimony of one who is not a police officer, just because Witness "1" is a police officer and for no other reason?

Q. The mere fact we—or in any trial, and the District Attorney himself, Mr. Curry, is appearing in the litigation as one of the Counsel for the Prosecution, and he is an elected official, elected by the people of this County to this office, but would that fact in and of itself have any tendency to cause you to give greater credibility to Prosecutorial theories than you would if he were not participating in the trial?

Q. All right.

Is there—is there a—you have seen—been in here now for some considerable period of time undergoing this examination and you know essentially what it is we are trying to do. Both sides. Both sides are endeavoring to determine, as best we can, what sort of person you are, and what sort of person you will be. We are not entitled to anything more than a fair juror with an open mind; correct?

Q. Can you think of anything that perhaps you haven't been asked about by either side, but anything that would bear upon your qualifications to serve as a juror that we ought to know about? That either side ought to know about?

Q. Some folks take a position that they judge books by the cover, and I suppose to some extent we all do. We make judgments on the basis of how people look and how people act. They may only be temporary impressions. They may only be impressions that do not influence us in making serious judgments, but nonetheless we tend to do that. Some people form impressions by looking at a face or a body that they are unable to overcome, that interferes with their ability to impartially consider everything else after that impression is formed. You may see a face that reminds you of an uncle you didn't like or bill collector or teacher or coach or—or you may see a face that reminds you of someone you did like, may create favorable impressions.

In this particular case—Mr. Davis, would you mind, sir, standing up just a moment?

Q. Is there anything about the way that Thomas Cullen Davis—thank you, sir.

Q. —that—that—anything about his looks that in any way creates any bi—and prejudice isn't a good word. It is a word. It's meaningful.

Any bias, any prejudice, any leaning one way or another, or at least any leaning against Thomas Cullen Davis as a consequence of the way he looks?

Q. Is there—is there anything that you have heard about these whole proceedings or this litigation, Thomas Cullen Davis, any of the people involved, anything you've heard from whatever source that in any way creates in your mind or your heart right now any—any feeling against the man who's on trial?

Q. Which were legitimately made, I think. We may, any of us during the course of the trial, demonstrate by our conduct that the first impression was to some extent in error, perhaps, but would—in that event, were that to happen, that certainly would not preclude you from fairly sitting in judgment on Thomas Cullen Davis? That's what's important.

Q. Okay. Is there anything now that I have asked of you that has in any way offended you or you deem to be abrasive or anything of that sort?

Q. Is there any answer that you have given to any question asked of you by either side that you would like to add to or to qualify or elaborate on or discuss to any extent?

Q. I think, then, that is all the questions I have of you at this time, (name). Thank you, sir.

2. *Determine Media Exposure*

In a publicized case the trial attorney must determine what preconceived notions, if any, the prospective juror may possess because of exposure to the media. It has been my experience that during a lengthy trial a prospective juror often recalls a fact (which was read in the newspaper and never presented in court) from the media but incorrectly attributes such testimony to a witness.

Q. Now you indicated that since the time you have received the notice that folks have brought it up, talking about this lawsuit, I guess; right?

Q. The Cullen Davis trial—ma'am?

Q. Okay. And that you listened and let them express themselves?

Q. All right. Now, these people who would bring it up, that would be just adult people in casual conversations to you once they knew you had received a summons to be a juror?

Q. These would be people you see, where, please, ma'am?

Q. Okay. That would be there when you would be as a—as a client or customer in the beauty shop?

Q. And did the ladies in attendance there in the beauty shop have any conversation about this particular lawsuit, about the Cullen Davis trial in your presence?

Q. In any way. Just tell me generally what it is that was said and how it was said in your presence. You may say exactly.

Q. This was in the beauty shop?

Q. All right. The person who said he's guilty, was that a person that you knew or stranger to you?

Q. All right. And the person who said he was innocent, was that a person that you knew or a stranger to you?

Q. And those people who mentioned that to you, were they friends or casual acquaintances or how would you describe how it is you knew them?

Q. Business associates of yours or—

Q. Of the shop? All right.

Now, in—in addition to the beauty shop where—where people have expressed their ideas about it and opinions about it, have other people at other times in casual conversations expressed their ideas about it one way or the other?

Q. All right. And—and where would that be, for example?

Q. They were guests in your home?

Q. And they are from somewhere in Texas or outside Texas?

Q. Kinfolks or just friends?

Q. Well, what was the nature of the relationship? Brother-in-law? Cousins? Uncles? What?

Q. (Name), in addition to—of the folks at the beauty shop and in the one conversation you had with kinfolks, have you heard any other adult people discussing their impressions about the case or discussing the case, period?

Q. Has (name) ever in any way discussed the case, that is, verbalized his feelings about the case or his opinions from having read the papers or from any other, on any other basis?

Q. You came out and asked him what he thought?

Q. And he—he just told you, "I couldn't give an opinion"?

Q. That's all that he has said about the Cullen Davis case?

Q. Ma'am? That is?

Q. Okay. And, now, was there anybody else at any time, either since, before you received your summons, or after you received your summons at any time up to this point in your life who have before expressed or talked about the Cullen Davis case?

Q. All right. Have you since you have been in attendance upon the court several times coming here to be a prospective juror, heard anybody in the halls or in the jury rooms commenting about the case and expressing an opinion in any way?

Q. All right. Have you, (name), at any point in your life, up to this very moment in your life, ever expressed an opinion about the guilt or innocence of Cullen Davis?

Q. Have you ever at any point in your life, up to this very moment in your life, ever verbalized, talked about your impression of this case?

Q. Is that a question that makes sense?

Q. Well, I didn't want to get—you may be right, and I didn't want to get locked in on the word "opinion." I had said in the other question have you ever before in your life given anybody your opinion?

Q. All right. And so because we might be—the word "opinion" might mean something different to you than it does to me, I ask you then, the next question: Have you ever given a, verbalized—spoken, given an expression of how you thought about the case, in any capacity, to anyone, up to this point in your life?

Q. All right. Thinking back, now, (name), to some of the publicity that has attended the incident made the basis of this lawsuit, were you—were you and your husband in town in August of 1976?

Q. All right. And did you, in August of 1976, subscribe to the *Fort Worth Star-Telegram*?

Q. And also to the—the other newspaper, the *Mid-Cities Newspaper* in August of 1976?

Q. Do you recall and I think you did, but I think you said you read about it when it first occurred?

Q. All right.

That would be, then, somewhere in August of '76; correct?

Q. All right.

And in reading about it, did you determine from reading about it where the incident was supposed to have occurred?

Q. All right.

And you had up to that point in time never seen the mansion on Hulen Street, I take it?

Q. All right.

After it was publicized in August of 1976, did you have a change—did you after that time ever see the mansion on Hulen?

Q. Nobody has ever pointed it out to you?

Q. All right.

Do you know anybody who claims to know any of the people involved?

Q. Do you know anybody who says they are either friends or acquainted or related in any fashion to any of the witnesses whose names have been listed on the juror information sheet?

Q. As a consequence of reading about it back in August of 1976, did you learn how many people were supposed to have been involved in the particular episode? I mean, what is your recollection about that?

Q. And can you recall any of the names of any of the people who are allegedly involved in the episode that appeared in the article that you had an opportunity to look at back in August of 1976?

Q. Do you recall what the—what Priscilla was related to? That was a first name, obviously, was it not?

Q. What does your recollection permit you to tell us now as to how that fits into the litigation? What do you recall about what was said about Priscilla?

Q. Yes, ma'am?

Q. Running—

Q. All right. What else do you recall?

Q. Just if you would, (name), just tell me just briefly what it is you recall now, not only from having read about it in August, but from having read headlines or seen things on TV or radio since that time in August, up to this very point in your life, what it is you recall as to what the media says, what the press says, what the TV says, and what the radio says. Tell me what you—is that a lot?

Q. Do you remember what connection his—that person figured in the story?

Q. Do you recall anything from having read about it or seen it on TV or radio as to what Priscilla claimed according to the media? As to what she claimed on the evening in question or early morning hour in question?

Q. Whose name, please?

Q. All right.

Q. Now, I gather you haven't had—you haven't read anything about the case since you were called up here initially by the Court in February on the 22nd, I think it was. Am I right?

Q. You don't believe you've read anything about it since then?

Q. All right. Did you in reading those articles in order to keep up with where you might be so you could sort of schedule yourself, read any of the articles that related to selection of the—the jury selection process?

Q. Don't you recall reading anything about any of the reasons why any jurors might not have been accepted or anything about those who have been accepted?

Q. All right. And do you—did you as a consequence of reading about it in the paper conclude that at least the newspaper version, the *Fort Worth Star Telegram* version of the facts, tended to indicate that Cullen Davis was guilty or not?

Q. You didn't get that impression —

Q. — from reading the *Fort Worth Star Telegram*?

Q. Did anyone ever from August of '76 to this point in your life state in your presence that "According to the papers, he must be guilty," or, "He probably is guilty," or, "I think he's guilty," other than those people you have told us about?

Q. And that was not your impression from reading the paper in any way?

Q. All right. Did what you read and what you heard on the radio and saw on the TV, did that create any impression in your mind, however slight, about the guilt or innocence of Cullen Davis?

Q. Do you have any feeling that the—at all that the newspapers are essentially accurate, 80% accurate, 50% accurate, or any feeling at all about the veracity of those things that appear in newspapers —

Q. I guess the question is: Do you take with a grain of salt what you read or do you believe it verbatim when you read it and again you are entitled to any opinion you want on it.

Q. Okay. Well, that's fair enough. I'm going to have to borrow that from you to ask the prospective juror about. I like that.

Let me ask you about—I'm going to get off this subject now in just a second. It's so vital that I be sure about it, (name). It's so important that no person get on the jury and sit in judgment on—I'm talking about right now—on Cullen Davis, if they have as a consequence of what has been publicized, formed any sort of a—an opinion or have any sort of a feeling, however slight, that's against the man on trial. Do you agree that it's important we not have a jury if they start off with a feeling against him?

* * *

Q. All right.

Do you know, (name), as a consequence of anything you have read, seen on the TV, or heard on the radio or heard discussed in your presence from any source, have any feeling in your heart or your mind now against Cullen Davis?

Q. All right.

Not even the slightest? You recognize that he's by law presumed innocent, do you not?

Q. Confining this inquiry to just what you have read in the newspapers, seen on the TV, heard on the radio, and heard other people discuss in front of you, what other people have said, do you have any feelings at all now, however slight, that Cullen Davis is probably guilty or might be guilty?

Q. Okay. I realize you don't have an opinion. Do you have any feeling in your heart that he's probably guilty? Just a feeling?

Q. Well, it's—a feeling is a matter of just what's in your heart right now as a consequence of just those things I mentioned—TV and radio and what other people have said. A feeling, however slight. Might be just the slightest feeling, but if it's to the effect that he's guilty or he's probably guilty, then I would need to know, wouldn't I?

Q. All right.

And more especially, because that's what your belief is, does that same belief apply now with the same force and effect, as it is your philosophy, to Thomas Cullen Davis, you feel and believe that way now about the man who's on trial that he is innocent until proven guilty?

Q. Okay. You indicated that you had read something about the case when it appeared in the newspapers back in August. I believe I think you indicated exactly that you had read some article back in August?

Q. All right.

And that you do not subscribe to the *Fort Worth Star Telegram*?

Q. Or any newspaper?

Q. All right.

Do you get the Sunday paper?

Q. Okay. Was there anything contained in any of the Sunday issues of the *Fort Worth Star Telegram* that—that you specifically recall that related to either Cullen Davis or this—or this case or the facts that are made the basis of this case?

Q. All right.

Do you get any other Sunday paper other than the *Fort Worth Star Telegram*? The Dallas papers, for example?

Q. Okay. The *Shopper*, now, is a—is that a—a paper that's delivered to the home that contains information about shopping. Does that make sense?

Q. Does it have news in it?

Q. All right.

Has there been anything in the *Observer* about Cullen Davis or this case or the facts allegedly made the basis of this case that has caught your attention that you now remember in any way?

Q. All right.

Did anything your wife said, with reference to what she had read, create any feeling or impression in your mind or heart that would cause you to be less than totally fair and impartial to Cullen Davis?

Q. All right.

With references to matters that may have occurred, may have been disseminated by radio, was there any radio broadcast since August that you specifically recall relating to Cullen Davis or to the facts allegedly made the basis of this case?

Q. Is there a—has there been anything on the TV relative to relating to Cullen Davis or to the facts allegedly made the basis of this case or the incidents, anything about this case or Cullen Davis or any of the people allegedly involved, that you specifically recall?

Q. Did anything that you have heard about that part of it create any special feeling one way which would—well, I want to know one way. Any special feeling in your mind or your heart against Cullen Davis?

Q. Okay. It is not, certainly not against the law, nor would it be less than normal, to form opinions or impressions. We all do that. We form impressions about things we hear, read, and see. You perhaps are forming an impression right now about me or about anybody at that table or about this process. Just naturally it happens in the process of thinking. Nothing wrong with it.

If a person, however, has an impression or an opinion to the extent that that opinion would influence or has the probability of influencing judgment or judgment calls on evidence, then I need to know about it.

Has there been anything you have read, heard on the TV or radio that has created any impression or opinion, however slight, in your mind or your heart about this case?

Q. Okay. Have you had any discussions, casual discussions, coffee discussions, other than ones you mentioned yesterday where—you articulated an opinion about the guilt or innocence of Cullen Davis?

Q. Has anything that has been said casually by other adults, co-workers, family, friends, fellow jurors in any way created any special feeling in your mind or your heart or an opinion or an impression that would be adverse to Cullen Davis?

Q. Do you agree with me that would be unfair to start off a trial with any kind of special feeling against the person on trial in your heart?

3. *Determine Opinion of Defense Attorneys and Objections*

In conducting focus groups regarding respondents' attitudes about lawyers who defend citizens accused of crimes, the author has discovered that the majority of respondents attribute negative characteristics to defense attorneys. Interestingly, similar negative characteristics are attributed to plaintiff's attorneys.

Q. Okay. Now when you—because the jury has the—has the power and that obligation to be the judges of the facts, I tell you this: That I—that I—and I submit to you that my conceived—it is part of my obligation and the obligation of my colleagues in representing Cullen Davis as it will be the Prosecutors' to cross-examine witnesses—they will cross-examine witnesses. We will cross-examine witnesses. It may be that lawyers for either side out of zeal for their cause or because they believe it to be the best vehicle to illuminate the testimony, will be aggressive in cross-examination. I, perhaps; my colleagues, perhaps, will be aggressive in cross-examination.

That brings me to this: The—the tactical considerations of the lawyers because they make the decision as to how the best to illuminate, how best to get at the truth, should not be a thing that would turn the jury off as against a person on trial, correct?

Q. If I make a total fool of myself in some conduct that I have, that I perform, that I do some act or omission, you can score me saying total fool, but to permit feeling about the lawyer to interfere with your fair and impartial consideration of the person on trial would be unfair.

Q. Be kind of like striking at the man on trial over the shoulder of his lawyer.

Q. And you, if selected as a juror, tell me, and more importantly, tell Cullen Davis, that you would not permit that to happen to you. You would go by the evidence in this case?

Q. The—during the course of a trial as you have already experienced even during this session, lawyers on both sides will make objections. The objections made at a time because the lawyers are of the opinion that it's appropriate and—and again like—like anything else the lawyer does, should be understood for what it is and not to be held against the person on trial.

For example, if I seem contentious and make objections, you would understand, would you not, that I'm doing so out of regard for my obligation as Counsel. I think it's appropriate.

The Judge rules. That's what Judges are for. He either rules it's well taken or it's not, but you would understand when it is done that it's simply an obligation of the lawyers and would not hold it against the citizen on trial? In this case, Thomas Cullen Davis?

4. *Determine Attitude on Capital Punishment*

The author recommends that the attorney inquire about a prospective juror's position on capital punishment in any type of litigation. My research has consistently revealed that those individuals who favor capital punishment will more likely convict in any type of criminal accusation. In civil litigation, the stronger a person believes in the death penalty, the smaller amount of damages he or she will award.

Q. You indicate, (name), that you have no conscientious scruples against the imposition of death as a punishment for crime in a proper case.

Q. All right. Is that a—a view that you have long held or one that you have only recently subscribed to?

Q. All right. Well, was there any single act or episode or event which occurred that caused you to focus on the issue more sharply and decide that you were not conscientiously opposed to capital punishment?

Q. Nothing happened in history or nothing happened in connection with your own life that made you look at the question more closely and decide how you felt about it?

Q. All right. Nothing occurred, then, in history—you know, something that happened in history or in connection with your own life that caused you to focus more sharply on the issue to decide how you felt about it?

Q. All right. Is your feeling on the subject of the death penalty as a—based on religious tenets or being married to a person in law enforcement or combination or none of the above? Can you tell me the basis just generally and briefly for your belief in capital punishment?

Q. All right. Is your feeling that the Bible teaches that killing, taking the life of a person in the name of the State, is acceptable where the law permits it?

Q. All right. Is it predicated in any part on any feeling that sort of an eye for an eye or tooth for a tooth concept or sort of a revenge concept?

Q. You say not necessarily. Does that indicate that some slight extent, that maybe that aspect of it, might be appropriate?

Q. Is it—do you have a feeling that capital punishment is a deterrent to crime?

Q. All right. So that then might be a part of the basis why you personally feel that capital punishment is appropriate? That is, that it is a deterrent to crime and it would perhaps keep others from engaging in criminal conduct?

* * *

Q. You indicated yesterday, (name), that you have no conscientious scruples against the imposition of death as a punishment for crime in a proper case where the facts and circumstances justify it—

Q. Correct? All right. Is that a—a philosophical concept that you have adhered to for a long period of time or one that you have focused upon fairly recently in your adult life and—just how long have you held to the concept that it is an appropriate part of the sentencing option?

Q. Was there any single act or episode or event, either that touched your personal life or a family member or relative or friend or some act, episode, or event in history, that caused you to focus more sharply on the issue and decide as an adult how you felt about the issue?

Q. All right. Well, most adults—it is a contemporary question that thinking people come to grips with from time to time to just determine in their own mind how they feel about it and the citizens of the country are apparently in three camps. A—a—a philosophy that is in favor of capital punishment, a philosophy that's just diametrically opposed to it, and then those who are not decided. They really don't know whether they are or they are not in favor of it, and can you recall any period in your—in your adult life when you were in either of the other two camps? That is, either undecided or definitely against the imposition of death as a punishment for crime?

Q. I'm not talking—okay. I'm just talking about maybe a period in your life where you were not as fixed in your philosophical belief as you are now.

Q. When you were a younger person?

Q. Just starting your life as a—

Q. Sure. All right. Now, is your—this question sounds ludicrous, but it is not. Do you have any such fixed opinion about the propriety of capital punishment that you would automatically vote to impose that punishment for—upon one convicted of the offense of murder—that is, the intentional taking of another—another person's life without regard to the rest of the—the—without regard to the facts and evidence in a case?

Q. Okay. In other words—and the Prosecutor asked you yesterday how you felt about the wide range of punishment.

In capital cases there are—if a jury believes beyond a reasonable doubt that one is—is guilty of the offense of capital murder, then there are only two punishments available. Either the supreme punishment, that is, death by electrocution, or life in the penitentiary, and the way that's resolved as was explained yesterday to you is that the jury answers those questions. First question was, "Was the taking of the life deliberate and intentional," essentially. If the answer to the question is yes, then the next question is, "Do you think there's a probability that the person is likely to continue to commit acts of violence that constitute a threat to society?" If that answer is yes, then the Court has no alternative except to impose the supreme punishment. If the answer to either one of those questions is no, then it's automatic life, so in that area if a jury—and I'm not talking about this case. I'm just talking generally about the law, and this I think is important. When I talk to you about the range of punishment, in as much as the Prosecution talked to you about the range of punishment, I'm not endeavoring in any way on the part of Mr. Davis to negotiate in advance with any prospective juror for the lesser punishment. You see what I am saying?

Q. I am not. It is not a thing where the Prosecution says, "Could you impose the death penalty," trying to get that sort of commitment from you, and the Defense says to you, "Could you impose the minimum?" It's not that at all. It's simply that because the law provides that there is a wide range of punishment options for the offense of murder, that we're entitled to know how you feel about the law that permits that. You can have a feeling that perhaps the law is too severe or—in which case the Prosecution would be interested in that, and legitimately so. You could have a feeling that the law was too lenient, and that's the minimum, in which case I would be interested in that because what this exchange is, as you know, is simply a—a—a device that the law permits to enable the lawyers on either side to decide who here is going to serve on the jury, who's going to sit in judgment on the person accused, in this case, Mr. Davis, and that's what this is about.

In the event a jury, and not in this case, again, but a jury selected to serve to sit on a capital punishment case, capital case, first of all they are not—no one is really qualified under the law to serve as a juror in a capital punishment case unless they first say, "I have no conscientious scruples against the imposition of death as a punishment for crime in a proper case," because if they say, "I do have a conscientious scruple," they can't even sit because they have a feeling against that part of the law that the Prosecution's entitled to rely upon. They seek the death penalty. They therefore are entitled to have people serve on the jury who have no philosophical disagreement with capital punishment, but indeed say, "I believe in it."

If a person is in the camp that just is unalterably opposed to capital punishment under any circumstances and says, "I could under no circumstances, regardless of facts, impose the death penalty. My conscience wouldn't permit me to do that," that would be a feeling against the law of capital punishment. That would be a feeling against the law of capital punishment. That would disqualify that person for service in a capital case and the Prosecution would be legitimately entitled to urge it.

On the other hand, if—because the full range of the law is important, if a person said, "I'm unalterably opposed, just on my own philosophy about things, I'm just opposed to minimum punishments in murder cases, and regardless of fact or circumstance, whether someone else thought they warrant it or not, I could never—I could never impose a minimum sentence because I wouldn't—there's no fact or circumstance imaginable that would permit me to do it," just have a feeling against that range of punishment, then I would be entitled on behalf of Mr. Davis in this case, for example, to say,

"We challenge for cause," and in that same vein, there's no prohibition against a citizen feeling anyway he wants to about the law in advance of the time that he's sworn actually to serve as a juror. You may have any feeling you want about the law. That's—you're entitled to it, but once sworn to serve, then you have to follow the law, whether you like it or not, so the only time you get to tell us about whether you like it or not is now.

Q. You may—for example, there's a 55-mile an hour speed limit. You may disagree with that as being prudent or reasonable, but it is the law, but you would have a right at this time to say, "I don't agree."

This is not a speeding case, obviously. That's just a—an analogy I picked up that I'm not really sure is appropriate, but—perhaps it will serve for this purpose.

The—you would have a right in advance of the time that you serve on a trial to articulate your feelings about any phase of the law, to tell us now, to tell me now, because frankly if you have a strong feeling about some phase of the law about which I'm entitled to rely, then we would take that into consideration in determining whether or not you are qualified to serve on this jury and sit in judgment upon him.

Fair enough?

Q. All right. The range of punishment has been described for you as being in the—in a murder case, if a jury does not find beyond a reasonable doubt that the extenuating circumstances exist that make a murder a capital murder, that is, murder in the commission of a burglary or while attempting to commit a burglary, if they don't beyond a reasonable doubt believe beyond a reasonable doubt that either those facets of the capital punishment have been proved, it's not their—they are not convinced beyond a reasonable doubt but they do believe beyond a reasonable doubt that a murder was committed and the person on trial committed it, they then—then they are talking about what we call straight murder, where the penalty is from five years, any term of years up to and including life or 99 years, so my question to you is: Do you as just a matter of your own personal belief and philosophy have any quarrel or disagreement with that full range?

Q. Okay. And you have no conscientious scruple or—or personal belief that would prevent you in any case from imposing a minimum sentence if you thought the facts and circumstances justified it in a particular case?

5. *Ascertain Juror Sentiment on Punishment Range and Probation*

The strong advocates of the death penalty may be identified by their lack of consideration of probation and the minimum punishment.

Q. Now, you indicated yesterday in response to questions by the Prosecution that when you were—you and the Prosecutor were discussing the law of probation, that you would find it difficult or have a problem with—let me see if I can find the exact language—considering the law relative to probation in a murder case where there was any evidence of premeditation. I believe essentially that was your statement. Was I correct about that, ma'am?

Q. All right. Well, I can understand how that would—how that would be. This is a new experience for you and—

Q. —here with strangers asking a lot of questions, but I gathered from—from the responses that you made that you have a—have a high regard for the sanctity of life; am I right about that?

Q. All right. I suppose in part that's grounded on religious training and just general feeling about the preciousness that is life; am I right?

Q. All right. As a consequence of that, when you think about how you feel about the law and again as it has been explained to you by the Court and by the Prosecutor, a citizen has a right to have any opinion or any feeling they want about the law in advance of the time that they serve on the jury. You can now have your own—at this point in your life, have any feeling you want about the law. You can either agree with it or disagree with it or think it ought to be changed or think in your mind it's not a fair law, not a proper law. That's your right as a citizen, and yesterday when the Prosecutor was talking to you about the law of—of probation, I think you said you—in response to the question, he was talking to you about probation and how it applied as a law and then you indicated that you could not do it if it involved premeditation, at which time there was a discussion about the law that does not require the State to demonstrate, to prove premeditation. Do you recall now? The State doesn't have to prove premeditation in order to obtain a conviction for the offense of murder.

Q. I was trying to bring you back in focus with the discussions yesterday that we had or that you had with the Prosecution, that is, when you were talking about—when you said you couldn't consider probation in a case for—of murder as being appropriate because—if premeditation was involved.

Q. Can you think of a set of facts that would permit you to participate in a verdict that would result in the imposition of five years probation for one found guilty beyond a reasonable doubt of the offense of murder?

Q. Let me see—let me talk to you about probation, (name), and please understand that when we talk about punishment in a criminal case, we are just talking about it abstractly, not talking about this case. We are just talking about how you feel about the law. Fair enough?

Q. Okay. The law requires citizens to—who are eligible or contend they are eligible, to make an application in advance of the trial if they would have that eligibility considered by that jury. You, for example, because you have never before been convicted of a felony in this or any other state, are eligible to have, sort of a reward that you have as an adult human being for not before having ever been convicted of a felony, so if, God forbid, you were charged with a felony, you would have the right because of your eligibility to let the Court know about it, that you've never before been convicted, and you have to come into court in advance of the trial and swear that you have not before been convicted of a felony in this or any other state. Once you enter your oath to that, that brings the issue of your eligibility into the proceedings.

Q. Yes, I think yesterday when—when the Prosecutor was talking to you about the law relative to punishment, he continually used the word "man"—"when the man, when the man," meaning, of course, not suggesting to you that he's talking about this particular citizen who's on trial, Thomas Cullen Davis. I'm sure that was not the intent, but simply to express himself.

At any rate, a citizen who is eligible makes that eligibility known to the Court by filing a sworn pleading, by swearing they have not before been convicted of a felony in this or any other state. That then makes the question of eligibility a part of the proceedings.

Q. All right. Now, the incongruity of it, the paradox that appears for the layperson is that they come to court as prospective jurors. Again, not talking about this case, but they come to court and they are advised that the citizen on trial enters a plea of not guilty and wants a trial. He says, "I am not guilty," and the citizen demands that the Prosecutor prove it to the jury beyond a reasonable doubt. Says, "I am not guilty."

At the same time there's a—what they call an Application for Probation filed which, in effect, says to the jury, "But if you find me guilty, please—and believe that I have not before been convicted of a felony in this or any other state—please grant me probation or consider my application for probation," so it's sort of an inconsistency right off the bat, except that the law simply requires the citizen to make his eligibility known before the trial starts so that everybody can check it out, I suppose. At any rate, that's what the law says; you have to make your eligibility known by your sworn application in advance of the trial, and when I talk to you about punishment, I am in no way trying to negotiate with you as a prospective juror about how you would—how you feel about this particular case.

Have I made myself clear about that—

Q. In other words, I am not saying to you, (name), I want you to give Cullen Davis any special consideration, I want you to give Cullen Davis probation, I want you to give Cullen Davis anything except impartiality, so I am not negotiating with you about punishment. Okay?

Q. All right. I just want to make sure that I understand what it was that was said. It was a little confusing.

Now, a jury in a case, once they—let's make it a murder case. The jury, if they find the citizen on trial not guilty, if the proof doesn't persuade them beyond a reasonable doubt that the man—the person on trial is guilty, they say by their verdict not guilty. It's that simple. Then—at which time the trial is over, citizen goes home, back to his family.

If the jury finds from the evidence beyond a reasonable doubt that the citizen on trial is guilty, they so say. They find them guilty. Then it becomes the burden or the duty of the jury to determine what punishment is appropriate. The two-stage system that we talked about yesterday, so you don't even think about punishing someone until first you are persuaded beyond a reasonable doubt that they are guilty; right?

Q. All right. Now, when you consider the punishment in a murder case where one is—where there is an affidavit of eligibility on file, that is, an affidavit to the effect that the citizen on trial has not before been convicted of a felony in this or any other state, and the jury is of a mind that 10 years or less is in the appropriate range of punishment, the jury then considers whether or not probation would be appropriate as part of the sentencing option. Just part of the things that a jury can do.

Have I made that reasonably clear to this point?

Q. Okay. Now, murder—murder is an offense recognized by the law as one wherein the law of probation is applicable. A jury can consider probation for one found guilty beyond a reasonable doubt of the offense of murder. Some people simply, because of the high regard for the sanctity of life, could not ever, under any circumstances, impose probation simply because they feel that it's not an appropriate sentence. If that's the way they feel, they are certainly entitled to feel that way.

Q. At any rate some people, because of their high regard for life, simply feel it inappropriate, under any set of circumstances, to impose five years probation for the offense of murder and so that we know what we're talking about, since you expressed a reservation yesterday about the propriety of five years probation for the offense of murder where there was some evidence of premeditation, was I accurate about that, now?

Q. What did you mean when you said you couldn't consider probation if there was any evidence of premeditation?

Q. All right. So getting back to the area where we need to have a fuller understanding, the—you understand now that the question of punishment does not come up for consideration by a jury until they have first determined from the evidence beyond a reasonable doubt that the person on trial is guilty?

Q. All right. So we've passed that stage in our discussion. The jury, let's say, in a case, has found that the person on trial is guilty of the offense of murder, found that beyond a reasonable doubt and has so said by their verdict. Now, it is the jury's function to determine what punishment is appropriate and it is decided that 10 years or less under the facts and circumstances is appropriate. Further, no question about the fact the person on trial is eligible. Then the question is whether or not probation ought to be the punishment and in probation, the person who has just been found guilty of the offense of murder does not go to the Penitentiary, but leaves the courtroom with the jury, subject to some rules that are imposed by the Court; that he work at a steady job, and support his dependents, not associate or hang out with undesirable persons, not use any drugs or alcohol, just normal rules that apply to citizens who—you know, who—who do not get in such a situation.

Q. Well, I think that's accurate. Some rules are set down as to what those placed on probation can do. They can leave the County by simply petitioning the Court or the Probation authorities for approval to leave, but they don't go to the Penitentiary. That's the point, so long as they follow these rules.

Is probation now generally—have I made that reasonably well understood?

6. *Explore Presumption of Non-guilt, Guilt beyond a Reasonable Doubt, and Burden of Proof*

It is the author's experience that jurors believe the accused citizen is guilty or he would not have been charged; that the jurors are predisposed to vote guilty; and that the accused citizen must convince the jury of his non-guilt.

I like to recommend to trial counsel that he inquire of each of the jurors what reasonable doubt means to him or her personally and to use the jurors' definitions in the closing argument.

Q. Now, Counsel has talked to you yesterday about reasonable doubt. I think it—when you talk about reasonable doubt we need to—in my mind—think about it this way: First of all, the accused citizen, Cullen Davis, has a presumption of innocence, a legal presumption of innocence. Of course, that's sort of hand-in-glove with what you knew from the first grade, probably, that everyone is innocent until proven guilty, and we just sort of grew up with that because that was the law, but it is more than just a—just a saying. It's a legal presumption. Right now, under the law, he is innocent, presumed innocent.

If you as a juror or if you right now had a vote—guilty or innocent—you would have no alternative but to say innocent. You would have to say not guilty because he's presumed innocent and that presumption is legal and you abide by that presumption, do you not?

Q. I mean, you wouldn't change that anyway if you had the power?

Q. Okay. And the burden of proof is upon the Prosecution. The Defense has to prove nothing. Theoretically, under the law, if I did not want to, I wouldn't even have to put you through this. I can simply say, "I have no questions," could do that, but I have a right to ask these questions. Under the law I—the Defense doesn't have to prove anything, wouldn't have to cross-examine a witness, wouldn't have to put on a witness, wouldn't have to do anything. It would still be the burden of the Prosecution to demonstrate to you, as a juror, beyond a reasonable doubt the guilt as alleged. Otherwise, you would have no alternative under your oath as a juror but to find him not guilty—

Q. —because of that presumption.

The common thread that runs throughout the whole trial and even when you get to the time where the jury—the case is closed, both sides have argued, the Judge gives them a Charge on the law, the common thread that runs throughout the Charge is the presumption of innocence. "If you don't believe it beyond a reasonable doubt, resolve it in favor of the accused. If you have a reasonable doubt, you resolve it in favor of the accused." It's—and that's what you've known all your life and you have no quarrel or philosophical disagreement with that burden—

Q. —that being over here on the Prosecution and would not change it if you had the power, or would not, would you?

Q. If you had the power, would you change the law or do you think it is a good law that the Prosecution be compelled to prove if they accuse it?

Q. All right.

And the burden of proving that guilt is upon the Prosecution?

Q. And you agree with that?

Q. Okay. Reasonable doubt in that same connection will not likely be defined for you by the Court. Counsel gave his version of what reasonable doubt means to him. The Prosecution did. I have heard it said this way:—

Q. I don't believe the Court will instruct a jury in specific terms what reasonable doubt means, but essentially—and essentially it will be each individual juror's determination. It is not percentage, or is it? It is not—certainly not just a greater weight of evidence. That's not beyond a reasonable doubt. It has been defined this way because it is so ephemeral, I think. Reasonable doubt is that doubt which would cause a reasonable and prudent person to hesitate to act in the conduct of his own most serious, personal affairs. That's one definition. That's one explanation. All that suggests is that it is ephemeral. That there is no finite definition. It will be in—up to each individual juror to decide if he or she is convinced beyond a reasonable doubt and if they have a reasonable doubt, to resolve that doubt in favor of the accused.

Q. The—let me talk to you just briefly about the offense of murder itself. Some—and again, we all react different to different stimuli, to different things. Those of us with children, we come into court and we are told that the person on trial is a child-molester. Well, that offense, because we have children, is so personally noxious and repugnant to us that we begin to see the person accused in a new light, begin to dislike, have special feelings in our mind and heart against him without hearing any evidence, just because of the nature of the offense. It's repugnant. We hate people. We dislike people like that, you know, who are—who do that and if one is accused, maybe that feeling permeates the mind and heart there.

Now, some people have such a strong feeling about—about murder that it is so—that offense, just murder, the intentional taking of the life of another, just the accusation, just the nature of the offense creates a special feeling in their mind or their hearts against the person on trial without having heard evidence.

Because this allegation is murder, because it is alleged the intentional taking by one human being of the life of another, does that fact in and of itself create any prejudice in your mind or your heart against Cullen Davis?

7. *Try to Avoid a Group Verdict*

The attorney must commit the juror to voting his own individual decision as opposed to a group decision to prevail as a hung jury. out of a group of twelve persons, the actual decision will be made by three or four dominant personalities. A person whose life history has been slightly different from the norm is an excellent candidate to hang a jury.

Q. And in that same context, a jury—let's take a jury in a case such as this that is protracted, takes weeks. At the conclusion of that service if you were selected to serve on this jury and sit in judgment on Cullen Davis, you would have found out a lot about your fellow jurors because the jury can only work on the case when they are in the courtroom. They can't talk about it or discuss it or deliberate on it, not as a body. They are instructed by the Court not to deliberate on it, discuss it or talk about it until such time as it's been submitted to them with the Charge, so during the hours after Court's out of session, there's opportunity to discuss hobbies and interests and backgrounds and kids and jobs, and you learn a lot about each other, and you come to have respect for the intellect and integrity of the jurors. It is an experience, and sometimes you could come to have a disregard for the intellect or integrity. That's conceivable, you know, because they are people with whom you will be in close proximity, sharing a most unique experience, and at the conclusion of a case it is necessary then for all the jurors to reach judgments, to decide what the facts are, guided by the law given to them by the Court, at which point they are obligated to consider the observations and thoughts and suggestions of fellow jurors, you know, to discuss it, to deliberate, but in the final analysis it is the individual judgment, you know, if—if someone felt different than you, you are obligated to listen to the point of view, but if you are not persuaded that your own view is incorrect, then you are obligated to insist upon your view, you know, not to do anything that would offend, would violate your own conscience; correct? It's not a mob function. It has to be unamimous, but in that unanimity you can't give up in the name of expediency your own individual judgment.

Q. Makes sense? All right.

Do you feel that you are a man of such temperament, maturity, and persuasion, that if you made your mind up after a fact, about something as serious as a trial, and after you had heard all the reasonable discussion of everybody else, that you would do what did not offend your conscience?

Q. Now, when a jury is empaneled, you know, the Court will say to the jury, "You don't deliberate until you have heard the entire case."

I ask of you this: That you not make your mind up until such time as you've heard the total case, because as you can appreciate now the Prosecution goes first. If you were to reach a definite, finite, irrevocable conclusion as a consequence of just hearing part of it, and close your mind to want to hear the rest of it, that would deprive—you see what I'm saying?

Q. Okay. So while it's impossible not to have the brain function and I'm not asking any prospective juror to do that, because as things develop in the presence of a trial, a picture begins to form in the mind. Questions are asked in the mind. That's normal. That's logical. It wouldn't be a functioning jury without it, so I'm not saying don't think. I'm saying don't reach finite, definite conclusions until you've heard the whole case, because I think, that's what I think, the Court will charge you to do.

Fair enough?

II. *ANALYSIS OF THE JURY DURING TRIAL*

This section has a deceptively modest goal. It purports to tell you how to read a jury during trial, while indicating potential impediments to doing so. It does not suggest what you should say to or in front of a jury, or how you should say it. Those suggestions appear later, in an examination of effective argument style. Moreover, those suggestions are made from probability and analytical perspectives. For example, if an audience (a jury) is composed of only a few individuals having any college education, the *probability* is that they will respond less favorably to an attorney who says, "It is I" than to an attorney who says, "It's me." The *analysis* is that, while "It is I" is grammatically correct, only fairly well-educated individuals would (1) know that and (2) care about using the correct option over the colloquial one.

What rhetorical analysis (or speech criticism) usually does not do is interview each member of the audience and ask, "What was your reaction when the attorney said, 'It is I'?" The reasons for this are twofold. First, people may not be honest in attributing their motives. Since it is not logical to fault someone for using hypercorrect speech, audience members may be reluctant to do so. Second, people often cannot explain why they arrive at some of their judgments; they may not be able to trace a less than good feeling about another person to that person's speech idiosyncracies. Thus, the reactions elicted by audience members may not clearly relate to acts of the speaker.

This section does not predict how jurors *will* react. Again, earlier sections suggest the range of reactions that typify human behavior in social circumstances. Jurors, being individuals in a definable social environment, are likely to respond within this described range.

This section instead focuses on the nature of juror reactions and how viewers of jurors (the attorneys) may be guided in the interpretation of the reactions. Since jurors are human objects of observation, experimental conclusions as to nonverbal behavior may be reliably applied to jurors. Thus, such conclusions will be examined in greater depth than in the previous section on the *voir dire*. Although the same principles apply in analyzing the prospective juror during the *voir dire* as in interpreting the reactions of a juror during trial, the *voir dire* facilitates only a brief introduction to the observed individual, while a trial offers the opportunity to study nonverbal behavior as an indicator of response rather than personality.

Armed with an understanding of the interpretative tools, we will then examine the reactions of an actual juror in a seven-month trial. The reactions were not provided in response to a social psychologist's questions; they were recorded as a report of a juror's experience. With the responses admitted, there is no need to attempt to interpret what this juror was thinking; he tells us that. What we can do with the tools is attempt to figure out *how we could have known what he was thinking*, because he tells us what his nonverbal behavior was.

Prior to this exercise, however, what some may view as a simpler method of reading a jury is discussed: the mirror or shadow jury.

A. *The Mirror Jury*

Earlier chapters discuss mock jury experiments or mini trials in which the subjects have acted as juries in fictional trials. This procedure involves simulation of an actual trial with witnesses and evidence presented. Twelve mock jurors who are representative of the personalities who are most likely to appear on an actual jury in the area of the trial are employed as simulated jurors. The case is presented to this mock jury in a simplified and condensed fashion, usually in a one to three day presentation.

This procedure is invaluable for evaluation of witnesses' testimony and demeanor, reactions to issues and theories presented in the case, and testing a trial strategy. An attorney noted that "[b]ecause practice and rehearsal comprise a large part of trial preparation, it makes sense to practice the impact of a potential trial strategy on a mock jury."[93]

In still other research, surrogate jurors have daily sat in on trials and reported their feelings and observations about the case to a trial consultant who conveyed this information to the attorney.

The simulated jury was originally designated a "shadow" jury.[94] The author prefers the term "mirror" jury or "gallery" jury. A group of six to twelve people is selected which most nearly matches or mirrors the demographic characteristics and dominant psychological traits of the actual jury panel. This "mirror" or "gallery" jury is employed by the trial consultant to attend the trial on a daily basis. These surrogate jurors are to see and hear only the evidence which is presented to the actual jury. Ideally, they are to leave the courtroom when the real jury does. (However, for example, in a highly publicized and well-attended trial or in a small community, this may not be possible because the mirror jurors may not be able to retain their seats or the exit from the courtroom may draw too much attention to this process and therefore should not be done.) The mirror jurors are instructed not to discuss the case with anyone and to base their opinions only on what is presented in the courtroom. They are also instructed not to sit together in the courtroom, not to talk among themselves, and not to do any act which would draw attention.

The "mirror" jury provides information, both positive and negative, to the trial consultant each evening. The trial consultant conveys and interprets this information for the litigator. This procedure has the advantage of permitting the trial attorney to have unbiased feedback as to the status of the case on a daily basis at a time when the advocate has the opportunity to correct misinformation or clarify important points. In other words, the mirror jury is a method used by an attorney to gauge the reactions of jurors to the case. This method is accomplished by simply asking mirror jurors to report their feelings, impressions, reactions and understandings. One commentator has stated that the mirror jury "[b]ecomes an on-the-spot lay adviser for the trial lawyer."[95]

The author has conducted numerous mirror juries in both civil and criminal defense litigation. In civil litigation, the mirror jury after the close of evidence has reached an identical verdict to the actual jury's verdict on the liability issues and has been within seven to ten percent of the dollars awarded by the real jury. All trial attorneys have consistently acknowledged that the mirror jury was helpful in evaluating the understanding and comprehension of the jury. The comments of the mirror jury were utilized in presenting testimony in a more understandable manner and in focusing the final argument. This research procedure reduces considerably the unpredictability factor of the jury.[96]

The trial consultant selects the mirror jury and acts as the researcher and investigator. This selection process involves finding surrogate jurors who represent the traits of the actual jurors. There is no one-to-one correlation between surrogates and actual jurors. For example, in a highly publicized criminal defense trial in Fort Myers, Florida, one mirror juror reflected the traits of two actual jurors, and two mirror jurors were required to represent the dominant traits of another juror. (I assisted attorneys, Michael R. N. McDonnell and Jerry Berry in the *State of Florida v. Steven Benson* case. The ultimate question in this capital murder trial concerned whether or not the heir, Steven Benson, to a tobacco fortune planted bombs in the summer of 1985 that killed his mother and brother and maimed his sister. The tobacco money came from his grandfather's founding the Lancaster (Pa.) Leaf Tobacco Co.).

The trial consultant debriefs the mirror jury each evening. The debriefings may range from thirty minutes to two hours per person. The mirror juror is asked to respond to inquiries which have been designed to elicit feelings about and reactions to the trial proceedings, witnesses, exhibits, attorneys, and the case in general; in addition to their comprehension, their understanding and interpretation of the evidence. These comments are conveyed to the trial attorney. Presumably, the real jurors are reacting and understanding or not understanding in a similar manner to the mirror jurors. Information from the mirror jury allows for the compilation of a list of additional evidence which needs to be presented to satisfy the group, for example, of the negligence of a doctor in medical malpractice litigation. The mirror jury can examine the charge and reveal their understanding of terminology and responses.

While it is stated and supported in earlier chapters by other evidence, I have concluded from my research about juror decision-making with mock or mini trials and mirror juries that most jurors decide the case at the conclusion of the *voir dire* and/or the opening statement. The trial is then selectively perceived and support or rationalization for one's early decision is "pigeonholed" for the deliberation phase. The decision is a function of their life experiences, background, attitudes and beliefs.

In the Benson trial in Fort Myers, Florida, the mirror jurors each voted "guilty" or "not guilty" or "don't know" at the conclusion of the opening statement of the trial and placed the decision in a sealed envelope. The mirror jurors decided privately and individually the ultimate issue each evening. Of interest is the fact that less than one-third of the group ever deviated from the initial vote. I have conducted similar experiments in civil litigation and can categorize early the majority of mirror jurors as favorable to the plaintiff or the defense. The small remaining member jurors of the group can be labeled as undecided and will lean toward whichever group is perceived as more dominant and in control. It is enlightening to observe the jurors rationalize the decisions which were formulated very early in the trial.

The author has observed that jurors do decide the case very early in the trial. One often hears attorneys say that the decision isn't final until the final word of the final statement. These two positions are not as inconsistent as they appear. What has to be examined is whether or not the juror will maintain his initial position. As stated in an earlier chapter, one will view the evidence in a manner that is consistent with his background, life experiences, attitudes and beliefs. Variables such as his personality traits will determine whether or not he maintains that position. Also, the group dynamics of who are the most "powerful" persons on the jury and is his viewpoint consistent with the powerful ones are factors which determine whether or not he maintains this initial position.

Mirror jurors learn, without verbal communication, the position of other group members much in advance of a trial. Those who think similarly will associate with each other and form a subgroup. This is evidenced on the actual jury by who is friendly with whom, who goes to lunch together or rides together, and other cohesive behavior such as who sits together around the jury table. Also, it is clear that mirror jurors consider the judge to be the authority figure and to be the "13th Juror." They attempt to determine the attitude of the judge by his demeanor and facial expressions in addition to his verbal communication. The mirror jurors have a strong desire to please the judge and are influenced by what they perceive to be his position.

The simulated jurors retain and understand very little of complex and technical expert testimony. If they can not understand expert testimony, they will reject such testimony but will not acknowledge problems in comprehension. Attorneys would be wise to present their case in simple terminology and repeat simplistic themes numerous times. Presenting a case is analogous to teaching a class. The advocate has a captive audience in physical presence only, not attention. The central theme must be simple and repeated numerous times for the jury to retain and understand. Attorneys are often startled by how little mirror juries retain and the "wrong" interpetations which are applied to certain statements and evidence. It is usually the case that the most effective communicator prevails in the litigation arena.

Of interest is the fact that jurors often know they need help interpreting what they see or hear. Attorneys are often oblivious to the nonverbal pleas for assistance or unwillingly react themselves without realizing that the jurors are reading such reactions as the interpretation they are seeking. Thus, the expert witness, who has been prepped by attorneys, gives his testimony in a way that pleases the attorneys, not the jury. When the jurors become lost and look to the attorney for guidance, the attorney's nods of approval (directed toward the witness) may tell them simply "to follow along," while an unconscious expression of shock may signal that the witness has just misspoken.

Attorneys should realize that jurors are very observant and will without evidence interpret, rightfully or wrongfully, what they see and hear on their own, if left unexplained. For example, mirror jurors noticed in the Benson trial that the courtroom suddenly was more full when the sister of Steven Benson, Mrs. Carol Benson Kendall, testified and consequently imputed their own significance to the testimony of this witness.

Attorneys or their office staff should not attempt to conduct a mirror jury themselves. The likelihood is that the attorneys' own belief of what went on in court, as well as their familiarity with the facts, will affect the questions asked, as well as how the answers are perceived. It is "critical" that whoever conducts the mirror jury be able to suspend preconceived views, an ability usually possessed only by the behavioral scientist. If properly conducted, this courtroom tactic (which is relatively rare because of cost and novelty) provides a glimpse, which no other technique can match, into the hearts and minds of the actual jury.

B. *The Significance of Nonverbal Communication*

More than communicating what a person is *thinking*, nonverbal communication is a clue to what someone is *feeling*. This is apparent from the research. Facial and bodily expressions are characterized as "emotional cues."[97] Body positions deliver information about someone's "gross affect state, that is, whether the emotion is positive or negative," while body acts and facial expressions can reveal specific emotions.[98] Posture, distance, and orientation are thought to reveal a communicator's attitude ("degree of liking, positive evaluation, and/or reference of one individual toward another") toward his addressee.[99] And sustained eye contact is believed to indicate a personal or confidential relationship between people.[100]

How jurors may *feel* about a witness or a party or some evidence is significant only if jurors are guided by their emotions in arriving at verdicts. Some believe this is precisely how jurors reach their verdicts.

> [I]n reality it frequently is the emotional response, the indoctrination and coerciveness, the suggestibility of the material to which the jury has been exposed, that shapes and influences not only its general verdict but the determination of that general verdict which may be at considerable distance from the judge's instructions, from the legal issues involved, and from the "legal" intent of the law. The lawyer, in his address to the jury, does not confine himself to clear and concise legal arguments based on the objective summary of the evidence. He does quite the opposite. He uses every manipulation of oratory and acting to appeal to the atavistic emotions of the jury. He knows only too well that they will not objectively weigh the testimony or discriminatingly consider what the judge has told them of the law.[101]

In an earlier chapter, personality traits are examined as indicators of potential juror behavior, suggesting not only how an individual may view a set of facts but also the extent to which he (1) may be influenced by more powerful personalities on the jury or (2) may be a powerful, influencing personality himself. Personality traits can also cue attorneys as to which jurors are likely to be susceptible to which types of "behavioral manipulation [e.g., coercion, persuasion, identification] which is congruent with the goals of lawyer-jury confrontation."[102]

It has been suggested that when presented with conflicting and confusing evidence, jurors, looking for some basis to make a choice, may do so solely on their liking for a particular attorney.[103] Such a backing away from logical analysis necessarily results in a reliance "more upon empathy, emotional identification, and the extent to which the persuasive and suggestible influences of the court are perceived."[104] Therefore, the attorney who seeks to control the emotional reactions of the jury could naturally benefit from being able to assess whether such reactions are as he desires.

C. *Assessing Nonverbal Cues*

Nonverbal reactions are limited to facial and bodily expressions, movements, and position. As earlier noted, the face is more easily controlled than the body and can more easily be made to display false emotions.[105] However, overcoming the tendency to "read" the face rather than the body is not simple. In one experiment, face and body cues were placed in conflict before subjects consisting of psychotherapists and professional dancers. Psychotherapists were presumed to be aware of potential nonverbal messages from patients, and dancers were assumed to be more attuned to body movement than other people.[106]

The subjects were shown fifteen photographs; in five, the subject had a pleasant expression in face and body; in five, an unpleasant expression in face and body; and in five, a pleasant expression in face but an unpleasant expression in body. Subjects were first shown all photographs of the entire body; later, they were shown photographs of only the body. "When looking at the whole picture, all judges attributed more pleasant feeling than when looking at the body only." Also, when shown the body only pictures, the subjects commented with surprise as to how much information was revealed by the body. But when they saw the whole pictures again, their estimations of pleasantness changed very little, although the dancers' estimations changed more than the psychotherapists.'[107] Thus, even when alerted to conflicting body information, the subjects' tendency was still to interpret facial expressions.

One explanation for the reliance on facial expression is that it is an act, as opposed to just a position; the body tends to have a position. Any act may simply carry more information than a position:

> The likelihood that people will act when emotionally aroused could be explained by a number of possible causal factors: (1) movements might be neurophysiologically linked to emotional arousal; or (2) movements might illustrate pictorially an affective theme which is concurrently being verbalized; or (3) movements might be learned adaptive responses to arousal which modulate, enhance, reduce, or discharge the emotional arousal.[108]

A still body position can carry information about a gross affect state (such as positive or negative), based on how relaxed or muscularly tensed the body is, but usually not the particular emotion (anger, fear, disgust, happiness, surprise, interest), which the face is more capable of portraying. However, even such a general assessment must take into account the normal body position of an individual. Certain basal positions that most people would use for certain types of interpersonal interactions would reveal little about emotion, but deviations from basal positions may not be reliably interpreted without a consideration of the individual. For example, a slouched position may indicate a negative affective state by suggesting the emotion of apathy, or a positive state by implying relaxation. Also, tension could be read as indicating excitement and elation or discomfort.[109]

All of the foregoing may cause one to doubt that he could ever reliably interpret nonverbal behavior. However, living in society demands that we interpret the words and actions of others on a continuous basis. The nature of our relationships with others tells us whether we have interpreted correctly. Thus, most of us form rather reliable, implicit interpretative rules, which we apply to new acquaintances. An attorney often becomes a professional interpreter of behavior because his success may depend upon it. He can somewhat easily come to know the basic body position of each juror and, by watching how jurors interact with each other, learn their natural facial expressions. He can then detect when these positions and expressions change and attempt to correlate such changes with testimony, personalities of witnesses and counsel, and other trial events. Moreover, there are two types of nonverbal behavior that seem to be minimally susceptible to the control of the actor, are easily recognizable, and appear to have a clear relationship to the emotions of the actor: eye contact and seated body orientation.

Specifically, eye contact and seated body orientation can indicate the degree of liking between a communicator and an addressee. While this may initially appear to be an insignificant finding, it is invaluable to the trial attorney. With all that has already been said about the emotions guiding the verdicts of jurors, it follows that testimony from a witness whom the jurors do not like will probably not be believed or used. If it is your witness on the stand (as opposed to the opposition's) and you detect that the juror does not like him or her, it behooves you to try to bring out a more appealing side. Similarly, if you detect dislike of yourself while talking to the jury, you should also try to remedy that.

Based on experimental results, eye contact increases with the degree of unfamiliarity and decreases with the degree of dislike, regardless of sex. Orientation of individuals communicating with each other, to each other, is determined by the positioning of the shoulders, and differs with sex. For women communicators, shoulder orientation is most direct for neutral addressees, least direct for intensely disliked addressees, and moderately direct for intensely liked addressees. Males behave similarly, except when addressing other males whom they intensely dislike. Then, males have a more direct shoulder orientation and are relatively tense, as if anticipating physical threat or aggression. Relaxation is indicated by sideway lean, and female communicators signal dislike with greater degrees of relaxation, regardless of the sex of the addressee. Thus, a female communicator who is extremely relaxed is expressing intense dislike for addresses. On the other hand, extreme relaxation in males suggests intense dislike only for female addressees. As earlier indicated, males tense up when addressing males that they dislike intensely. The results of the experiment showed no connection between the communicator's attitude and the degree of relaxation or openness of arms and legs.[110]

An experiment concerning only eye contact revealed a difference between men and women in direct eye contact. In the experiment, a speaker delivered a monologue about himself or herself to a single listener (a stranger), who looked at the speaker the entire time, some of the time, only when the speaker said personally revealing things, or only when the speaker did not say personally revealing things. Based on the results, the experimenters concluded that "[t]he female speaker becomes more personal and revealing and likes her listener better when looked at, whether the gaze is constant or contingent upon self-disclosure. The male speaker, by contrast, responds with less intimacy and slightly less liking for his listener when faced with direct gaze rather than gaze avoidance." Apart from this difference, they also found that direct gaze may result in openness and liking when the level of intimate disclosure is low and within cultural limits of propriety. When the listener exceeds these limits by implicitly seeking, through direct gaze, more self-disclosure than the speaker is willing to provide, the speaker may become uncomfortable, tense, or embarrassed.[111]

The experiments described above regarding body positions, facial expressions, and eye contact specifically involved speakers and audiences. On the surface, then, as applied to the jury, the results would be relevant for someone analyzing not the jury, but a witness or an attorney from the perspective of the jury. However, whenever there is a live presentation before an audience, the audience is always aware of its being expected to respond, to participate in the communication, and it never fails to respond, even if in a different way than desired or expected. In the theater, audiences applaud, groan, laugh, gasp, or otherwise indicate their reactions. Members of an audience for a speaker may frown, move their heads in agreement or disagreement, mumble responses, roll their eyes, or make comments to their neighbors. Depending upon the formality of the occasion, theater and speech audiences may be extremely spontaneous and wildly varied in their reactions. It is natural to respond, verbally or nonverbally, to a performance, and the responses themselves become communications to the speakers or performers.

Jurors cannot respond verbally to witnesses and attorneys. And, because they are cautioned not to reach their verdicts until the end of the trial, they attempt to mask what would otherwise be very natural nonverbal responses, fearful that such repsonses will be viewed as an indication that they have reached a verdict prematurely. But for the most part, this calls for Herculean effort, being a task that they have never undertaken before, and nonverbal reactions will almost assuredly slip out at times. Moreover, most people do not realize that what they do unconsciously signals what they are feeling. For example, if jurors do not like a witness and cannot bring themselves to look at him or her, they probably do not know what that tells whoever is watching *them*. Simply, they cannot compensate for or correct what they do not realize they are doing. The communication from the jury will undoubtedly be there, for the astute attorney to interpret.

D. *The Juror's Reactions*

For our purposes, it would be ideal if one or more jurors on a panel could be filmed and recorded during a trial that was itself recorded, with the juror given the freedom to react, verbally and nonverbally, precisely as he wanted during the trial. Then, we could play both tapes, on side-by-side monitors, and determine what sparked each of his reactions. That, of course, has yet to be done. However, certain people having been jurors for famous (and infamous) trials, have written of their experiences. One such person, a skilled writer, made notes during breaks and recollected the daily events in front of his typewriter at home. Due to both his literary aptitude, which results in the descriptive detail so necessary for our analysis, and the seven-month trial, which provided a wealth of data, his account has been selected for examination.

Edwin Kennebeck was *Juror Number Four*; his book is subtitled *The Trial of Thirteen Black Panthers as Seen from the Jury Box*. Although the book is exactly what its title suggests, an account of the trial from the perspective of the jury, it amazingly verifies certain propositions concerning trials and juries that researchers and attorneys have formulated, from the other side of the jury box. The following analysis centers on those propositions.

1. *Jurors Are Affected by the Courtroom Environment*

This proposition may seem too obvious to state. The revelation is *how* jurors are affected by the courtroom. An earlier chapter argues that attorneys should realize they are before a demanding audience when they try cases and should seek tips from professional actors while on the "courtroom" stage. This receives clear verification in Kennebeck's account. When Kennebeck was sworn in, the clerk directed, "Juror, look upon the defendants. Defendants, look upon the juror." What did he think of this? "Ceremony. Living theater."[112]

When the last chapter discussed who should conduct the questioning during *voir dire*, the judge or the attorneys, it appeared that the judge is more able to instill in jurors a sense of responsibility and induce them either to admit or to overcome their prejudices. Kennebeck suspected that Judge Murtagh may have been "infected," consciously or not, by prejudices against the Panthers, simply because of the judge's advanced age and race (white). But the very trappings of the courtroom (the setting) and the judge's costume had a profound effect on the audience:

> [T]he majesty of the stern man in black robes, wearing horn-rimmed glasses, in his comfortable chair behind the bench, with his chrome carafe of water (the other participants had bright plastic pitchers) and his seasoned authority over guards and clerks and assistants—the awesome and austere power that the Judge represented made me feel old-fashioned respect, which I didn't shake off during the whole trial.[113]

A recurring question of jury researchers is whether jurors take literally the legal principle of innocent until proven guilty. These researchers may be surprised to know that some jurors will pick that principle apart. It was one of the first things that Kennebeck heard, and he heard it repeatedly. Though he admits that "most of us are willing to go along with that," he adds that "it doesn't mean what it says." The "*until* proven guilty" suggests that the defendants *will* be proven guilty. Moreover, "if the defendants were really presumed innocent, why were any of them kept in jail?" Some researchers posit that juries in criminal trials begin with a leaning towards guilty, simply because the defendants have already been indicted and may still be in jail. Kennebeck's reaction however, suggests an opposite leaning, almost an inclination to compensate for the prior incarceration—"There was no question of their having to be proven innocent. This is one of the beautiful wild claims that the American system makes."[114] Kennebeck calls himself "a good liberal."[115] Perhaps his interpretation of the innocent-until-proven-guilty standard suggests that a question to ask every "good liberal" in *voir dire* would be what his personal interpretation of that standard is. (The following statement is of particular interest concerning attitudinal bias. As previously mentioned, the author assisted attorneys Michael R.N. McDonnell and Jerry Berry in the defense of Steven Benson in Fort Myers, Florida. One of the Benson jurors, when asked by the media why the jury found Benson guilty, state on television that the "defense had not proven Benson's innocence.")

2. *Jurors React Personally to Attorneys, Parties, and Witnesses*

One of the cautions mentioned in the discussion of *voir dire* is the avoidance of offending prospective jurors, who may wind up on the jury and harbor some resentment against an attorney. Kennebeck describes the questioning session of one juror, Hiram Irizarry, a maintenance man who had come to New York from Puerto Rico thirteen years earlier. A peculiar exchange occurred between Irizarry and three of the defense attorneys. His answer to a question about discrimination apparently left them uncertain as to his complete understanding of the English language; the exchange contained not only conflicting answers, but also non-idiomatic English. One of the defense counsel asked the judge to excuse Irizarry because he might not be able to understand all of the English in the trial. Although counsel had attempted to make this request outside of Irizarry's presence, the judge had not allowed it. After the judge said that he considered Irizarry to be qualified as a juror, the assorted defense counsel evidently discussed at length whether to use a peremptory challenge on him, and decided against it. Halfway through the trial, Kennebeck was walking with Irizarry after the end of a day and asked whether he also got headaches during the day. The reply was "No. . . I just get angry." While Kennebeck then reflected that he had not thought Irizarry had been bothered by the *voir dire* incident, he admits, "I wasn't absolutely sure."[116]

Joseph A. Phillips and Jeffrey Weinstein were the prosecuting attorneys. Kennebeck usually refers to Phillips as "the DA." Kennebeck's comment on what is Phillips' opening statement and/or information imparted in the *voir dire* indicates a strong reluctance to believe the DA's story, though a fear that the evidence could demand the contrary: "But as the DA gives us the broad, dismaying outlines of his case, telling us about the dynamite that one secret agent discovered. . . I am hit hard by the possibility that something may indeed have gotten out of hand a couple of years before among those angry blacks."[117] Perhaps because Phillips was the prosecutor, perhaps because he acted the part too well, Kennebeck implies that Phillips received little sympathy from the jury. Two of the defendants, Michael Tabor and Richard Moore, apparently left the country during trial. On April 1, five months into trial, stipulations were entered that Tabor was in Algiers. Kennebeck reports that the DA had actually talked to him and recorded the conversation. The jurors joked among themselves about how the conversation might have gone: " 'Hello, Mike, this is Joe.' 'Joe who?' " One of them added that the DA probably called at night so that he could get the lower rates.[118]

One humanizing incident concerning Phillips came late in the trial, when the defendant counsel were resting for their respective clients. The DA noted that one more defendant, who represented herself, had not been heard. After she said, "I rest," two of the jurors said in sequence, "I rest." Kennebeck reports, "The DA smiled."[119] This almost stands out as a singular occasion of juror rapport for the DA.

For the closing statements, the six defense counsel preceded the DA. Kennebeck's comments about each of them reveals responses to personalities, and the good feeling he had about the defense attorneys seemed to set a difficult precedent for the DA. After Sanford Katz had given the first summation, Kennebeck notes that Katz had been "refreshingly free of jury-flattering, except by dry implication." His next thought was to wonder "if the DA will try cozening."

William Crain then spoke, and although Kennebeck found him "sometimes repetitious and overly rhetorical," he admits, "Crain did show us plenty of facts, contradictions, incompletenesses, absurdities." Carol Lefcourt went next; of her, Kennebeck says only that she was more forceful than usual and did not take long; he apparently viewed the latter to be a virtue. Robert Bloom then spoke, but was cut short when he commented on "the DA's enormous power, including the power to select the judge to preside in this case." After the jury had been whisked from the room, Kennebeck imagined that Bloom received a brief lecture. When his voice weakened at about 4:15, Bloom asked the judge for permission to break for the day. Although he consented, the judge attributed his reluctance to the length of the trial already, implying in Kennebeck's mind that the defendants were to blame for the lengthiness—"one of the most unconscionable remarks . . . in the course of this unconscionable trial." Charles McKinney, the only black attorney, closed last for the defense. Of him, Kennebeck wrote in his journal, "*He ended up most obviously eloquent—beautiful.*"[120]

From Kennebeck's description, the DA's closing was probably textbook-proper. Phillips seems to have done everything possible to identify with the jury, humanize himself to them, refresh their recollections, and cause them to see his interpretation of the facts. But, perhaps because he had a bad set of facts and witnesses, which may have thwarted any jury rapport from the beginning, all of his efforts appeared transparent and insincere. Kennebeck notes that

> [h]e tried hard enough. He joked with us, alluded to each juror personally in one way or another. . . . He interlocked his knuckles to show us how the evidence meshed to prove his case. . . . His appeals to our recollection, like his quips, were supposed to generate some kind of response in our faces; we were supposed to smile or nod our heads. . . . At one point [he said his younger colleague should be the one summing up]. It was a lodge-meeting pleasantry, the kind . . . meant to be laughed at. . . . We didn't laugh. . . .
>
> Cajoling, coddling, cozening.

And although Kennebeck had cited certain of the defense counsel for taking a long time, Phillips erred more so by promising to take only a day and a half but going twice that long. "It was grueling." One day at lunch another juror observed, Phillips "simply doesn't know the audience he's talking to." In their general complaining about the length of the speech, Kennebeck joked that he wished they *could* say they remembered whenever Phillips asked about certain evidence—"That might speed him up."[121]

One remarkable thing about the apparent antipathy regarding the DA is the seemingly positive description Kennebeck gives of him just prior to the closing statement: "Mr. Phillips of the bright, large, pleasant face and glittering blue eyes. Dressed in a plain black suit...like a genial priest. Father Joe explaining dogma to the parishioners."[122] It is as if Phillips had just taken the wrong side of an unattractive case.

Kennebeck's description of the defense counsel suggests that, if they were not more appealing people in their own right than the DA, at least they were more so due to their association with the opposite side of the case. Bloom, "relaxed and 'bearlike,' had a deceptively gentle manner"; he smiled so much that he almost forced Kennebeck into smiling back, despite his determination not to respond. McKinney, with "his elegant dark face and gentle tone," was simply "[c]ourtly."[123] It was McKinney, perhaps in part because he, like the defendants, was black, who moved Kennebeck the most. During the defense summations, as the jury filed out of court at the end of one day, Kennebeck writes that McKinney looked up at each of them as they passed. "*I would give him an encouraging look if it weren't for the officers and other court types sitting nearby. Jesus—watching and waiting and wondering; sweating it out.*"[124]

Kennebeck describes the defendants as if they were works of art or fabulous fictional creations. First, he notes that some of them were known both by "resonant astonishing African names" and "original ordinary 'slave names.'" At no point does he seem put off or prejudiced by any cultural difference. The face of Afeni Shakur, he writes, was "a study in African beauty," though she "lounged against the table, bored, chewing gum." Robert Collier had a thin, dropping mustache, which "gave him a mandarin look." Richard Moore, a/k/a Dharuba, had almond eyes and a Levantine nose. Although the *voir dire* lasted six weeks, the defendants were so numerous that the jury had trouble differentiating them and at last asked the judge to have them introduced individually. "Most of them gave a restrained clenched-fist salute."[125] But neither this nor any of the other behavior of the defendants throughout the trial, which may have appeared disrespectful in another court, seems to have affected the jury negatively.

Kennebeck had a particularly "strong emotional reaction...intensely negative" to a certain witness, Carlos Ashwood. His description of his response to Ashwood shows that Kennebeck's nonverbal reactions should have betrayed his feelings. Kennebeck says that he "found it impossible to smile at [Ashwood]. . . . he disconcerted me with his long pauses before and during replies and with the fierce resentment he seemed to feel at defense questions." Ashwood apparently listened very carefully to questions and answered them literally, instead of answering the questions that were clearly intended, which Kennebeck read as "verbal ducking-dodging." Kennebeck confesses to being so upset by Ashwood's testimony style that he was almost induced to "blow [his] cover as an undemonstrative juror." For relief (or revenge?), Kennebeck "developed a habit of staring at him."[126]

3. *Jurors Repress Natural Reactions*

Kennebeck repeatedly tells that he, as well as the other jurors, were always aware of the need to show no reaction and attempted to repress their responses to personalities and evidence. A review of some of these incidences suggests that certain of these repressions probably appeared to be exactly that, which in turn would be significant nonverbal behavior. Kennebeck mentions defendant outbursts as they occurred throughout the trial. In one instance, the judge, who used his hand for a gavel, pounded the wood in front of him to protest an interruption. As the defendants pounded their table "in antiphon," Kennebeck "made an effort not to frown and not to smile."[127] Early in the case, the DA passed around a souvenir sword cane seized as a weapon at the apartment of one of the defendants. As Kennebeck withdrew the sword from its sheath and ran it over his wrist, he was amazed at how blunt the edge and tip were. He thought, "*Cripes, Mr. Phillips—this is a Black Panther revolutionary weapon?*" But he refused to let his face reveal his feelings.[128]

In addition to the interruptions by the defendants, the attorneys engaged in "many courtroom wrangles," so much so that Kennebeck admits that the defense counsel "sometimes went beyond the bounds of proper procedure." However, on one particular occasion the premise for the trial itself became so oppressive that Kennebeck seemed close to bursting and one juror actually did cry out in protest:

> I got uptight-angry not so much at the quarreling as at some of the nonsense that it seemed to me the State of New York was asking us to swallow. My outrage, oozing from my head to my stomach, would spread tension into my feet, which I usually

> braced against the oak-paneled partition in front of us; I'm surprised that it didn't crash to the floor. There did come a moment when defense lawyers and the DA and the Judge were arguing so discordantly that Steve or someone cried out "Stop!"[129]

At another time, apparently anxious for a bit of comic relief, Kennebeck overreacted when a fellow juror whispered a wry comment: "*At which I nearly broke up, but fortunately heaven has sent me a sore throat in which I can to some degree drown my laughter. It came in handy during the day.*"[130]

During the DA's closing, Kennebeck's description of how the jurors so consummately resisted responding suggests that they were trying to signal to him the futility of his cause, and simultaneously let the defense know that the DA was not among friends:

> [W]e were supposed to smile or nod our heads. But we sat like stones. . . . It was. . . . meant to be laughed at. . . .We didn't laugh.
>
> . . .The DA looked at us and said, "How about a break? Seconded?" Nobody said a word or moved a muscle, as far as I could tell. . . .
>
> I've always found it difficult to keep from smiling or laughing out of politeness when some genial person is trying to make a joke. So I had to stop looking at Phillips.

When the DA summarized a critical point about the existence of dynamite, he expressed a certainty that caused Kennebeck to put on "one of my finest moments of straight-face." Then, the DA explained that he had not put on a particular witness because it would have extended the trial even more. Kennebeck admits that his nonverbal response got away from him:

> [It] struck me as so absurd that I must have made a face or something; I turned my eyes toward the spectators inadvertently, and a young woman in the front row saw this and smiled. Then I looked at Bloom, and I thought he must have noticed. I quickly tried to gather my features into a blank.

At one point in the closing, the DA addressed Kennebeck directly, explaining why the spy witnesses had to rely so heavily on their reports for their testimony. As Phillips shook his finger at Kennebeck, Kennebeck did not maintain eye contact, though Phillips was speaking specifically to him. But instead of believing that Phillips had proved his point, all Kennebeck thought was that, "Yeah, he could get me rattled on a witness stand."[131]

4. *Jurors View from Their Own Perspectives*

The above heading does not imply that jurors are immune to the suggestions or persuasiveness of attorneys; it is a simple verification of the belief that jurors come into the courtroom with their own means of interpreting testimony and events. Sometimes observant attorneys can tell that jurors are not adopting the desired interpretations, as the DA might have been able to conclude had he seen Kennebeck rubbing the blade of the sword cane across his wrist. Moreover, as was noted in an earlier chapter, if a juror does not see the relevance, from his perspective, of a piece of evidence, he simply will not integrate it into his piecing together of a story, regardless of the significance that the law may impute to it. An example in this trial was a pair of handcuffs that the DA passed to the jury, reportedly found when one of the defendants was arrested. Kennebeck "felt a little put-upon. . .while we examined the pair of handcuffs. . . .The cuffs didn't seem to be worth much time, so I gave them a glance and handed them on to Fred Hills." Also found at the defendant's apartment was a copy of the *Black Panther*, a newspaper, which contained an article on explosives. As that was passed around, Kennebeck reflected that just because literature is in your home, you haven't necessarily read the whole thing or even any part of it. He took the time to read the entire paper himself and then scanned the article on explosives, noting that it bore no underlining or any other marks to indicate that it had been read. The sword cane was also passed to the jury that day, and it was that afternoon that Kennebeck "first felt the strain of not being able to talk about the case." He badly wanted to point out that the "*sword cane is no weapon*."[132]

The evidence against the defendants included tape recordings of their alleged conspiratorial plans. After an arduous process of having the tapes transcribed and then having the court approve the tapes and transcription, the jury was allowed both to hear the tapes and follow along with a type transcription. Kennebeck describes how the impurity of the recording and the wealth of boring discussion caused him and other jurors headaches and other discomfort, but they were nevertheless "supremely attentive." He suspected that the others, like him, were "looking for some operative conspiratorial words to supersede. . .'shucking and jiving.'" He realized that the jury had the "power and the freedom [to] interpret words and intentions for" themselves. To Kennebeck, the tapes "seemed. . .just wild talk."[133]

At one telling point, one of the jurors actually caught a witness in a crucial mistake. Reportedly, a bullet had gone through a pouch and a pad of paper inside. As the DA passed the pouch, one of the jurors examined the pad, which was "miraculously intact." The juror, receiving permission to ask his question, verified how the pad was positioned in the pouch. This testimony had also been before the grand jury, but Kennebeck supposed that they had not asked to examine the pad. "[The witness] had been mistaken. *Cripes*." In his own attempt to piece together the picture, the story of what happened, Kennebeck says "[t]here was a point where I could half-see that frenzy. . . the two patrolmen. . .'scrambling' for cover behind their own car to duck bullets fired by the two 'male Negroes.'. . . But that picture really wasn't there to be seen."[134] Earlier Kennebeck had noted that "[t]he DA would like us to see a picture of the conspiring Panthers. . . But we didn't get enough scenery or dialogue through Phillips to fill it out."[135]

E. *Conclusion*

Although it does not appear to have been his intent, Kennebeck has suggested the nonverbal cues on which attorneys can rely to interpret what jurors are feeling, how they are receiving evidence, witnesses, and counsel. As earlier indicated, one of the jurors cited the DA in his summation for not knowing his audience. The reported reactions of the jury, which quickly absolved the defendants on all counts, imply that the prosecution had little idea of how even the subject matter of the trial, let alone its component parts, would affect a jury. Kennebeck's account is also filled with many humorous examples of juror interaction. To the extent however, that trial events were the subjects of the jokes, the humor appears to have been a means of dealing with an unpleasant subject. For example, after the testimony concerning the tape recordings, which were generated by one of the men who spied on the Panthers wearing a microphone, it was a standing joke for Murray Schneider, one of the alternate jurors to say, "Speak into my necktie, please." Although this made everyone laugh, Kennebeck reports, "even now I can get a sinking feeling in my stomach as I imagine somebody wearing one of those at a business conference, say, or group discussion."[136] Even the formalities of trial procedure itself, perhaps unavoidable, began to grate on the jurors. When one witness was called back to the stand after having not been heard from for several weeks, he was reminded that he was still under oath. Kennebeck asked another juror how long it took for an oath to wear off.[137]

Finally, as a supreme example of a presentation of evidence that was meant solely for the record and *not* for the jury, in the midst of a stream of expert testimony, one of the jurors joked to Kennebeck that they should start chanting, "We want Detective White." Kennebeck retorted that they should carry banners saying "No More Ballistics."[138]

And as a parting affirmation of both primacy and a juror's clinging to his own piecing together of the story, Kennebeck recalls that, the DA, in his summation, urged the jurors to look again at any evidence that concerned them. Kennebeck thought to himself that he would like to see just one thing, the "sword cane. [He] couldn't remember any mention of it in the DA's summation."[139]

III. *EFFECTS OF JURY SIZE AND DECISION RULES*

This section would have had a more imaginative title had all of the good ones not already been taken. From "And Then There Were Twelve" to ". . . And Then There Were None," and "Six Will Do!" to "Twelve Is Just," legal and psycholegal scholars have waxed eloquently and persuasively on the topics of appropriate jury size and decision rule (unanimity as opposed to a majority). That the literature continues to flow, both from legal scholars and the social scientists, proves that the appropriate size and decision rules are still in dispute. That size and decision rules ever changed from the unanimous twelve in the first place is symptomatic of the unresolvable nature of the issue. In other words, had there been an original clear-cut rationale for a unanimous twelve, it might have withstood the scrutiny of modern times. But "[t]he origins of the twelve-member jury are shrouded in obscurity." Searches for the justification of this number have ended with a discovery of the appearances of the number twelve in history and its associations then, such as the twelve Apostles of Christ, the twelve officers of Solomon, and the twelve members of the community that were required in the Norman Inquisition to report to their king under oath about his subjects.[140]

> The origin of the twelve-person unanimous jury is lost in history. . . . For our purposes, it will suffice to know that the twelve-person unanimous jury was established in England by the end of the fourteenth century. And, more important, that in the man-

ner of most venerated social institutions, no one has any sound ideas about the rationale that guided the institution into existence.[141]

In 1970, in *Williams v. Florida*, the Supreme Court held that a decrease in the size of a criminal jury from twelve to six did not violate the Sixth Amendment. Although the "studies" that the majority relied on, supposedly indicating that the reduction would produce no discernible differences in the juries' results, are still being criticized, a less responsive tribunal might have taken a different approach. That is, since there was as yet no articulated rationale for a unanimous twelve, the Court could have asked simply for such a rationale: "Why shouldn't we change, or what is the justification for twelve?" The Court however, felt it knew the answer to that; had there been a rationale, the framers of the Constitution would have suggested it or specified the number twelve. In the absence of any such rationale, the Court, though it theoretically did not need to, then ostensibly yielded to the "persuasiveness" of the studies, which at least seemed to present a rationale for a smaller number. The point is, even if the data were flawed, they presented more of a basis for six-member juries than history alone could for twelve-member juries. In a similar vein, by 1952 many states had replaced twelve-member civil juries with six members, as had fifty-four federal district courts by 1973, when such a reduction was upheld by the Supreme Court in *Colgrove v. Battin*. Apparently, these state and district courts had already addressed the "Why shouldn't we change?" question and arrived at the same answer as the Court. Although the Court is criticized both for buttressing its finding in *Colgrove* with the *Williams* support and for justifying *Colgrove* and *Williams* with four recent experimental studies, the issue is the same—the experiments were probably less responsible for the holding than the lack of a rational basis for the traditional twelve-person jury.[142]

The literature following *Williams* and its progeny has taken three forms: legal, psycholegal, and social-psychological. Discussion of the purely legal literature, which dissects the Court's reasoning, is best left to another forum, for at least two reasons. First, it would require reporting and analysis of majority and minority dicta from case to case, which is more suited to legal treatises. Second, such an analysis presumes that the answer to jury size and decision rules is legal. That would probably be true only if the rationale for a unanimous twelve were set forth in common law tomes or other legal sources. The psycholegal literature though, examines the psychological findings cited as support for case decisions and examines other experimental results in relation to supposed requirements of the jury. The psychological-sociological literature more directly considers experimental results. What emerges from a review of these latter two types of literature is the bare conclusion that twelve- and six-member juries are likely to have different compositions, behave differently, and produce different verdicts. Those who criticize the move from the twelve-member jury are primarily saying that these differences make the six-member jury undesirable, but they do so without ever establishing the independent rationale for the traditional unanimous twelve. In other words, the comparison of six and twelve shows six to be undesirable just because the results are different; for the results of six to be "bad," it must be shown that the results of twelve are "good." Thus, this chapter ends with the potential differences, so that, to the extent choice is available, client and counsel can decide which jury best suits their needs and make an informed selection.

A. *The Psycholegal Approach*

There may be a logical flaw in the expressed reliance of the Court in first *Williams* and then *Colgrove* on the studies. On the one hand, the Court says that there is nothing magic about the number twelve. But on the other, it justifies the acceptance of six-member juries by saying that the studies indicate there is no difference between the results of twelve-member and six-member juries. What the Court has done therefore, is validate the findings of twelve-member juries (while rejecting the idea of any rationale for twelve-member juries). Thus six-member juries, by the Court's implicit criterion, must behave like twelve-member juries to be acceptable. It is precisely this requirement that has spawned much of the critical literature, initially with the attack on the studies showing that they fail to demonstrate that results of twelve- and six-member juries are the same, and later, with almost indisputable evidence of differences.

In *Williams*, the Court cites six studies as indicating that jury size produces no discernible differences in results. While Hans Zeisel characterizes these studies as "nonexistent evidence,"[143] a more descriptive summary follows:

> The six studies . . . are primarily expressions of opinion based, if on any evidence at all, upon uncontrolled observations that might be likened to clinical case studies. . . .
>
> . . . .

> Thus, of the six "experiments," the first was a mere assertion with no evidence; the next three were casual observations of the verdicts rendered by smaller juries, two of those reports being of the same set of juries; the fifth was merely a report that a smaller jury had been used; and the sixth was a discussion of economic advantages, irrelevant to the questions the Court posed as the critical questions of jury functioning.[144]

Zeisel has led the charge against the "empirical" evidence that the Court cited in *Colgrove* and analyzed each of those studies in an article written with Shari Seidman Diamond. The first study examined concerned civil jury trials in Washington, which are held before six-member juries unless one of the litigants requests twelve members. The study concluded that in 128 workmen's compensation trials, the juries found in equal proportions for the plaintiff, regardless of jury size. But the opportunity to choose the jury size causes Zeisel to dismiss this study. He suggests that when an attorney has a choice, he selects six or twelve members for a reason, and that a larger jury is likely to be more favorable to a larger award. Thus, the attorney's choice could have affected the size of the award in these cases. A second study was also conducted in a jurisdiction in which the litigants had a choice of jury size; additionally, various types of cases were involved. Zeisel notes that the larger juries tried the more complicated cases, which he believes accounted for the larger awards and longer deliberation time for the twelve-member juries. Based on the difference in the cases, though, no conclusions as to comparisons between six- and twelve-member juries could be drawn.[145]

A third study avoided the problem of different cases by showing a videotaped case to six-member and twelve-member mock juries. But since the evidence was so overwhelmingly for the defendant (not one jury found for the plaintiff), "any jury under any rules would probably have arrived at the same verdict." In addition, deliberation time is a consideration in the selection of jury size. In the study, the vote of the jurors before and after deliberation was taken. However, Zeisel points out that due to the evidence so strongly favoring the defendant, six of the twelve-member juries and four of the six-member juries had reached the required majority before deliberation began. Thus, for ten of the juries deliberation was an empty exercise, and any conclusions about comparable deliberation time were invalid. The last study purported to compare trial results before and after Michigan replaced its twelve-member jury with six members in 1970. Zeisel suggests that such a comparison could be valid but for other changes that might have accounted for trial results. Two such changes were the institution of a mediation board and the modification of procedural rules to allow for the discovery of insurance policy limits. Zeisel sees "a disconcerting picture" in the Court's reliance on these four studies to conclude that "there is no discernible difference" between twelve- and six-member juries.[146]

Three topics continue to arise in the discussion of jury size: cost, representativeness, and accuracy. Clearly they are not on the same plane. Cost and time savings, however, are thought to be as important as (if not more important than) other arguments for reducing jury size.

1. *Cost*

Zeisel agrees that based on 1974 per diem rates of $20 in the federal system, reducing juries from twelve to six would result in savings of a substantial sum, $4 million. However, this "is only a little more than 2% of the total federal judicial budget and a little more than the thousandth part of 1% of the total federal budget." As to the time saved in empaneling a jury, he points out that most federal *voir dire* is conducted by the judge, who takes no longer to ask questions of twelve than of six; the time differences in their responses would be minimal. Finally, he suggests that if deliberation time if shorter, this is not necessarily an attribute.[147]

Each of Zeisel's conclusions is refutable with opposing arguments of the same ilk, but since his conclusions are only responses to opposing arguments in the first place, to say there remain these issues is merely to suggest that they are inherently unresolvable. On another level of response, it may be that neither Zeisel's arguments, nor those that he was answering, are the issues to be addressed. For example, legal professionals can debate cost in similar terms. It could be pointed out that Zeisel has overlooked cost savings that would accrue from the relative ease of "[h]andling, corraling and supervising a jury of six" and finding jury rooms that require only half the physical space in courthouses, where space is valued so highly; these were savings noted by the Civil Court of the City of New York after having used a smaller jury for three years.[148] However, the jurors themselves may have a different perspective on cost, and many are likely to welcome a solution that will keep them away from their jobs less often and for a shorter period of time (assuming deliberation time really is shorter).

The argument Zeisel makes about the *voir dire* is an example of considering jury size in a vacuum. He suggests that *voir dire* conducted by the judge goes rather quickly anyway. That is precisely why so many attorneys (and quite a few judges) are trying to make attorney-conducted questioning a requirement. Therefore, if the rules change, the rationale for Zeisel's argument fails. On the other hand, if *voir dire* is conducted with the thoroughness that many attorneys recommend, then it logically should take less time to decide upon six jurors than twelve unless, of course, it is supposed that even more thought should be put into the decision of the six, since each of them will have the impact of two jurors in a twelve-person panel.

The fear of Zeisel, and others, that a smaller jury will not deliberate as long as a larger jury is based on the presumptions that deliberation in general has some ascertainable value and that the kind (length, depth, scope) of deliberation in twelve-person juries is inherently more valuable than the kind that occurs in smaller juries. First, Kalven and Zeisel, in their book *The American Jury*, explode the myth that jurors do not reach their decisions until after deliberation; they found that deliberation produces not a decision, but only consensus.[149] It would seem to follow that consensus would be more readily produced with a smaller number; thus, if the practical function of deliberation is to produce consensus, that goal is more efficiently met with smaller juries. That route of logic is not the one taken, however. Instead, the hypothesis is twisted so that consensus is a *bad* thing, more likely *not* to be reached with a larger jury, which results in a greater chance of hold-outs and hung juries, less likely to occur in small juries. Second, it is presumed that whatever now occurs in and comes out of twelve-person juries is by some standard correct and that any deviation from that product is somehow incorrect. Such a conclusion is logically impossible, with twelve-person juries lacking a theoretical foundation. What happens with and emanates from twelve-person juries is exactly that—behavior and results of twelve-person juries—not idealistic behavior and results of any jury.

2. *Representativeness*

> The Federal Supreme Court has said that whatever limitations were inherent in the historical concept of the jury as a body of one's peers do not prevail in the United States, in which a jury

> should be a body truly representative of the community and not the organ of any special group or class.[150]

Zeisel argues that when the jury's size is reduced from twelve to six, it will necessarily be "less representative of the community from which it was drawn." He admits that even though "twelve jurors cannot really represent the whole community," six would be even less representative.[151] Most who defend twelve jurors on the basis of greater heterogeny begin with the statement that the more heterogenous the population, the larger the sample must be to be representative of it; therefore, twelve is not an ideal number; it is simply better than six. Then, they frequently use a one in ten ratio as an example. That is, they suppose that 10% of the population is black or Hispanic and compute that, of 100 twelve-member juries, seventy-two will have at least one representative of the minority but that, of 100 six-member juries, only forty-seven would have a minority representative.[152]

Almost each time the above computation is made, the respective authors add something like the following:

> Obviously, ethnic status is used only as an illustration. We could speak, with equal facility, of the probability that no juror will be predisposed to favor a police officer's testimony over that of an accused's, that no juror will be a corporate executive, that no juror will be a man, that no juror will have anti-authoritarian attitudes, and so on. Much of the value of the jury system inheres in its ability to bring persons with conflicting biases (and varied expertise) together to deliberate as a group.[153]

First, notice that there is again the presumption that the jurors will "deliberate as a group," pooling opinions based on diverse backgrounds to arrive at a joint decision. There is simply no evidence that this is what deliberation accomplishes. Second, ethnic status is *not* like having an anti-authoritarian attitude. One could not go to a judge and request a new panel on the basis of an absence of anti-authoritarians, but very likely could if there were no Hispanics on the panel when the community had a 25% Hispanic population. Third, the foundation of *voir dire* is that it weeds out prospective jurors who are biased. With unlimited challenges for cause, an attorney is theoretically assured of an unbiased panel, even if they do not happen to embody ideal attitudes, from the perspective of his client. "The law is well settled that a defendant has no right to a trial by any particular jury or jurors, but has the right only to a trial by a competent and impartial jury."[154] Finally, the one in ten ratio, as well as the resulting percentages, always neglects different actual ratios in different communities.

3. *Accuracy*

"[S]ocial-psychological research into group decisionmaking and problem solving has isolated two related factors—size and heterogeneity—that suggest that smaller juries are more prone to error than are larger bodies."[155] This observation naturally stems from the assumption that juries behave like groups such that conclusions as to group discussion are applicable to jurors. As indicated in an earlier chapter, this view is flawed.[156] The statement that "smaller juries are more prone to error" suggests that the task put to a jury is a eureka task, having an obvious correct solution. With such tasks, larger groups may well be better able than smaller groups to arrive at that correct solution. But that is not the kind of task that confronts jurors. Instead, they deal with a human relations task, in which the data are simply too "problematic" to be sorted and judged precisely the same way by individuals with different perspectives. Also, because of the human relations aspects, it is not a task that responsible people trust to others. This probably explains why most jurors have already made up their minds when they leave the jury box, before deliberation begins.

Thus, to say "smaller juries are prone to error" is to misconceive the function of juries: they interpret the evidence and judge guilt in light of the court's instructions. The interpretation phase occurs before they leave the jury box; having fifty or five jurors will not insure a "correct" interpretation of the evidence because such does not exist; it is a judgment in the mind of each juror. Perhaps what defense counsel mean by "correct" here is the way their clients would have the evidence interpreted. Interpretation of the court's instructions, however, can be correct or incorrect, but there is no way to insure by sheer *number* that the court's instructions will be understood. Ironically, those who would interpret the court's instructions to the letter might also be those who would fail to see the defendant's version of the facts. Also, there are jurors who will clearly disregard the court's instructions and the applicable law: "while the jury is moved to leniency by adding a distinction the law does not make, it is at times moved to be more severe than the judge because it wishes to override a distinction the law does make."[157] Those who allude to the "correctness" of a twelve-member jury forget its lack of any theoretical justification.

But those who point to one rather clear difference between the results of twelve- and six-member juries, the likelihood of "fewer examples of that treasured, paradoxical phenomenon—the hung jury," suggest that six-member juries will be less correct because of that difference. Zeisel predicts the diminishment of this "treasured phenomenon" because of fewer holders of minority positions on a six-member jury and because any dissenter on such a jury is likely to be the only one in such a position and unable to maintain it. He emphasizes that it is not the proportion of minority representatives to the majority that matters, but whether the minority hold-out has an ally. That means that two vs. ten is not the same as one vs. five; though both are in the same ratio to the majority, the lone hold-out has no ally. As empirical verification of his hypothesis, Zeisel points to the frequency of hung juries in the Miami Circuit Court in six-member juries of criminal trials as compared with hung juries in twelve-member juries nationwide. The six-member juries hung 2.4% of the time, and the twelve-member juries hung 5.0% of the time.[158]

Zeisel therefore implies that even if a minority representative is on a six-member jury and if he decides differently than the majority, his voice is likely not to be heard, he will give in, and the ultimate vote will not truly be a consensus. However, when a group reaches the size of twelve, it tends to break into factions of three or four. In addition, as a group increases in size, the inequality of the members' participation also increases. Thus, "[t]o the extent that groups larger than six produce decisions (verdicts) based on the strength or vociferousness of factions of three or four members a verdict of six will represent a greater consensus of the group than will a verdict of twelve." Although hung juries may be attributable to two dissenters providing social support for each other, the more serious the crime, the more support even one voting in the majority may require. With a felony then, a juror in a six-member panel may not feel that he is adequately supported by only five other jurors and may therefore prevent a verdict rather than accept responsibility for a consensus. In this way, six-member juries could hang more often than twelve-member juries with serious crimes, and the difference in the crimes may account for the difference in Zeisel's figures for hung juries.[159]

Still concerned with the elimination of the effect of the minority, Zeisel points out that abandoning the unanimity rule accomplishes the same end. "Minority viewpoints fare better on a jury of ten that must be unanimous than on a jury of twelve where ten members must agree on a verdict." To explain this, he returns to the minority's probable appearance on seventy-two of 100 juries. Of that seventy-two, one minority representative is likely to appear on thirty-eight juries, two are likely to appear on twenty-three juries, and three are likely to appear on eleven juries. If the jury of twelve has a decision rule of ten, then the one minority member (for thirty-eight juries) and the two minority members (for twenty-three juries) can be completely disregarded. Thus, only on eleven of 100 juries can the minority member expect to influence the jury. With a unanimous decision rule, the minority can expect to influence seventy-two of the juries.[160]

Zeisel's concern about the minority viewpoint under non-unanimous decision rules was expressed in 1971. In 1977, Saks proposed the very question in Zeisel's mind: "Under a non-unanimous decision rule, are arguments of the minority given less attention, perhaps even ignored (when that minority coalition is inadequate to block a verdict)?" Considering rationales for affirmative and negative responses, he deems both "eminently plausible," but notes neither to be supported by evidence, "largely because no evidence exists on the question."[161] But there need be no evidence to point out two critical but unproven assumptions that underlie Zeisel's concern: (1) that the minority representative on the jury is the same person or persons who are in the minority in the vote, and (2) that the minority representative will voice the reasons for his vote or otherwise seek to alter the opinion of the majority.

Concerning the first, no one has yet demonstrated that the 10% minority of, for example, the corporate executive, if he is the only one of his kind on the jury, will be the hold-out in the conviction of a corporate executive on trial for a felony. Similarly, if in the community of a trial, the Hispanic population is 10%, it has not been demonstrated how the single Hispanic juror will vote. On the one hand, Zeisel is concerned about representing any number of minorities (recall that he purportedly includes *all* minority *attitudes*, a practical impossibility, regardless of jury size); on the other hand, he is concerned about these attitudes, once represented, being swept away by the majority; but he has not linked the two.

Concerning the second, a jury of twelve could have as many as three to five minority votes after the first ballot. Depending on the personalities of the people in the minority, they could be swung to the majority merely by the force of the initial count. Even if one or more of them held their positions, there is no indication that they will voice their reasoning or try to persuade the majority. Similarly, a very strong personality, alone, could persuade weak personalities in the majority to decide with him. Undoubtedly the lack of evidence as to the force and effect of minority opinions in a jury is due to the uniqueness of the jury's task (which is really not a "group" task) and the strength or weakness of individuals on the jury.

B. *The Psychological Approach*

An experiment reported in 1975 appears to have been designed to answer many of the questions posed in the legalistic view presented above. "Juries of six or twelve persons listened to a simulated trial of a rape case, deliberated, and then rendered verdicts according to the unanimity or two-thirds majority social decision rule assigned." The experiment involved 720 subjects, consisting of 221 females and 499 males. After hearing the trial but prior to deliberation, each subject indicated his or her individual verdict. At that time, 22% thought the defendant was guilty. Not a single jury brought back a guilty verdict, and in a unanimous twelve-member jury, the jury hung 28% of the time, and voted not guilty 72% of the time.[162] Although it is only by chance that the 28% of the cases that apparently hung because of minority beliefs as to the defendant's *guilt* matches the 28% that Zeisel notes as the frequency of a minority representative's appearance on a jury (which he feels is a safeguard for the defendant), the coincidence helps to make a point. Juror response is more than a function of the make-up of the individual juror (which is *not* totally defined by observing that one or more of his personal or attitudinal traits places him in some recognized minority); it is also intricately related to the nature of the crime.

The experimenters admit that their study was prompted in part by the Supreme Court's decision that a reduction in jury size and departure from unanimity would not result in materially different verdicts. Concerning that, they conclude, "[t]he efficacy of the rule assignment and size manipulations together seem to suggest that from this study we cannot argue against the wisdom of the recent Supreme Court decisions described at the outset." However, two outcomes for the ⅔ majority decision rule for both six- and twelve-member juries are disturbing. At a 67% certain probability of guilt, as determined by the individual assessments before deliberation, twelve- and six-member juries would both convict about 80% of the time (the frequency of joint conviction rises thereafter in proportion to the probability of guilt). Similarly, at a 33% probability of guilt, both twelve- and six-member juries would acquit about 80% of the time. However, at a 50% probability of guilt, a twelve-member jury will convict 20% of the time, while a six-member jury will convict that often on only a 33% probability of guilt. Conversely, 20% of the time that there is a 50% probability of guilt, a twelve-member jury will acquit; a six-member jury will acquit that often when there is a 60% probability of guilt. The conclusion is that a switch from twelve to six jurors "would promote more guilty verdicts for weak prosecution cases [when the probability of guilt is low] and result in more acquittals for strong prosecution cases." The authors then glibly explain that majority models tend to exaggerate high probabilities and depress low probabilities in the group outcome distribution that were apparent in the individual distribution. This explanation, without more, is neither illuminating nor comforting.[163]

The above results, however, indicate a correlation between apparent guilt and jury size or decision rule, and the jury's verdicts. Such a correlation was found in another experiment, "designed to assess. . . the influence of jury size and apparent guilt upon rate of conviction, hung juries, and acquittals in simulated juries." Subjects (360, male and female) were divided into twelve- and six-member juries, and each size of jury heard two types of cases, one slightly favoring the defendant's guilt (high apparent guilt) and one slightly favoring his innocence (low apparent guilt), before arriving at unanimous or hung verdicts. The results are summarized on page 259.[164]

Number of Convictions and Nonconvictions (Acquittals Plus Hung Juries) by Experimental Condition

Condition	*Twelve Members*	*Six Members*
Low apparent guilt		
Acquittals	6	8
Hung juries	2	0
Total nonconvictions	8	8
Convictions	2	2
High apparent guilt		
Acquittals	2	1
Hung juries	6	0
Total nonconvictions	8	1
Convictions	2	9

The researchers observe that when the evidence suggests low apparent guilt, jury size has no significant effect, but "a defendant's safeguards against conviction, where apparent guilt is relatively high, are substantially reduced by use of a six-member jury rather than the traditional twelve-member jury." They also conclude that, when the case for the prosecution is very weak, "the defendant might be expected to have a better chance for acquittal with a smaller jury."[165]

Postexperimental questionnaire data revealed that the least satisfied of the four types of juries was the six-member jury in which the defendant had a high appearance of guilt. Members of this type of jury did not feel that their group allowed the free expression of divergent opinions and were not satisifed with their participation in these juries, which took "significantly less time" to reach their decisions than the other three types of juries. Members of the six-member juries that had innocent-appearing defendants, though, were very satisfied with their groups.[166] The expressed dissatisfaction of the convicting six-member juries verifies the earlier expressed idea that six members may not be enough to make juries feel comfortable in their convictions for serious crimes. Here, the defendant had been charged only with assault and battery.

A 1985 experimental report begins with a summary of the studies that had already compared six- and twelve-person juries and the conclusion that "[t]he nearly universal finding is one of no reliable jury size effects on jury verdicts." However, it adds that "intuitively plausible" and "empirically validated" jury decision-making models "have all led to the prediction that larger juries should hang more often." This result is not thought to stem from some differences in the decision-making process for juries of different sizes. Rather, unanimity is more likely when there is a preponderance of support for one of the verdict alternatives at the beginning of deliberation, and sampling theory reveals this is more likely to occur in smaller groups.[167]

The experiment sought to discover any differences between deliberation processes for twelve-, six-, and three-person juries. The results showed virtually no differences in the deliberation process with the twelve- and six-person groups; "[f]or example, factions of the same relative size were equally able to attract converts and to ultimately prevail in six- and twelve-person groups." In addition, the time required for a decision shift was comparable for those two groups. As to absolute deliberation time, the shorter times for the smaller groups could be due to the greater probability of the smaller groups being at or near unanimity at the beginning of deliberation. Behavior of three-person groups, however, suggested that they did use different deliberation processes. Even when their initial verdict splits were comparable to those of the larger groups, the three-member groups "had markedly different final verdict distributions; they were generally less likely to hang, were more likely to convict when the majority favored conviction, and were less likely to acquit when the majority favored acquittal."[168]

The experimenters conclude that aside from the occurrence of hung juries, "group size had no effect on the relative likelihood of conviction or acquittal," but they do recognize that a hung jury "is a relatively favorable outcome for a defendant."[169] This is a common association of a hung jury, but notice that it rests on the assumptions that the majority of the jurors have found the defendant guilty and that the minority is actually "corrected." First, "it is impossible to measure directly the quality of the group product in juries, because we never know which is the correct verdict. Does a particular hung jury prevent injustice or does it impede justice?"[170] A hold-out opinion on a jury is simply a different opinion from the majority, and "[t]he larger the sample of individuals that is drawn from a given population, the greater will be the probability of that sample's containing one individual who will disagree with his fellows."[171] Second, if a hung jury represents a majority for an acquittal and a minority guilty vote, then the defendant is harmed, not helped, by the hold-out. An example in this experiment is seen in the fact that no twelve-person groups began with a 0-guilty-12-not-guilty split, but three six-person groups voted unanimously for acquittal at the beginning of deliberation.[172]

An experiment reported in 1976 examined the relationship between decision rule and jury verdicts when the standard of reasonable doubt varied. One instruction contained no definition of reasonable doubt; a second defined reasonable doubt as "a serious and well-founded misgiving about the defendant's guilt"; and a third provided a stringent definition: "the prosecution must have convinced you to a moral certainty, with absolute and positive proof."[173] Although the mock juries *all contained six members*, the number of hung juries fluctuated widely, in apparent concert with the nature of the instruction on reasonable doubt. When reasonable doubt was undefined, the unanimous and majority juries had an equal number of hung juries. This suggests that court instructions comprise another dimension to examine in the attempt to account for the differences between results of twelve- and six-person juries; simply looking at jury outcomes from a particular jurisdiction for juries of different sizes will not provide a comparison of the instructions. In addition, the individual reactions of the mock juries were recorded prior to deliberation. In almost all cases, the results of the juries were less harsh (more towards not guilty) than the individual verdicts, suggesting the strength of the minority opinions, regardless of the decision rule and despite the fact that most of the majority-rule groups stopped deliberating once the required majority had been obtained.[174] The verdict results are summarized on page 262.[175]

Frequency and Relative Frequency Distributions of Predeliberation, Individual Verdicts, and Jury Verdicts

Assigned Decision Rule

	Unanimous			*Majority*		
Criterion of reasonable doubt	*Guilty*	*Not guilty*	*No opinion*	*Guilty*	*Not guilty*	*No opinion*
Predeliberation, individual verdicts						
Stringent	49	52	13	55	48	11
	.430	.456	.114	.482	.421	.096
Lax	69	34	11	67	35	12
	.605	.298	.096	.588	.307	.105
Undefined	32	24	10	44	24	16
	.485	.364	.152	.524	.286	.190
Column total	150	110	34	166	107	39
	.510	.374	.116	.532	.343	.125
Jury verdicts						
Stringent	2	10	7	7	11	1
	.105	.526	.368	.368	.579	.053
Lax	8	3	8	11	8	0
	.421	.158	.421	.579	.471	.000
Undefined	3	4	4	6	4	4
	.273	.364	.364	.429	.286	.286
Column total	13	17	19	24	23	5
	.265	.347	.388	.461	.422	.096

C. *The Differences between Six-person Juries and Twelve-person Juries and Unanimous and Majority Juries*

Following are some of the differences between juries of different sizes and decision rules that Saks provides;[176] the comments and considerations next to those differences are not necessarily Saks', but flow from the issues raised above.

1. *Large juries spend more time deliberating than small juries.* If this is an advantage, it must be because deliberation has a clear function. The only discoverable result of deliberation is the facilitation of consensus, a result that seems furthered by six-person juries, since twelve-person juries may be more likely not to reach consensus, i.e., hang.

2. *Large juries engage in more communication per unit time, although small juries allow more communication per member.* Before the value of the communication can be assessed, it must first be known of what the communication consists. If, as revealed in the section "The Juror as a Unique Subject," the communication consists of each juror validating his own verdict, the amount of communication may be of little consequence. If however, the communication involves explanation of court instructions and definitions of law, the bases of most changes in juror opinion, then the amount of communication could be meaningful.

3. *Large juries manifest better recall of testimony, although small juries better recall arguments as a percentage of the total arguments.* Also as indicated in "The Juror as a Unique Subject," only if, by the time of deliberation, his version of "what happened" is incomplete, will a juror incorporate into his version any testimony or arguments mentioned in the jury room. In addition, although the percentage of collective recall may be high for twelve persons, it is still likely to be incorrect or contain faulty emphases; theoretically, the more people there are to misrecall the facts, the more they will be misrecalled.

4. *Large juries represent the community better.* For this to be relevant, the effect of "better" representation must be shown. That is, there must be demonstrated a correlation between six-person juries that survive *voir dire* (and are, therefore, supposedly unbiased) and unfavorable findings for defendants, when similar defendants charged with similar crimes have received favorable verdicts from twelve-person juries in the same or similar jurisdictions.

5. *Large juries tend to favor the defendant when his apparent guilt is relatively high; when the prosecution's case is weak, small juries are more likely to acquit.*

6. *Unanimous juries deliberate longer.* Again, the value of deliberation must be clear for this to be an advantage.

7. *Unanimous juries are more likely to hang.* This is an advantage for the defendant only when the jury hangs in his favor; that is, but for a hold-out juror, the defendant might be acquitted.

D. *The Practical Effect of Personality Dominance on a Six-member or Twelve-member Jury*

The trial attorney must consider the effect of group dynamics and dominant personalities on the verdicts reached to be successful in predicting jury results. In the jury selection process each prospective juror must be considered as dominant, passive, or flexible in personality type. Twelve or six individuals are not selected independently of each other as a jury. People react differently in groups depending on the composition of the group. It is surprising to learn how many attorneys incorrectly conceptualize the jury as being composed of twelve or six independent people with a foreman. This is never the case. A leader or various leaders and subgroups will emerge.

It has been the author's experience that the six-member jury more readily conforms to single person dominance. One strong, verbal personality can impose his or her views on the other five jurors more easily than in a twelve-member jury. In a six-member jury the decision will be made by one or two strong persons, with the remainder of the group passively in agreement. A twelve-member jury dilutes a single dominant personality and sometimes in fact, will reach an opposite verdict, isolating the vociferous juror to a one- or two-person minority. The dynamics of a twelve-member jury are such that it always breaks down into three or, more rarely, four subgroups. The results obtained by twelve-member juries indicate that this group is more likely than six-member juries to find the defendant guilty of negligence or of producing a defective product. Also, twelve-member juries award a larger amount of damages. The twelve-person verdict is a reflection of the fact that this group is generally controlled by three or four individuals. Therefore, the verdict is most likely the consensus of those three or four persons with a "me too" stamp supplied by the rest of the group. I have found that a six-member jury is more conservative than a twelve-member jury in the amount of damages awarded. Also, the six-member jury is more likely to require the plaintiff to prove the case by *stronger* evidence as to guilt or wrongdoing for an award of damages. It can be said that trying the case to a six-member jury is almost like trying the case to the judge. One dominant personality will emerge (at the most, two dominant persons) and the other five or four will be passive. These strong verbal people are more inclined to be negative than positive to the plaintiff's position.

Despite the numerical difference in six- or twelve-member juries, the single most important factor in either group is the existence of one or two strong personalities in the six-member jury and three or four strong personalities in the twelve-member jury who will determine the outcome of the litigation. It is the trial advocate's function in jury selection to identify and examine these strong personalities to determine whether they are likely to agree with his position in the litigation. If so, keep them on the jury. If not, eliminate them, as the attorney can not proselytize this type of juror. If the prospective juror's background, social experiences, and personality are consistent with the advocate's position in the lawsuit, the juror will be for him through the verdict. If this prospective juror is negative, he needs to be eliminated from the jury. The strong juror can usually be identified as the male who is in an executive position, with a high salary, much responsibility, and decision-making authority, and he is usually more educated than the average juror. He is used to making decisions and requiring others to follow as a component of his job responsibilities. He will hold firm in the face of adverse argument. This personality is motivated by: "Will the verdict that he is required to render in this case be acceptable to his executive peer group to which he reports? Will they like his decision?" Peer pressure is enormous on this type of individual. His own views may be suppressed in order to meet the approval of the "boardroom."

To crystallize this discussion, suffice it to say that several strong personalities control the juries and in fact, return the verdicts. The best trial insurance is to locate such a personality and have him on your side, or just as important, eliminate him if he is "probably" for the other side.

Most attorneys, as they present the evidence, try to determine which of the jurors will lead the group. If *voir dire* has been done well, strong personality types were identified and are favorable or they have been eliminated and the jury is a sea of passive people who are leaderless and ready to rubberstamp whichever side they trust, respect, and believe. They will endorse the side who seems the most organized, prepared, and reliable (that is, *perceived* as more in control of the courtroom and possessing more knowledge).

NOTES

1. Frates & Greer, *Jury* Voir Dire: *The Lawyer's Perspective*, 2 Litigation, Winter 1976, at 17, 18.
2. Atkins, *Jury* Voir Dire: *The Judge's Perspective*, 2 Litigation, Winter 1976, at 19, 50.
3. Covington, *Jury Selection: Innovative Approaches to Both Civil and Criminal Litigation*, 16 St. Mary's L. Rev. 575 (1985).
4. Cone & Lawyer, *The Art of Persuasion in Litigation* 256 (1966).

5. See "Theory: Primacy vs. Recency," section I of Chapter 2.
6. Cone & Lawyer, *supra* n.4, at 256.
7. *Id.* at 258.
8. *Id.* at 256.
9. *Id.* at 256.
10. *Id.* at 260.
11. See the explanation of "reactance" in "Theory: Primacy vs. Recency," section I of Chapter 2.
12. Cone & Lawyer, *supra* n.4, at 256.
13. *Id.* at 261.
14. Bush, *The Case for Expansive* Voir Dire, 2 Law & Psychology Rev. 10 (1976).
15. *Id.* at 11–14.
16. *Id.* at 15–20.
17. Fed. R. Civ. P. 47(a); Fed. R. Crim. P. 24(a).
18. Bush, *supra* n.14, at 16.
19. *Id.* at 16–19.
20. *Id.* at 23–24.
21. *Id.* at 20.
22. Carlson, *Successful Techniques for Civil Trials* 325–26 (1983).
23. *Id.* at 324.
24. See "The Juror as a Unique Subject," section III of Chapter 2.
25. Cone & Lawyer, *supra* n.4, at 263.
26. Atkins, *supra* n.2, at 19–20.
27. Bush, *supra* n.14, at 17.
28. Atkins, *supra* n.2, at 20, 50.
29. Wiseman, *Lawyer* Voir Dire, 11 Litigation, Winter 1985, at 5, 6.
30. Will, *Judicial Independence and* Voir Dire, 11 Litigation, Summer 1985, at 5, 6.
31. *Id.* at 6, 59.
32. See "The Expert Attorney," section I of Chapter 1.
33. Sullivan & McMeans, *Judge or Jury,* 10 Litigation, Summer 1984, at 18, 19, 62.
34. McCullough & Underwood, 2 *Civil Trial Manual* 559–60 (1980).
35. *Id.* at 561.
36. *Id.* at 562.
37. Lees-Haley, *The Psychology of Jury Selection,* 47 Tex. B.J. 918, 920 (1984).
38. *Id.* at 920–21.
39. See "The Juror as a Unique Subject," section III of Chapter 2.
40. Frederick, *Jury Behavior: A Psychologist Examines Jury Selection,* 5 Ohio N.U.L. Rev. 571, 575–76 (1978).
41. Author's unpublished research on the authoritarian personality and jury decisions.
42. *Id.*

43. Author was retained by a law firm to design and conduct such research.

44. Desired or ideal juror pattern reinforced the attorney's idea, from his experience, as to the type of person that he was seeking.

45. Frederick, *supra* n.40, at 577.

46. Covington, *State-of-the-Art in Jury Selection Techniques: More Science Than Luck*, 19 Trial, Sept. 1983, at 84.

47. Frederick, *supra* n.40, at 580–81.

48. *Id.* at 580.

49. Worthy, Gary, & Kahn, *Self-Disclosure as an Exchange Process*, 13 J. Personality & Soc. Psychology 59 (1969).

50. *Id.* at 60–63.

51. Hamlin, *What Makes Juries Listen* 72 (1985).

52. Jordan, *Jury Selection* 283 (1980).

53. Suggs & Sales, *Using Communication Cues to Evaluate Prospective Jurors during the* Voir Dire, 20 Ariz. L. Rev. 629, 630–31 (1978).

54. Hunt & Lin, *Accuracy of Judgments of Personal Attributes from Speech*, 6 J. Personality & Soc. Psychology 450, 451 (1966).

55. *Id.* at 452.

56. Zaidel & Mehrabian, *The Ability to Communicate and Infer Positive and Negative Attitudes Facially and Vocally*, 3 J. Experimental Research in Personality 233, 235 (1969).

57. *Id.* at 240–41.

58. Mehrabian & Wiener, *Decoding of Inconsistent Communications*, 6 J. Personality & Soc. Psychology 109, 110, 113 (1967).

59. *Id.* at 113.

60. *Id.* at 114.

61. Suggs & Sales, *supra* n.53, at 634–35.

62. *Id.* at 640.

63. Covington, *Use of Expert Assistance in Jury Selection*, 90 Case & Comment 20, July, August, 1985.

64. Covington, *supra* n.3, at 579.

65. D'Agostino & Brown, *Loaded for Acquittal? Psychiatry in the Jury Selection Process*, U. West L.A. L. Rev., Winter 1975, at 199, 212.

66. Appleman, *Preparation and Trial* 159 (1967).

67. Johnson, Johnson, & Little, *Expertise in Trial Advocacy: Some Considerations for Inquiry into Its Nature and Development*, 7 Campbell L. Rev. 119, 141 (1984).

68. McGarry, *Do-It-Yourself* Voir Dire, 10 Litigation, Winter 1984, at 38.

69. *Id.* at 39.

70. *Id.* at 39–40.

71. Appleman, *supra* n.66, at 162.

72. *Id.* at 160.

73. *Id.* at 162–63.

74. *Id.* at 163–65.

75. *Id.* at 165–70.

76. *Id.* at 171.

77. *Id.* at 176.

78. Hanley, *Brush Up Your Aristotle*, 12 Litigation, Winter 1986, at 39.

79. Appleman, *supra* n.66, at 161.

80. McGarry, *supra* n.68, at 39.

81. Covington, *supra* n.46, at 86.

82. Liebenson & Wepman, *The Psychologist as a Witness*, 164 (1964).

83. Blue, *Nonverbal Communication*, Mississippi Trial Lawyers' Seminar, Jackson, Mississippi, Spring 1984.

84. Broeder, Voir Dire *Examinations: An Empirical Study*, 38 S. Cal. L. Rev. 503, 510 (1965).

85. Suggs & Sales, *supra* n.53, at 639.

86. Gordon, *A Psychological Strategy for Jury Selection*, Seminar, Dallas, Texas, May, 1978.

87. Mulroy, *Getting an Edge with Mock Juries*, Nat'l L.J., Sept. 24, 1984, at 15, col. 2.

88. *State of Texas v. Davis*, No. 16,838, in the Criminal Court No. 4 of Tarrant County, Texas, 1979 (not guilty verdict).

89. *Marion T. Phillips v. Heinr, Wilhelm, Huss & Co., a/k/a Huss Mfg. Co., Continental Park Attractions, Inc., & Rick Polkentons*, No. 83-13587-K, in Dallas County, Texas, 1983.

90. *Phillip J. Birchfield et ux. v. Texarkana Memorial Hosp. et al.*, No. 76-C-1206, in Bowie County, Texas, 1984. Appellate opinion, *Hall v. Birchfield*, at 718 S.W.2d 313 (Tex. App.—Texarkana 1986).

91. Mulroy, *supra* n.87, at 16, col 1.

92. Interview with Aubrey Roberts, attorney, regarding use of systematic jury selection techniques, March 27, 1984.

93. Mulroy, *supra* n.87.

94. Vinson, *Shadow Juries: Monitoring Jurors' Reactions*, Trial, Sept. 1983, at 75.

95. Mulroy, *supra* n.87, at 16, col. 1.

96. Covington, *supra* n.63, at 24.

97. Dittman, Parloff & Boomer, *Facial and Bodily Expression: A Study of Receptivity of Emotional Cues*, 29 Psychiatry 239 (1965).

98. Ekman & Friesen, *Head and Body Cues in the Judgment of Emotion: A Reformation*, 24 Perceptual & Motor Skills 711, 718–19 (1967).

99. Mehrabian, *Relationship of Attitude to Seated Posture, Orientation, and Distance*, 10 J. Personality & Soc. Psychology 26 (1968).

100. Ellsworth, *Intimacy in Response to Direct Gaze*, 11 J. Experimental Soc. Psychology 592 (1975).

101. Kline, *The Role of Suggestibility in Lawyer-Jury Relationships*, Social Psychology & Discretionary Law 93, 95–96 (L. Abt & I. Stuart ed. 1979).

102. *Id.* at 98.

103. Marshall, *Law and Psychology in Conflict* 84 (1986).
104. Kline, *supra* n.101, at 99.
105. Suggs & Sales, *supra* n.53, at 629, 634–35 (1978).
106. Dittman et al., *supra* n.97, at 239.
107. *Id.* at 240–243.
108. Ekman & Friesen, *supra* n.98, at 718.
109. *Id.* at 718–19.
110. Mehrabian, *supra* n.99, at 28–29.
111. *Id.* at 608–609.
112. Kennebeck, *Juror Number Four* 26 (1973).
113. *Id.* at 32.
114. *Id.* at 29.
115. *Id.* at 32.
116. *Id.* at 104–107.
117. *Id.* at 19.
118. *Id.* at 179.
119. *Id.* at 188.
120. *Id.* at 190–99.
121. *Id.* at 203–207.
122. *Id.* at 202.
123. *Id.* at 28–29.
124. *Id.* at 191.
125. *Id.* at 26–27.
126. *Id.* at 167–73.
127. *Id.* at 31.
128. *Id.* at 62.
129. *Id.* at 128.
130. *Id.* at 129.
131. *Id.* at 203–209.
132. *Id.* at 62–66.
133. *Id.* at 79–82.
134. *Id.* at 142.
135. *Id.* at 179–80.
136. *Id.* at 78.
137. *Id.* at 99.
138. *Id.* at 143.
139. *Id.* at 212.
140. Thompson, *Six Will Do*, Trial, Nov.-Dec. 1974, at 12, 14.
141. Saks, *Jury Verdicts* 6 (1977).
142. Kaye, *And Then There Were Twelve: Statistical Reasoning, the Supreme Court, and the Size of the Jury*, 68 Cal. L. Rev. 1004, 1005 (1980); Wick, *The Half-Filled Jury Box: Is Half a Loaf Better Than None?* Litigation, Winter 1976, at 11, 13.
143. Zeisel & Diamond, *"Convincing Empirical Evidence," on the Six Member Jury*, 41 U. Chi. L. Rev. 281, 290 (1974).

144. Saks, *supra* n.141, at 9–10.

145. Zeisel & Diamond, *supra* n.143, at 283–86.

146. *Id.* at 286–90.

147. Zeisel, *Twelve Is Just*, Trial, Nov.-Dec. 1974, at 13.

148. Thompson, *supra* n.140, at 14.

149. Kalven & Zeisel, *The American Jury* 489 (1966).

150. 47 Am. Jur. 2d *Jury* § 24 (1969).

151. Zeisel, *supra* n.147, at 14.

152. *Id.* at 15; Zeisel, *...And Then There Were None: The Diminution of the Federal Jury*, 38 U. Chi. L. Rev. 710, 716 (1971); Saks, *supra* n.141, at 19; Kaye, *supra* n.142, at 1018.

153. Kaye, *supra* n.142, at 1018, n.58.

154. 47 Am. Jur. 2d *Jury* § 27 (1969).

155. Kaye, *supra* n.142, at 1019.

156. *See* "The Juror as a Unique Subject," section III of Chapter 2.

157. Kalven & Zeisel, *supra* n.149, at 494.

158. Zeisel, *supra* n.152, at 719–20.

159. Rosenblatt & Rosenblatt, *Six Member Juries in Criminal Cases: Legal and Psychological Considerations*, 46 N.Y.S.B.J. 259, 263–65 (1974).

160. Zeisel, *supra* n.149, at 722.

161. Saks, *supra* n.141, at 20–22.

162. Davis, Kerr, Atkin, Holt, & Meek, *The Decision Processes of 6- and 12-Person Mock Juries Assigned Unanimous and Two-Thirds Majority Rules*, 32 J. Personality & Soc. Psychology 1, 5–7 (1975).

163. *Id.* at 11–12.

164. Valenti & Downing, *Differential Effeccts of Jury Size on Verdicts Following Deliberation as a Function of the Apparent Guilt of a Defendant*, 32 J. Personality & Soc. Psychology 655, 658–60 (1975).

165. *Id.* at 662.

166. *Id.*

167. Kerr & MacCoun, *The Effects of Jury Size and Polling Method on the Process and Product of Jury Deliberation*, 48 J. Personality & Soc. Psychology 349, 350 (1985).

168. *Id.* at 356, 358, 360.

169. *Id.* at 360.

170. Saks, *supra* n.141, at 13.

171. Rosenblatt & Rosenblatt, *supra* n.159, at 264.

172. Kerr & MacCoun, *supra* n.167, at 355.

173. Kerr, Atkin, Stasser, Meek, Holt, & Davis, *Guilt Beyond a Reasonable Doubt: Effects of Concept Definition and Assigned Decision Rule on the Judgments of Mock Jurors*, 34 J. Personality & Soc. Psychology 282, 286 (1976).

174. *Id.* at 292.

175. *Id.* at 287.

176. Saks, *supra* n.141, at 105.

CHAPTER 5
THE WORDS OF THE WITNESS

SYNOPSIS

CHAPTER 5
THE WORDS OF THE WITNESS

A trial attorney is scarcely out of law school (if it takes that long) before he realizes the importance of a witness, apart from that to which the witness will testify. The reasons for this are explained in the previous chapters,[1] but can be briefly summarized as follows: (1) Jurors are as susceptible as other human beings to the physical attractiveness of parties (and counsel), and if the physical attractiveness precedes any other information about the parties, it can color the jurors' interpretation of later information, in favor of the attractive individuals. (2) In the absence of clear-cut evidence, or in the presence of strong evidence on both sides, jurors may base their decisions simply on the attorney they like best and/or the testimony of the witnesses that that attorney seemed to like best. (3) Jurors cannot help but rely upon their sense of values in resolving doubts about factual issues, determining "where the equities are," even if that means ignoring existing law or applying a standard more stringent than the law requires.

Despite the most precise and complete presentation of evidence, jurors can improperly weight what they hear, focusing on legally irrelevant details but determined to ferret them out so as to complete their versions of what happened. Jurors often forget major witnesses and confuse witnesses. Expert testimony is frequently used to support the conclusion the testimony actually disputed.[2] The jurors' selective perception of the evidence may result in evidential anomalies. In making a decision, jurors will rely upon their basic beliefs, attitudes, and values. It is man's nature to strive for consistency in behavior. The psychologist Leon Festinger believed that when there is an inconsistency, for example, between new information and old attitudes, the person will employ procedures to reduce this discrepancy so that both the old and the new are in agreement.[3] In a jury trial, cognitive dissonance may be evidenced by rejection of the contrary information or minimization of its importance or distortion of the information. In a well-publicized murder trial, the jury rejected the testimony of several eyewitnesses. Post-trial interviews revealed that the dominant jurors believed that wealthy, handsome men do not commit murder. Similarly, in a case in which much scientific evidence indicated an act of medical negligence, the persuasive leaders of the jury felt that the local physician was skillful and rejected or minimized the importance of expert medical testimony.

Surely, in both of these cases, the jurors also had to believe that the defendants were what they represented; i.e., that the wealthy man embodied their ideas of refinement and morality imputed to a high social class and that the doctor was a competent and respected member of the medical community. Thus, it is common for the trial attorney to have one ear on what the client or potential witness is saying, another on how it is being said, and both eyes on the appearance of the speaker—dress, mannerisms, gestures, and the like.

Considerations of the implications of dress and nonverbal behavior appear in an earlier chapter, primarily as a guide for the attorney in analyzing prospective jurors during *voir dire*. Naturally, however, the very kinds of analysis that an attorney may consciously conduct of visual cues are subconscious tools of jurors as they attend to witnesses and counsel. While jurors are affected by what they see, though, whether or not it is intended to be evidence, most evidence takes the form of words. And while two witnesses may deliver essentially the same evidence, the testimony style of each witness can affect the credibility and estimation of the witness by the jury. The first section below, therefore, examines the effects of different styles of testimony, as well as recommended methods for conducting direct examination, presenting expert testimony, and handling cross-examination. The second section concerns reducing witness stress to enhance effective communication. The third section considers hypnotically-induced testimony. Presented in the fourth section is a discussion of the attributes and shortcomings of eyewitness testimony.

I. *TESTIMONY STYLE*

A. *The Elements and Their Sources*

As will become apparent, courtroom testimony involves a power struggle, with the witness pitted against the questioning attorney or, when questioning is conducted by the court, the judge. Because "[t]he adversary system of legal procedure specifies that testimony be presented through the witness's response to the lawyer's questions. . .control over the content and to some degree, over the style of the testimony conversation is vested in the lawyer."[4] Therefore, when the attorney relinquishes control to a witness, the jury may conclude that it is because of the attorney's regard for the witness and/or the witness's ability to present the testimony. A prime indicator of control relinquishment lies in the method of questioning. The attorney can ask many questions, each eliciting only a brief response from the witness (fragmented style), or can ask only a few questions, to which the witness might respond with long, narrative answers (narrative style).

While earlier chapters suggest the difficulty of making assumptions about juror behavior when jurors cannot be contacted for their reactions during trial and cannot be recorded during deliberations, "court speech is publicly available and, with appropriate safeguards and permissions, [can] be tape recorded and subjected to sociolinguistic analyses to discover style variations that occur in actual speech." Thus, an experiment reported in 1978 relied upon actual trial tesimony, but had actors rerecord it so as to eliminate references to actual persons, places, and dates, to provide for difference in sex of the speakers, and to create different testimony styles. The results were a male witness and a female witness using the narrative style, and a male and a female witness using a fragmented style, with all four tapes containing the same substantive information. The table below indicates the specific differences between the testimony styles:[5]

Measure	*Narrative* *witness male*	*witness female*	*Fragmented* *witness male*	*witness female*
No. of question/answer pairs	30	30	131	131
No. of words in lawyer's questions	424	424	1039	1042
No. of words in witness's answers	1265	1290	1090	1111
Average no. of words in lawyer's questions	14.13	14.13	7.93	7.95
Average no. of words in witness's answers	42.17	43.00	8.32	8.48

The subjects, comprised of eighty-two undergraduate students and forty-three law students, were asked to respond to questions from the attorney's viewpoint and from their own, and to give their perceptions of the attorney. The attorney's evaluation of the witness, from the juror's viewpoint, consisted of their estimation of his perception of the witness's competence, trustworthiness, intelligence, strength, and activity. For the undergraduate subjects, the attorney appeared to favor most the male witness using the narrative style of testimony; the attorney least favored the male witness using the fragmented style. For the law students, the attorney most favored the female witness using the narrative style and least favored the female witness using the fragmented style. Based on the same criteria (competence, trustworthiness, intelligence, strength, and activity), the undergraduate and the law school subjects both favored the female witness with the narrative style. Thus, regardless of the sex of the witness and the perspective (the attorney's or the jurors'), narrative style was associated with the most favored witness.[6]

Law students made up part of the subjects because of the many cases that are tried to the court, a fact finder with legal training. Also, law-trained subjects were expected to react differently than laymen to testimony styles. The results showed that law students did indeed react to the testimony of a female witness, explained by their presumed heightened interest in legal sex discrimination issues. Therefore, the examining attorney who appeared to yield the floor to a female witness impressed the law students. The subjects who were undergraduate students were not expected to be as attuned to the sex discrimination issues. Accordingly, when an attorney used narrative style with male witnesses, he has viewed as favoring those witnesses about three times as much as when he used narrative style with female witnesses.[7]

Narrative or fragmented style refers only to the questioning process. A related topic is simultaneous speech by the attorney and the witness, which establishes a power struggle, particularly when the clash reflects hostility. When simultaneous speech occurs frequently, one party can come to dominate by perseverance, while the other acquiesces. An experiment designed to test observers' reactions to such verbal battles used only male actors, since subjects appear to be more sensitive to speech conflicts between male attorneys and witnesses.[8]

When the attorney had low perseverance (and acquiesced to the witness), he was perceived to be more intelligent and fairer to the witness and to allow the witness more of an opportunity to present evidence, regardless of the sex of the subject, than when the attorney had high perseverance. This suggests that, "once the attorney had lost some of his social control by participating in an overt verbal clash with the witness, an attempt by the attorney to re-establish his dominance by 'overpowering' the witness verbally was viewed unfavourably." On other measures, results differed with the sex of the subject. The attorney who had high perseverance was viewed as skillful by male subjects, but not as skillful as the attorney with low perseverance was viewed by female subjects. Witness competence, to any degree, existed only with low attorney perseverance and female subjects, and the witness was likeable by female subjects only with low attorney perseverance; the male subjects found the witness likeable only when there was high attorney perseverance. The experimenters formulated an explanation for the subjects' different responses:

> The male subjects, who are postulated to be focusing on the outcome of the interpersonal conflict between the attorney and the witness, may have felt that in view of the attorney's power in the court it was foolish for the witness to be too assertive, as he was in the low attorney perseverance tape. . . .The female subjects may have been more concerned with what they saw as the fair presentation of the evidence than with the outcome of the verbal clash and may have given the witness higher evaluations in the low attorney perseverance conditions since it was in this condition that the witness was seen as securing greater opportunity to present his information to the court.[9]

The type of testimony style, fragmented or narrative, and the extent to which the attorney perseveres when verbal conflict with the witness occurs, result in jurors attributing characteristics to a witness due to something other than just the witness's actions. That is due to the attorney's theoretical ability to control the style of testimony and verbal conflict. However, unless the witnesses are trained or rehearsed, it is unlikely that they will change their ordinary ways of speaking for the courtroom. And their ordinary ways of speaking may stand in the way of their being "good" witnesses. Moreover, if they do try to change their ways of speaking without guidance, the results may be even worse.

The courtroom is one social situation (school is another) in which working-class speakers, unlikely to be familiar (or as familiar as middle-class speakers) with standard language rules, may be at a disadvantage. The experimental results indicating such a conclusion are based on a study of trials in a special courtroom in Vienna that hears cases dealing with serious automobile accidents. More than being the fact finder in this courtroom, the judge also asks the questions. The experimenter selected automobile cases because the defendants would span a wider range of classes than theft, murder, or corruption. In all cases, at least one death had occurred, and the purpose of the trial was to determine the defendant's degree of guilt.[10]

Information drawn from the defendants at the beginning of trial established their social status. The fifteen defendants were middle-class, lower middle-class, and working-class; of the eight working-class defendants, five were first-time offenders, and three had prior convictions. The experimenter believed that the middle-class defendants would perform well in the courtroom because of an ability to speak and act well and the working-class defendants would perform poorly, as they would be unfamiliar with courtroom norms. He predicted that those from the lower middle class would also be insecure but would have different speech behavior than those from the working class. The defendants with previous convictions, though, despite their class, were expected to perform better due to their past courtroom experiences.[11]

The class information of the defendants, being revealed early, apparently determined the way they would be questioned thereafter; "[p]eople with prestigious occupations, like 'university assistant' or 'student,' were treated in a completely different manner from nonacademic defendants." Also, a middle-class defendant capable of performing both the role of the guilty person, as well as the contrite person, in the same breath, presented himself as "contrite, capable, and socially acceptable." An example of such adroitness appeared when a defendant said, "Although I certainly was wrong, I was very shocked. . . . I tried to change [lanes]. . . . It never happened before." Working-class defendants who came into court with their testimony memorized were unable to adapt when the judge asked questions; thus, their spontaneous versions differed from their memorized accounts, and they were not able to demonstrate flexibility.[12]

The most interesting result of the class difference in the testimony is that the judge tended to allow the middle-class defendants to use a narrative style but restricted the working-class defendants to a fragmented style. The examples below suggest that the judge was merely responding to the words that had already come from the witness. That is, the middle-class defendant anticipated and provided the information the judge wanted; the working-class defendant did not, and when the judge interrupted to try to draw out the needed information, the defendant appears to have become flustered and unable to respond.

Middle-Class Male Speaker

J: = Judge; D: = Defendant

J: G.F.?

D: Yes. Good morning.

J: You are a Ph.D.?

D: Yes.

J: In what field?

D: Philosophy.

J: Philosophy? How does that relate to your athletic activities?

D: I have been a member of the Austrian Alpine Club for several years. I have led expeditions and have undertaken difficult climbs.

J: You are single? You live at...

D: Yes.

J: Average income?

D: 6000 shillings.

J: 6000 shillings? No capital? No maintenance obligations?

D: No.

J: No previous convictions. Do you plead guilty or not guilty.

D: Yes, I plead guilty to not having seen the woman, even though I was paying full attention...

J: [Naming the place of the accident.] Flotzersteig, near the Wilhelminespital. Now, what happened?

D: Yes, I was in the second lane because there were cars parked on the right-hand side, and about at the place where the accident occured, the row of parked cars ended. I wanted to change lanes because the right lane was clear ahead, and so I looked in the mirror, and then suddenly I saw in front of me, or rather, to the left of me, a figure, and my first thought was that it's completely impossible, and I was really quite shocked that something could appear in front of me to my left at all, and before I would start braking, the collision happened and somehow I also realized that the vehicle behind me had skidded. Together with this, I realized that the woman had been thrown toward the curb, and this was my first thought: no further accident if, behind me, cars crash into me, and—therefore—eh, I set—I had subjectively the impression that the car went to the left. After this, after thinking it over, this had to be explained; it was due to the deformation of the wings on the right side; I braked. I wanted to steer the car to the right in order to stop it at the curb, so I had the impression that the car went to the left. Then I would be able to orient myself and brake the car and stop at the curb. . .

[After sentence has been passed]

D: I wish to thank you for the conduct of the trial and, especially, for the mild sentence.

J: I hope it will go alright in June. Then you will become a professor?

D: This can be applied for, after a certain time, the professorship, after the habilitation, after three years it can be applied for. . . . It is difficult.

J: Will you earn more then?

D: Professorship: Yes, one can live on that quite well.

J: More than now?

D: I think the starting salary is about 10,000 shillings, the starting salary.

J: Okay. Thank you.

Working-Class Speaker

J: Religion?

D: Catholic.

J: Married?

D: Yes.

J: And you live. . .?

D: In the 22nd [district].

J: Vienna 22. . . . So, and now we need the education.

D: Primary and secondary school.

J: Each four years.

D: Yes. . .

J: Yes, and what else?

D: Yes, I was near the crossing, suddenly the car came from the right. I saw it, but I couldn't manage to brake, so. . .

J: You couldn't brake? Couldn't you try to swerve somehow?

D: No.

J: Do you know what that is?

D: No.

J: You can't answer that question either?

D: Yes, to steer somewhere else did you mean? Or. . .?

J: Yes. Every vehicle has a steering wheel. If one turns it around the direction changes, doesn't it? If it's not broken. If one turns this thing, it is called "swerving," to put it briefly. Understood? Yes?

The experimenter adds that the working-class defendant above repeated "I couldn't brake" twenty times during the trial; she was "unable to draw on her verbal resources to defend herself," evidently due to her "situational discomfort and the judge's overt hostility."[13]

The middle-class defendants and the previously-convicted defendants shared a certain ease in the courtroom. The middle-class defendants were able to use the appropriate language, and to use it consistently. The previously-convicted defendants did not engage in the style-shifting that the working-class attenpted when the judge asked for spontaneous responses; instead, they spoke in the same vernacular as when they were at ease. However, the content of their speech revealed their familiarity with the courtroom situation.[14]

An experiment conducted with the same data used when the subjects were law school and undergraduate students produced results that facilitated a description of the language style used by witnesses and characteristics of the style that most favorably impressed the subjects. In general, the words of the witnesses were classified as "powerful" or "powerless" speech. The concept of powerless speech, however, emerged as a description of language previously noted as being used by women. Robin Lakoff, credited with the identification of "women's language," begins with the premise that "[a]s much as our choice of forms of expression is guided by the thoughts we want to express, to the same extent the way we feel about the things in the real world governs the way we express ourselves about these things." She then concludes that the way we speak can be used "as a diagnostic of our hidden feelings about things."[15]

In tracing the sources of women's language, Lakoff explains that because of the dominant influence of a mother and other women in the lives of children, both boys and girls probably learn women's language at the same time. However, as they age, boys begin to experiment with "rough talk," an activity discouraged in little girls, and at about the age of ten, split off into same-sex peer groups. She suggests that boys then totally throw off the women's language and adopt a new way of speaking. They use this language for the rest of their lives. Girls, however, in effect become bilingual. Once they reach college, they learn that a neutral language is more appropriate than women's language in certain circumstances, such as job interviews or talking to professors. However, "[l]ike many bilinguals, [a girl] may never really be master of either language, [and] though her command of both is adequate enough for most purposes, she may never really feel comfortable using either, and never be certain that she is using the right one in the right place to the right person."[16]

Lakoff contends that women's language, in combination with other aspects of female behavior, denies women access to power by suggesting that they are unable to hold it. The first example she provides of this is the distinction women make among colors, which men find to be a trivial subject, "irrelevant to the real world." Thus, a woman might call a wall *aquamarine* or *lavender,* words not found in the vocabulary of most men, but she would not evoke any particular reaction, since color distinction is a subject within the realm of female concern. If a man were to use such words, however, "one might well conclude he was imitating a woman sarcastically or was a homosexual or an interior decorator."[17]

Another trait of women's language is that it is devoid of strong expletives. Once adults, men can rage without risking social ostracism, but women can do no more than fuss and complain.[18] Support for Lakoff's suggestion appears in experimental results reported in an earlier chapter. Women were found to be much better than men at expressing negative feelings through nonverbal behavior, theoretically because, in our culture, men are given far greater latitude in the explicit expression of negative attitudes.[19] In expressing positive attitudes, men tend to use a range of sexually neutral adjectives, like "great," "terrific," "cool," or "neat," while usually only women say "adorable," "charming," "sweet," "lovely," or "divine." Again, when a man uses words from the second list, he either risks damage to his masculine reputation or is thought to be joking. Concerning these "feminine" adjectives, however, their exclusive relegation to women does not exist in England, as long as their use is restricted to the upper or middle class (where such langauge is apparently an indication of gentility or nobility).[20]

Another linguistic indicator of women's powerless position in society is their tendency to use tag questions with declarative statements. With a direct question—"Is John here?"—a listener could be expected to answer "yes" or "no." However, when one hears, "John is here, isn't he?" the inclination is to answer "yes," since that is what the speaker obviously would like to hear. In other words, tag questions seek to induce the listener to respond as the speaker would like, as if the speaker were too weak to withstand some other response. In another form of the tag question, such as, "The way prices are rising is horrendous, isn't it," the speaker avoids making a commitment and possible conflict with the listener, who may not agree.[21]

A similar linguistic device is the question intonation that women often give declarative statements, as if they are uncertain of the effect of the statement and are seeking approval in an answer from the questioner. The exchange Lakoff cites follows: "When will dinner be ready?" "Oh. . .around six o'clock. . .?" This same reticence appears in the request form used much more by women than men. Men are more likely to use an imperative, such as "Close the door," or to insert a token request word, such as in "Please close the door." Women, however, tend to qualify the request, as in "Won't you please close the door?" which conveys the assumption that the addressee is much freer to refuse. Therefore, the greater politeness seen in women's language is thought to derive from their perceived position of inferior power.[22]

Later researchers, O'Barr and Atkins, examining courtroom speech, found that "trial practice manuals. . .often had special sections on how female witnesses behave differently from males and thus special kinds of treatment they require." Specifically, although attorneys are instructed to behave, in general, the same way towards men and women witnesses, they are also advised to be particularly courteous to women and to avoid making women cry. In addition, since "women hate to say yes" and even intelligent women "will very often be evasive," attorneys are told how they can use this trait to advantage, such as in discrediting the testimony of women. Thus, the researchers designed the experiment for detection of speech patterns supposedly unique to women.[23]

O'Barr and Atkins begin by naming the various characteristics that Lakoff describes or mentions:

1. *Hedges.* ("It's sort of hot in here," ; "I'd kind of like to go."; "I guess. . ."; "It seems like. . ."; and so on.)
2. *(Super)polite forms.* ("I'd really appreciate it if. . ."; "Would you please open the door, if you don't mind?"; and so on.)
3. *Tag questions.* ("John is here, isn't he?" instead of "Is John here?"; and so on.)
4. *Speaking in italics.* (Intonational emphasis equivalent to underlining words in written language; emphatic *so* or *very* and so on.)
5. *Empty adjectives.* (*Divine; charming; cute; sweet; adorable; lovely;* and so on.)
6. *Hypercorrect grammar and pronounciation* [sic]. (Bookish grammar; more formal enunciation.)
7. *Lack of a sense of humor.* (Women said to be poor joke tellers and to frequently "miss the point" in jokes told by men.)
8. *Direct quotations.* (Use of direct quotations instead of paraphrases.)
9. *Special lexicon.* (In domains like colors where words like *magenta, chartreuse,* and so on are typically used only by women.)
10. *Question intonation in declarative contexts.*

The cases from which testimony was drawn for the experiment included offenses of traffic violations, drug possession, robbery, manslaughter, and rape. Although the researchers admit that the ten weeks of testimony that these cases involved did not produce a large number of witnesses, they saw "considerable variation in the degree to which women exhibited" the above characteristics in their speech and initially felt "at a loss" to explain why some females used only a few examples of women's language.[24]

In addition, the results indicate that the testimony of male witnesses also contained examples of women's language. The table below indicates the frequency of some of these characteristics in the speech of six witnesses.[25]

	Women			*Men*		
	A	*B*	*C*	*D*	*E*	*F*
Intensifiers	16	0	0	21	2	1
Hedges	19	2	3	2	5	0
Hesitation Forms	52	20	13	26	27	11
W asks L questions	2	0	0	0	0	0

	Women			Men		
	A	B	C	D	E	F
Gestures	2	0	0	0	0	0
Polite Forms	9	0	2	2	0	1
Sir	2	0	6	32	13	11
Quotes	1	5	0	0	0	0
Total (all powerless forms)	103	27	24	85	47	24
# of Answers in Interview	90	32	136	61	73	52
Ratio (# powerless forms for each answer)	1.14	0.84	0.18	1.39	0.64	0.46

The respective social classes of the witnesses suggest reasons for the differences indicated above. A was a housewife, fifty-five years old. B was married and thirty-five years old, and there was nothing to indicate that she had a job outside the home. By contrast, C was a pathologist in a local hospital, thirty-five to forty years old; since she was addressed as "Dr.," there was no indication of her marital status. Although the table indicates that she had close to the same number of powerless forms in her speech as B, notice that C provided more than four times as many answers as B; that is, the focus should be on the ratio of the powerless forms to all of the answers. F had the lowest ratio among the males; he was an experienced member of the police force, in the same age range as C. Also, he and C testified in court frequently. The researchers point out, however, that not all of the witnesses in the experiment who had few appearances of women's language also had expert witness experience. D was an ambulance attendant, around thirty years old, and had been at his job for about six months. E was D's supervisor, thirty to thirty-five years old, and more experienced than E. The marital status of all of the men is unknown. Based on the background data of these and other witnesses, the experimenters summarize that the women who used relatively few examples of women's language "were typically well-educated, professional women of middle-class background." Similarly, men whose speech exhibited traits of women's language tended to have "either subordinate, lower-status jobs or were unemployed."[26]

Because of the association of women's language with powerless social positions, regardless of the sex of the speaker, O'Barr and

Atkins have substituted "powerless language" for "women's language," with the same traits characterizing both. "Powerful language" is language missing those traits. The experiment was constructed to reveal the effects of powerless and powerful language in testimony. While the substance of actual testimony was not changed, it was rerecorded to omit references to actual people, dates, and locations, and to reflect powerful and powerless styles, with a female speaker and a male speaker. The linguistic characteristics of the resulting tapes appear below:[27]

	Female Witness		*Male Witness*	
	Powerful	*Powerless*	*Powerful*	*Powerless*
Hedges	2	22	2	21
Hesitation forms	13	73	18	51
W asks L questions	2	5	2	6
Use of *sir* by W	0	3	0	4
Intensifiers	0	35	0	31
Running time of tape	9:12	11:45	9:35	12:10

Subjects were then asked to rate the witnesses as to convincingness, credibility, competence, intelligence, and trustworthiness. In all cases, for both male and female witnesses, the powerful witness received a higher rating. On two measures—competence and intelligence—the powerless female witness scored higher than the powerful male. That could be because women are not expected to reveal their intelligence and competence by their language; since men probably are, then when their language was powerless, they seemed even less intelligent and less competent. Similarly, the powerful female witness was rated as being more intelligent and more competent than the powerful male witness.[28]

Reported elsewhere are the results of testing along another measure, social attractiveness. Given Lackoff's beliefs that women are taught to behave a certain way from childhood and that deviant behavior does not receive social approval, it is reassuring to see that powerful testimony delivered by female witnesses is not deemed socially unattractive. On that measure, female witnesses received a rating of 2.48 in contrast to the 2.52 rating for powerful male witnesses. Moreover (although this may defy an expectation), powerless female witnesses received a much lower rating (.54) than powerless male witnesses (1.23).[29]

Another phase of the experiment tested for the difference in response to powerful and powerless witnesses, depending upon the sex of the subject. The report of those results provides an example of the two types of testimony the subjects heard:[30]

Q: Then you went next door?

A: (Powerless:) And then I went immediately next door, yes.
(Powerful:) Yes.

Q: Approximately how long did you stay there before the ambulance arrived?

A: (Powerless:) Oh, it seems like it was about uh, twenty minutes. Just long enough to help my friend Mrs. Davis you know, get straightened out.
(Powerful:) Twenty minutes. Long enough to help get Mrs. Davis straightened out.

Q: Now how long have you lived in Durham?

A: (Powerless:) All my life, really.
(Powerful:) All my life.

Q: You're familiar with the streets?

A: (Powerless:) Oh yes.
(Powerful:) Yes.

Q: You know your way around?

A: (Powerless:) Yes, I guess I do.
(Powerful:) Yes.

Subjects, who consisted of seventy-three male and seventy-nine female undergraduate students, rated the witnesses as to credibility and attractiveness. As in previous results, powerful speakers were perceived as more credible than powerless speakers, but this difference was even greater when the witness and the subject were of the same sex. The powerful speakers were also more attractive overall than the powerless speakers.[31]

As to the credibility effect of powerful speech, it is assumed that "[t]he more definite powerful style. . . may lead to the attribution that the communicator does indeed believe the statements to be true." Thus, listeners may feel "less confident about attributing the speaker's speech style to his or her level of certainty when the speaker [is] not of the same sex and when the listeners [can] not use their own speech behavior as a referent." Since the attractiveness scale did not show this correlation (recall that male subjects found powerful female witnesses the most attractive), the suggestion is that attribution of attractiveness does not follow the same process as attribution of credibility. That powerful female witnesses fell in attractiveness when the testimony was transcribed could be explained by stereotyped bias against female speakers. Voice qualities provided in the spoken testimony may have provided additional information that allowed subjects to modify (or ignore) the traditional stereotyped image of women speakers.[32]

B. *Direct Examination*

"The function of direct examination is to construct the case in an understandable form before the jury."[33] Direct examination often supplies the opportunity for the client to tell his story, or at least to provide the outline, which will be completed with the details of other witnesses and evidence. The ideal is that the jurors will form their versions of "what happened" in strict accordance with the story told. There are, of course, many impediments to the realization of the ideal. Some of those, consisting of roadblocks from opposing counsel in the form of interruptions and objections, as well as problematic accounts from other witnesses, are somewhat beyond the control of an attorney and his client. Thus, those factors that are *within* the control of the attorney and client should reach their maximum effect potential.

Clearly, when curable signs of powerless speech threaten to undermine an otherwise strong version of the facts, the attorney owes it to his client to attempt to purge those signs from the testimony. As indicated in an earlier chapter, rehearse the client in his testimony and, if possible, in an actual courtroom, so that he can become familiar with the surroundings. Some clients, just like some people, know no fear and have never met a stranger. These people often need to be restrained rather than encouraged, which usually requires that the attorney convince them that he knows far more about law and evidence than they do and that if they do not acquiesce to his lead in the courtroom, they may not like the legal consequences. These witnesses, too, however, need to practice their testimony, so they will learn how the attorney can draw out details by asking more questions, which relieves them of the burden of having to paint a complete picture in their first answer.

The less assertive individual, though, may require a certain amount of confidence building. Also, the typical client could feel anxiety because of the courtroom situation, in which he/his cause will be judged; the public speaking required by testifying; and the fear that he will forget everything this attorney has told him about testifying. Hamlin recommends explaining to the client the potential value of his testimony: "Probably no one can really do this job any better than you, because you are an expert on your own experience with what happened in this case." The client should come to know that if he omits a detail, is unclear, or simply starts to ramble, his attorney will interrupt or otherwise give him a chance to clarify or simplify. The attorney should explain that unless he specifically asks the client to "tell the jury thus-and-such," he is to respond to and look at the attorney. When a witness answers while looking at a jury, without explicit direction, "it looks prearranged and contrived, like a performance." If a lawyer stands next to the jury while asking questions, though, the witness can answer the lawyer but still face the jury. When clarification of an answer is needed, Hamlin suggests that the attorney ask the witness to "tell us" what was meant; asking the witness to "tell the jury" implies that the attorney understood but feared the jury did not.[34] If it could be done without appearing contrived, counsel could ask instead, "Could you tell *me* what that means?" allowing the jurors to believe that he thought some of them could have understood, even if he did not.

Leading witnesses away from powerless language could begin with a list of prohibitions and, by way of an explanation for each, a short course in confidence building:

1. *Do not use hedge words.* One example is "I think," which literally has no meaning, since we first think before we ever speak. The only time the phrase is appropriate is when the question concerns varying viewpoints on a controversial issue; the proper emphasis then is "*I* think." If, during rehearsal, an attorney catches his witness using the phrase a few times and points it out, the witness will become conscious of it himself and should learn to avoid it. "You know" is one of those verbal tics discussed in an earlier chapter; often, simply pointing out to someone the use of such a phrase is enough to focus his own attention on it.

2. *Do not be overly polite.* Unless the witness is a child, "ma'am" and "sir" either will appear artificial or will cast doubt on the witness's own status. An attorney should explain to the witness that he does not want to elevate respect for opposing counsel at the cost

of a loss of respect for himself. It is worth telling the witness ahead of time that, should the judge ask a question (which occasionally happens), the proper form of address is "your honor," regardless of sex.

3. *Do not overuse intensifiers.* Each time the witness uses an intensifier ("*very* late," "*definitely* speeding") during rehearsal, the attorney should stop him and say, "Okay, you've conveyed your enthusiasm, but you haven't told me anything concrete. *What* is '*very* late'—one hour? two hours? a day? *What* is '*definitely* speeding'—faster than you were going when you were going the speed limit, faster than other cars on the road, faster than a speeding bullet?"

4. *Do not use hypercorrect speech.* Counsel should emphasize to the witness that the courtroom is not the place to experiment with higher forms of grammar or try out new words, as we all make mistakes even with the vocabulary and grammar that we think we already know. College professors may speak a certain way and farmers another, but what jurors detect is inconsistency. And when someone fails in an attempt to speak above his profession or education, jurors are likely to recognize the error and wonder why the atempt was made—was the speaker ashamed of his station and trying to disguise it? Was he trying to indicate his superiority to the jury? Nothing succeeds more in detracting from intellect than a failed attempt to display it. Examples could bring this point home to the witness, and a couple come to mind. A secretary, twenty-eight years old, with a high school degree and a few college courses to her name, aspired to a higher professional status and attempted to reflect her ability for same by using formal speech, both with her employers and peers. In relating the story of how she was robbed of her cash and credit cards, she ended with the statement that she was determined to "regroup" her losses. An employee, commenting on what she perceived to be her employers taking unfair advantage of the situation of the employees, summarized that her workplace was a virtual "den of inequity."

Sometimes, signs of powerless language may be so engrained in a person's speech that only professional counseling can ensure their removal. "[W]here the witness proves incapable of avoiding powerless, hypercorrect or fragmented speech, the lawyer may be able to compensate for the problems to which he is now alerted by giving the witness an opportunity to show, through the structure and content of his testimony, that he is indeed credible, competent and intelligent."[35]

An attorney can assist the client during the testimony of the client and other witnesses in still another way. Recall the notion that jurors seek to piece together their own versions of "what happened." How does this occur?

> While listening, [jurors] construct in their minds an "image" of an incident that was, of course, never witnessed by any one of them. . . . It is important, then, to understand the factors that influence the construction of an incident in the minds of jurors, as a way of understanding their verdicts.[36]

An earlier chapter made a point concerning the effect of vivid testimony as compared with pallid accounts. The conclusion is that jurors are more likely to recall an argument supported by vivid testimony ("knocking a bowl of guacamole dip onto a white shag carpet") than non-vivid versions ("knocking a bowl to the floor").[37] It also appears though, that the very wording of questions can affect jurors' perceptions of what happened in that they tend to incorporate language of the questions into the facts. This is first seen in the effect of wording on witnesses who had watched a film of a car accident and were then asked about the speed of the cars. When the attorney's question was "'About how fast were the cars going when they smashed into each other?'" witnesses gave higher estimates of speed than when the word "hit" was substituted for "smashed." Also, witnesses who were asked with the word "smashed" tended to report seeing broken glass, although no broken glass was in the film. "The particular words in the question had apparently led the witness to develop a 'memory' for the accident that was more severe than the accident actually had been."[38]

Jurors could naturally be similarly affected. In an experiment conducted at the University of Washington, subjects received one of two versions of a case and were told to act as jurors. The reported incident involved two men meeting at night at a marina, one being a blackmailer and the other being the blackmail victim. After an argument, the blackmailer wound up in the water and drowned, and the other man was arrested. A witness testified to having seen most of the incident, but the account was purposefully vague to allow for both a murder and an accident interpretation. In one version of the case, the witness was asked questions filled with words associated with violence, designed to evoke emotion, and suggesting that the blackmailer was pushed into the water (e.g., "How much of the fight did you see?"), while the questions in the other version contained neutral language (e.g., "How much of the incident did you see?"). Of the jurors who read the emotional version, 41% returned a guilty verdity; of those who read the neutral version, only 22% returned a guilty verdict. Then, individual interviews conducted with the jurors revealed that those who had read the emotional version "had a different image of the incident. They tended to think of it as a relatively violent struggle."[39] The attorney, therefore, should be always mindful of his client's position when formulating questions to any witness, since the attorney's word choice alone can influence the jury's perception of the evidence.

Careful consideration of language by the client in his testimony is also of critical importance, particularly when the client is a defendant in a criminal case. Therefore, "the client must understand counsel's theory of the case so that his answers will be framed in language that supports inferences consistent with the defense." Whether to put a defendant in a criminal case on the stand involves a number of legal issues and turns on the particular facts in each case, the alleged crime, and the impression the defendant is likely to make on the particular jury. When a defendant testifies, however, he must persuade the jury, above all, of his credibility. Concerns explored in earlier chapters, such as physical attractiveness, grooming, clothing, and the order in which unfavorable facts are revealed, as well as whether the defendant employs powerful or powerless language, all contribute to the effect he will make on the jury. As a final comment on the effect of his testimony per se, however, a testifying defendant with shortcomings as a witness should be the first witness. Then, the entire rest of the trial provides an opportunity to overcome any negative impact. "Where a client is particularly articulate or otherwise favorably impressive he should testify last."[40]

Experts summarize that "[b]y far the most sophisticated technique on direct examination is the short, clear question. . . .While it looks easy, it is not, because it is contrary to nearly all of our legal training." Examples of such questions include the following: "Where did he go? What did he say then? Who else was there? When did they leave? Why did you stop? Tell us what happened. Would you explain how it works?" The virtue of such questions is that both the jury and the witness understand what is being asked. Also, notice that even in their apparent simplicity such questions allow for narrative and brief responses. An example of testimony based on questions like these follows. While the resulting testimony is itself informative and clear, the attorney had an added motive here. The witness did not follow standard operating police procedure in his handling of evidence, and the attorney anticipated that opposing counsel would have a heyday with that slip-up. Therefore, the questioning attorney took the opportunity to diffuse the expected attack. Also below, notice how the attorney gets the officer to repeat the non-standard procedure and even explain what he should have done instead. The effect is to place the officer's actions under a bright light of examination and determine that although they were non-standard, that made no difference.[41]

A: Now then, Sergeant Herr, would you tell us what you did with the revolver, People's Exhibit 5 for identification, when you returned to the station house?

A: I tagged it and then put it in my desk drawer.

Q: I'm sorry, Sergeant, you *what*?

A: I tagged it and then put it in my desk drawer.

Q: Is that standard police procedure for dealing with evidence taken from the scene of the crime, to put it in your desk drawer?

A: No, sir.

Q: But that's what you did?

A: Yes, sir.

Q: What was the proper procedure, Sergeant?

A: To tag it and turn it over to the evidence locker and obtain a receipt for it.

Q: Why didn't you follow the correct procedure?

A: There was a new man at the desk in charge of the evidence locker, and he was backed up about twenty minutes. As I was waiting to turn it over to him, my partner and I got an emergency call, so I put the gun in my desk drawer and locked the drawer, and I didn't take it out of the drawer until the next morning.

Q: Sergeant, do you know the reason for turning exhibits over to the evidence locker?

A: Sure, it's to keep the evidence safe, and to keep it from being tampered with.

Q: Does anyone else have a key to your desk drawer besides you, Sergeant?

A: No, sir. Just me.

Q: When you came back to your desk the next day, was the drawer locked or unlocked?

A: It was locked. I had to open it with my key.

Q: What did you find?

A: The gun—just as I had left it.

Q: Did it appear to have been tampered with or altered in any way from the night before?

A: No, sir. It was just as I left it.

Q: Thank you, Sergeant.

The instances in which the police officer calls the attorney "sir" do not detract from the officer's status, since we expect people in the military or similar uniformed professions to call their superiors "sir." Also, we are aware that police officers are trained to be formally courteous to citizens. Thus, "sir" is a part of their professional language.

C. *Expert Witness Testimony*

"It is a rare case today that does not include some opinion testimony."[42] Probably everything that could be said about what the client should project in his testimony could be said about what the expert witness should project: honesty, personal appeal, knowledge concerning that about which he is testifying. And part of the personal appeal will, of course, be founded in such traits as dress, mannerisms, and powerless vs. powerful language. The difference between a client and an expert, however, is that the latter can usually be selected from a number of possibilities, based on honesty, personal appeal, knowledge, and experience.

The very criteria that cause attorneys to select one expert over another as a witness explain why experts are more likely to be better witnesses than the average individual. First, experts are supposed to be involved on a regular basis in the activity about which they will testify. Therefore, they will speak to the jury with firsthand experience and thereby generate credibility. Second, experts should be recognized leaders in their field. Since their credentials will precede their opinions, the former is likely to make the latter more believable. Third, an expert witness should be able "clearly and persuasively to articulate his ideas in simple terms, readily understandable to the layman." At first blush, this criterion would suggest that college professors would make excellent expert witnesses. But in refutation, all we must do is recall the poor college professors we have encountered and the fact that publication in one's field insures college tenure as much or more than good teaching. In addition, the fourth requirement is that an expert witness be able "to think quickly and correctly under hostile questioning." Unless a college professor has had especially demanding (and rude) students, he is unlikely to meet this requirement based solely on his teaching experience.[43] Many professors, however, have developed into competent expert witnesses (and there are actually clinics established to teach the art of testifying as an expert witness).

Concerning actual testimony, the most important of the above requirements is the ability to put sometimes complicated ideas into a layman's language. The attorney can assist the expert in this regard during practice sessions by requiring the expert to stop and explain each and every technical term he uses. Ideally, the expert can learn to stop himself so that the attorney does not need to interrupt the testimony during trial. In addition, the expert should be encouraged to use analogies and examples that are or should be familiar to the jury; this is a technique to draw the jury into the testimony and enable them to relate to it.[44]

It goes without saying that the questioning attorney must come to be as familiar with what the expert will say as the expert himself. This will allow the attorney not only to guide the direct examination of his expert but also to repair, in re-direct, any damage done and to cross-examine the opposition's expert. This necessary familiarity, however, can also be the bane of an attorney. In his zeal to learn to speak medicine like a doctor, he can lose his perspective at the time of trial. If he and his expert engage in Q&A like colleagues, the jurors may well think, "Here are a couple of extremely smart fellows. I wish I knew what in the world the two of them are talking about." Thus, attorneys should never forget their state of mind when they initially sat their expert down and asked him to walk them through his intended testimony in detail.[45]

Following are two excerpts from the testimony of opposing expert witnesses in a case concerning the possibility of a high-voltage transmission line near a school producing cancer in children (proper names have been changed). Before each of the following answers, existing scientific literature on topics such as cancer and the effects of electric and magnetic fields had been reviewed. Both experts answered similar questions. However, Expert 1 could be talking to colleagues; while he does not use a great deal of scientific jargon, the amount he does use, when combined with his abstract way of speaking, obscures his testimony. Expert 2 seems at least as qualified as Expert 1, and he uses jargon as well, but he explains what he says and relates it to members of society, not just the scientific community.

Expert 1

Q: How do you relate laboratory studies, and your study of them, to possible biological effects of transmission lines?

A: My approach to this has been to just as exhaustively as possible study each one of the reports which have been published which indicate that they are biological effects.

Now, I haven't limited myself to any particular range of fields. I have concentrated on the frequencies between about one or two hertz, and three hundred, maybe a thousand hertz in general, because it's clear that direct current fields could produce qualitatively different actions that alternating current fields. And also illuminating the high frequencies, because they have different interactions with biological material. So that's been my area.

There's been several hundreds of papers which I've now analyzed. In each case I have looked at the nature of the biological effect that's claimed. I have looked at—checked out the frequency. But if it's a nice, simple sine wave that's used to change the direction of the field, then it's quite simple.

I have also looked at the magnitude of the field that's used. And in some cases that again required the use of field theory in order to determine what the effective field strength would be. I have looked at the magnitude of the fileds, and had to develop a special scale of my own in order to represent the magnitude of the effects.

The thing that's important in terms of whether the biological effect will be of any real significance, health significance, is how big the effect is. Of course, what its qualitative nature is, as well. So what I have tried to do is express the magnitude of the reported effect in terms of this biological variability that I have been talking to you about, the range of variabilities.

And finally, of course, the question is, is this a believable effect.

Now, if the effect is very large—that is, if it's much, much larger than the variability, and if it's directly related to the magnitude of the field, as you get bigger effect when you increase the strength of the magnetic field, then—a single paper can have frequently been believable. However, when the magnitudes of the field are comparable to, in some cases even less than the normal variability, we have to be very cautious in taking those kinds of studies at face value. And the best way to determine whether one of these subtle, small-scale effects is real, is to see if it can be confirmed by an independent investigator.

So this is the kind of analysis that I have done in each one of these studies that's been reported.

Expert 2

Q: But the effect that electromagnetic fields have, or the alleged effect that electromagnetic fields may have on humans, is just one of a category of things that you have studied in the past, is it not?

A: Well, this whole issue comes down to our society, and things that we can see and feel as differentiated from those that we can't see or feel. When we see a giant trailer truck on the freeway, and see it coming in our direction, we know we best get out of the way. But if you don't see something or don't feel something, you may come to the conclusion that it's harmless. And I have already alluded to the studies on x-ray. You cannot see an x-ray, you cannot feel an x-ray, but it's there. And it can do you great good if you use it carefully, and great harm if it's improperly used.

There are other kinds of radiation that I have lectured about which are produced by molecular species, radioactive molecules, such as radioactive iodine. We use radioactive iodine in medicine to treat thyroid diseases. It localizes in the thyroid. Now, the right dose can control thyroid activity, the wrong dose can kill the thyroid, and you may damage the person.

Similarly, there are other kinds of waves that we are concerned about. And what we all know is that there is a great unknown that we don't know anything about. That's why these initial reports are a subject of concern.

And indeed, in Smith, et al.'s report in 1985, they said these are worrisome. Everybody agreed more work needed to be done.

In 1985 there have been three major reports in relationship of cancer to electromagnetic wave of the sixty hertz variety that we have in this school setting. One of these is a report from Blake and his associates from Australia, who deal with again, another report on increasing incidents of leukemia—this is 1985—as a result of exposure to electromagnetic waves.

Carter has done a study on what's called silent keys. Silent keys are ham operators who have died. And he's asked the question, "What is the relationship of their deaths to electromagnetic waves?"

And Carter has come to the conclusion that the incidence of leukemia in that group of people is much higher than it is in the population as a whole. That is, it's double or more.

The final report is that of Morse, and their associates from the University of Tennessee and Johns Hopkins University. And they have found that there is an increase in brain cancer—gliomas, gliblastomas and astrocytomas, just technical terms for brain cancers—that have occurred in the population of individuals who are exposed to electromagnetic waves.

So there is not just a stationary body of evidence, there is an increasing body of evidence which is the basis for our concern about the children.

D. *Cross-examination*

This section does not aspire to be a primer on cross-examination techniques. Instead, it examines certain aspects of verbal style that characterize recommended cross-examination. In contrast to testimony of a client or one's own expert witness, almost never will an attorney purposefully allow testimony elicited from the opposition's witness to take the form of a narrative. In fact, an attorney conducting cross-examination usually strives to formulate questions that can be answered with a "yes" or a "no." This is true for the same reason that an attorney should allow his own witness to give narrative answers, because the attorney has regard for his witness and his ability to present his story clearly. The other side's witness should not appear to have counsel's trust and confidence; he should not be allowed to have the stage to himself, unless in those rare Perry-Mason-case instances in which he can be worked up into spilling out an emotional confession.

Even if he is supplying only one-word answers, an adverse witness should not be on the stand long. Not only does his prolonged appearance imply an importance to his role that the questioner seeks to diminish, but jurors fast reach saturation. "There is a very low limit on the capacity of the juror to absorb information by ear. Once that limit is reached, he can absorb no more. Ask him to do so by dragging out the cross-examination and he becomes bored and sullen." Counsel is cautioned that his goal in cross-examination should be to obtain only enough information to support one argument (three at the maximum) in summation concerning the witness's credibility.[46]

Adverse witnesses should not testify long for another reason. It is difficult for an attorney to continue to ask questions (both to phrase them correctly and to seek the precise information) that can only be answered honestly with "safe" responses. The longer the witness is on the stand, the more his chances increase that counsel will err in his questionings, and the witness will be able to win a point. Moreover, attorneys frequently do not realize that unless they have totally charmed the jury with their own personality or their client's cause, they are playing the scoring game under a handicap:

> The jury identifies with the witness, not with you and your magic power. It sits there during your cross-examination just waiting for the witness to score a point. It is amazing how clever even the most unsophisticated witness can be when he is cornered. Little victories for the witness are magnified. Your victories had better be big ones. Jurors will continue to empathize with the witness until you show them that he is not worthy of their trust and sympathy.[47]

Following is an excerpt from a reported cross-examination that occurred in England. Sir Percy was questioning the manager of the company that had employed the defendant and the victim, whom the defendant was accused of murdering. In his direct examination, the witness had provided a strong chain of circumstantial evidence suggesting the defendant's guilt. While the questions may not be as short as some purists would recommend, and the answers reflect elaboration beyond a simple "yes" or "no," the answers nevertheless are, in content, favorable to the defendant's case. (The additional verbiage could well be due to the difference in speaking norms for middle-upper class England as compared to the same class in America. Recall that certain aspects of "powerless language" are characteristic of middle-upper class English speech without carrying the same powerless effect as they would in the United States.) Sir Percy, however, then makes a critical error; in asking a question that allows for other than a yes-no response, he provides the opportunity for a soliloquy, which this witness takes as if he has been reading for the part for months:

Q: Now, Quigley, you admit that my client, Jacob Jones, was not the only employee with a key to your office.

A: That's quite right, Sir Percy.

Q: And my client wasn't the only employee who had expressed a strong dislike for the deceased, Smyth, was he?

A: No, Sir Percy, Smyth wasn't very well liked at all.

Q: And my client wasn't the only driver who returned his lorry late on the night of Smyth's death, was he?

A: No, Sir Percy, there were several others.

Q: And my client wasn't the only employee who went on holiday the day after Smyth's death.

A: No, Sir Percy, there were others. (Pause)

Q: Well, sir, then how in the name of heaven can you possibly contend that my client Jacob Jones murdered Samuel Smyth?

A: Sir Percy, I can answer your question in seven parts: First, Jones told me and everyone within earshot that he would kill Smyth if Smyth didn't stop playing around with his daughter. Second. . .[48]

In the discussion of powerless language, tag questions are explained as emanating from a weak person who is encouraging the addressee to respond affirmatively, as if the questioner would not be able to withstand a negative answer. However, in the context of cross-examination, tag questions become challenges to the witness; he is not being *requested* to respond affirmatively; he is almost being demanded to verify a statement that the questioner already believes to be true. The attorney's belief in the statement appears so strong by this technique, that the witness could well expect a negative response to bring a shocking, "*No?*" as a retort:

Q: You were in your car, were you not?

A: Yes.

Q: You were, at that time, seated, were you not?

A: Yes.

Q: And your car was then parked, was it not?

A: Yes.

Q: Parked next to the curb, isn't that a fact?

A: Yes.

Q: The radio was on, was it not?

A: Yes.

Q: And while sitting in your car which was parked next to the curb with the radio on, you noticed the light, did you not?

A: Yes.

Q: And the light was red, was it not?

A: Yes.[49]

One other technique of cross-examination is also an echo of a recommended direct examination method. Recall the suggestion that the witness can be helped to eliminate intensifiers ("very," "really") from his speech by being encouraged to provide the factual details that justify the intensifiers. (Q: You say you "really" liked him; how much did you in fact like him? A: Enough to marry him.) In expressing intensity of feeling, intensifiers also contain information about personal judgment. Adverse witnesses realize that their personal judgment will be brought into question. Therefore, they will resist adopting language of an attorney that indicates personal judgment, as they suspect he is trying to foist words with his own meaning onto them. Thus, in the question, "The radio played loudly, did it not?" *loudly* is a personal judgment, and the adverse witness may respond with "Oh, I wouldn't say loudly," "What do you mean by loudly?" "That depends," or "As a matter of fact, I could barely hear it." What the attorney should do is draw facts from the witness on which the jurors can reach their own conclusion that the radio was playing loudly:

Q: The radio was on, was it not?

A: Yes.

Q: Had you turned it on?. . .

A: Yes.

Q: You turned it on to listen to it, did you not?

A: I turned it on for background music.

Q: You turned it on to hear it in the background, did you not?

A: Yes.

Q: And you could hear it, could you not?

A: Yes.

Q: It was loud enough to hear, was it not?

A: Yes.

Q: Louder than the street noise, wasn't it?

A: Yes.

Q: Because you could hear it, could you not?

A: Yes.

Q: Above the noise of the traffic, did you not?

A: Yes.

Q: Above the noise of the people on the street, isn't that a fact?

A: Yes.

Q: It was loud enough to hear above the traffic and the people, was it not?[50]

E. *Conclusion*

"As a trial lawyer, you must take the witnesses you find, train them in simple exposition and teach them how to communicate, simply, clearly and accurately. You must become a teacher in effective communication."[51] Clearly the author of these words is referring to verbal, and primarily oral, communication. Teaching that to a witness is indeed a task, for any teaching rests on the presumption that the teacher has first mastered the subject that he is teaching, and oral communication is a difficult subject to master. Apart from the words themselves—their denotations and connotations and the ways they are combined with other words—are meaning-interferences and meaning-additives, supplied by vocal delivery, personal appearance, life experiences and accomplishments, and reputation. The attorney may not be able to teach these aspects of communication to witnesses but should himself be aware of them, so that he can anticipate and counter or make use of their effects.

II. *REDUCING WITNESS (AND ATTORNEY) STRESS*

Benjamin Franklin once said that in this world "nothing is certain but death and taxes." The author would be willing to bet that most trial lawyers would additionally insert "and an unpredictable witness." When a witness gives testimony in a courtroom, there is a feeling of uncertainty and conjecture. What will he say? How will he say it? How will the judge or jury react to him? Will his testimony be persuasive? These questions concern all attorneys who ask a witness to testify for them in court; yet most attorneys do little ahead of time to relieve their own tensions, and more important, those of the witness. These are the same attorneys who would be the first to tell you that a witness can win or lose a case for you.

The fields of social and behavioral sciences offer these attorneys relief in the form of an abundance of research discussing how people perceive each other. A trial consultant applies the results of these studies to the legal setting. Acting as an advisor to the attorney, the trial consultant is able to improve the courtroom situation and benefit the attorney by preparing the witness, or by advising the attorney or his staff on how to prepare the witness. After all, a prepared witness is a more persuasive one, and a persuasive witness can affect the eventual judgment. This in turn can affect the amount of the attorney's fee and his reputation. This causal link is important to keep in mind when considering whether to hire a trial consultant.

Although this section focuses specifically on preparing a witness for a jury trial, the suggested advice can also be applicable to a bench trial. At least one judge has openly encouraged the lawyer to prepare, to the maximum extent possible, his witnesses for a non-jury trial as he would a jury trial.[52]

The attorney's goal in either type of case is to present his client's side as persuasively as possible. One of the important means he has in doing this is through witness testimony. A witness's ability to persuade a verdict in favor of the side for which he is testifying is enormous. However, much can go awry between a well intentioned witness's testimony and how that testimony is perceived by the jury.

When a witness enters a courtroom, he will bring in more than his memory. Studies show memory to be very questionable as reliable evidence.[53] The witness will also bring with him a multitude of other factors that will influence how he is perceived. A persuasive and eloquent attorney can have the effectiveness of his case undermined by ineffective witnesses.

Persuasive communication is more than the witness testifying about the facts of a particular case. As the jurors hear the testimony, they form opinions about the facts of the case, as well as about the witness who is testifying. Annoying mannerisms and negative styles of speech can get in the way of the substance of the testimony. How the witness speaks, sits, dresses, and gestures are additional factors the jury looks at to decide what type of person the witness is and whether he is telling the truth. If any of these additional factors works as distractions, the witness's ability to persuade is lessened. It is even possible a witness would not be able to persuade at all. This occurs when one or more of these external factors greatly impede the witness's testimony.

How the testimony is presented must be viewed apart from the substance of the testimony in order to improve its effectiveness, and therefore its persuasiveness. Ineffective communication can be eliminated by adequate preparation of the witness.

Often the idea of "preparing the witness" conjures up negative thoughts. To many it suggests that the witness is given a "script" of answers to the attorney's questions. The witness is then expected to "memorize" his "lines" verbatim for when he later testifies in court. The biggest mistake an attorney can make is not giving his witness advice on how to handle "stage fright." After all, a nervous witness may actually have experienced the facts he is testifying about, but if he cannot effectively communicate these facts to the jury, his testimony will not be persuasive.

However one wishes to view the process of getting a witness ready to testify in court, the main goal of the attorney should be to help reduce the stress the witness will inevitably feel in the courtroom. When a witness is under less stress, his or her testimony and behavior will become more predictable, which in turn will result in less stress for the attorney. Everyone benefits!

Preparing a witness to do an effective job in court demands a great amount of time. Every attorney has his own favorite method. It is important to realize that because an attorney has prepared his witnesses the same way for years, he has not necessarily been able to present them as effectively as he can.

Each method and its degree of effectiveness varies greatly. Some attorneys prepare the witnesses themselves. If done properly, this will consume a good deal of the attorney's time. This method usually results in the attorney being able to prepare only his client. An attorney, however, should never underestimate or overestimate the effect any of his witnesses can have on a jury. All witnesses need and deserve some degree of preparation. By only preparing his client, in effect the attorney is putting all his eggs in one basket.

Other trial attorneys have their secretaries, paralegals, or newer associates in the office do the job. This saves valuable time and is ideal if these people have been properly trained to handle such an important task.

Some attorneys even feel that giving their witnesses "scripts" of questions and answers to memorize is sufficient preparation. The result is that the witness tells the facts the way the lawyer wants them told and not necessarily the way they happened.[54] Jurors more often than not see through this and are left with the impression that the entire case has been concocted. The "script" method can also backfire if the witness is cross-examined with questions that the witness has not been "prepared" to answer. There simply is no substitute for a witness's own words.[55]

Another method many attorneys employ is to leave the success of all their witness's performance in court to fate. Some of these attorneys are under the mistaken belief that their witnesses were born public speakers. An ideal thought, but a greatly mistaken thought, nonetheless.

Still other attorneys give handouts to their witnesses that discuss some of the basics of testifying in court. Common words of advice to the witness are, "Try not to be nervous: there is no reason to be." If these "seasoned" attorneys could replay their very first day in the courtroom in their minds, they would quickly remember that there is much for the witness to be nervous about. Newer attorneys who also give this same advice should keep in mind that their witnesses are likely to be more scared than they are. In either case, this type of advice is very naive, and of no benefit to the witness or the attorney in the long run.

Attorneys, unlike trial consultants, are usually not trained in understanding why a witness incurs problems in a courtroom. A trial consultant has the time and expertise to see to it that a witness will be as persuasive as possible. Ideally, it would be beneficial to attorneys if they developed skills for training witnesses, and also knew when to solicit the help of a professional.[56]

The two feelings that witnesses experience most frequently in the courtroom setting are anxiety and anger. Many of the witness's negative behaviors are ways of covering up these feelings.[57] Sources of anxiety can include the impersonal and unyielding feel of the courtroom, the judge's looking down, uncertainty of court procedures, feeling no control over courtroom events, the ritualistic type rules, awareness of being center stage, the experiencing of a new situation, worrying about forgetting important facts, expecting the opposing attorney to attack the witness's credibility, and knowing that the witness may make a difference in what the final verdict will be.[58]

Sources of anger include suspense as to what will happen, the lack of control in a threatening situation, feeling insulted by having credibility doubted, and fear of personal life being inquired into.[59]

A trial consultant knows that these are ample reasons why a witness has every reason to be nervous and angry, and prepares the witness with these in mind. She sees flippancy, condescension, a nervous smile, or an extremely quiet demeanor as behavior that may be covering up feelings of anger and anxiety.[60]

A witness's reaction to anger and anxiety is negatively perceived by the jury. This is usually not done intentionally. As we people are constantly making judgments about other people.[61] We categorize people for various reasons. A thorough study on the subject shows that categorizing (1) reduces the complexity of the environment; (2) is the means by which the objects of the world about us are identified; (3) minimizes the need for constant learning (if appropriate attributes of an object are present, we can identify it even though we have never encountered this particular object before); (4) gives direction for our responses; and (5) allows for restructuring of our knowledge of the world by linking new categories to old ones.[62] By categorizing people as we do, we are able to form fast and very real impressions of others based on a minimum amount of information.[63]

Behavior resulting from a witness's anger or anxiety is not the only factor by which the jury perceives the witness. The gestures he uses, his physical appearance, his facial expressions, and the way he speaks are just a few of the other factors.

The ability to identify negative speech habits or styles is a first step towards preparing the witness to come across well to others. A witness's speaking style may be looked at by a jury to decide the witness's credibility. This may be unfortunate when a lower social-status witness, by virtue of the way he speaks, is seen as having less credibility.[64] With less credibility comes a lesser chance of a fair hearing than a higher status witness would receive. And, a lesser chance of finding the truth so justice will prevail.[65]

Changing the way in which a witness speaks takes time. The witness has often grown accustomed to his way of speaking and usually gives no thought to how he speaks or the words he chooses. The witness's manner of speech reflects his background, and any change must be done with acute awareness of this factor. Making the witness aware of how his speaking style comes across to others is key to encouraging the witness to change it.

A famous study published in the Duke University Law Journal (mentioned in the previous chapter) looked at the language a witness uses to testify, and its effect on jurors' perception. The study resulted in finding that "subtlo differences in the language we use can communicate more than the obvious surface meaning."[66] The additional communication cues, in turn, greatly influence the way our spoken thoughts are understood and interpreted.[67] The researchers, William M. O'Barr and John M. Conley, concluded that "seemingly minor differences in phraseology, tempo and length of answers, by the covert messages they convey, can have a major effect on the jurors."[68]

O'Barr and Conley's taping of ten weeks of criminal trials held in Durham County, North Carolina[69] has direct relevance for the trial attorney. Identifying characteristics of a tentative style of speech,[70] they labeled it "powerless" language,[71] a phenomenon earlier described by linguists and attributed mainly to American women.[72] While it was originally thought to be unique to women,[73] O'Barr found this type of language common among any societal class that had not traditionally held power.[74] The results of the researchers' transformation of the powerless language into a powerful style (reported in detail in the previous section) are instructive. If counsel wants his witness to appear competent, convincing, and trustworthy, regardless of sex, he should attempt a similar transformation with the speech style of any powerless speaker.[75] Even a male witness (who may, purely by his sex, *appear* powerful) can lose favor by powerless speech.[76]

The researchers also looked at another pattern of speech they termed "hypercorrect." This type of speech occurs when a witness, perhaps trying to live up to the courtroom's formal atmosphere, tries to sound educated and cultured.[77] An example of the difference between hypercorrect testimony and less formal testimony is illustrated by the following:

Question: How did you feel after you fell over the crate?

Hypercorrect Answer: A feeling of animosity had manifested itself in me and I was militant to say the least.

Less Formal Answer: I was angry she had left it there.

The hypercorrect testimony and less formal testimony were presented to mock jurors. The mispronunciations and incorrect word choices resulted in the converse effect of what the witness had hoped to convey. As referred to in the previous chapter, the speakers using the less formal style were rated more intelligent, competent, convincing, and trustworthy than speakers who used hypercorrect language.[78] It may be that jurors resent the efforts of the witness to appear to be something he is not.[79]

Some people have verbal habits that affect their credibility but that are not necessarily based on their social status. Expressions like "In all honesty" and "To be honest with you" may indicate to the jury that the witness is telling the truth only at that point in the testimony. Responses like "O.K." after each question may indicate that the witness remembers a prepared question and answer.[80]

Another irritating habit that may affect the credibility of the witness is the expression "you know," said throughout the testimony. The person preparing the witness should see how frequently these verbal habits occur. If they occur infrequently, then there is no reason to call them to the attention of the witness. The witness has enough to worry about without feeling self-conscious over irregular habits.

The sound of a witness's voice may also have a bearing on his credibility. A witness will not be persuasive if he speaks without feeling. Speed, intonation, and inflection of the voice can all convey feeling.

As a witness presents his testimony, the jury also observes the witness's nonverbal behavior. Often verbal and nonverbal are read and judged separately. A person's behavior without verbal communication is interpreted differently than with it.[81] Jurors routinely evaluate the cognitive and emotional states of witnesses. The judgments made are based on their "reading" certain witnesses' behaviors and expressions. They are not based on scientific or technical tests. The jury members ask themselves whether the witness is trustworthy, does he have shifty eyes, is he shaking, and whether these behaviors are a result of his nervousness in being there or are signs of lying.[82]

Some jurors will not even give the benefit of the doubt to the witness. They will hear and see so many variables, and then they will evaluate his performance. It is as though the witness is up for an Emmy, but she must put on the performance of her life before she will even be named a winner.

A person is capable of either reinforcing or contradicting his verbal messages by his nonverbal behavior.[83] A witness is even capable of communicating when he is silent. How a witness sits, dresses, and gestures all communicate something to the jury.

Gestures must be read together to truly understand how a person feels, just as a sentence must be fully read to understand the meaning of a word.[84] If all gestures are congruent, then the real attitude of a person can be determined. However, if prior or subsequent gestures are contradicting or confusing, the ability to persuade is lessened.[85]

When verbal and nonverbal communication contradict, we instinctively rely on the nonverbal—factors we have less control over.[86] Nonverbal responses may be more revealing than verbal responses. Lying with words is easy, but nonverbal behavior speaks a language of its own. The old saying that it is not *what* is said but *how* it is said takes on an important meaning in the courtroom setting.

Since it is impossible not to communicate, everything the witness says or does influences how others perceive him.[87] Before a witness opens his mouth to testify, the jury has already begun evaluating the type of person he is.[88] The witness's own ability to persuade jury members starts from the moment the jury sees him. Everything the witness says or does can affect how persuasive he is. The witness does not even have to be on the witness stand testifying to affect how the jury will perceive him. For example, jury members could see him somewhere in the courthouse setting acting obnoxious and cocky. The testimony the witness has already given or, is about to give, can be colored by their perception of him in his nonwitness role. For this reason, witnesses, other than important ones such as the client himself, should not be allowed to remain in the courthouse after testifying. Sequestering the witness prior to testifying is also highly recommended.

While an attorney may be able to have his witness sequestered prior to testimony, it is impossible to have his witness's facial expression sequestered during testimony. A witness sitting on the witness stand will probably not have her hands or feet exposed for the jury to see. Facial expressions are very revealing and can reflect the witness's true feelings, his moods, or his emotions. For these reasons, facial expressions of the witness are important to view as a source of communication.

Since facial expressions are difficult to hide, the jury can easily see that the witness is avoiding eye contact, frowning, smiling nervously, or raising his eyebrows in a delayed and phony manner. Where conflicting messages are sent, the observer will rely more on facial expressions than on what is being said and how it is being said.[89]

Jurors are influenced by the choice of expression the witness uses to convey his feelings. A person's facial expressions reveal 55% of the emotional meaning of a message, verbal language adds 7% of the meaning, and vocal characteristics add the remaining 38%.[90]

These findings suggest that feelings are indicated more through action than through words.

Several studies have shown that the amount and type of eye contact a person gives to others also influences their perception of him. If a person avoids eye contact, he is often perceived as feeling poor, hostile, depressed, or guilty.[91] Too much eye contact may be perceived as threatening.[92] This may be especially so if a defendant has an intense, piercing look, and is on trial for a triple axe murder.[93]

A witness's clothing can also influence the jury's perception of him. While dress and appearance receive a thorough treatment later, they are a deceptively simple means by which an attorney can set himself at ease, assured that he and his client look the (appropriate) part. One study found that a person's attire was a good indicator of personality[94]; in fact, of subjects viewing four hundred women, 72% of the women were accurately assessed based solely on their clothing.[95]

The witness's attire during his courtroom appearance must not be overlooked. The subject must be addressed with every witness. A witness should wear clothing that is clean and neat, and appropriate for this occasion. No one should be dressed beyond his ability.[96] A witness who works in a factory may not be creating a good impression if he sits there in a suit looking stiff and uncomfortable.[97]

If the witness is the client, the attorney should suggest to him what he should wear in court and make sure he sees what the witness actually is wearing *before* going into the courtroom.[98] This procedure is recommended for all of the attorney's witnesses. If possible, the attorney should have the witness meet the attorney at his office, or outside the courthouse before proceeding to the courtroom. Doing this will also make the witness less apprehensive about going in to testify.

The client's Rolex watch, Gucci loafers, or silk chemise may be impressive and appropriate in some settings, but the courtroom setting is certainly not one of them. Additionally, it is highly recommended that all witnesses leave their "I'm so happy I could. . ." T-shirts at home.[99]

An extreme example of why the final "dress" rehearsal of the witness should occur outside the courtroom was illustrated in a Texas courtroom. A new assistant U.S. Attorney was planning to call his principal witness, who was a secretary with a federal agency. It was around Halloween, and the supervisor told everyone to come to work in a costume. The secretary had not been told by the attorney what to wear to court, so she walked into the courtroom as Minnie Mouse, complete with mouse ears, a short red skirt, and a long black tail![100] An attorney should never assume anything when it comes to a witness. A trial consultant sees to it that he doesn't.

Although factors like appearance, style, and delivery can all reflect on trustworthiness, males and females observe people differently. Males look more at what others say, and slightly more at their physical appearance. Females, on the other hand, look more at actions and verbal styles.[101]

Several studies have indicated that the client's attractiveness influences how a judgment is rendered. In one such study, the subjects read accounts of an automobile accident in which the driver, who had been drinking heavily, struck and killed a pedestrian.[102] The defendant was presented as either an attractive, neutral, or unattractive person. The subjects were more lenient with the neutral and attractive defendants than they were with the unattractive defendant.[103] Furthermore, if the unlawful behavior has to do with the attractiveness of the female, for example where an attractive female entices the victim with her charms, the attractive defendant will be treated worse than if she had been unattractive.[104]

It is unlikely to find a person who has all positive traits. A juror normally weighs all of the positive and negative traits that he has perceived to determine his final impression of the person.[105] A "halo" effect may occur, however, when a person is physically attractive. An attractive person will be judged as having other positive characteristics, though in reality, the person may not have as many as believed.[106] An attorney can benefit by knowing what events and processes, like the halo effect, distort impression formation.

If the person is unattractive, the attorney or trial consultant may have to use imagination to try and improve him. If they are unable to do so, they may want to sharpen the witness's skills as a communicator to try and balance the negative trait. The attorney must bear in mind that he is helping himself as well as the witness who hopes to save face.

The perception of another may also be influenced by whether he sees a witness as likable.[107] Mock jurors were read two conflicting testimonies of two witnesses (a plaintiff and a defendant) regarding which one ran the light. They also were given written descriptions of the witnesses. One description was written in positive (likeable) terms, and the other in negative terms. The descriptions allowed the jurors a basis on which they could form impressions of the witnesses. (In a real trial, the jurors would be able to observe the witness first-hand.) The jurors were then asked to decide the guilt or innocence of the witnesses and rate their credibility level. The witness who was described in likable terms was perceived as more credible. This factor made the jury less certain about his guilt.[108]

Other factors like the witness's name may also affect whether the witness is perceived as likable. If a witness has an unusual name, the attorney may want to have her shorten it when she is on the witness stand, for example, from Louise Annabelle to Lou Ann. We associate various characteristics with a name. A study of children found that those with unusual or disliked names may be discriminated against by others.[109] Whether we carry these attitudes into adulthood has not yet been studied.

It is amazing the things one takes for granted. It is hard for a witness to believe that he is being judged on factors other than the content of what he says. The fact remains that he is, and the attorney, with the help of a trial consultant, can take the results of these studies and make them work for him.

There are two goals every attorney should have in mind when he prepares the witness for court. First, the attorney must develop techniques to reduce the anxiety that the witness presently feels, or will inevitably feel, when he actually testifies. Second, the attorney must present his witness in the most persuasive manner he can. The second goal overlaps the first goal since a less tense witness can be a more persuasive one. However, the second goal further involves identifying and altering any witness characteristics which may reflect upon the witness's credibility. Both goals are equally important.

The goal for the witness is to get through his testimony without inadvertently harming the case.[110] The attorney must see that the witness has every possible chance of doing that. Hiring a trial consultant helps the attorney establish his goals. In fact, showing interest in the person may even make him want to be a better witness for the attorney.

Getting the witness ready for his court appearance should begin long before the actual trial. Doing this will lessen the chance of any last minute surprises. It will also allow the attorney and the witness more time to work on making the witness more effective at testifying.

From the onset, the attorney or trial consultant should explain to the witness that feelings of anger and anxiety are normal, even for him. It is productive to tell the witness that the preparation will make him feel more comfortable in court.[111]

The main reason a witness suffers stress and anxiety in the courtroom is fear of the unknown.[112] Our bodies react to tension. Tension often reveals itself in unproductive ways. For example, when we become tense, our vocal cords and upper bodies tighten and we forget the most obvious things. The end result is that we look stiff and uncomfortable, and we sound weak and unconvincing. A witness must be taught to control anxiety, not let it control him.

Before the attorney can achieve his first goal of reducing a witness's anxieties, he must first find out what they are. Witnesses, like most people, do not like to admit their fears to anyone. The attorney may wish to discuss his own fears or common fears of other witnesses. The attorney must work at developing and maintaining a comfortable and honest atmosphere. Having the attorney express his own fears may get the witness to open up and express his anxieties about his upcoming testimony. Ask the witness to express his greatest fears. Some of these fears may be imagined, others anticipated. Make a point to alleviate these fears in particular. Once the fears are identified, the attorney should ask the witness what he believes causes these fears.[113]

The most common reason a witness fears testifying is that the witness has never experienced the courtroom situation before. The witness lacks confidence in his ability to be a good witness. He also feels insecure.

If possible, take the witness to the courthouse and let him sit in on a trial. Then take him to an empty courtroom. At this point the witness should be brimming with questions. Familiarize the witness with the various key people in the courtroom and explain what they do. Have the witness sit in the judge's chair, the jury box, and on the witness stand. Remind the witness that the judge and jury are not his enemies. Explain the role of the jury who has to hear hours of conflicting testimony from different witnesses. Tell the witness how important it is to have his testimony believed and understood. Explain that the jury consists of people like him who have fears and make mistakes. Anything the attorney can do to demystify the courtroom will be helpful in relieving witness anxiety.[114]

Each phase of the trial should be explained to the witness. Explain the basic rules for testifying. For example, show how the witness will be sworn in, the order and purpose of direct and cross-examination questions, the type of objections that can be made, and how a judge can rule on them. A judge's response of "overruled" or "sustained" is part of every day trial language for an attorney. Any witness who wasn't raised watching Perry Mason every Friday night will find these words very confusing and discomforting. Not only are these terms unfamiliar to the witness, but the witness knows that it was his testimony that elicited the attorney's objection and the subsequent ruling by the judge. Emphasize that these reactions to his testimony must not be taken personally.

It is important that the attorney gain the trust of the witness. The witness will be feeling mixed emotions in the courtroom. Few if any of these emotions will be positive if the witness has not been trained effectively. If the witness knows that he has even one person he can depend on to make him a little less uncomfortable in this strange environment, he will be less tense. His testimony will also reflect this fact. One way to gain the witness's trust is to explain the concept of re-direct. Tell the witness that even if the opposing attorney elicits unfavorable information from him, re-direct will allow the witness to clarify any misconception.

Explain the overall strategy and theme of the case to the witness. Habituate him to the major facts of the case prior to trial. Let the witness know how his testimony will fit into the overall strategy of the trial. The witness and his testimony now take on a sense of importance.[115] Be sure the witness knows what parts of his testimony will be focused upon during direct and likely focused on during cross-examination. Show him how you will break down his testimony so it will be clearer to the jury. Explain the opposing side's viewpoint as best you can so the witness will have some idea where the opposing attorney's questions are coming from.

The witness should be given copies of previous answers to interrogatories, any depositions, any previous testimony, and any oral or written statements he may have given. These will help freshen the witness's memory. The witness, with the help of the attorney, will be able to see any inconsistencies that may later lead to impeachment in court.[116] The witness should be told to admit or clarify any ambiguities if questioned about them.[117] Determine at this point whether the witness's present memory of the incident differs in any way from how he had earlier recorded it.

The witness should also be given the opportunity to look at any available exhibits that the witness will later be asked to use or identify during testimony. Explain to the witness how you will use the exhibit. Additionally, explain the necessary foundation requirements for each exhibit. An awkward or unfamiliar exhibit can itself be a distraction to a witness's testimony.

Revisiting the scene is a good way to refresh the witness's memory. Revisiting is not recommended, however, if changes have occurred that may affect his memory of the scene at the time of the original occurrence. The goal here is to refresh the witness's memory, not confuse it further.

Practice the expected testimony with the witness in an empty courtroom, or in as close to a courtroom setting as possible. Generally cover what will likely be covered in court. Stress to the witness that the questions likely will not be asked in the same order, nor in the same wording. Focus on any specific areas of the testimony that will be pertinent to the case. The witness will probably want a set of written questions and answers, but discourage this type of crutch. Remind the witness that he personally experienced the incident and therefore does not need any aids.

Most witnesses are unaccustomed to public speaking. Encourage the witness to view the jury as his peers by speaking in a conversational tone, maintaining frequent eye contact, and avoiding a monotone voice.

Initial tension is normal. Explain to the witness that tension will go away during the preliminary questions normally asked of every witness on direct. Questions concerning his name, address, education, and hobbies are familiar questions to which the witness can relate, and at the same time allow him to become more comfortable speaking to the jury.

How a witness is allowed to testify also can affect the jury's perception of him. For years trial strategy books have advised attorneys to allow their witnesses to testify in a narrative form on direct. By doing this, the witness would appear to be telling the story as he actually saw it, not the way the attorney wanted him to see it. The testimony, broken down into small segments, and interrupted by numerous questions did not make the story come across as well. With the narrative form of testimony came greater credibility of the witness.[118]

Researchers O'Barr and Conley tested this hypothesis. To their surprise, they found that the questioning style affected the subjects' perception of the lawyer, more than the witness.[119] Attorneys who allowed their witnesses to testify in a narrative, rather than a fragmented style, were seen as having more confidence in their witnesses. The subjects also believed that the attorney saw his witness as more intelligent and assertive. As a result, the jury started viewing the witness in the same manner as they believed the witness's attorney viewed him.[120]

However, not every witness should be allowed to testify in a narrative style. The witness's personality and speaking style should influence which method of questioning on direct is used. A witness who is rather verbose, overexaggerates, and testifies to more than he personally knows, is not going to leave a favorable impression on the jury if he is allowed to testify in a narrative style. The number of times the opposing attorney will (should) interrupt with objections will distract from the witness's testimony. This is the type of witness who will come across more effectively if he is giving brief answers to frequent questions.

The quiet, shy witness on the other hand, who is unable to tolerate tension very well, will not be effective if he is allowed to testify in a narrative style. With less talking, the jury will be able to "listen" better to ineffective nonverbal language. The silence that exists during the witness's verbal testimony will be screaming for a more fragmented style of testimony.

If the attorney has prepared the witness to testify in the most efficient and comfortable way possible, then there should be no waste of time on direct. The longer the testimony takes, the more likely the jury's attention span will wane. The attorney must see to it that the witness is prepared to give clear, concise, and convincing testimony—nothing less, and definitely nothing more. Knowing how to use a witness effectively is a trial strategy technique that should not be overlooked.

The witness must be reminded that he can only testify to things he personally saw, heard, or did. The witness must be told to stop if he is interrupted by an attorney's objection, or if the judge interrupts. He should also wait for an objection before he answers.

If the witness remembers that something he previously testified to is incorrect, he should correct it as soon as possible. Remind the witness that the cross-examiner is not friendly so the witness should pay particular attention to his questions. The witness must also listen to all instructions given by the judge or attorney.

The witness must not appear to be cocky because the jury will not have any sympathy for him when the opposing attorney demolishes him on cross.

Testifying for lengthy periods of time can be very tiring for the witness. Tell him to remain polite, conscientious, and steadfast in his beliefs. If necessary, he should not be afraid to ask for a short recess.

The witness should concentrate on the question being asked, and not worry about potential ones. He should also not worry whether something he testifies to on direct will come back to haunt him during cross-examination. This will only cause extra stress.

The witness should not volunteer additional information as it will just open up his testimony to objections by opposing counsel. Instruct the witness not to conclude his testimony with phrases like "nothing else happened." Such finality is a prime target for cross-examination.

The thought of being cross-examined is undoubtedly the greatest fear of a witness. During this time, the witness's credibility and perception are most often attacked. Common witness fears include fear of forgetting, fear of making a mistake, fear of the opposing attorney trapping him, fear the witness will not make a good impression, and fear of being discredited. There are several ways to help reduce this fear.

Every trial attorney has his own way of eliciting damaging testimony during cross-examination. If the witness can become exposed to the opposing attorneys favorite tactics and idiosyncrasies before trial, he will feel less threatened.[121]

An ideal way of exposing the witness is by having the witness sit in on another case in which the opposing attorney is involved. If this is not possible, have an unfamiliar person, like an associate, paralegal, or trial consultant act out the role of the opposing attorney. The role-player should cross-examine the witness with questions covering every possible subject matter the opposing attorney is likely to cover. It is wise to go over any questions the adversary may use to trap the witness or make the witness uncomfortable. Common trap questions include the amount of money a witness is getting paid to testify and whether the witness has discussed his case with anyone. Impress upon the witness that he should answer all questions honestly, but that truth is best conveyed in a confident, rather than hesitant manner.[122]

The witness should be taught that he can control the cross-examination to some degree. For instance, if the opposing attorney asks questions the witness does not understand, or hear, the witness should not hesitate to ask that the question be rephrased or repeated. Additionally, if the attorney asks that a question be answered with a simple yes or no, and the witness feels that the question cannot be answered without clarification, the witness should indicate this fact. At that time it will be up to the judge to decide whether to let the witness clarify his answer. Even in the unlikely case that the judge refuses, the jury will know what kind of predicament the witness is in. The witness who employs these types of methods on cross-examination, yet remains polite and firm in his testimony, will be viewed as in control over the situation.

A witness is not anxious or angry if he is relaxed. The witness learns to relax by concentrating on positive thoughts.[123] A witness who knows what the courtroom looks like, knows what is expected of him, and knows what type of questions the opposing attorney is likely to ask will be much more relaxed than a witness who has not had this thorough preparation. Having this knowledge is positive! The energy that the witness saves by being exposed to the unknown can now be channeled productively into effective testimony.

A witness who is full of anxiety simply cannot be as convincing as one who is not. Preparing the witness helps to decrease his anxieties and thereby make him more persuasive. Testifying can even be viewed as a challenge that can be enjoyed.[124] Improper preparation, or no preparation at all, is an injustice to the client's case.

The attorney or his staff using the advice of a trial consultant, or the trial consultant herself, can prepare the witness to be the most persuasive witness he can be. This is the second goal of the attorney.

Witnesses must be prepared individually. What works for one may not work for another. When the attorney or trial consultant begins preparing the witness, the witness must be told that he is a significant part of the legal process, that his previously learned behavior may or may not apply to the courtroom setting, and that any change will be temporary.[125]

The personal style of the witness must be looked at to determine his positive and negative qualities. The witness can help make this assessment. The objective is to develop the positive qualities and decrease the negative ones.[126] Certain witness characteristics are likely to produce certain perceptions in others. Factors to look at include the witness's body posture, his manner of dress, use of hands and gesturing, ability to interact, use of eye contact, ability to project the voice, use of facial expressions, and reactions to stress.[127] All of these factors can have a negative effect on the jury's perception of the witness. This is so even if the witness is telling the truth.

Many behaviors that are negatively perceived are actually physiological responses to stress. The attorney and witness should identify physiological and nonphysiological cues that will help the witness realize when feelings like anxiety or anger are occurring.[128] Examples of these cues include sweaty palms, tension in shoulders or neck, clenched fists, rapid speech, or a nervous smile.[129] These cues may also be misinterpreted as signs of deception. Recognizing these cues will enable the witness to identify the feeling early on and hopefully be able to switch to new behavior.

It is beneficial for the witness to know what types of behavior are associated with credibility and deception. It is imperative that the witness knows exactly what behavior characteristics need to be changed or minimized and specific ways to alter them.

Other negative witness characteristics may be the result of the witness's personality or style. The attorney with the help of the witness can assess traits or behavior that may need modification.[130] For example, together they should look at whether the witness lacks eye contact (a sign of evading the truth), if the witness unnecessarily uses professional jargon (putting on a false air), or if the witness dresses inappropriately (a sign of indifference). Other negative qualities that need modification include distracting body movements, mumbling, extreme tension, ramrod posture, and distracting facial expressions like fast blinking and grimacing.[131] All of these can be irritating habits which affect the witness's credibility.

Do not be overly critical of a witness's physical mannerisms. This will only increase his fear of testifying. Work on changing only the ones which affect the witness's credibility.

Testifying in front of a jury is like having to put on a performance that wasn't auditioned for. Role-playing is the next best thing to actually testifying in court. Not only does the witness become more comfortable in his new "role" as a witness, but the attorney is able to view behavioral and personality traits that may need to be improved. Role-modeling will also allow the attorney to determine which style of questioning on direct will be best suited to that particular witness.

Role-playing is time consuming and requires great patience, but the desired benefits are produced each time role-playing is practiced.[132] It results in the development of new skills that appear very natural.[133]

Role-playing allows the attorney and witness to see how the witness reacts to conflict during cross-examination. A witness who reacts to stress by being defensive or aggressive will not be viewed as in control of the situation. As a result, he will not be positively perceived.

Trial consultants sometimes recommend videotapes to focus on problem areas. This is a good way for the witness to understand why some of his behavior is ineffective. Before watching the videotape of the role-playing, it is effective to have the witness identify what makes a person believable and persuasive.[134]

Trial simulations can also be videotaped. It is effective to have the trial run in an empty courtroom. Mock jurors can provide valuable feedback to the witness.

If videotape equipment is unavailable, tape record the witness's voice during role-playing. Allow him to take the tape home so he can listen to how his voice reacts under stress.[135] Few people are aware of how their voice sounds to other people. The witness should not be expected to change his voice overnight, but being made aware of potential problems, is the first step to encouraging change.

The best way to get a witness to change is by subtle suggestion and criticism. An insensitive lawyer will only be effective at one thing—offending the witness's vanity.[136]

Even witnesses who frequently testify in court can be helped by trial consulting. In some cities like Denver, attorney-consultants are teaching police officers how to be effective witnesses in court.[137] The attorneys initially focus on the officers' distrust of the legal system (the source of their anger) and then help them to better understand it. The attorneys inform the officers that in their attempt on the witness stand to see that the defendant gets what he deserves, the jury may perceive it as a personal vendetta against the defendant. They are also informed that their courtroom credibility may be lessened when they wear their uniforms. The uniform may indicate that the officer is not an objective witness. However, if the officer is perceived as likable and comes across as competent, the uniform (toned down a bit) will be good for the authority it represents.[138]

Before a jury can ever begin to deliberate in an attorney's favor, they must believe the testimony of the attorney's witnesses.[139] It is a mistake not to give a case every chance possible to win a favorable verdict. Hiring a trial consultant improves that chance.

Most witnesses, however, are not given the advantage of trial consulting. There are numerous factors for this. These factors include the extra cost to the attorney, the lack of time between some attorney's preparation of the witness's testimony and the actual trial, confidence in the attorney's own ability to prepare his witness, and a lack of awareness of how invaluable a trial consultant's expertise can be to an attorney.

Whatever excuse an attorney gives for not hiring a trial consultant, there is a growing number of attorneys who are hiring them—and, rehiring them for subsequent cases.

Should a witness be viewed as a product that is tested in the courtroom? There is a recent trend to spend the time and money necessary to prepare the witness properly for the courtroom experience. If a witness looks and sounds good, the attorney not only relieves himself of unnecessary stress, he puts himself a step closer to swaying the judge or jury in his favor. After all, verdicts are based on facts as well as perceptions, despite the fact that perceptions are not formally introduced into evidence. The end result is that success in the courtroom is no longer solely dependent on the attorney's legal skill, but rather on how skilled the attorney has become in using persuasive techniques. Tipping the scales of justice in favor of one side is now within the attorney's reach.

Why are these techniques so important? Look at the following example to best understand the answer.

> A murder trial hinges on the testimony of one witness. The jury's belief in this witness, which will determine their decision, depends almost entirely on the impression they form of him in his brief time on the witness stand. They examine his face, his features, his clothes, the quality of his voice, and his answers and try to decide what kind of person he is. . .[140]

A trial consultant is able to present an attorney a silver platter of very useful research and advice on how to make a witness more persuasive. But the decision of whether to take from the platter rests solely in the hands of the attorney.

III. *HYPNOSIS AND THE COURTROOM*

Dr. Martin T. Orne, Professor of Psychiatry at the University of Pennsylvania, has been involved with the field of hypnosis for more than thirty-five years and the "special expertise on hypnotically induced testimony and its use in the criminal justice system.[141] Several years ago, defense counsel in New Jersey planned to use Orne's analysis of the plaintiff's hypnotically refreshed recollection to discount her testimony. The Assistant Deputy Public Defender and an attorney report the case as follows.[142]

An attempted rape victim, who escaped attack by telling two men who had abducted her of her pregnancy, was threatened with harm to her family if she went to the police. She reported the incident, however, and picked one man from the mug shots in police files but was unable to identify the second. At the request of the police, she agreed to undergo hypnosis. Prior to hypnosis, she had selected a photograph from police files as a close look-alike of the second man. After hypnosis, however, she reconstructed the crime and felt she could positively identify him. Coincidentally, she saw him on a street shortly afterwards and telephoned the police. He was the same man that she had earlier identified as a close look-alike.[143]

Defense counsel sought Orne's interpretation of the plaintiff's hypnotically refreshed recollection. Orne suggested that, when the victim was regressed back to the night of the attack, she was unable to put aside the photograph of the close look-alike, and it became a part of her recollection. Thus, she became "an honest liar." Defense intended to use Orne's analysis to show that the plaintiff's statements were sufficiently unreliable to be admissible in court. The prosecutor's office, however, moved for dismissal for other reasons. The Assistant Deputy Public Defender and the attorney decided to chronicle this story anyway to "point out the deficiencies of hypnosis as a barometer of truth."[144]

Further details of the case make that point even better. In his account, Orne describes that, after the woman had gone to the police, she received threatening notes, which she turned over to them. It was then that they urged her to submit to hypnosis. Because the public defender's office promised to combat the use of hypnotically refreshed recollection, the district attorney began to examine the facts of the case more carefully. The handwriting of the threatening notes, which the district attorney had earlier thought was peculiar, was submitted to an expert for analysis. It was determined that the alleged victim had written the notes and had fabricated the entire rape attempt "in an effort to reawaken the interest of her husband who was in the process of filing divorce proceedings against her." She had never even met the two men that she had accused.[145]

This example, however, stands in sharp contrast to others. In one case, a woman was raped at knifepoint by an assailant who dropped his wallet and then later returned to retrieve it. While he was gone, she locked herself in a bathroom and attempted to examine the wallet's contents but had time to see only his name and a photograph.

Under hypnosis she was unable to recall his name; since it turned out to be a complicated Middle European name, it may not have completely registered in her mind when she saw it. However, in reliving the experience, she was able to "see" his photograph again and then selected the man from mug shots. When the man was apprehended, his fingerprint was found to match a print in her bathroom.[146]

These cases clearly illustrate the range of success of forensic hypnosis. What is not clear on superficial examination is why such dramatic permutations comprise the range. The answers lie in the meaning and characteristics of hypnosis itself, which are set forth in the first section below. The second section presents results of laboratory experiments designed to test or elicit the meaning and characteristics of hypnosis relevant to testimony. The third section discusses inherent differences in laboratory and forensic conditions, along with the potential effects of these differences. The next section examines the use of forensic hypnosis, in light of recommended conditions, and closes with possible effects on the jury of hypnotically-induced testimony.

A. *Background and Definitions*

"Hypnosis has never completely recovered from its mystical past."[147] Because of its "highly fictional background," many people believe hypnosis to be a myth, "on a par with fortune telling, astrology, and spiritualism."[148] A common dictionary definition is just accurate enough to perpetuate some of the misconceptions about hypnosis: "a state that resembles sleep but is induced by a hypnotizer whose suggestions are readily accepted by the subject."[149]

The association between hypnosis and sleep is due to the term's derivation from the Greek word *hypnos* and the unfortunate selection of that word by James Baird, the Father of Modern Hypnotism.[150] In actuality, hypnosis is described as anything but sleep: "a state of alert, attentive, receptive, integrated concentration characterized by a parallel awareness." By this, the author means that the hypnotized subject can relate to another individual while being "intensely involved in another facet of his own life experience."[151]

Hypnosis has spawned more than one scientific definition, probably due to "the unknown" that still envelops certain aspects of hypnosis, such as an explanation for "its unique ability to pull up seemingly irretrievable data from our memory bank." The many theories of memory and memory recall, indicating in their number how much is still unknown about those subjects, undoubtedly account for the uncertainties about hypnosis.[152] Results of the experiments reported below, along with insights offered by the authorities already cited, suggest the following simplified view of hypnosis. The mind registers empirical data on both a conscious and an unconscious level. The conscious level is subject to certain pressures that do not invade the unconscious. These pressures act as impediments to recall; when they are relieved, the information becomes available. Thus, the super-alert description is accurate, because the subject is aware of more than he would otherwise be. He is intensely involved in a personal experience in the very act of retrieving a past, subconscious thought. And he relates to another individual in the sense that he has probably been assisted in his undertaking by a hypnotist.

The suggestion in the dictionary definition that the hypnotist in fact places the subject in a hypnotic trance is "utter nonsense. . . he simply taps the natural trance capacity that is inherent in the subject." The ability to be hypnotized is determined by genes and/or learned during the early developmental years. Within less than ten minutes, the degree of intensity of one's trance capacity can be measured, on a 0-5 scale. This ability does not change during the adult years unless altered by forms of mental illness or drugs that hamper the ability to concentrate and begins to reduce only slightly after the age of 70. "In everyday life, when a person is highly motivated or highly charged for a specific goal, he is prone to spontaneously shift into his own trance level to facilitate the achievement of a task." All the hypnotist does is tap the subject's natural trance ability, with his cooperation and agreement.[153]

Dr. Goodenough, a licensed, practicing clinical psychologist with a law degree, refers to the notion of the hypnotist having control over the subject's mind as "the big lie that dominates the perversion of hypnosis and still confounds judge and jury alike." He observes that everyone is hypnotized at one time or another, either through putting oneself into a trance or by being hypnotized by various stimuli, such as the endless highway on a long drive. Even in a session with a hypnotist, the subject hypnotizes himself. Moreover, if neither the subject nor the hypnotist ends the trance, it terminates automatically. Because hypnosis induces if not emanates from relaxation, allows acute concentration, and creates a heightened receptivity in the subject, Goodenough suggests that self-hypnosis could assist the client in preparing his own testimony and counsel in absorbing factual data, writing and researching briefs, and even taking bar exams.[154]

This triad of relaxation, concentration, and receptivity also explains the successes of hypnosis. As an example, if a witness to a slight auto mishap sees a vehicle long enough to scan the license plate but later cannot recall it, since the event was an ordinary, non-stressful occurrence, spontaneous concentration and collateral associations could cause the memory to emerge. Hypnosis merely effects this in a more formal trance and produces a more efficient flushing of the memory.[155]

Additionally, the psychological pain accompanying a dramatic event could further deter recall. Thus, in the incident of the Chowchilla kidnapping, the bus driver had seen and tried to memorize the numbers of the van license plate but had been too afraid to concentrate under the watchful eyes of the kidnappers.[156] Only under hypnosis could he recall the numbers.[157] When certain pressures of the conscious mind repress memories of a rape victim, the hypnotist can suggest to her that she is viewing the scene anew, but as a spectator, not a participant. Since she is now "divorced from traumatic involvement," she can recall and report the incident. "The forensic and therapeutic results are at times nothing short of miraculous."[158]

Forensic hypnosis is an artificial carving out of a section of hypnosis, as distinguished from clinical hypnosis, with the main difference being the purpose of recall. Forensic hypnosis is primarily used for investigative purposes.[159] Different methods of hypnosis can produce the same results. Hypermnesia is simply greater recall than that experienced in the non-hypnotic state and can be induced with proper stimulations or associations. Revivification is the reliving of an incident by the subject and requires posthypnotic suggestions as to the exact date of the incident; it is thought to require a deeper trance, since the subject must be able to superimpose surroundings of the past over those of the present. Age regression, while a separate technique, is also inherent in revivification, since the subject acts out past events, at the age when he or she experienced them, but in the framework of the present.[160]

Although Goodenough contends that we all undergo hypnosis, self or externally imposed, the measure of intensity of trance capacity is relevant if different hypnotic techniques require different trance levels. On the 0-5 scale, about 70% of the population is capable of some degree of trance (the "everyday" hypnosis Goodenough suggests we all experience may not be frequent or deep enough to reflect on the scale). About 15% of these can go into no more than a light trance, 15% can go into very intense trances, and the others are somewhere in between in trance capacity. The Hypnotic Induction Profile (HIP), which measures hypnotic capacity, also indicates relative mental health and personality style. In one case, a military policeman charged with the kidnapping, rape, and murder of three teenagers claimed he was not guilty by reason of insanity. A videotaped interview of the supposedly hypnotized defendant allegedly proved that he was suffering from dual personality and that his "bad" side had committed the crimes. But since multiple personalities have high trance capacity, his HIP score, in revealing that he was barely able to sustain a trance, neutralized the drama of the videotape by indicating that he was faking this "bad" side.[161]

This last example reveals the defendant's reliance on what he felt certain the fact-finder would conclude about the reliability of a hypnotic trance, that the subject could not be lying. Notice, however, how the defendant was thwarted: not by the prosecution refuting the idea that a hypnotized subject could not lie but by its showing that the subject was not actually hypnotized. As the experimental results below indicate, even legitimately hypnotized subjects can "lie."

B. *Experimental Results*

An experiment reported in 1944 sought to discover the type of information that is better recalled under hypnosis than in the waking state. The experimenter built upon contributions of others, such as Freud's theory that emotionally disturbing experiences are repressed while pleasant or non-anxiety-producing experiences are recalled (i.e., different memory of emotional vs. non-emotional events) and Bartlett's idea that memory is an organized reconstruction of "meaningful" events (suggesting that nonsense information is treated differently for recall purposes).[162] Therefore, even though emotional memories are suppressed and nonsense information is simply not pieced together into a conscious memory, theoretically both are within the subconscious, retrievable with hypermnesia.

The procedures were the same for all of the experiments, with only the type of material to be learned and recalled changing. Each of thirteen subjects participated in seven experiments twice, once as a member of the control group and once as a member of the experimental group. The control group would learn material, recall it in the waking state, and then recall it again in the waking state. Then, at least ten days later, the experimental group would learn similar material, recall it in a waking state, and then recall it again in a hypnotic state. To test the effect of hypnosis, hypnotic recall (after waking recall) was to be compared with waking recall (also after waking recall).[163]

The first experiment involved three-letter nonsense syllables on flash cards. In the second experiment, meaningful words were interspersed at random in lists of nonsense syllables. No hypermnesia appeared in the hypnotic or waking recall for either experiment. In the third experiment, subjects were again asked to recall meaningful words from lists of nonsense syllables but were also told that the number of words they recalled indicated their "innate intelligence" as accurately as the college entrance tests. The subjects were told they would pass or fail and that, even though they might do well on one test, the material on it could be easier, which meant they could fail overall by doing poorly on another test. Words incorrectly recalled were "failing" words while words correctly recalled were "successful" words. In the second session of the experiment, waking recall or hypnotic recall (depending on the group), the subjects were told they would be given a second chance to improve their scores, since they were so low. There was almost no increase in recall for the waking recall group. However, there was marked hypermnesia for the hypnotic recall group. In fact, the increased memory of the failing words brought them up to the number of successful words recalled.[164]

The difference between the second and third experiments was the presence of anxiety in the subjects when presented with the possibility and, later, the confirmation of failure. This was confirmed by the experimenters in the "blanched faces" of many subjects during the experiment and the fact that, although the subjects had been forewarned that the experiment involved "psychic tension," two men asked to drop out in the third experiment.[165] The author explains how reasonable it is that one would recall less well those words, tasks, or events having unpleasant associations, such as those reminding of failure. However, that kind of filtering is a device only of the conscious mind.

> The characteristic relaxation of hypnosis, however, makes possible a lack of anxiety and insecurity, an elimination of the need to sustain confidence in one's abilities; under these conditions, the need

> for ego enhancement is gone, and the [subject] can remember his unpleasant experience because he is free from fear of feelings of inadequacy or from criticism. . . . in relaxation, the ego functions are under no stress to protect themselves. . . because the [subject] has attained. . . a feeling of confidence in the hands of the hypnotist that makes for neutralization of negative emotions.[166]

It is suggested in the earlier example of the rapist with a complicated Middle Eastern name that perhaps the name failed to register with the victim, even in her subconscious. To Americans, certain foreign names conform to no recognizable pattern and often combine letters in ways that defy English spelling rules. Thus, such names become like nonsense syllables. When a subject is on the analyst's couch, the relaxation often produces a free association of ideas, which allows for the recovery of memory or the proper reconstruction of independent memories. Free association succeeds only if there is some connection between a thought and a memory.

> [I]solated nonsense words lacking any organized context or varied associations will not show enhanced recall in a relaxed state simply because the disconnected, disparate character of nonsense material precludes the spontaneous flowing together of meaningful memories that relaxation in hypnosis facilitates. In such a state there would be a search for one specific associate, one and only one right nonsense syllable.[167]

The need for an "organized context" is further verified by the results of the fourth experiment, in which the subjects attempted to memorize four five-line poems. The hypnotized subjects showed increased recall over those in the waking state. In the fifth experiment, subjects learned ten poems, each consisting of twenty to twenty-two words. They also underwent a success-failure anxiety-producing process like that in the second experiment. However, despite this added feature, there was no increased recall in the hypnotic state for "successful" or "failing" poems. The offered explanation is that the poems were so numerous that the subjects had difficulty associating a particular failure with any given poem. "In other words, the memory material became so undifferentiated and blurred, that there would be no identification with the appropriate affect." The subjects demonstrated tension and anxiety, but those emotions simply were not correlated with particular memories.[168]

In the sixth experiment, memory for profane vs. innocuous words was tested, with the goal of comparing "emotionally disgusting stimuli with neutral stimuli." While there was no hypermnesia for either type of words in the hypnotic or waking state, the profane words were better recalled than the innocuous words.[169]

The final experiment tested for recall of tasks the subjects performed under high anxiety conditions. Half of the group was predetermined to fail, and half was predetermined to pass. As with the third experiment, there was hypnotic hypermnesia for naming or describing those tasks that had been designated as failure during performance. Successful tasks showed no hypermnesia in either state, and failure tasks showed no hypermnesia in the waking state.[170]

Given the apparently controlling effect of relaxation in hypnosis and the 30% of the population that evidently cannot sustain a measurable hypnotic trance, it is not surprising that some psychologists advance relaxation techniques as much as hypnosis. In 1982, Dr. Wagstaff, of the Department of Psychology of the University of Liverpool, summarized his research on hypnosis, which had been prompted by the increased use of hypnosis in police investigations in the United States and Israel but only occasional use in the U.K. The goal of his research was to determine whether hypnosis, as opposed to waking recall, actually helps people to recall material relevant to police investigations.[171]

One difference Wagstaff detected between hypnosis and waking recall was eye closure, with those undergoing hypnosis being more likely to have their eyes closed. Because closed eyes would result in fewer distractions (and should therefore enhance concentration), he tested waking subjects with their eyes closed and found that "eye closure had a small but significant effect on facilitating recall for pictures of everyday items." Next, he showed subjects slides of people, cars, license plates, etc. Some of the subjects were put under hypnosis, some were given relaxation instructions, and the others remained untreated. Not only did the results show that hypnosis did not aid memory, but for those who were not hypnotically susceptible, hypnosis seemed to cause them to perform worse than the other groups.[172]

In a third experiment, the subjects watched a realistic videotape on crime and violence and were assigned to one of three groups: a group that was hypnotized and given revivification suggestions, a waking group that was given comparable guided memory instructions, and a control group that was untreated. Their recall was tested immediately after the videotape was over and then one week later. While the results differed little among the three groups, "there was a slight, non-statistically significant trend for the hypnosis group to do rather worse than the other two groups." The fourth experiment tested for face identification. Subjects examined a set of photographs approximating mug shots and, one week later, were either hypnotized or untreated and asked to pick out a face from a collection of photographs as being one they had seen earlier. Again, hypnosis did not improve memory. "The only significant finding was that hypnosis increased the number of false positive responses, i.e., incorrect identifications which the subjects were 'sure' were correct."[173]

Concerning the poorer performance by hypnotized subjects, Wagstaff suggests that the hypnosis simply made them feel drowsy. He concludes from this that the "standard hypnotic relaxation techniques. . . may be counterproductive with witnesses who are not in a debilitating state of anxiety." In recognizing that witnesses to crimes are often under stress not shared by experimental subjects, he also observes that many of the forensic "breakthroughs" occur before the witness is even hypnotized. In such cases, the hypnotist has evidently managed to assure the witness that he will be in no danger and that embarrassing or frightening details can be revealed without shame or fear. He also credits individual forensic hypnotists with the ingenuity of determining the appropriate mode of interrogation and response (free association, drawing pictures, playing roles) for each witness. Such individual interaction is usually missing from laboratory experiments. Thus, he concludes as follows:

> (1) Arguments based on ill-controlled studies of 'supermemory' under hypnosis may be misleading. (2) The real value of hypnosis may lie more in the special interaction or rapport that the hypnotist creates. (3) By emphasizing the less mystifying aspects of hypnosis in the form of the use of relaxation, concentration and imagination, many of the techniques presently applied by forensic hypnotists may be more widely accepted and be applicable to a greater number of witnesses.[174]

The incorrectness of hypnotized subjects in recall is a result of another experiment. Based on a Stanford C Scale of Hypnotic Susceptibility, fifty-four subjects were selected with either high or low susceptibility. They were shown sixty black and white line drawings of common objects, at the rate of three and a half seconds per slide, and then given a sheet containing sixty blank spaces and asked to reproduce as many of the items as possible. After three such trials with brief rest periods in between, they were allowed to leave and were told to repeat the recall procedure once each day for six days and deposit their sheets of drawings in a collection box. The mean number of items initially recalled was thirty but had risen to thirty-eight by the last trial. Then, the subjects were placed in a hypnosis or task-motivated condition and told to recall as many items as possible. Hypnotized subjects reported over twice as many new memories as the other subjects but made three times the number of new errors. The correct information reported by each group was proportional to the total output shift. On an individual basis, none of the highly hypnotizable subjects reported more than five new correct items, and six did not retrieve any new information at all. But these new items were accompanied by nearly three times as many errors as in other subjects.[175]

The researchers point out that "the probability of correctly recalling new items under hypnosis seems directly related to the number of items a subject is willing to report as memories." With a less judgmental criterion while under hypnosis, the subject may be willing to report as a memory an item that he would not report, for lack of certainty, if he were not hypnotized and subject to more rigorous, conscious restraints. This conclusion is consistent with the absence of ego involvement and less need to perform to certain standards that is thought to accompany a hypnotic state. But the great number of reported memories that were not memories at all caused the researchers to advance another theory:

> If hypnosis enhances the vividness of mental imagery, perhaps the vividness with which the subject is able to envision these possibilities becomes compelling. Under these circumstances, the [central processor or] editor could mistake vividly imaged possibilities for memories of the stimuli; the enhanced vividness could lead to a false sense of recognition and hence the inflated output as well as the surprising certainty that subjects have about their hypnotically enhanced recall.[176]

The above theory is especially interesting in light of the results of another experiment, which indicate that "fantasy generation induces [a subject] to adopt a laxer criterion for reporting so that he recalls low-confidence memory contents which he would not have otherwise have reported." The researcher takes off from the ending point of other studies, which show that initially unreported briefly flashed stimuli tend to emerge in later fantasy products of the perceiver, such as daydreams, doodling, and free associations. This event has been called the "emergence effect" or "activation," among other terms.[177] In relation to the experiment just described, this would mean that the subjects might later recall some of the line drawings that they had always failed to name in the recall trials, while daydreaming or doodling. Moreover, the subjects who ultimately participated in the task-motivated (as opposed to the hypnotized) group may have relied on free associations in thinking of the new items.

Because previously unreported stimuli have, in other experiments, emerged in fantasy, the researcher inquired whether a recall trial *following* a fantasy activity might result in the report of even more stimuli. In other words, can fantasy encourage the memory flushing procedure? In the experiment, subjects were shown slides of twelve ordinary items (broom, chair, TV, boy, lamp, telephone, pitcher, table, toaster, cat, clock, and cup) arranged in three rows of four items each, for 500 msec. Two versions were shown, with the only difference being placement of the items, and no item held the same position in both versions. Subjects were in one of three groups: experimental, dart, and yoked.

After viewing the slides, all the experimental and dart subjects filled in a 3 × 4 matrix, in which they were to reproduce the sequences of pictures they had seen, via labeled drawings, "as much as possible, short of outright guessing."

The experimental and yoked subjects then engaged in a free association exercise that lasted thirty minutes. Subjects were to look at blank screens and call out any ten words. Then, the experimenter sought phrases and sentences associated with those words for one minute, and, next, single words until ten more words were generated, which were used for more phrase and sentence and then other single word associations. The dart subjects, instead of free associating, threw darts for half an hour. Then, all subjects were asked to complete another recall form for the stimuli originally shown. Last, in a forced recall trial, they were asked to make guesses about the possible content of any empty boxes and draw them in.[178]

The scoring was done on two levels. Structural scoring examined the physical congruences between the items drawn and the stimulus items, regardless of the labels or conceptual relations. Conceptual scoring disregarded structure and concentrated only on the extent to which the labeled items approximated in concept or association the items in the stimuli. The results are depicted on page 333.[179]

Scoring	*Group*	*First Recall*	*Second Recall*	*Forced Recall*
Structural	Exper'l	1.48	2.08	3.50
	Dart	1.65	1.83	3.73
	Yoked	1.44	1.70	2.91
Conceptual	Exper'l	1.95	2.40	3.95
	Dart	2.17	2.33	4.46
	Yoked	1.94	2.10	3.01

While the dart group scored higher structurally and conceptually in the first and forced recall, the experimental group scored higher in the second recall on both dimensions. The focus of the researcher, though, is on the difference between the initial recall and the second recall, which is a marked increase for the experimental group for both types of scoring in comparison with a much lower increase for the other groups. Therefore, the free association (fantasy production) experienced by the group that had actually seen the stimuli (as opposed to the yoked group, which did not) resulted in a greater increase in the number of items recalled.

In a second experiment, much like the first, subjects also indicated the degree of confidence they had in the recall of items. The results of this experiment, when combined with those above, suggest that fantasy causes subjects to retrieve recoverable information by inducing them to be less critical of the certainty of their recollection and to report memories that they might not otherwise. Clinicians note the patients sometimes state that they recall "lost" memories after a course of therapy sessions, which are essentially free-recall associations. The results here support that clinical observation, as subjects recalled "inputted material following free associations which they seemed unable to recall before.[180] Since there is no report here of the number of erroneous responses given by the subjects, these results do not rebut those of the researchers who report that an increase in correct answers under hypnosis was offset by three times the number of wrong answers.

The implicit claim in the above findings is that a characteristic of hypnosis, in this case, the relaxing, free-association procedure (which lacks guidelines other than the instruction to concentrate on one word or idea and think of *anything* it may trigger) causes the subject to state a memory with the certainty that it is a memory. That certainty, however, is not the same certainty that a less relaxed state of mind would admit. Therefore, the accuracy of the alleged memory is left to someone else's determination; that burden is not placed on the subject. Ironically, therefore, even if the subject is told that he will remember and report only the truth, his perception of what comprises the truth is altered, as his standards seem not as stringent.

Another technique of hypnosis that is criticized for inducing the subject to speak less than the level of truth he would speak if he were not hypnotized, is the leading nature of the questioning often used by the hypnotist: "Did you see *the*...?" "Was there *a*...?" Because of the connection between anxiety and repressed recall, researchers testing the effect of leading questions compared hypnotic with waking recall of events observed under stressful conditions. The stimulus was an eight-minute excerpt from a film entitled *It Didn't Have to Happen*, which displays a number of shop accidents interspersed with instructional material concerning shop safety. The accidents include a vivid and unexpected amputation of a finger by a router and a worker's impalement on a board ejected from a circular saw. The researchers relied on findings of others as to the physiological and subjective stress that the film created in viewers, and the subjects signed informed consent statements acknowledging that they would be exposed to emotionally arousing stimuli.[181]

Subjects consisted of thirty-six introductory psychology students who scored in the medium-high range on the Harvard Group Scale of Hypnotic Susceptibility. They were assigned to either a hypnosis or waking group at random except as follows. Because the subject was thought to have more appeal to men than women, an equal number of women and men were assigned to each group. Also, the hypnotic susceptibility of each group was arranged to be approximately the same.[182]

After the film excerpt, subjects in the hypnosis group were individually placed in a room with an experimenter different from the one who had previously dealt with them. After the first experimenter had left, the second experimenter said he would hypnotize the subject and inquire about the film, the projection room, and the physical description of the first experimenter. The "T.V. Technique" of hypnosis was used, with the subjects being asked to imagine that they were in their living rooms, watching a large television screen, which would display the events from the time they entered the projection room. (This was done in part to distance the subjects from any anxiety they may have associated with the accidents in the film.) They were told that they would be able to slow, quicken, or freeze the film speed. The subjects faced away from the experimenter (so that the subject could not see the experimenter's reactions) while he read fifteen nonleading questions and five leading questions, all thought to be "analogous to those commonly asked in the course of an actual criminal investigation." The leading questions appear below:[183]

*Leading Questions Used in the Present Experiment**

1. Did you see the man wearing safety goggles at the beginning of the film?
2. Did you notice the safety poster that was shown after Armand severed his finger?
3. As the man was struck by the board, did you see the large tool fall out of his pocket?
4. Did you see Lucky take off his hat after his friend died?
5. Did you see the large, red book on the desk next to the projectionist?

*The correct answer to all of these questions is "No."

Subjects gave their answers with ideometer finger responses. The experimenter acknowledged each answer, and the subjects redisplayed their answer if the acknowledgment was wrong. The subjects also provided a confidence rating of one through five for their certainty concerning an answer, with one indicating a guess and five, absolute certainty. Subjects in the waking group sat idly for twenty minutes, which corresponded to the hypnosis induction time period of the other subjects. Then, they were asked the same leading and nonleading questions.[184]

Wrong answers accompanied by a confidence rating of more than one counted as an error, "don't know" was not counted as an error, and correct answers were computed without regard to confidence ratings. The results show that, for the nonleading questions, both groups had the same mean number of correct answers, 8.77 (out of 15) and approximately the same number of errors (5.22 for the hypnosis group and 4.89 for the waking group) and confidence ratings (3.59 for the hypnosis group and 3.34 for the waking group). However, of the leading questions, the waking group scored 4.39 correct answers (out of 5), .56 errors, and a confidence rating of 3.42. The hypnosis group had 3.61 correct answers and 1.28 errors, but a similar confidence rating as the waking group, 3.38. The authors conclude that, not only did hypnosis fail to enhance recall for the nonleading questions, but subjects "in the hypnosis group responded more frequently in the direction implied by the leading questions, and thus were led into erroneous responses."[185] Concerning the comparable confidence ratings of both groups for the leading questions, the authors found a correlation between hypnotic susceptibility and confidence ratings in both groups. They explain that subjects "highly responsive to hypnosis have a tendency to be confident of their answers, even when such confidence is not warranted."[186]

For purposes of better understanding the phenomenon of hypnosis, the correlation of hypnotic susceptibility and confidence ratings, even when the subject is not hypnotized, has significant implications. Obviously, the "T.V. Technique" calls for subjects to visualize, or to imagine, that they see on a television screen what they have seen before. It would follow that the more clearly they "see" something, the more certain they are of it. However, a similar degree of certainty appears to accompany the decisions of persons with high hypnotic susceptibility who are *not* hypnotized. Therefore, the ability to imagine may be greater in persons who have high hypnotic susceptibility. When this ability is combined with the increased relaxation and possibly reduced mental criteria that accompany hypnosis, those with high susceptibility are likely to incorporate outside suggestions, such as those in leading questions, into their visualizations. Thus, what they "see" is a combination of past and present data, but the fact that they clearly see makes them certain.

Purposeful lying, without a strong motivation to deceive, is rarely a problem with hypnosis. However, because the situation may encourage the subject to be helpful, he may "experience suggested alterations of perception, memory, or mood [and] honestly report [them] as real." This explains why a hypnotized subject looking at a white wall, when told it is blue, will report seeing a blue wall. Similarly, a subject told to recall a person that he saw only once at 100 yards may be asked, under hypnosis, to use binoculars to "see" the person more clearly.

> [T]he subject may describe the person in detail down to the pattern of his necktie, even though the "perception" of such detail is beyond the physical ability of the human eye at a distance of 100 yards. In other words, the hypnotized subject responds to the suggestion to observe with binoculars by hallucinating or imagining the details. This fantasizing of information that seems plausible is called *confabulation*.[187]

Therefore, the goal of forensic hypnosis should be to tap the memories of witnesses without adding to them. Some of the ways for accomplishing this goal derive from recognizing the differences between laboratory results and anecdotal experiences.

C. *Laboratory vs. Forensic Hypnosis*

For the experiment just reported, the researchers sought to explain why the results conflicted with those of individual case studies and anecdotal reports indicating that hypnosis effectively increases the recall of witnesses of traumatic crimes.[188] First, they point out that the stimuli material did not produce even approximately the trauma that might be experienced by a crime victim, implying that hypnosis is most effective in calling up memories buried in response to a high degree of stress. In other words, the film was simply not traumatic enough to cause the subjects to repress information that could be retrieved only with hypnosis. On the other hand, they note that many eyewitnesses are not victims, observe non-violent events, and therefore might be subject to even less stress than the subjects watching the film. The response here appears in the results of the poem-learning exercise, being that hypnotized subjects showed increased recall over those in a waking state. When material fits into an "organized context," hypnosis (or even relaxation technique) does seem able to assist with its retrieval.[189]

Second, the authors suggest that since the subjects were forewarned of the stressful stimuli, they may have reacted to it more calmly than crime victims or witnesses. They then rebut this by noting that anticipated stress can create more anxiety than sudden exposure. Regardless of the degree of stress produced by the film and/or its warning, it is important to realize that the subjects, in watching the film, engaged in the identical process that the hypnotized subjects did in visualizing the film on a television screen. In other words, the "T.V. procedure" is intended to distance the subject by convincing him that he is watching a re-enactment, which will not involve or harm him. No matter how vivid a film may be, viewers know that it is a re-enactment that does not involve and cannot harm them. Even if a film of a real incident is played, viewers know that the events on the screen have already happened; there is no chance that those events will now happen to them. Crime victims, however, are actual participants, and witnesses view events as they are happening. Therefore, causing viewers of recreated scenes to experience the same emotion as victims and witnesses may be theoretically impossible.

Formulators of an experiment reported in 1981 point out that both practical and ethical difficulties accompany subjecting individuals in an experiment to stress in order to arouse them emotionally. "Even if the ethical problems could be overcome," subjects would still be likely to believe that any threat was just part of the experiment. Therefore, traumatic arousal would not occur, and no memories associated with stress would be repressed. However, they rely upon the findings of others indicating that "emotionally arousing films produce physiological and psychological responses somewhat similar to those in real-life situations." Thus, they constructed an experiment designed to create traumatic arousal, sexual arousal, and low arousal in the subjects. While changes in skin conductance and heart rate, along with the subjects' own reports, indicated that the respective types of arousal were created, "[t]he hypothesis that aroused states would differentially influence recall received only marginal support." The authors conclude that "[i]t remains a challenge for ingenious researchers to devise experimental situations more closely approximating the real world."[190]

However, other results of this experiment explain the reported successes of forensic hypnosis. Besides stress, laboratory experiments and actual crimes are also different in that the material learned for experiments is (1) usually meaningless—even if it is something other than nonsense syllables, like poems or drawings, it is not meaning*ful* to the subjects, and (2) intentionally learned—witnesses tend to learn information incidentally, sometimes not realizing the import of what they have seen. Therefore, in this experiment, the subjects were exposed to a variety of stimuli (posters, a film, and recorded messages), which did interest or involve them (i.e., was meaningful), as indicated by the levels of sexual or traumatic arousal. While the results were independent of the degree of arousal, they showed that "a hypnotic induction with task motivating instructions yielded greater recall than task motivating instructions alone." The researchers found this significant, in light of studies indicating that there was no difference in recall between hypnotic induction and task motivating instructions. They suggest the difference is due to the meaningfulness of the material and its incidental learning in their experiment.[191]

The researchers add that the hypnosis may have lent credibility to the task motivating instructions "and thereby increased [subjects'] confidence and motivation in recalling the information." They also recognize the implication of this:

> Nonhypnotized subjects may be less willing to give an approximate memory as a response. In other words, fragments of memories which are considered too sketchy to be reported by nonhypnotized [subjects] may more likely be reported by hypnotized [subjects]. . . .This implies that in criminal investigations hypnotic induction might be viewed by witnesses/victims as enabling them to recall information more readily. This would increase confidence and motivation for recalling while reducing critical judgment [which] could lead in increased reports of inaccurate as well as of accurate memories.

They caution, however, that, future studies should report the hypnotic susceptibility of the subjects. If only moderate to highly hypnotizable subjects show greater recall after hypnosis, then the result is due to hypnosis. But if subjects all along the range of susceptibility show greater recall, then "the difference would be attributable to motivational aspects of the hypnosis *situation* and not to hypnosis per se."[192] This would mean that either (1) aspects of the hypnosis situation, such as relaxing and assuring the subject, could be used to induce greater recall without the subject being hypnotized (and thus without the incurrence of many of the evidentiary objections to hypnotically refreshed recollection), or (2) the hypnotic situation could be carefully monitored to eliminate or severely reduce influences on memory that may lie in leading questions and reactions of the hypnotist.

The very aspects of hypnotically refreshed recollection that make it valuable to the clinician can pose problems for the forensic investigator. "Hypnosis does not pretend to ascertain the truth; it just refreshes and flushes out more memory. It has all the defects found in eyewitness testimony."[193] Clinicians seek the subject's *perception* of past events and encourage the reporting of even hazy memories; they are unconcerned about the accuracy of the report, except to the extent that it provides insight into the way the subject views life. Hypnotized or not, "[p]eople will tend to remember what they want to have happened. . . .We all believe what we often make up and what we want to believe." If this natural tendency is combined with an increased motive to provide detail, such as a witness's desire to help the police or the injured party or the victim's desire to extract revenge, the results of any testimony can be questioned. "Eye witnesses not hypnotized can and do lie, exaggerate, fake, mislead, and struggle to cope with that fickle finger of memory."[194]

Age regression and revivification produce some of the most convincing results of hypnosis. For example, an adult can be told that he is six years old and at his birthday party. He may act, talk, and apparently think like a child, as he addresses other children he "sees" there and describes the surroundings.

> The naturalness with which these descriptions are given and the conviction that is communicated by the individual are compelling even to trained observers. The feelings which are expressed appear appropriate to a child more than to an adult, and the entire phenomenon is such that it is generally described as beyond the skills of even a professional actor.

Despite the convincingness of the subject, though, there is no way to be certain of his accuracy without independent verification. In fact, Freud long believed that a child's seduction by a parent was the cause of eventual hysteria. "It was some years later that Freud realized the seduction scene that the patients relived in treatment accurately reflected the fantasies of the patient but did not accurately portray historical events." Drawings elicited from adults age-regressed to six years old have looked very much like the drawings of the children but, when analyzed by experts, have been deemed not to be drawn by children at all, reflecting instead "sophisticated oversimplification." (In other words, they were an adult's conception of how a child would draw.) In other instances, subjects named or described their classmates with such conviction that the researchers who checked the school records were surprised to discover that some of those people had not been in the subject's class.[195]

The hypnotic suggestion to relive a past event is often accompanied by questions concerning details, which the subject will feel pressured to supply. While his memory may be jogged to the extent of recalling the event in general, the hypnotic situation "will also cause him to fill in details that are plausible but consist of memories or fantasies from other times. It is extremely difficult to know which aspects of hypnotically aided recall are historically accurate and which aspects have been confabulated."[196]

The following example seems to rebut arguments about how in control and alert the subject remains during hypnosis. However, it is offered to demonstrate that a subject susceptible to suggestion can be absolutely convinced of the truth of his statements, and such conviction could be accepted by an observer as an indication of truthfulness. What it instead indicates is that the subject truly believes in what he is saying, not that his perceptions are accurate. It also illustrates the ability of the mind to create, of past memories and fantasies, supporting details for propositions believed to be true. It should be pointed out that the subject scored a five on the HIP scale, which means that he was among the top 15% of the highly hypnotizable population. He was a successful businessman, "somewhat left of center," politically, who agreed to participate in an experiment and joined the researcher and Frank McGee at the NBC television studios. Under hypnosis, he was told that Communists were taking control of the television networks and that, if anyone challenged that fact, he would be even more convinced of it. Then, with the suggestion imposed, he came out of the trance, and McGee talked to him while they were being filmed. McGee challenged him about the takeover, and, the more he did so, the more adamant the subject became. He even gave names of individuals who met at a specific location to discuss the plot and physically described the leader. After he was given the signal to come out of the trance, he had total amnesia for what had occurred. (It is not clear whether this was coincidental or a hypnotic suggestion.) When he was shown the movie five months later, he was "astounded" and did not know anyone with the names and description he had given. "During the experiment, in response to the hypnotic signal, the subject created a totally false story to rationalize his compliance. He sincerely believed it to be true. Since he was locked into the hypnotic bind, he suspended his own critical judgment."[197]

D. *Forensic Hypnosis*

Orne observes that a "deeply hypnotized individual" can be given the suggestion that he is living in the future, such as the year 2000, and when requested, describe the surroundings in detail, though he could have no memory of these surroundings. The concern is that the same process that allows for this kind of hallucination can also be involved when the subject is asked to recall what happened several days, weeks, or months earlier, particularly if he cannot recall details accurately with his waking memory. "Unfortunately, if such pseudomemories relate to events which occurred six months ago and are eminently plausible, there is no way for either the hypnotist or the subject or a jury to distinguish between them and actual recall of what occurred." Orne explains that the sources of pseudomemories are at times detectable, such as a recent viewing of a science fiction movie as an explanation for a description of the future. He compares this with a hypnotist's own beliefs about the facts and his unconscious but almost unavoidable guiding of the subject to reporting what the hypnotist believes happened.[198]

The "creation of memory" during hypnosis is most dangerous because of the difficulty, if not impossibility, of detecting what the subject's recollection was prior to the memory created at the unwitting suggestion of the hypnotist. Orne gives a convincing example of a subject whom the hypnotist knows, by verification, to have gone to bed at midnight and arisen the next day at 8 a.m. Under hypnosis, the subject can be made to relive that night; he is then told that it is now 4 a.m. and asked whether he has heard the two loud noises. Orne reports that "a good subject" will say that the noises actually awakened him. Instructed to tell what the time is, the subject will say a few minutes after 4 a.m., perhaps elaborating that he has just looked at his digital clock and noticed that it is 4:06. When asked what he did after hearing the noises, he may report going to the window or just wondering about the noises. If he is then told that, once out of hypnosis, he will recall everything that happened then, as well as what happened that night, he will later include in his account the noises at 4 a.m. and "will be convinced that his description. . . is accurately reflecting his original memories." Insofar as faulting the hypnotist for inquiring about the noises, Orne asks rhetorically, "if the hypnotist knows that two shots have been fired at approximately 4 a.m. . . . what seems more natural than to inquire of a witness whether he heard any loud noises?"[199]

Successful examples of forensic hypnosis indicate conditions under which pseudomemories will not pose problems. Two examples, the case of the Chowchilla kidnapping and the case of the rape victim who could not recall the complicated Middle Eastern name of her assailant, have already been mentioned. The bus driver in the kidnapping was able to recall a license plate number, which led to the apprehension of the kidnappers; and the rape victim recalled the man's face and picked it out of mug shots, and his fingerprint matched a print in her bathroom.

In another case, a man abducted and raped two girls, aged seven and fifteen. He left them at a motel in Mexico, telling them that if they went to the police their parents would be killed. Because of the traumatic nature of the event, the girls were unable to provide much concrete information. When the older girl was hypnotized, however, she recalled such details as where the man had stopped for gas, what he told the attendant, the colors on the gas credit card he used, the crudely repaired gear shift knob, the noisy front passenger window, and the brand name of tissues and cookies in the car. The gas station and credit card led the FBI to the suspect's home. "Examination of the car confirmed every single detail supplied by the girl when she was under hypnosis."[200]

Schafer and Rubio present cases based on their use of forensic hypnosis in 1972-1973 in and around Orange County, California. The case involving the assailant with the Middle Eastern name is one of theirs. Among the others is a case in which a policeman was a participant in a shootout at a store. The criminal used the elderly wife of a store owner as a shield to effect his escape, during which he killed a policeman. Policemen are trained observers, and the descriptions of the many policemen on the scene had resulted in the suspects being narrowed down to two people. However, when one of the policemen was hypnotized, he recalled a distinguishing feature of the criminal—a space between his teeth—which eliminated one of the suspects. A confession was later obtained from this man. In another incident, a twelve-year-old girl was abducted and sexually molested. Within hours after she had been returned to the site of her abduction and then taken to the police, she was hypnotized for recollection of further details. At that time she recalled the last number of the license plate, which she could not remember in the waking state. This information resulted in "the quick apprehension of the child molester."[201]

The above examples all have one thing in common: in each instance, information supplied by the hypnotized subject was corroborated by other data. Because of the potentiality of pseudomemories, "[t]he most one can legitimately expect from hypnotic interrogation is further data, which may serve as *leads* for more conventional evidence gathering. Data elicited through hypnosis by itself deserve low or no priority until they are supported by other data."[202] Orne points out that, if the singular goal of the hypnotic session is to provide clues that may lead to incriminating evidence, then the facts that these clues emerged under hypnosis is irrelevant. Thus, he suggests that when the facts are neither known nor presumed, the risks of created memories pose no danger if such memories will be independently investigated. However, when significant facts are known or presumed, if a victim's hypnotically refreshed recollection suddenly *confirms* a fact (such as the identity of an assailant), the reliability of recollection being precisely that becomes the issue. "Though it is possible that accurate information is recovered, the important effects that motivation can exert on memory—hypnotically enhanced or otherwise—must be taken into account in assessing the 'memories' that are obtained."[203]

As a guard against the effect of leading questions, Orne also suggests that a narrative statement of events first be elicited from the subject. Although such an account is still subject to confabulation, it is less likely to introduce the bias of the hypnotist, who can later ask questions about the account itself.[204] He also warns against the hypnotist's use of encouraging comments, such as "Good," "Fine," "You are doing well." While these remarks have a definite purpose in the clinical setting (to encourage the patient to divulge whatever thoughts he might have), they tend to act as rewards. The subject naturally wants to continue to receive the praise; thus, if the hypnotist fails to make an approving comment, "he clearly communicates that something more is wanted" and unwittingly urges the subject to provide more.[205] The following guidelines for forensic hypnosis are based on Orne's recommendations:[206]

Guidelines for Forensic Hypnosis

1. *The hypnotist should be a mental health professional who knows nothing or little about the case.* Obviously, without knowing details about the case or the particular kinds of facts the police are seeking, the hypnotist should be less likely to lead the witness into "recalling" facts that support a certain view. If any information about the case must be transmitted to the hypnotist, it should be done only in writing, so as to provide a record of such information. Aside from being more expert at hypnotic induction, a mental health expert will also have an independence from the police, which would be helpful to any effort to introduce as evidence any hypnotically refreshed testimony.

2. *All contact between the hypnotist and the subject should be videotaped.* If there is a challenge to the reliability of the witness's recollections, a record of all verbal and nonverbal contact between the hypnotist and the subject could indicate the degree to which the recollections may have been influenced by words or acts of the hypnotist.

3. *No one but the hypnotist and the subject should be present for the interview and any pre-induction discussion.* Others, particularly if they have knowledge of the case, may react to what the subject

does or does not say and thereby influence later reports from him. If operation of the video equipment requires a technician to be in the room, he should have no knowledge of the case and should indicate this in writing. If the psychologist conducting the hypnotic induction has no training in forensic interviewing technique, then it may be necessary for a policeman or someone else with such training to ask the questions. In such an event, any knowledge transmitted to him should be documented in writing, and he should write out a list of any facts he knows about the case from other sources.

4. *The subject should undergo a prehypnosis evaluation.* One goal of this step is to provide a record of what the subject recalls before hypnosis; thus, the subject should be asked to give a narrative description of the facts, with the hypnotist being careful not to invite new details through suggestion. If information emerges in the narrative description that has not surfaced before, Orne recommends considering whether to stop the procedure then, in an effort to deter objections based on hypnosis. If that decision is made, then the witness should be interviewed as to whether he thought he was under hypnosis at the time he recalled the new information. The subject should also be evaluated psychologically and should sign a consent to the procedure.

5. *The memory retrieval techniques used in hypnosis should be free of suggestion.* First, the witness should be requested to give a narrative account. While minimal verbalization by the hypnotist is the goal, if he needs to move the subject through the story, he should make comments that invite progress but not concern over content, such as " 'Go on,' 'Continue.' " The witness should never be encouraged to report details that it was physically impossible for him to see.

6. *Communication with the hypnotist should be surreptitious.* Ideally, the hypnotist and the subject can be viewed through a one-way screen or television monitor. The hypnotist should take breaks, such as at the end of the prehypnosis interview or the narrative recall obtained during hypnosis to allow for the police or other observers to make suggestions to the hypnotist as to areas that deserve further inquiry. Such suggestions should be written and should be retained.

7. *The subject should participate in a posthypnosis discussion.* During this discussion, posthypnotic suggestions about the nature of the subject's nonhypnotic memory (e.g., implying that he will be able to recall things that he has not remembered before) should be avoided. Instead, the subject's experiences during hypnosis should be explored, along with what the subject thinks occurred and why.

E. *Possible Effects on the Jury*

The primary concern is presenting hypnotically refreshed memory to the jury is that what will be placed before the jury may not be memory or evidence at all. Despite all of the faith placed in the ability of twelve men and women to serve as fact finders and accurately detect who is telling the truth and who is lying, if an adult can portray a convincing six-year-old in front of a psychiatrist and cause that psychiatrist to believe that he is hearing actual memories, what judgmental criteria can we dredge up from our own realms of experience that are superior to those of the psychiatrist? It is the witness's state of conviction in the truth of what he says that may cause the jury to be "wholly unable to determine the credibility of his testimony." The argument is therefore made that "[t]he only way to avoid the misleading effects of confabulation is to exclude testimony from the present, hypnotically refreshed recollection."[207]

Moreover, even the fact of hypnosis could bias the jury towards testimony obtained under that condition:

> All things being equal, if we place two parties before the average lay jury with its modest reading level, hypnotize one of the parties and so inform the court and jury, that party will probably stimulate the interest, awe, and belief of the jury. All too many lay jurors will feel that that party is imbued with some special power and truthfulness and that the non-hypnotized opponent speaks with "forked tongue."[208]

Ironically, although the witness is the one who has been hypnotized, "jurors may become so *mesmerized* by the induction procedure that they give the testimony undue credibility, regardless of the truth of the matter asserted."[209]

F. *Conclusion*

Currently, general rules concerning the admissibility of hypnotically induced evidence allow (1) a witness to testify at trial about matters on which his memory was restored through pretrial hypnosis, (2) an expert to describe the uses, techniques, and general reliability of hypnosis, and (3) a hypnotist to opine on the reliability of memories induced in a prosecution witness by pretrial hypnosis.[210] Thus, to the extent that hypnotically refreshed recollection is used for other purposes than generating leads to evidence, counsel will undoubtedly attempt to educate the fact finder as to the nature, benefits, and shortcomings of hypnosis, using material not unlike that presented above.

IV. *EYEWITNESS TESTIMONY*

The previous section quoted this statement by Dr. Robin Goodenough: "Hypnosis does not pretend to ascertain the truth; it just refreshes and flushes out more memory. It has all the defects found in eyewitness testimony."[211] The comparison of eyewitness testimony with hypnotically refreshed recollection may be discouraging. With hypnosis, it is thought that aspects of induction that can cause the supplementation or alteration of memory bear the primary blame for skepticism. While it may be true that "[i]t will never be possible to completely sanitize the interaction between hypnotist and subject. . . the act can be cleaned up."[212] In other words, there is at least a theoretical model for a hypnosis session that will not add to or alter the subject's memory, even though the literal realization of that model may be difficult if not impossible.

Perceptions of an eyewitness, however, are unique to the perceiver and within the perceiver, simply waiting to be extracted and placed before the fact finder, right? Of course, but therein lie the problems. Elements inherent in the memory process can cause two individuals to see the same person but not to register the same characteristics of that person, with the result being that one may say that person was the culprit and the other may say he definitely was not. Even if similar characteristics about someone were to register in the minds of two or more perceivers, different methods of extracting the memories from the perceivers can alter or supplement the memories. These results stem from many of the same techniques that produce the same results in hypnosis sessions.

Potential shortcomings of eyewitness testimony comprise only half of the issue; the other half concerns the jury's reactions. Do jurors realize intuitively that even highly convincing witnesses may really not have seen what they thought they did? Do jurors, and the system of justice, benefit from having psychologists explain how and why eyewitness testimony can be flawed? Solutions to the problem of jury interpretation of eyewitness accounts are presented below, following an examination of memory processes and extraction techniques that exacerbate potential weaknesses of recall.

A. *Memory Processes*

While the terms may differ, there are basically two main theories to explain memory. One is reconstructive, which posits that memory is supplemented by later events. This means that certain characteristics of a suspect mentioned in a police officer's questions (or read in a newspaper account, overheard outside the district attorney's office, etc.) could be integrated into the witness's "recollection" of that suspect. The "exact copy" or tape recorder theory "assumes that information is stored accurately and that forgetting is the result of an inability to retrieve the information." The exact copy theory is often believed by police investigators, and it is on the basis of this theory that hypnosis is often employed.[213]

Naturally, the memory theory of the examiner will affect the way a witness is questioned. If the examiner believes in the exact copy theory, he will not be concerned about the effects of leading questions or other means of suggesting responses to the witness. But if the reconstructive theory is correct, then the examiner may well add to or alter the witness's recollection. The certainty of the witness will also be no clue, since experimental subjects that have formed support for a reconstructive theory appear convinced that details suggested to them were in fact their own memories.[214]

In one experiment, subjects viewed an accident between a car and a bicycle on videotape, being told to watch it as if it were an event they had seen while walking around campus. The film showed the car approaching an intersection, stopping, and then turning right, at which point it cut in front of a bicycle passing on the right. The bicycle and its rider were knocked to the ground. Subjects were either then sent home, returning the next day (long delay group), or given a fifteen-minute cognitive exercise (short delay group). Subjects from each type of delay group were either hypnotized or not hypnotized.

Then, fifteen questions were asked of all subjects, six of which were leading: "Did you see the stop sign at the intersection? Did you see the passenger in the car? Did you see the license plate number of the car? Did you see the broken glass from the bicycle light? Did you see the bent wheel on the bike? The last leading question concerned the color of the hair of the woman in the film, which was black. Just before the questioning procedure, though, the experimenter had asked whether the subject had recognized any of the people in the film, such as "the blond woman who witnessed the accident." Just as with results reported in the previous section, the subjects made more errors in answering leading questions under hypnosis than in the waking state. More dramatic is that the findings for the hypnotized subjects support the reconstructive theory of memory. The hypnotized subjects were just as confident of the accuracy of their responses as the other subjects; the hypnotized subjects did not know they answered many of the leading questions incorrectly. In other words, they believed, as memories, what actually consisted of memories altered by the suggestion of the leading questions. One hypnotized subject reported having a mental image of the woman in the picture, and she had blond hair. When she saw the film again, with the woman with *black* hair, the subject said that the face clearly in her mind simply did not match that on the screen. She also indicated that part of her confidence was based on the fact that the women in the film looked like her roommate. "It seems possible that she constructed the image from a combination of her memory of the accident, the suggestion of [the experimenter], and her roommate's hair."[215]

The reconstructive and exact copy theories both describe the process of memory. Prior to memory, however, there is perception, which is determined by at least three types of input, in addition to the thing perceived. First, bias or expectation either assists us to see what we do or causes us to interpret what we see in the way we do.

> If a person expects to see a woman's figure rather than a man's face or a bunch of guilty hoodlums rather than a peaceful lot, the attributes corresponding to those expectations are clearer and more vivid in perception. They stand out more. We pay more attention. . . .expectations have an enormous impact on what a person claims to have seen.

Similar to expectations is knowledge (or what we take to be knowledge) about an incident before it occurs. For example, if we see a man on a side street in broad daylight attempting to open a car door with a coat hanger, we may conclude that it is his car and pay him little attention. However, if we see him doing this at 2 a.m., we are likely to conclude that he is a car thief and will attempt to make a mental record of his description for reporting to the police. Finally, the activity a witness is engaged in, besides observing a crime, can determine the elements of the crime on which he is likely to focus. A hidden witness to a crime may attempt to remember details for reporting to the police. A victim, however, may be so emotionally involved that, despite seeing the criminals up close, his concentration on escape could cause him to be registering how they are carrying their weapons, whether they are watching the exit, etc.[216]

How the mind records and recalls faces is a study in itself. Time enters into the equation, but in two different ways. First, the longer a person views another face initially, the greater is the later recognition. In one experiment, the viewing times were exceedingly short by standards we might apply to walking past someone on the street or standing next to someone in an elevator: .25, .50, 1, 2, and 4 seconds. However, the recognition index for 1 second was almost twice that for .25 second, and the recognition index for 4 seconds was half again that for 1 second. The length of time a face is initially seen is more significant for recall than the interval between seeing a face and being asked to recall it, with often only slight deterioration in recall following more than three or four weeks after the initial viewing of a face. Apparently, what is more important than the time elapsed until the second viewing is the kind of experiences the viewer has. Specifically, viewing many faces in that interval, such as what a witness might do in looking at mug shots, tends to obliterate or distort the memory traces associated with the initial face.[217]

In addition, people of one race are poorer at recognizing faces of people of a different race. This was confirmed by an experiment conducted in Scotland and Rhodesia. European subjects were better at recognizing white faces than black faces, and African subjects were better at recognizing black faces than white faces. Part of the explanation for this is that people of different races focus on different parts of the face. When subjects were asked to write descriptions of photographs of faces, the features described were classified as upper (eye level and above) or lower (below eye level). Europeans noticed first the hair, then the eyes. Africans, however, rarely mentioned the hair and eyes, and described upper and lower facial features with equal frequency.[218]

Using similarity groupings of faces provided by subjects, researchers applied a mathematical procedure known as multidimensional scaling to arrive at the most important features used to judge similarity in faces: length and style of hair, general shape of the face, and apparent age of the face; eyebrows, lips, and mouth were also important. The suggestion was then made that such features be taken into account when persons are being selected for police line-ups, in which there is a great potential for leading witnesses to select a particular suspect, such as placing a black youth in a line-up with five white youths. As one experiment indicated, even the nature of instructions given to persons viewing a line-up can affect identification. Soon after sixty subjects had been shown ten faces, they were asked to pick out any familiar faces from twenty-four faces, which were presented either simultaneously or sequentially. None of the ten target faces was among the twenty-four faces. Half of the subjects were told not to worry much about making a mistake. The other half were told that the target faces might not be among the twenty-four faces and that no faces should be selected unless the subject was sure. While the subjects given the lax instruction made almost twice as many misidentifications as the group receiving the strict instruction, even the latter group averaged three misidentifications per subject. Misidentifications are thought to occur when the faces are similar to those of the culprit, the memory image of the culprit's face is not clear, and information other than memory influences the witness's decision.[219]

Whether a reported memory is exactly that, or is a base memory embellished or otherwise altered through subsequent information, the degree of confidence or certainty expressed by the one reporting the memory can convince others of the validity of the recollection. "Eyewitness confidence or certainty is a belief in the accuracy of one's memory report." Not only have studies verified the connection between eyewitnesses' confidence and the credibility of their testimony, but the witness's level of certainty has been named as a guideline for judging eyewitness testimony in court.[220]

Given the effect of witness certainty, a number of researchers have tried to determine whether there is a correlation between such confidence and accuracy. Of thirty-one studies conducted between 1974 and 1982, thirteen reported a correlation of statistical significance between eyewitness certainty and accuracy; eighteen showed nonsignificant correlations. The interpretation of the statistically significant correlations is not encouraging:

> [S]tatistical significance simply means that the correlation is not likely to be attributable to chance. Statistical significance does not mean that the correlation is useful or socially significant. . . .
>
> [A]n overall analysis of [the studies] (not just an analysis of the studies showing statistical significance) indicates an estimated correlation of only .07. A correlation of such magnitude is relatively useless in any applied sense.[221]

Witness certainty also loses some of its persuasiveness in the wake of the foregoing section on hypnosis and the examples of subjects who are convinced of the accuracy of their recollection, which turns out to be a composite of memory and suggestion. As is indicated in that section, being able to relax and concentrate (and, in one sense, say whatever comes to mind through free association) may be as successful in retrieving memories for some individuals as hypnosis. In addition, there may be personality types that are susceptible to suggestion, even without hypnosis.

In one case, Peter Reilly was found guilty of murdering his mother, primarily on the strength of a confession he signed within hours of being interrogated. Despite the confession, the teenager said he did not recall the murder and accepted the police's explanation of amnesia. However, his friends in the community said that he was gullible and unsure of himself. A HIP examination revealed that he was unlikely to develop amnesia and that he could not be hypnotized; his low score was also indicative of an immature personality and poorly developed sense of self. With the discovery of this information concerning his personality, a new trial was ordered, where evidence placing him five miles from the scene at the time of the murder was presented (it had been withheld by the prosecution in the first trial).

> The new information about Peter's personality style and immaturity indicated that his having no memory for the event was not due to amnesia but rather was due to the fact that he had not actually been present and had not, in fact, committed the murder. However, he was unable to withstand the accusatory pressure of the police.[222]

In this case, the witness was "certain" enough to sign a confession, and it was his own supposed activity that he thought he was reporting.

The audience of a witness may discount the credibility of a witness, despite his professed certainty, when he is elderly, due to the stereotyped image of the elderly as being "highly dependent, psychologically helpless, and intellectually inferior." Studies have shown that the elderly and the young have different degrees of recall for certain kinds of items.[223] The results of such studies suggest to attorneys potential weaknesses in the eyewitness testimony of both clients and other witnesses. Moreover, knowing that many people embrace the stereotype about the elderly, the attorney familiar with the truth about perception and recall in the elderly will be able to question his own witnesses in a way that lends credibility to their testimony. In addition, if he understands why the elderly tend to have different recall than younger people, counsel himself may not be defensive about his own witness's testimony and can convey his confidence to the jury. Yarmey summarizes the results of several studies about recall in older people as follows:

> Older persons may be more susceptible to such things as unconscious transference [confusing a person in one context with another seen in the same context] and negative stereotypes, which are more likely to influence their misidentification of peripheral figures, such as innocent bystanders. This may be especially true when the observational conditions are ambiguous and short in duration.[224]

If the increased susceptibility to negative stereotypes is true, it is probably less a result of diminished mental capacity in the elderly than a result of living many years and having contact with many people. Stereotypes, after all, derive from reality. Young persons are still in the process of encountering different types of people; based on their years of experience, older individuals may feel that they have met most types and, for ease of reference, rely on these types, which they feel they know, to categorize new people. In addition, older people may not have the same interest in new faces that younger people might have, particularly if the older people have settled into a fairly routine existence. Usually, younger people are often thrust into new social, educational, and professional situations, which are defined, for the most part, by the people they meet. Finally, it may also be that older people are more proficient at recognizing *older people* (1) than they are at recognizing younger people and (2) than younger people are. After a certain age, a number of facial and hair features are shared by many people, which may cause older faces, as a rule, to be somewhat indistinguishable to younger people.

B. *Memory Extraction*

Even if the exact copy theory of memory is correct, particular questioning techniques and/or the personality of the witness can result in the production of *testimony*, which may or may not be the reporting of recollection. The following excerpt reveals a fragmented questioning technique, which allows the examiner to maintain control and to put together pieces of a story through the questions. In the alternative, if a witness can tell the story in the way that the attorney finds helpful (e.g., including relevant details, maintaining chronology, speaking loud enough), then the attorney might opt for a narrative questioning technique. Thus, consideration of the relative strengths and weaknesses of each witness, as well as his testimony, could guide the attorney in court. By the point of trial, an attorney will know, in general if not in detail, what each witness he intends to call will say; thus, there is little fear that the mode of questioning by the attorney at that time will create new memories for the witness. However, the excerpt below is *not* testimony. It is from a victim's account to the police of a rape, several hours after it occurred. Apparently, she had already told the story to the police, and they were having her repeat it, as she might then provide more details. The paragraph that precedes the excerpt summarizes what the victim had already told the police.

Recently in a town in Idaho a man raped a young woman, Jane, while forcing her friend Susan to lie with them on the bed. The two roommates had been asleep in their apartment when Susan heard Jane screaming. Since Jane often had nightmares and occasionally talked in her sleep, Susan began to get up from her bed to go into Jane's room and awaken her. Then she heard a male voice. Before she could even get up, her own bedroom door opened and revealed the intruder holding Jane. The stranger was standing directly behind Jane, with his left arm across her upper chest, holding her close to him. He held a long knife—possibly a kitchen steak knife—in his right hand. Jane was forced to lie down on the bed with Susan and both women were told to cover their faces. But Susan looked up periodically. . . .

Q: What was he doing when you looked up?

A: I don't know, he was trying to bother Jane and I just took the pillow away from my face and started to say something to him and he saw me and told me to get my face back down.

Q: What do you mean bother?

A: He was starting to—you know.

Q: Have intercourse with her?

A: Yea, he was just kind of fondling her I guess, I don't know, I didn't see anything he was doing that, you know, she was telling him to stop and please don't do that.

Q: All right, let's go back, you heard the scream?

A: Yes.

Q: And you heard a man's voice?

A: Yes.

Q: The next thing you knew your door opened?

A: Right, it was partway open to begin with.

Q: And then it was just pushed open?

A: Yes.

Q: And then he brought her into your room, into your bedroom, with his hand around her throat, or did he have her in a head lock or. . .?

A: Yea.[225]

Loftus explains the obvious danger of this questioning technique: its potential of imparting information to a witness while ostensibly extracting information. She notes that this can happen whether the examiner has a theory of the case (in which instance he might unconsciously guide the witness to support that theory) or not (and might toss out alternative responses—"or. . .a head lock"—from which the witness might choose).[226] Clearly, this portion of the interview was transcribed/recorded. However, it is unlikely that all discussion between the witness and the police, from the time they came to her apartment or she went to the police station, was transcribed. One question is, how much of the original statement of the facts (as summarized in the paragraph preceding the excerpt), was extracted through similar questioning?

When someone is confronted with a leading or multiple-choice question as opposed to an open-ended question, the effect has been described in terms of cognitive set. Leading questions restrain the cognitive set by allowing only a yes or no response, and multiple-choice questions limit the witness to only stated choices. Thus, particularly when the witness is trying to be helpful, "there is an implicit imperative to respond to a question even if unsure." The yes/no or choice selection question restrains a witness's flexibility and freedom of telling the story as he or she recalls it; moreover, because such questions are specific, it is likely that the witness is unable to answer the question accurately. Because of the "implicit imperative," the quantity of responses will be high, but because of the restrictions in the questions themselves, the accuracy of the responses will be low. On the other hand, open-ended questions provide the witness with a wider cognitive set, "there is less likelihood of being confronted with a question about which no response can be made, and it is unlikely for witnesses to volunteer information about which they are unsure." Thus, while the number of responses will be lower, the accuracy of those responses will be higher than with specific questions. Accuracy should be even higher (and quantity even lower) with totally unstructured testimony—free elaboration without any questioning; the absence of questions removes any imperative to respond.[227]

The above theories were tested/verified in an experiment designed to simulate trial testimony. Forty each of male and female students viewed a film depicting a peaceful park, in which a man is suddenly robbed and shot. They were led to believe that the film was of a real event, had been made by a photographer filming in the area at the time, and was on loan from the district attorney's office. After the film, subjects were either immediately questioned or released, to return a week later and then report what they recalled. Testimony was either structured or unstructured, and questions were either leading, multiple-choice, or open-ended and had either a positive, neutral, or negative bias. The questions concerned 144 items in the film, which had been noted by 23 independent raters who had also been asked to view the film carefully and then write down as much about the film as they could recall.

The results showed that accuracy fell 4.3% from immediately after the film to the week later; quantity, however, fell 18%. The neutral questions were answered most accurately (83%). Unstructured testimony (91%) resulted in more accuracy than structured testimony (70%). The results also contained a surprise: "Female witnesses responded significantly more accurately to the questioning than did male witnesses. . . though the difference in quantity was nonsignificant."[228]

Based on experiments concerning eyewitness testimony, as well as hypnotically refreshed recollection, leading questions may alter memory by adding to it (explained by the reconstructive theory of memory). Memory may be supplemented with details supplied through other techniques, as indicated in the results of experiments described below. Counsel should be aware of these techniques, for both offensive and defensive purposes. For example, Loftus explains that she has introduced nonexistent objects into students' recollections by only casual mention. In one instance, students watched a film of a car accident on a country road. She then asked some of the students how fast the white sports car was going as it passed the barn. A week later, she asked whether they had seen a barn, and over 17% of them said they had. Only 3% of the students not previously told about a barn said that they had seen a barn. There was no barn.[229] In another experiment, her students staged a crime in a public place. A couple of them took names and telephone numbers of witnesses, and a bogus insurance agent later called these witnesses and inquired whether they had seen the thief take a tape recorder. Over half of the witnesses remembered the event, and almost all could describe the tape recorder fairly well. There, of course, was no tape recorder.[230]

Skillful cross-examination could result in a witness testifying to details that did not exist. Once this is revealed, the witness will lose credibility. This is also instructive when one's witness is being cross-examined. Counsel should attend carefully to the questions to see whether an attempt is being made to lure the witness into "creating" memories. If an attorney sees that his client or witness is not alert to the cross-examiner's technique, the attorney should make objections, pointing out to the witness and the court that the examiner is taking liberties with the facts and/or existing testimony.

In a number of facets of the law, something other than objective description becomes a necessity. For example, the reasonable person standard inquiries of the behavior of the reasonable person in a particular circumstance, and degrees of elements in that circumstance can determine expected behavior. If a man is running fast towards another man, yelling, and looking furious, the expected behavior of that other man would be different than if the first man were merely walking fast, talking loudly, and looking unhappy. Therefore, witnesses are often called upon to give value judgments in reporting their recollection. These, too, can be manipulated in memory.

Loftus participated in an experiment reported in 1975 in which students were shown an excerpt of a film called *Diary of a Student Revolution*, in which eight demonstrators disrupted a class in a relatively noisy but nonviolent manner and then left the classroom. The subjects were then asked to complete one of two questionnaires. The neutral/passive questionnaire asked questions like "Did you notice the demonstrators gesturing at any of the students? Did the professor say anything to the demonstrators? The emotional/aggressive questionnaire asked questions like "Did you notice the militants threatening any of the students? Did the professor shout something at the activists?" The subjects were not told they would be questioned again, but when they returned a week later, they were given a new series of questions to answer about the disruption and asked to give their answers on a five-point scale:

1. The incident could be described as: quiet ____ ____ ____ ____ ____ noisy
2. Would you describe the incident as: peaceful ____ ____ ____ ____ ____ violent
3. Do you recall that the demonstrators were: pacifistic ____ ____ ____ ____ ____ belligerent
4. In general, the students' reaction to the demonstration was: sympathetic ____ ____ ____ ____ ____ antagonistic

The results showed that "the subjects who were interrogated with questions worded in an emotional, aggressive manner reported that the incident was noisier and more violent, that the perpetrators of the incident were more belligerent, and that the students in the classroom were more antagonistic than did those subjects whose questionnaires were neutral and passive."[231]

An interesting parallel exists between memory and the piecing together of "what happened" that jurors attempt. As indicated in an earlier chapter, "once jurors' constructions of the evidence, their stories of what happened, were formed and stabilized, these stories were relatively resistant to persuasive argumentation from other jurors."[232] It is as if each juror's version of what happened becomes his own recollection. In one experiment, subjects watched a series of slides depicting the theft of a wallet: a man bumps into a woman, causing her to drop her shopping bag; she places her purse on the ground, she turns around to gather the spilled items, and he pulls out her wallet, which happens to be red. In a following questionnaire, 98% of the subjects identified the wallet as being red. Then they were given written versions of the incident, with the supposed task of critiquing the writing. In one version, four significant objects in the incident were incorrectly described (the subtle suggestion). In the other, in addition to those objects, there was an obvious error: the red wallet was described as being brown (the blatant suggestion). The subjects next participated in a brief "filler" activity, and then completed multiple-choice questions about the theft. The results support two main conclusions. First, subjects were more susceptible to the suggestibility in the subtle version; that is, they more readily adopted the erroneous descriptions of the objects. The blatant mistake in calling the red wallet brown appears to have made them more resistant to other suggestions by the author. Second, "subjects were better able to resist a suggestion about an item if they had initially been accurate on that item than if they had not," whether the later suggestion was subtle or blatant. The figure below demonstrates this relationship.[233]

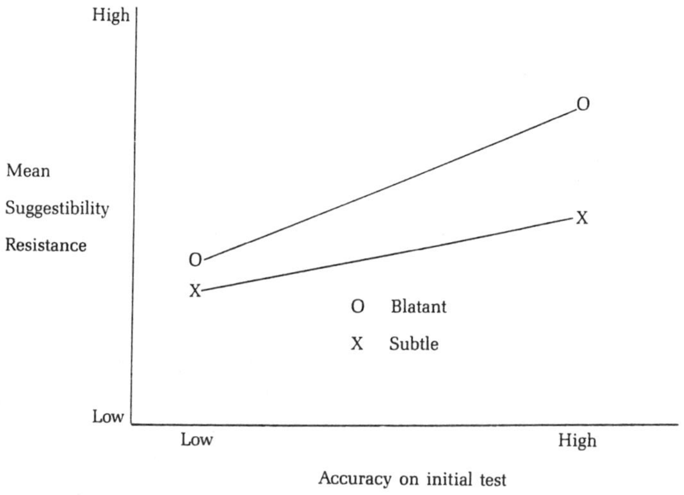

What the above suggests is that, if witnesses have an opportunity first to give their version of "what happened," such as in an unstructured, narrative fashion, they will be more resistant to either subtle or obvious influences by those who later question them.

A critically important example of how additional information and subtleties can affect "recall" is the police line-up or photo array. As earlier indicated, a line-up can be so grossly biased as to include one black youth with six young white men; also, if all persons besides the suspect have similar upper facial features, then the suspect will strike the witness as being different (since our culture tends to focus on upper facial features). Loftus suggests that a line-up is biased if, given six people in a line-up, persons who did not witness the crime would pick out the suspect with greater than a one in six probability (she adds that the probability would be one in seven if "none" were a choice). In an actual case in California, a suspect was arrested and charged with armed robbery. A victim described the suspect to the police as a male, 5′7″–5′8″, 21–23 years old, 150–160 lbs., with medium-length black hair. The victim later picked the suspect out of six photographs containing only one or two pictures of people with medium-length hair. Loftus then devised an experiment with these data, reading the physical description to twenty subjects individually and then having them look at the pictures. (Real witnesses might see the description of a suspect in the newspaper or a police report, or overhear police officers or other witnesses discussing physical descriptions.) If the one in six ratio were correct, then only three or four people would have selected the suspect. Thirteen identified him. This experimental result is more than only interesting, since the prosecution in the actual trial "placed a police officer on the stand who testified that in his opinion the photo array was extremely fair."[234]

Psychologists have studied eyewitness accounts in laboratory settings for some time, seeking the ways that events are initially perceived, how accurately they are reported after time has passed, and conditions under which the reports are more accurate than not. While laboratory experiments "can never simulate completely the unexpectedness of witnessing an accident or criminal event as it occurs, or the emotional accompaniments that are present on such an occasion . . . the laboratory provides opportunities to be much clearer about the influences upon memory and the nature of the distortions that occur." In an experiment, the effects of kinds of questions, among other things, can be examined, with false information in one set of questions and true information in another. Thus, changes in accuracy that fluctuate with the kind of question can be detected. This would be difficult, if not impossible, to do in a police interrogation.[235]

A frequent criticism of laboratory experiments is that the subjects are not motivated to perform at the same level as if they were in a real situation and that motivation is necessary for accuracy. In the previous section on hypnosis, experimenters appeared to motivate subjects by intimating that correct results were a sign of intelligence. In one experiment, Loftus offered cash rewards for the recollection of the type of traffic sign in a slide subjects had seen earlier; to one group, she offered no reward. The absence of any effect of the reward on the accuracy of the subjects is indicated below.

Reward	*Number of Subjects Who Were Correct*	*Percentage of Subjects Who Were Correct*
None	5	25
$1	4	20
$5	6	30
$25	3	15

She also appealed to the intellect, by saying to one group of subjects that only the "most intelligent" people could recall the correct slide; only 25% performed accurately.[236]

After a review of the research on eyewitness interrogation, Hilgard and Loftus observe that time limitations prevent everyone in law enforcement, defense, and prosecution from engaging in such studies.

> But if new methods are to be taken seriously and the interests of justice served, some ways of providing studies of process and outcome of interrogation methods are obviously needed. The background provided by the laboratory studies is relevant to the extent that they show the questions which must be answered if interrogation methods are to improve completeness of witness reports without sacrificing their accuracy.[237]

C. *Jury Reactions to Eyewitness Testimony*

If all of the potential shortcomings of eyewitness testimony were known by the jury *and* if the jury were provided with the details of each interrogation of the witness, there would be no problem. The jury could then be supposed to be able to weigh the accuracy of the witness's "recollection" against the nature and format of the questions; the witness's age, knowledge, and expectations; and any other potential influences on perceptions and memory. That supposition is an ideal insofar as jurors always being given interrogation information; whether human beings have the critical skills to assess accurately eyewitness testimony without such information is still being examined by the experts. So far, we have not made a great showing of ability.

In one experiment, the researcher began with the findings of three other studies and one "fact." The findings showed that an eyewitness to a staged crime who had identified an innocent suspect was just as credible as someone who had identified the actual criminal. The fact was that "eyewitness confidence can account for up to 50% of the variance in jurors' decisions to believe eyewitnesses." From that, the researcher sought to discover what information, besides credibility, jurors might rely on in judging the accuracy of an eyewitness identification. Subjects were shown videotapes of cross-examinations of eyewitnesses, and the subjects were asked to express their thoughts about the witnesses. While "[r]eference to confidence, certainty, or composure was obviously of paramount import," there was also "an equally consistent reference to the witnesses' memory for detail." For example, a subject said that one witness was "really paying attention" because he remembered the color of a suspect's shoes. (The assumption, of course, was that the color was correct.) Another subject expressed distrust of a witness's memory because of no recollection about the kind of calculator that was stolen.[238] This last comment is especially meaningful in light of the experiment reported above in which students of Loftus's "created" in eyewitnesses detailed memories of a recorder that didn't exist. In addition, if peripheral data are the benchmark for accurate recall, testimony of the elderly may bear a particular strike against it, since the earlier reported experimental results suggest that the elderly may simply pay less attention to bystanders (and anything or anyone else deemed insignificant) than young people do.

Existing literature on information processing suggests that inattention to peripheral detail is probably consistent with increased focus on the face and, as a consequence, better memory of facial features. The researcher tested this conclusion, while trying to determine the weight mock jurors assign to trivia reported by witnesses. In the experiment, each subject was individually exposed to a "thief" and later asked to select him from a photo line-up, to indicate the degree of confidence in the identification, and to describe environmental details. The correlation of the accuracy of the identifications with the recall of trivia is presented below; the results suggest that the more peripheral items there are recalled, the less accurate the identification will be. Also, the confidence level of those who incorrectly identified the suspect was approximately that of the correct witnesses.[239]

Witnesses' Performance on Identification Task, Confidence in Identification, and Performance on Memory for Details Test

	Witness Behavior on Identification Task (Photo Spread)		
Measure	*ID of Thief*	*Inaccurate ID*	*No ID*
Frequency	57	32	18
Confidence*	5.12	4.93	3.00
Performance on 11-item memory for details test (no. correct)	6.36	8.50	5.11

*Higher values represent greater levels of confidence.

The second phase of the experiment tested the effect of recall of trivia on the credibility of the witness. Ninety-six subjects were told that they would play the role of jurors in assessing whether a witness to a staged crime correctly identified a criminal or mistakenly identified an innocent person. The subjects viewed cross-examinations of the witness, in which the witness was either asked about details or allowed to give a narrative answer, and was then challenged as to certain details and shown to be wrong about them or was not questioned about the details.[240]

The subject-jurors indicated that a high recall of detail convinced them that the witness was accurate about the identification. As a result, they often believed witnesses who made *inaccurate* identifications but recalled many details. When questioned, the subject-jurors freely disclosed that they discounted testimony when the witness made repeated errors in simple recall of documented details. The researchers hypothesized that, quite to the contrary, those witnesses who did not recall details had been focusing more on the thief.[241] The disturbingly high belief in the accuracy of the incorrect witnesses may be explained solely by the witnesses' confidence (an explanation that, in itself, is disturbing), since only the witnesses with high confidence in their identifications submitted to cross-examination.

The researchers close with a tip for attorneys. If cross-examination reveals that a witness has not recalled details, the jurors' natural inclination will be to discount an identification made by that witness. Therefore, counsel would be wise to follow with redirect or possibly even expert testimony concerning the import of recall of trivial details as compared with remembering faces.[242]

Juror intuition for the significance of recall of trivial details appears rebuttable. What is more resistant to refutation is the weight (or lack thereof) that jurors tend to ascribe to nonidentifications when paired with identifications. In general, if it creates reasonable doubt, is viewed as evidence of innocence, or offsets or otherwise changes the weight given to identifying testimony, nonidentification should theoretically influence jurors toward a not guilty verdict. In practice however, jurors may underutilize "disconfirming evidence, or. . .view nonidentifications as a *failure* to remember."[243]

Two experiments reported in 1985 tested the weight of nonidentifications. In the first, subjects were told to play the role of jurors receiving evidence in court. They were presented with a fact situation involving a theft of $300 from a store and an identification by the owner. Other subjects were presented with those facts plus either an identification by a bystander, a nonidentification by a bystander, or conflicting statements from bystanders. The following diagram indicates the percentage of subjects who found the defendant guilty under those different conditions.

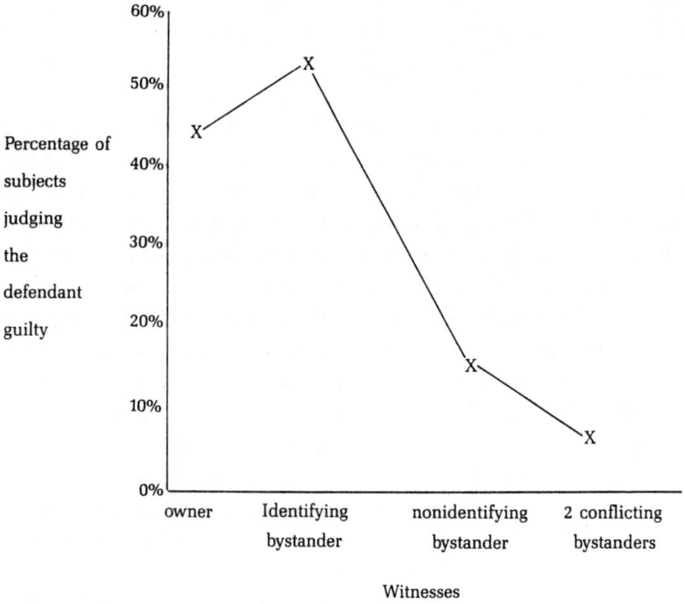

The researcher suggests that the dramatic effect of a nonidentification ("this defendant is not the criminal I saw") on the verdict, even when countered by two identifications (the owner and the identifying bystander in the last condition), may have been due to the directness of the testimony. That is, it was not an ambiguous statement or a lack of recognition; "the nonidentifier indicated his confidence that the defendant was not the robber." The subjects also prepared written comments, and thirteen of the twenty-one subjects in the last two conditions (which both had a nonidentifying bystander) said that the nonidentification was a major reason for the not guilty verdict.[244]

In the second experiment, one witness said in court that the defendant was not the culprit, and the other was reported in court as saying simply that no one in the line-up looked more familiar than any other. Then, this added type of nonidentification and the mode of reported as opposed to actual testimony were added to the conditions in the prior experiment, which resulted in the following conditions:

Victim ID, bystander ID and testimony

Victim ID, bystander non-ID and testimony

Victim ID, bystander non-ID and no testimony

Victim ID, no bystander

No victim ID, bystander ID and testimony

As would be expected, guilty verdicts resulted most often when the victim and the bystander identified the suspect. However, guilty verdicts were least frequent when the victim identified the suspect but the bystander did not and testified to that in court. In other words, the bystander's nonidentification seemed to have more weight than the victim's identification. However, an absent nonidentifying witness, whose nonidentification is merely reported, may do the defendant more harm than good. Presumably that witness is not on the stand because he indicated only that the defendant was familiar but could not say that the defendant was the culprit. (The assumption is that the witness would be present if he could say, "That is not the man.") Jurors tend to realize that the familiarity noted by the witness corroborates the victim's testimony and results in "two *occurrences* of memory," which convinces the jury of the defendant's guilt.[245]

This last observation suggests that jurors may make use of even hints of negative information about a defendant and disregard them only if they are clearly found to be false. This notion is supported by another experiment concerning nonidentification. The conditions were a single witness who identified the suspect, one who did not, and one who said he could not say; and two witnesses who identified the subject, two who said he was not the man, and one who said he was and another who said he was not. "Comparisons with the single eyewitness control revealed that both single and multiple eyewitness identification produced significantly higher perceptions of guilt and longer sentences, whereas the multiple, but not the single eyewitness non-identification condition, produced significantly lower perception of guilt and shorter sentences." The researcher reasons that, if identification and nonidentification testimony were given the same weight, they would cancel each other out. This, however, is not the case. Instead, the results show that identifications have more weight than nonidentifications.[246]

The conclusion expands to include exonerating evidence as a whole with the results of a related experiment conducted by the same researcher on fingerprint nonidentifications. The control group had no fingerprint information. As expected, identification through fingerprints resulted in a greater finding of guilt and longer sentences than for the control group. However, nonidentification through fingerprints produced results very much like those for the control group. "The underweighting of nonidentification evidence points out a rather large bias in favor of the side using identification information (typically the prosecution) and against the side using nonidentification information (typically the defense)." It is suggested that the underweighting may be due to the jury's expectation from the outset that a defendant is guilty, "since people do not optimally use information that disconfirms a hypothesis they have."[247]

In another experiment, the ability of jurors to detect accuracy in eyewitness accounts was assessed; the hope was that, as witness accuracy decreased, juror belief would fall proportionately. First, the correlation between the accuracy of witnesses and their confidence was examined. Witnesses were placed in one of three situations, designed to induce different degrees of accurate recall. Each subject was assigned to an individual cubicle. In the low-accuracy situation, a thief entered the cubicle wearing a knit cap that covered all of his hair and part of his ears, asked whether a calculator sitting there was the subject's, then took the calculator and left, having stayed a total of twelve seconds. In the moderate-accuracy condition, the thief behaved as before, except that the cap was pulled up so that his hair and other facial features were visible. In the high-accuracy situation, the thief stayed about twenty seconds, preceded the calculator question with one about the experimenter, and wore no cap. About thirty seconds after the thief had left, the experimenter entered the cubicle, explained that the event had been staged, and asked each subject to select the suspect from a set of six photographs; the subject could also select none. In addition, the subjects indicated their degree of confidence on a seven-point scale. The accuracy results and confidence ratings appear in the table below:

Situation	*Accuracy*			*Mean Confidence Rating*	
	Correct	*Incorrect*	*No ID*	*Correct*	*Incorrect*
low	8	16	3	4.3	3.4
moderate	14	14	4	4.3	3.8
high	32	12	5	5.0	3.9

These results indicate "a weak but statistically significant difference between accurate and inaccurate witnesses in confidence."[248]

The second experiment involved videotaped cross-examinations of the witnesses in the first experiment, which were viewed by subject-jurors. The witnesses were asked questions that were open-ended, that asked them to use specific dimensions (such as in describing the room), that suggested inaccurate recall ("Was that really long enough to get a good look at the thief?"), and that challenged the witnesses' credibility (such as suggesting that the defendant only reminded the witness of someone seen at some other time). After each examination, the subject-juror indicated confidence in a witness's identification on a seven-point scale, from "not at all sure" to "extremely sure." The results below indicate that juror belief in a witness is a function of the witness's confidence (which is, in turn, a function of the situation) *and* the situation:[249]

Percentages of Subjects' Decisions to Believe Witnesses As Functions of the Confidence and Situational-Accuracy Conditions of Witnesses

	Situational Accuracy			
Witness Confidence	*Low*	*Moderate*	*High*	*Mean*
Low	47	54	76	59
High	76	76	78	77
M	62	66	77	

The researchers note that (1) per the first experiment, witnesses are just as likely to make an identification and be cross-examined about it whether they are twice as likely to be wrong than right (in the low situation), equally likely of being wrong or right, and more than twice as likely of being right than wrong and, (2) per the second experiment, that jurors adjust their belief according to the situation, knowing that the situation can affect the witnesses' accuracy. However, "subjects' compensation for the witnessing conditions fails to match the slope of change in witness accuracy rates." This leads to the conclusion that jurors are apparently "overbelieving of witnesses when the probability of witness accuracy is low and particularly if witness confidence is also high." As ameliorations of this tendency in actual courtroom situations, the researchers point out that eyewitness testimony is only a single kind of evidence considered by jurors. Also, cross-examination in court will probably be much longer and more thorough than that in the experiment, which might bring out more reason for the jurors to reject the testimony of certain eyewitnesses.[250]

In his analysis of the above results, Wells finds an answer to the question of whether jurors can discriminate between accurate and inaccurate witnesses. He concludes that they cannot, being able only to discriminate between situations that have a high probability of producing accurate witnesses and those situations with a high probability of not producing accurate witnesses. He also notes these results as indicating that jurors do not take these situations into account when the witness is confident of his testimony.[251]

D. *Suggested Solutions to the "Eyewitness Problem"*

Greene and Loftus identify the "eyewitness problem" as stemming from "the inherent unreliability [of] human perception and memory," "human susceptibility to suggestion," and the probable unawareness of laypersons (jurors) of the potential unreliability of eyewitness testimony. They consider four proffered solutions to the problems. First, courts could simply overturn any convictions based on the uncorroborated testimony of a single eyewitness. This solution is found unacceptable because many eyewitness accounts are quite reliable (if, for example, the witness and the defendant have been neighbors for years) and such a move would take from the jury a task with which it has always been entrusted. A second solution is requiring the presence of counsel in pretrial line-ups. Noting that problems in line-ups account for only a small part of misidentifications, Greene and Loftus further point out the underinclusiveness of this suggestion: "A witness may have erred long before law enforcement officials were called into the picture." As to the third solution, providing expert testimony about the unreliability of eyewitness testimony, Greene and Loftus briefly summarize the pro and con positions in both the psychology and legal fields, concluding in the only way that the literature and cases allow—"some judges will allow expert testimony to be introduced in court and others will not; some psychologists will advocate its use and others will not." The fourth solution is to have the court instruct the jury on evaluating eyewitness testimony. Even if such instruction would be effective, its opponents argue that cross-examination has the potential for demonstrating weaknesses in eyewitness testimony. But

> [some critics] suggest that if a witness honestly believes he has a good memory for faces when in fact he does not, no amount of cross-examination will reveal otherwise. Cross-examination is designed to elicit facts that a witness knows but has not disclosed. But because a witness [is] often not cognizant of the many suggestive influences that can bias her identification, even the sharpest cross-examination would not daunt an honest, but mistaken witness. Likewise, counsel's closing arguments are thought to be ineffective at pointing out the inherent unreliability of some identifications. Although attorneys can suggest certain deficiencies in an eyewitness's memory, they are not allowed in argument to present scientific evidence that relates to the reliability of an identification.[252]

With the apparent difficulty of selecting a solution, the temptation is to ask, given that there might be an eyewitness "problem," what are its results? Many presenters of the "problem" seem to anticipate this question and begin their treatises with a singularly heinous example of an innocent man, guilty of nothing more than looking like someone else (real or imagined), who has been released after years of imprisonment, countless trials, and, usually, the apprehension of the real criminal. Without question, these accounts are shocking, and the audience is often led to believe that they are only the tip of an iceberg. From time to time, an entire volume is devoted to telling a series of such stories. The effect is chilling:

> The present collection of sixty-five criminal prosecutions and convictions of competely innocent people exemplifies the manner in which these mistakes in the administration of justice occurs. . . .
>
> Perhaps the major source of these tragic errors is an identification of the accused by the victim of a crime of violence. This mistake was practically alone responsible for twenty-nine of these convictions. Juries seem disposed more readily to credit the veracity and reliability of the victims of an outrage than any amount of contrary evidence by or on behalf of the accused, whether by way of alibi, character witnesses, or other testimony.[253]

But what such accounts do not reveal is that the ratio of conviction of the innocent to conviction of the guilty is unacceptably high. "Documented cases of wrongful conviction resulting from mistaken eyewitness testimony obviously represent only a very small fraction of 1% of the cases in which defendants were convicted at least in part on the basis of eyewitness testimony." While a reading of even a single report of the tragic results of misidentification could convince one that no more of such errors should be allowed, a fraction of 1% is not on its face an unacceptable ratio. Therefore, "the cases of erroneous convictions fail to demonstrate that jurors are too willing to believe eyewitness testimony." It is often argued that the known accounts only serve as a clue to the number of innocent people convicted by misidentifications. However, absent a means of estimating the number of these "undocumented cases of wrongful convictions, [they] cannot be used as evidence that erroneous conviction on the basis of eyewitness testimony occurs too often."[254]

In fact, there are data that refute the existence of an eyewitness "problem." In one experiment, a defendant was identified by a bank teller. The defendant's mother explained the cash found on her son by saying she had given it to him to buy a car that day; she testified further that she believed he had been at home when the robbery occurred, but admitted that she could not be sure, since his door was closed. In one condition, the twenty-four subjects received only the foregoing information. In another condition, the forty-eight subjects were exposed to the expert testimony of a psychologist, who discussed the effects of such things as stress on eyewitness accounts. Only two of the twenty-four subjects did not hear the expert testimony found the defendant guilty, compared with three of the forty-eight who did hear the expert testimony. All subjects, in explaining their decisions, said that "although the defendant may well have been guilty, it was possible that the teller had made an erroneous identification."[255]

There is also a suggestion as to how to weigh the results indicating that, although jurors alter their beliefs of witnesses in accordance with witness accuracy, jurors start out overbelieving eyewitnesses and do not alter their beliefs in the same ratio that witnesses become incorrect across various situations. If 90% of witnesses made accurate identifications and 100% of the jurors believed the witnesses had a 90% probability of being accurate, then the juror belief rate of 100% would exceed the witness belief rate of 90%. "Data suggesting that jurors overestimate the probability that eyewitnesses are accurate do not necessarily imply that jurors are too willing to convict on the basis of eyewitness testimony." Also, before it can be said even that jurors place too much weight on eyewitness testimony, it must first be shown what weight they place there, relative to weight placed on other types of testimony.[256]

It could be that the perceived inadequacies of solutions to the eyewitness "problem" solve that problem about as well as it has been defined. But while statistics alone may suggest that there is really no problem at all, they do not refute the tragic results of misidentifications of innocent people. (It was estimated that in 1986 approximately 8,500 people would be convicted of a crime which they did not commit; more than one-half of these wrongful convictions would involve mistaken eyewitness identifications.)[257] Statistics fade in importance when the innocent person is your client. Thus, the experiments described above suggest possible reasons for those results, as a caution to the responsible attorney.

NOTES

1. *See* "The Juror as a Unique Subject," section III of Chapter 2.

2. Observation by author from numerous interviews with mirror jurors in varied types of litigation.

3. Maddi, *Personality Theories* 162 (1972).

4. Lind, Erickson, Conley, & O'Barr, *Social Attributions and Conversation Style in Trial Testimony*, 36 J. Personality & Soc. Psychology 1558, 1559-60 (1978).

5. *Id.* at 1559-62.

6. *Id.* at 1563-64.

7. *Id.* at 1564-65.

8. Lind & O'Barr, *The Social Significance of Speech in the Courtroom, Language and Social Psychology* 66, 80-81 (H. Giles and R. St. Clair ed. 1979).

9. *Id.* at 83-85.

10. Wodak-Engel, *Determination of Guilt, Discourse in the Courtroom, Language and Power* 89, 91-92 (1984).

11. *Id.* at 93-94.

12. *Id.* at 94-95.

13. *Id.* at 95-96, 98-100.

14. *Id.* at 96-97.

15. Lakoff, *Language and Woman's Place* 3 (1975).

16. *Id.* at 6-7.

17. *Id.* at 7-9.

18. *Id.* at 9-11.

19. See section I of Chapter 4, "Voir Dire."

20. Lakoff, *supra* n.15, at 12-13.

21. *Id.* at 14-16.

22. *Id.* at 17-19.

23. O'Barr & Atkins, *"Women's Language" or "Powerless Language"? Women and Language in Literature and Society* 93, 94-96 (S. McConnell-Ginet, R. Borker, & N. Furman ed. 1980). The reported research was supported by National Science Foundation Law and Social Science Program Grant No. GS-42742, with William O'Barr as the principal investigator. This same research spawned the above-referenced articles by Lind, Erickson, et al. and by Lind and O'Barr, as well as the article referenced below by Erickson, Lind, et al.

24. *Id.* at 96-97.

25. *Id.* at 100-101.

26. *Id.* at 102-103.

27. *Id.* at 104-105.

28. *Id.* at 107-108.

29. Lind & O'Barr, *supra* n.8, at 73.

30. Erickson, Lind, Johnson, & O'Barr, *Speech Style and Impression Formation in a Court Setting: The Effects of "Powerful" and "Powerless" Speech*, 14 J. Experimental Soc. Psychology 266, 270 (1978).

31. *Id.* at 269, 274.

32. *Id.* at 276-77.

33. McCullough & Underwood, 2 *Civil Trial Manual* 587 (1980).

34. Hamlin, *Effective Direct Examination*, Litigation, Winter 1986, at 15, 16, 18.

35. Conley, O'Barr, & Lind, *The Power of Language: Presentational Style in the Courtroom*, 1978 Duke L.J. 1375, 1395.

36. Loftus, *Psychological Aspects of Courtroom Testimony*, 347 Annals N.Y. Acad. Sci. 27, 28 (1980).

37. See section III of Chapter 2, "The Juror as a Unique Subject."

38. Loftus, *supra* n.36, at 28.

39. *Id.* at 29.

40. Rosner & Taikeff, *To Testify (Or Not) in a Criminal Case*, Litigation, Winter 1977, 24, 27.

41. McElhaney, *More on Direct Examination*, Litigation, Fall 1981, at 43, 45.

42. Hanley, *Working the Witness Puzzle*, Litigation, Winter 1977, at 8, 12.

43. Castles, *Selecting and Preparing the Expert Witness*, Litigation, Winter 1977, at 28.

44. *Id.* at 28.

45. Hanley, *supra* n.42, at 12.

46. Younger, *A Letter in Which Cicero Lays Down the Ten Commandments of Cross-Examination*, Litigation, Winter 1977, at 18, 19.

47. Hanley, *supra* n.42, at 11.

48. *Id.*

49. Walter, *Controlling the Witness on Cross-Examination*, Litigation, Fall 1980, at 36.

50. *Id.* at 54.

51. Hanley, *supra* n.42, at 8.

52. Walker, *The Demeanor of the Witness*, 59 Fla. B.J., 44-45 (Nov. 1985).

53. Levine & Tapp, *Psychology of Criminal Identification; The Gap from Wade to Kirby*, 121 U.P. L.R., 1074-1131 (May 1973).

54. Steingas, *A Judge's 10 Tips on Courtroom Success*, A.B.A. J., Oct. 1985, at 70.

55. *Id.*

56. Follingstad, *Preparing the Witness for Courtroom Testimony*, Trial, Jan. 1984, at 50.

57. *Id.* at 54.

58. *Id.* at 50, 54.

59. *Id.* at 54.

60. *Id.*
61. Yarmey, *The Psychology of Eyewitness Testimony* (1979).
62. Bruner, Goodnow, & Austin, *A Study of Thinking* (1956).
63. Yarmey, *supra* n. 61.
64. Andrews, *Exhibit A: Language,* Psychology Today, Feb. 1984, at 32.
65. *Id.*
66. O'Barr, & Conley, *When a Juror Watches a Lawyer,* Barrister, 1976, at 8.
67. *Id.*
68. Andrews, *supra* n.64, at 32.
69. Conley, O'Barr, & Lind, *The Power of Language: Presentation Style in the Courtroom,* 1978 Duke L.J. 1375-1399.
70. *Id.; See also* Johnson, *Mind Your Mannerisms,* Student Law., Oct. 1979, at 8.
71. *Id.*
72. *Id.*
73. *Id.*
74. *Id.*
75. Andrews, *supra* n.64, at 31.
76. O'Barr & Conley, *supra* n.66, at 9.
77. Johnson, *supra* n.70, at 9.
78. *Id.*
79. *Id.*
80. McElhaney, *The Horse Shed,* Litigation, Summer 1981, at 44.
81. Geidt, *Comparison of Visual Content and Auditory Cues in Interviewing,* 19 J. Consulting Psychology 407-16 (1955).
82. Yarmey, *supra* n.61.
83. Peskin, *Nonverbal Communication in the Courtroom,* Trial Diplomacy J., Summer 1980, at 8.
84. Argyle, *Bodily Communication* (1975).
85. *Id.*
86. Peskin, *supra* n.83, at 8.
87. Swanson & Wenner, *Sensory Language in the Courtroom,* Trial Diplomacy J., Winter 1981, at 13.
88. *Id.*
89. Bugental, Kaswan, & Love, *Perception of Contradictory Meanings Conveyed by Verbal and Nonverbal Channels,* 16 J. Personality & Soc. Psychology, 647-55 (1970).
90. Mehrabian, *Communication Without Words,* Psychology Today, Sept. 1968, at 53-55.
91. Knapp, *Nonverbal Communication in Human Interaction* (1972).
92. Ellsworth, Carlsmith, & Henson, *Staring as a Stimulus to Flight in Humans: A Series of Field Studies,* 21 J. Personality & Soc. Psychology 302-11 (1972).
93. McElhaney, *supra* n.80, at 44.

94. Reed, *You Are What You Wear*, Human Behavior, July 1974.
95. *Id.*
96. McElhaney, *supra* n.80, at 44.
97. *Id.*
98. *Id.*
99. Walter, *supra* n.52, at 44-45.
100. McElhaney, *supra* n.80, at 44.
101. Mazanec & McCall, *Sex Factors and Allocation of Attention in Observing Persons*, 93 J. Psychology 175-80 (1976).
102. Landy & Aronson, *The Influence of the Character of the Criminal and His Victim on the Decisions of Simulated Jurors*, 5 J. Experimental Soc. Psychology 141-52 (1969).
103. *Id.*
104. Sigall & Ostrove, *Effects of Offender Attractiveness and Nature of the Crime or Juridic Judgment*, 31 J. Personality & Soc. Psychology 410-14 (1975).
105. Anderson, *Adding Versus Averaging as a Stimulus Combination Rule in Impression Formation*, 70 J. Experimental Psychology 394-400 (1965).
106. Dion, Berscheid, & Walster, *What is Beautiful is Good*, 24 J. Personality & Soc. Psychology 302-11 (1972).
107. Garcia & Griffith, *Impact of Testimonial Evidence as a Function of Witness Characteristics*, 11 Bull. Psychonomic Soc. 37-40 (1978).
108. *Id.*
109. McDavid & Harari, *Stereotyping of Names and Popularity of Grade School Children*, 37 Child Dev. 453-59 (1966).
110. Follingstad, *supra* n.56, at 50.
111. Hamlin, *Preparing a Witness to Testify*, A.B.A. J., Apr. 1985, at 82.
112. Hinkel, *Ten Ways to Reduce Courtroom Jitters*, A.B.A. J., July 1985, at 74.
113. Hamlin, *supra* n.111, at 82.
114. *Id.*
115. Rothblatt, *Vital Elements in Preparing the Witness*, Trial, July 1982, at 50.
116. Dombroff, *100 Days to Trial (Part II)*, A.B.A. J., Nov. 1985, at 75.
117. McElhaney, *supra* n.80, at 45.
118. Andrews, *supra* n.64, at 32.
119. O'Barr & Conley, *supra* n.66, at 11.
120. Andrews, *supra* n.64, at 32.
121. Rothblatt, *supra* n.115, at 50.
122. *Id.*
123. Hinkel, *supra* n.112, at 75.
124. Rothblatt, *supra* n.115, at 50.
125. Follingstad, *supra* n.56, at 50-58.
126. *Id.*
127. *Id.*

128. *Id.* at 55.
129. *Id.* at 56.
130. *Id.* at 54.
131. *Id.*
132. *Id.* at 56.
133. *Id.*
134. Van Camp, *Preparing the Criminal Defense Case,* Trial, 1978, at 38-41.
135. Hinkel, *supra* n.112, at 75.
136. Nizer, *Witness Examination,* Trial Diplomacy J., Fall 1980, at 21.
137. Daviss, *Legal Aids,* Student Law., Apr. 1984, at 8-10.
138. *Id.*
139. Walker, *supra* n.52, at 44-45.
140. Freedman, Carlsmith & Sears, *Social Psychology,* 30 (2d ed. 1974).
141. Orne, Soskis, Dinges, & Orne, *Hypnotically Refreshed Testimony: Enhanced Memory or Tampering with Evidence?* ii (1985) (hereafter cited as Orne & Soskis).
142. Waldman & Posnock, *Hypnosis Under Question,* Soc. Action & Law, Nov. 1979, at 47.
143. *Id.* at 47-48.
144. *Id.* at 48.
145. Orne, *The Use and Misuse of Hypnosis in Court,* 27 Int'l J. Clinical & Experimental Hypnosis 311, 333-34 (1979).
146. Schafer & Rubio, *Hypnosis to Aid the Recall of Witnesses,* 26 Int'l J. Clinical & Experimental Hypnosis 81, 86 (1978).
147. Goodenough, *Hypnosis in a Trance,* Fed. B. News & J. 490 (1983).
148. Fountain, *Hypnosis: Understanding Its Use in the Criminal Process,* 11 Tex. Tech L. Rev. 113 (1979).
149. *Webster's New Collegiate Dictionary* 563 (1974).
150. Fountain, *supra* n.148, at 115.
151. Spiegel, *Hypnosis and Evidence: Help or Hindrance?,* 347 Annals N.Y. Acad. Sci. 73 (1980).
152. Goodenough, *supra* n.147, at 490.
153. Spiegel, *supra* n.151, at 73-74.
154. Goodenough, *supra* n.147, at 492.
155. Speigel, *supra* n.151, at 75.
156. Smith, *Hypnotic Memory Enhancement of Witnesses: Does It Work?* 94 Psychological Bull. 387, 390 (1983).
157. Orne & Soskis, *supra* n.141, at 5.
158. Goodenough, *supra* n.147, at 493.
159. *Id.* at 490.
160. Fountain, *supra* n.148, at 118-19.
161. Spiegel, *supra* n.151, at 74, 81.

162. Rosenthal, *Hypnotic Recall of Material Learned Under Anxiety- and Non-Anxiety-Producing Conditions* 34 J. Experimental Psychology 369, 370-71 (1944).

163. *Id.* at 371.

164. *Id.* at 372-77.

165. *Id.* at 376.

166. *Id.* at 386.

167. *Id.* at 385-86.

168. *Id.* at 378-80.

169. *Id.* at 380, 388.

170. *Id.* at 382, 388.

171. Wagstaff, *Hypnosis and Witness Recall: Discussion Paper,* 75 J. Royal Soc. Med. 793, 795 (1982).

172. *Id.* at 795-96.

173. *Id.* at 796.

174. *Id.* at 797.

175. Dywan & Bowers, *The Use of Hypnosis to Enhance Recall,* 222 Sci. 184-85 (1983).

176. *Id.* at 185.

177. Erdely, *Recovery of Unavailable Perceptual Input,* 1 Cognitive Psychology 99, 111 (1970).

178. *Id.* at 101-03.

179. *Id.* at 103-04.

180. *Id.* at 104-05, 111-12.

181. Zelig & Beidleman, *The Investigative Use of Hypnosis: A Word of Caution,* 29 Int'l J. Clinical & Experimental Hypnosis 401-06 (1981).

182. *Id.* at 404, 406.

183. *Id.* at 405-06.

184. *Id.* at 406-07.

185. *Id.* at 407-08.

186. *Id.* at 410.

187. Orne & Soskis, *supra* n.141, at 10.

188. Zelig & Beidleman, *supra* n.181, at 409.

189. See section III(B), "Experimental Results" in this chapter.

190. DePiano & Salzberg, *Hypnosis as an Aid to Recall of Meaningful Information Presented under Three Types of Arousal,* 29 Int'l J. Clinical & Experimental Hypnosis 383, 387-90, 395-96 (1981).

191. *Id.* at 385, 390, 395-96.

192. *Id.* at 396.

193. Goodenough, *supra* n.147, at 492.

194. *Id.* at 493.

195. Orne, *supra* n.145, at 316-17.

196. *Id.* at 317-18.

197. Spiegel, *supra* n.151, at 78.

198. Orne, *supra* n.145, at 322.

199. *Id.* at 323.
200. Smith, *supra* n.156, at 389.
201. Schafer & Rubio, *supra* n.146, at 85-86.
202. Spiegel, *supra* n.151, at 79.
203. Orne, *supra* n.145, at 328, 332.
204. Orne & Soskis, *supra* n.141, at 33.
205. Orne, *supra* n.145, at 326.
206. *Id.* at 335-36; Orne & Soskis, *supra* n.141, at 43-49.
207. Pelanda, *The Probative Value of Testimony from the Hypnotically Refreshed Recollection*, 14 Akron L. Rev. 609, 621, 630 (1981).
208. Goodenough, *supra* n.147, at 493.
209. Fountain, *supra* n.148, at 134.
210. *Id.* at 143.
211. Goodenough, *supra* n.147, at 490, 492.
212. *Id.* at 493.
213. Putnam, *Hypnosis and Distortions in Eyewitness Memory*, 27 Int'l J. Clinical & Experimental Hypnosis 437-39 (1979).
214. *Id.* at 440.
215. *Id.* at 441-45.
216. Loftus, *Eyewitness Testimony* 47-48 (1979).
217. Ellis, Davies, & Shepherd, *Experimental Studies of Face Identification*, 3 Nat'l J. Crim. Defense 219, 223-25.
218. *Id.* at 225-28.
219. *Id.* at 229-31.
220. Wells & Murray, *Eyewitness Confidence, Eyewitness Testimony* 155 (G. Wells and E. Loftus ed. 1984).
221. *Id.* at 160-62.
222. Spiegel, *supra* n.151, at 80-81.
223. Yarmey, *Age as a Factor in Eyewitness Memory*, *supra* n.61, at 142, 150-51.
224. *Id.* at 152-53.
225. Loftus, *supra* n.216, at 74-75.
226. *Id.* at 76.
227. Lipton, *On the Psychology of Eyewitness Testimony*, 62 J. Applied Psychology 90, 91 (1977).
228. *Id.* at 92-94.
229. Loftus, *supra* n.216, at 60.
230. *Id.* at 61-62.
231. *Id.* at 71-72.
232. Hastie, Penrod, & Pennington, *Inside the Jury* 169 (1983); *also see* section III of Chapter 2, "The Juror as a Unique Subject."
233. Loftus, *supra* n.216, at 124-27.
234. *Id.* at 145-46.
235. Hilgard & Loftus, *Effective Interrogation of the Eyewitness*, 27 J. Clinical & Experimental Hypnosis 342, 352 (1979).

236. Loftus, *supra* n.216, at 118-19.

237. Hilgard & Loftus, *supra* n.235, at 354.

238. Wells & Leippe, *How Do Triers of Fact Infer the Accuracy of Eyewitness Identifications? Using Memory for Peripheral Detail Can Be Misleading*, 66 J. Applied Psychology 682, 682-83 (1981).

239. *Id.* at 683-84.

240. *Id.* at 684.

241. *Id.* at 685-86.

242. *Id.* at 686.

243. Leippe, *The Influence of Eyewitness Nonidentifications on Mock-Jurors' Judgments of a Court Case*, 15 J. Applied Soc. Psychology 656, 659-60 (1985).

244. *Id.* at 662-63.

245. *Id.* at 665-69.

246. McAllister & Bregman, *Juror Underutilization of Eyewitness Nonidentifications: Theoretical and Practical Implications*, 71 J. Applied Psychology 168, 169 (1986).

247. *Id.* at 170.

248. Lindsay, Wells, & Rumpel, *Can People Detect Eyewitness-Identification Accuracy within and across Situations?* 66 J. Applied Psychology 79, 80-82 (1981).

249. *Id.* at 82-84.

250. *Id.* at 86-88.

251. Wells, *How Adequate is Human Intuition for Judging Eyewitness Testimony? Eyewitness Testimony* 256, 269-70 (G. Wells & E. Loftus ed. 1984).

252. Greene & Loftus, *Solving the Eyewitness Problem*, 2 Behavioral Sci. & L. 395, 396-403 (1984).

253. Borchard, *Convicting the Innocent, Errors of Criminal Justice* 1 (1932).

254. Egeth & McCloskey, *Expert Testimony about Eyewitness Behavior: Is It Safe and Effective? Eyewitness Testimony* 283, 286 (G. Wells & E. Loftus ed. 1984).

255. *Id.* at 287-88.

256. *Id.* 288-89.

257. Statistics quoted on H.B.O. television program, week of October 13, 1986, regarding the analyses of four cases where individuals were wrongly convicted of crimes.

CHAPTER 6
EFFECTIVE ARGUMENT STYLE

SYNOPSIS

CHAPTER 6
EFFECTIVE ARGUMENT STYLE

If the subject matter of this entire section were not courtroom events, a more appropriate title might be "Effective Presentation Style." However, probably everything counsel say and do from the moment they step foot into the courtroom, if not before, has or theoretically *should* have a persuasive purpose. For the uninitiated (as well as for many of us, long after the initiation session should be over), such is an ideal. During the first half dozen trials and the first few days of even later trials, we are understandably still learning the rules of the particular judge, along with the names and faces of opposing counsel's assistants and the courtroom officials. And these matters have only a peripheral bearing on the facts of the case, the order and examination of witnesses, the necessary making of timely objections, and the sometimes impromptu legal research required by motions *in limine* or the like.

In other words, merely keeping track of who's on third is a challenge for quite a few trials. One of the few advantages of the passing of time, however, is the gaining of experience (and, hopefully, assistance at the counsel table). Once the procedural and logistical details are under control, there is the opportunity to focus on language, persona, and interaction in general with others in the courtroom, always with the awareness of potential effects on the audience, the fact finder.

Attorneys are public speakers, but not only in the same sense that, for example, politicians are. People who speak before an assembled audience often read from prepared speeches. Particularly for politicians, this is a safeguard against being misquoted and against misspeaking. Moreover, memorable and quotable phrases and sentences are much more likely to be the product of thought and consideration *before* the presentation than momentary inspiration. Speakers who have less concern about particular phrases coming back to haunt them in the press usually do not read their speeches, since the very act of reading is less appealing to an audience than apparent extemporaneousness. Such speakers work from written or mental outlines, which may contain pre-devised "quotable" phrases or sentences, to be dropped in when and if appropriate. The Reverend Jessie Jackson would exemplify this methodology, in speaking to a group of college students. In one such speech, his purpose was to motivate the students to develop academic skills, not just athletic skills, so as to be better prepared for the world after college. He was casual enough to be talking to his own children, but his constant reiteration of the theme revealed the structure and organization of a planned speech.

Speakers also know ahead of time approximately what their audience wants to hear. This is determined by the occasion of a speech. People attending a ground-breaking ceremony want to hear about city progress. People coming to a commencement want to hear the graduates complimented on what they have done so far and prepared for what the future can hold for them. Thus, speakers can be fairly certain of predispositions of their audience. Jurors are not supposed to have predispositions before the time that the verdict is decided, jointly, with other jurors. Although conclusions reached in earlier chapters suggest this may be only a myth, jurors often do their part to maintain the fiction by trying not to let counsel know what they are thinking. The report by Juror Number Four confirms that.[1] Thus, attorneys cannot suspect, on the basis of occasion or other obvious signs, what the jurors would like to hear. Instead, an attorney tries to convince jurors to believe in what he is saying. Sometimes that belief is created because the jurors have come to like the attorney. Thus, whatever he says becomes what they would like to hear.

Attorneys differ from speakers per se in another important way. Although attorneys address those in the courtroom, they are constantly aware that they are "making a record." This reality has a number of implications. In a witness examination, even though an attorney may extract half-syllable responses or nonverbal reactions that indicate to jurors that the witness has given the testimony the attorney has sought, a deficient record could be support for an appeal of a judge's refusal to render a verdict n.o.v. In addtion, in front of a judge who is openly hostile, an attorney may be intimidated into not making objections properly or not making them at all. The attorney must realize that even if he state, "Objection," and the judge barks, "Overruled!" the objection has not been stated for the record. And though he may incur the wrath of the judge, the attorney owes it to his client to request respectfully that he be allowed to state the nature of his objection for the record. Attorneys or other legal personnel are often surprised, after having been present at a hearing or deposition that has been heated, to see how calmly the report appears in a transcript. Skilled attorneys, although they may appear to allow their emotions to take control at times, may simply be dealing with opposing counsel in kind but maintaining close control on their words, which, in print, never disclose the heat of the moment.

Despite the obvious differences in the situations, perhaps the best analogy between speaking occasions and trials is that of opposing campaign speeches or a debate delivered to uncommitted voters. What the audience wants to hear is why they should vote for one candidate instead of the other. They listen to the first speaker and may identify with what he seems to find important, like him as a person, and otherwise believe that he will represent their interests well. Then they listen to the second candidate, considering whether his values are even closer to their own, whether his intelligence or expertise causes his conclusions to be more trustworthy than those of the other candidate. While each candidate would like to win the vote of every member of the audience, they both know that they cannot adopt the unique stance on every issue of each individual. Therefore, they both explain the rationale behind their respective positions, hoping that, even though they will not express exactly what is in the minds of all of their listeners, they will at lease achieve acceptance in principle. Similarly, counsel is bound by the facts of a case and applicable law, and is committed to presenting them in the way that will most advance his client's cause. He knows that he may be calling upon the jurors to think totally new thoughts, but he tries to show them a rationale for arriving at the urged conclusion that is not unlike principles that guide them in their daily lives.

Because of the overlap in speaking tasks, it is no surprise that many people in high school and college debate programs often become trial attorneys, usually excelling in advocacy competition while in law school. Depending on the particular program at each educational step, students may study speech theory and technique in detail. Regardless of their backgrounds, though, successful trial attorneys are generally known for speaking skills, whether it be their cross-examination or *voir dire* methods, or their opening or closing arguments.

Teaching speech with the study and analysis of speeches presumes that there is a discoverable technique in successful speeches that can be described, analyzed, and, in the best of all worlds, emulated. The assumed validity of that presumption is the basis for the second section below, which provides a rhetorical analysis of selected actual "arguments" by attorneys. As that section reveals, and as intuition would suggest, successful speeches combine individual elements chosen from a wide variety of options; it is the particular *selection* that is inspired. Therefore, the first section below examines the available verbal choices, the stylistic elements, along with their expected effects on the audience. The third section below, exploring the means and successes of demonstrative evidence, is a prime example of visual style.

I. *THE STYLISTIC ELEMENTS AND THEIR EFFECTS*

What is style? Several definitions on the term found in an ordinary dictionary incorporate either the word "manner" or the word "mode." Thus, based on these definitions, style is *how* one lives (as in maintaining a certain lifestyle), speaks, writes, dresses, addresses others (as in using titles), and acts. The *how* suggests a way, and the designation of *a* way implies the existence of other ways. Thus, style is the choice one makes, among the many options available, of, for example, dressing.

The concept of persona is examined in an earlier section "Dress and Appearance," where it is explained that the way one dresses can assist in conveying the "person" that the jury or judge sees. Choice of dress, as well as the way one speaks, conveys the impression of a certain lifestyle. In turn, choice of lifestyle tells the jury or judge something about the values of counsel, parties, and witnesses. Despite the various manifestations of style, the focus of this section is on verbal style. Recall that "verbal," meaning "of words," includes both writing and speaking.

A. *Written Style*

Since this chapter is a lead-in to a rhetorical analysis of oral arguments, some may wonder why written style is discussed. There are at least three reasons. First, almost all speech is reduced to writing before being analyzed in any detail. The most ideal situation for speech analysis is the live event of the speech. This is because, even though the setting and occasion can later be described, along with the audience composition and reactions, such descriptions can never be as vivid and complete as the actual event. In addition, a speech critic seeks to ascertain the desired and presumed effects on the live audience. If, at the time the effects are noted, the critic is swift enough to quote words and phrases of the speaker and connect them to the effects, then the critic is performing an ideal task. However, he is unable to keep this up for the entirety of the speech, unless it is very short indeed. What most often happens is that the speech is studied, in print, for some time after the live event has passed. It is at that time that the most appreciation results for the speaker's structure, support, analysis, word choice, phrasing. The conclusion is then reached that the dissected parts of the speech, with their respective strengths and weaknesses, worked together in a complex fashion with the persona of the speaker, on the particular occasion, in the particular setting, to produce the audience response that occurred. In addition, such a critique of a speech is itself written.

The second main reason that written style is an important topic is that attorneys produce great quantities of writing. And in case you have missed this, legal writing has been maintaining a defensive posture for quite some time. The *Texas Bar Journal* has run a column for several months written by an English Ph. D. whose sole purpose is to point out what's wrong with legal writing and offer suggestions for improvement. She is a part of the Continuing Legal Education Program at the University of Texas at Austin School of Law, which, like other programs at other law schools, provides periodic writing mini-courses for practicing attorneys. The University of Texas at Austin, also like other law schools, began using English Ph. Ds. for teaching certain aspects of the writing courses for law students. For the most part, people with a background in literature and teaching composition are simply shocked at legal writing and attempt to translate it into "normal" writing. When this is done absent an understanding of the sources and meaning of legal terms and purposes, the end result may be clearer, but may accomplish few or none of the original objectives.

The linguists have taken an anthropological view, opting to tag and study the disparate parts instead of killing the beast. Their apparent confusion is admitted:

> [I]t is unclear how best to characterize legalese: it is not a register, as only a small proportion of the population controls it, and it is acquired only through a very special type of schooling. It also differs significantly from normal usage. It is more than a professional jargon, as it contains its own peculiar syntactic constructions. However, it may not qualify as a dialect of English, because most of its odd syntactic structures are not productive, and because it is not acquired in a "natural" manner.[2]

Distinctions of "legal and bureaucratic language" at various linguistic levels illustrate its uniqueness. The observation at the level of discourse is that it "appear[s] to violate many rules of ordinary usage," such as the avoidance of pronouns (e.g., "the said document" for "it," and "party of the first part" for "him" or "her"). Also, legal and bureaucratic documents often do not contain contextual information, which "would allow readers to relate the information in the document to their own experience, or alert them to the fact that what they are about to read is not connected to any of their pre-existing notions." On the syntactic level, legal and bureaucratic language includes unique word combinations: doublets ("any and all," "cease and desist"), word lists ("A witness who has special *knowledge, skill, experience, training, or education* in a particular *science, profession or occupation*"), and unusual prepositional phrases and clauses ("as to," "until such time as"). Finally, at the lexical level, there are common terms with uncommon meanings ("consideration," "assign"), legal terms ("eminent domain," "trespass"), and terms that are either quite vague ("as soon as is practicable," "all the rights and remedies") or quite precise ("any and all manner of actions, cause and causes of action, suits, debts, dues, sums of money, accounts, reckonings, bonds, bills, specialities," "no animal of the dog kind").[3]

In short, what many laymen have done is complain that they cannot understand legal writing. What linguists and English professors have attempted to do is explain why the misunderstanding exists and suggest what can be done about it. The aspiration of this and the next chapter is simply to create an awareness of the kind of language used and the kind that is more likely to make the desired impression on the jury (which, as you might suspect, is not legalese).

The third reason that writing deserves study is that there is a limit to the number of well-turned phrases or sentences that can be devised and kept in the head. A convincing example of this appears in the challenge to work the following problems without pencil and paper:

$$\begin{array}{r} 6 \\ \times\ 7 \\ \hline \end{array} \qquad \begin{array}{r} 68 \\ \times\ 7 \\ \hline \end{array} \qquad \begin{array}{r} 96 \\ \times\ 87 \\ \hline \end{array} \qquad \begin{array}{r} 6723 \\ \times\ 376 \\ \hline \end{array}$$

The first is easy, and the second only slightly less so. The third can be worked, with concentration, but not the fourth, unless one has a memory aid, like a pencil and paper. The explanation is that the mind can hold only five to nine units in short-term memory. The fourth problem involves more steps than that; "when mental tasks become sufficiently complex, that is, when they require that we hold more than seven or so separate units in our minds at one time, we must use some sort of a memory aid." Only by using a system that reduces the number of steps and the resulting strain on short-term memory, can one work the fourth problem in his head.[4]

The five-to-nine-units limitation on short-term memory may not apply if items to be recalled are chronologized (which eases the strain on memory), grouped into larger units (which would make the number of items recalled a multiple of the larger units times the number of items in those units), or conventionally prescribed units already (such that we know by experience what items are within those units). However, if "analytic/synthetic thinking necessary to invent theoretical principles or the linguistic and conceptual originality now prized in poetry, pencil and paper appear necessary."[5]

Attorneys have the opportunity to write out their opening and closing arguments, and some write out examination questions. A successful trial attorney, with over thirty-five years of experience, observes that

> [a] jury argument can be more flowery, rhetorical, and argumentative than the opening statement, but it must tie into the opening statement. I always outline my thoughts on paper so I can present them in a cohesive, methodical manner. To flounder confuses the jury more than anything else. In a complex matter, I will even write out every question [for the jury], even though I sometimes do not use them all.[6]

While this is not to suggest that attorneys should read their closing arguments, or even memorize them word for word, it is through writing that memorable words and phrases emerge. Once written, and reviewed, they tend to be retrievable at the time of oral delivery. An outline of a closing argument on paper can also incorporate the specific words and phrases devised in the writing stage. "Why write? One important reason is that unless we do there are mental acts we cannot perform, thoughts we cannot think, inquiries we cannot engage in."[7]

B. *Elements of Style*

In writing, selections are made from these categories of elements: sentence structure, order within sentences, punctuation, and word choice. Depending on which system of classification is used, there are four main types of sentence structure: simple, compound, complex, and compound-complex. Essentially, each type after "simple" merely combines other grammatical elements in a set fashion so as to pack more information into a single sentence. It is amazing that, even though the majority of native English speakers often correctly use the last two types in speech, the correct writing of these types poses problems for many people. However, when speech is reduced to print, the sentence structure may depend in part on how comfortable the transcriber feels with writing more complicated sentences. That is, one transcriber could "hear" and transcribe a series of simple sentences, while another could "hear" and transcribe a lesser number of compound sentences (a compound sentence combines two or more simple sentences). If a listener fails to understand what a speaker has said, it is probably not because of his sentence structure. As listeners, we tend to take the words of the speaker and translate them into sentence structures that we understand. Therefore, the attorney need not concern himself with designing his oral presentations on the basis of the types of sentence structures.

Within each type of sentence structure is the order of words, and ordering is significant to both the reading and listening audience, as indicated by the following examples. (1) A simple sentence, "I like that man," can be converted into "That man, I like." (2) Similarly, a complex sentence like "One-one/hundredth of one percent is a hundred thousand dollars to somebody that's got a billion dollars" can become "To somebody that's got a billion dollars, one-one/hundredth of one percent is a hundred thousand dollars."[8] (3) And "May I make this claim with right and conscience?" can be converted into "May I with right and conscience make this claim?"[9] In the first example above, the shift in word order creates interest, since it is something that one would not expect to hear. The order of "That man, I like" causes the sentence to have more of an impact that it would otherwise have. In the second example, the effect of the order change is to place the "somebody" before the listeners sooner than in the more conventional order; therefore, the effect is to emphasize the "somebody." In the third example, the second order produces a more melodic sentence than the first (the second sentence is actually iambic pentameter; the first is not); the second sentence, therefore, is more appealing to the ear than the first, and is more likely to be recalled.

A caution should be entered here as to selecting among elements purely for dramatic effect. That is, "That man, I like" is effective because the order of the sentence is rare. If, however, every other sentence took this order, the order would no longer have its dramatic effect. Also, the effect produced by "That man, I like" would be greatly diminished. Extemporaneous speakers often develop unconscious fetishes for unique words, such as "poignant." The first time the word is used, it has its dramatic effect; the second time it is used, the word had lost its uniqueness. If it is used a third time, the audience is probably subconsciously listening for it, as with a verbal tic (like "you know"). Unique, meaning one of a kind, implies a singular occurrence. Therefore, if a word or sentence order (or any stylistic device) is to be unique, it should appear only once.

Different from the repetition of a unique word or structure is a planned pattern. An effective technique, often used by televised evangelists, is to sum up a set of details with a single word or phrase. Then, a new set of details, similar to the first set, may be presented, again summed up by that same word or phrase. What the speaker is trying to do is induce the audience themselves to apply that word to other sets of similar details he may mention, *before* he uses the word. Comedians also rely on this technique. Early in their routine, they may state a punch line, which they revive at various other times with similar joke data; if all goes as planned, the audience will yell out the punch line themselves in later parts of the routine. The effectiveness of planned pattern appears in the following excerpts of a closing argument:

> Ladies and gentlemen, the Kluczynskis were party to an agreement. They entered into an agreement to go to Orlando, Florida. . . . *They could have been* neurosurgeons going down there to operate on somebody's head that had to be there at a certain time. *They could have been* going down to get married and miss the church. *They could have been* somebody working for the government, very important, who didn't want to fly in a government plane. . . .[10]

Counsel had the choice of variety or pattern in the introduction of each possible type passenger. Although it is not known whether he took advantage of it, by opting for the pattern, he also allowed himself the opportunity to *vary* his pronunciation of each of the patterned phrases: *They* could have been, They *could* have been, They could have *been*. Thus, he actually could have used both variety and pattern here. Because of one or both of these techniques, this portion of the argument could have stayed with the jurors.

Punctuation is the element of writing that attempts to substitute for a variety of oral stylistic elements. Pauses in speech between groups of words forming individual ideas appear in writing as commas, semicolons, colons, and periods. A semicolon is "stronger" than a comma only in writing; a pause the "equivalent" of a semicolon in speech sounds no different than a comma, a dash, or a period. Long pauses in speech probably have no equivalent in writing but can be effective, because of their drama, in speech, unless they convey that the speaker is lost. Exclamation points and underscoring in writing indicate emphasis but are relatively poor simulators of the volume, tone, gestures, and expressions available to a live speaker. However, just as exclamation points and underscoring tend to lose their effectiveness when they are overused, so do repeated increases in volume and flamboyant gestures. Stylistic elements designed to indicate emphasis succeed in doing so only when they are placed in relief; if the norm is wild ranting, what does one do to draw increased attention to particular points? Also, especially in opening argument, counsel is likely to invite objections with an emotional delivery. Not only might the objections be sustained, but the argument will be interrupted. Thus, the following caution:

> The third rule for avoiding objections is a restrained delivery. It is amusing to note that the same words delivered forcefully will cause an objection but if delivered softly will not. Ironically, the soft delivery will scream far more loudly than the raised voice could ever do. You should never draw an objection during your opening statement if you are careful and well prepared. This is true although your goal is to argue your case and even inflame the jury.[11]

Word choice is a deceptively simple category; the deception lies in the variety of sub-categories within word choice. Grammar, meaning simply a description of a language, is such a sub-category. Most people do not make word selections on the basis of grammar; they assume there is only one grammatical way of saying something and, if they think about it, believe that they are probably using that way when they write or speak. They are correct about grammar being an absolute term; either speech or writing is grammatical or it is not. On the whole, they are also probably correct about adhering to the rules of grammar when they write or speak, but they do not do that consciously. Non-native speakers of English who learn English in a systemized program (studying English as a foreign language) usually know the rules of grammar far better, and adhere to them more religiously, than do native speakers.

If a speaker, however, knows and can apply rules of grammar, he may be able to assess the extent to which his audience would recognize and appreciate the application of these rules and can then make a conscious choice between grammatical or ungrammatical constructions. For example, the sentence "It is I" is grammatical. Many people, knowing its correctness, though, would be uncomfortable saying that, fearing that they would sound too formal or stilted. Therefore, the usual translation is, "It's me," which is so colloquial (popular) that even sticklers for grammar would probably not hold its utterance against the speaker. However, the upper class British often speak beautifully correct English; an audience of such a composition could think less of someone who used the colloquial form. Another example is "Bill and I went to dinner" versus "Me and Bill went to dinner." Most people with a college education would recognize that the second sentence is not grammatical. However, even if they could recall the grammatical distinction—assuming they cared to think about it—residents of a small Texas town might identify more with someone who said "Me and Bill" (with the "and" converted to "an") than "Bill and I." Sometimes, people who flaunt grammar do so merely to indicate that their values are placed on more important concerns, and they seem to relish saying things like "It don't matter." Speaking the "lingo" of the jurors may at times require counsel to adopt creative grammar.

A category similar to grammar is the degree of formality in both phrasing and word selection. Formal phrasing usually requires more words, and formal words are often longer than more casual words; the result is probably a precision that is matched only by the nonverbal tone, expressions, and gestures of more casual speakers. Perhaps it is no coincidence that those who tend to speak formally also tend to be reserved in dress, manner, and gestures. People who have learned English as a second language are more prone to speak formally (and to be more restrained in expressions and gestures) than are native speakers, and native speakers are generally more prone to speak formally around strangers than around friends and acquaintances. When native speakers are formal in casual circumstances, they induce reactions to the formality itself. One college professor instructed her students to speak formally outside of the classroom and report on the reactions. The following exchange occurred in a dormitory:

Trish: Would it be possible for you to wait for me after class?
Ann: Yes, of course it's possible. Why are you talking so proper?

Apparently, Trish would normally have said something like, "Could you wait for me after class?" And Ann, who seems to be mocking Trish's formality in her reply, would normally have said, "Sure." This exchange reportedly occurred in a cafeteria:

Tom: Is this seat taken?
Al: Why no. Won't you join us?
Tom: [looking puzzled] How was logic today?
Al: Very instructive.
Tom: Oh, was it? What did he talk about?
Al: He talked about fallacies and associated topics.
Tom: [laughs, looks puzzled, mimics Al and hits him] Would you care to come over for tea?[12]

Evidently, Tom would have thought the exchange was more natural had it proceeded as follows:

Tom: Is this seat taken?
Al: Nah—sit down.
Tom: How was logic today?
Al: Not bad!
Tom: Oh, was it? What did he talk about?
Al: Fallacies, stuff like that.

As a part of the exercise, students were also instructed to use formal, "polite" speech at home. "The results were disastrous. Mothers cried. Fathers became furious. Since politeness indicates formality, therefore social distance, their reaction was perhaps to be expected."[13] Recall the discussion of hypercorrect speech in "Testimony Style" in Chapter 5, and its appearance with super-polite forms of speaking in a list of characteristics of powerless language. But also recall the conclusion that, for certain professions (such as academia) or cultures (such as the British), hypercorrect and super-polite speech is not associated with weakness but merely with professional goals or class differences. The caution, therefore, simply is to use the proper level of speech formality in the proper circumstances. Although there are exceptions, federal court is generally more formal than state court (but at either level, counsel may be addressing both a judge and a jury, which may have different requirements of formality), circuit courts of appeal are more formal than federal district courts, the Supreme Court is more formal than the appellate courts, and the English courts are more formal still. The increased degree of formality at each step in procedure and decorum could be properly echoed in the formality of the language used in each court.

Another category of word choice is verb selection. The legal profession is notorious for using passive verbs, as opposed to active verbs. Active verbs indicate people doing things ("Joe threw the ball") instead of things being done by people ("The ball was thrown by Joe"). English teachers urge that legal writing could be made far more interesting, less distant, and clearer with the elimination of passive verbs, and they often pull examples of boring, distant, vague passive constructions from statutes and court opinions. A strong argument, however, could be made for the use of passives in statutes and other legislative materials, as well as court opinions. Statutes are not designed to be "personal"; they are meant to relate to the public as a whole. Also, legislators would be surprised to think that the public expected statutes to be "interesting," as if laymen would pick up a volume of statutes instead of a novel if only the writing were different. Finally, statutes must be sufficiently "vague" to allow for the myriad examples of activities that might be suggested in a single prohibition. Similarly, court opinions are not written to entertain the reader; they comprise reference materials. Also, an opinion must speak to a fact situation at hand but cannot be so specific as to anticipate any and all variations of that fact situation that may occur in the future. Therefore, the more general expression of principles allows later courts in the same jurisdiction to rely on prior decisions.

Writing *to* judges, however, is much different, as is writing to clients. In both cases, the attorney should strive for clarity and economy of words and, with the client, probably a more personal approach. Passive verbs literally give the reader more words to consider, since a passive verb consists not only of the base verb, but also a form of the verb "be"; plus, if the "doer" of the action appears in the sentence, it will be connected to the base verb with a "by," which adds another word. Compare the number of words in "Jim threw the ball" with those in "The ball was thrown by Jim." Although passive constructions create distance through their indirectness, this result is most apparent on the written page, when the only personality of counsel is his writing style. In oral delivery, the entire persona of the speaker, created by appearance, mannerisms, arguments, etc., often blurs certain stylistic techniques on a first hearing (although analysis of videotapes or the written text can uncover them). However, the repeated use of passives may well leave the audience with an overall impression of the speaker being ponderous and wordy.

One attorney, advising as to persuasive techniques in the courtroom, suggests using the active voice simply because the "passive voice is weak." The examples he contrasts are "I shall always remember my first trial" and "My first trial will always be remembered by me." He also advocates the use of concrete words ("This corporation called John Smith a thief" instead of "The defendants slandered and defamed the plaintiff") and words that evoke definite images or elicit certain feelings (e.g., "tyranny, wench, miser, traitor, coward, and mother").[14] Clearly, active verbs are more consistent with the dynamic type of presentation he urges than are the more sedate passive constructions.

This same attorney also advocates the avoidance of "[m]echanical repetition," which he says "avails little and irritates judges and jurors," but recommends the (planned) repetition of "parallel words or phrases in the same sentence or series of sentences." The difference, of course, is that the former looks to the audience like lack of imagination while the latter, instead of appearing to be a stylistic technique, may simply do a better job of conveying the message. He cites a number of examples of this technique from John F. Kennedy.[15] Perhaps the best known of these, however, is "Ask not *what your country can do for* you, but *what* you *can do for your country*."

Modern verbal parallelism has its roots in "Greek art, architecture, and oratory [which] all reflect the importance of balance and symmetry." A brief cataloging of the kinds of parallelism possible, along with examples, indicates the potential of this stylistic device. (As the precision of the examples suggests, however, this is one of those tasks that is best achieved with pencil and paper instead of extemporaneously.) One category is the repetition of key words, as in this excerpt from Martin Luther King's "I Have a Dream": "I have a dream my four little children will one day live in a nation where they will not be judged *by the* color *of their* skin but *by the* content *of their* character." A second category contrasts opposites, as in Proverbs 22:7: "The *rich* ruleth over the *poor*, and the *borrower* is servant to the *lender*." Notice that the challenge in this example is not only to set the opposites in the first clause, but also to find opposites for the second clause *and* to make sure that the second clause is an echo, in content, of the first. In a third category, grammatical elements are repeated; that is, more than one instance of the same part of speech appears, as with gerunds ("the *beating* of wings and the *roaring* of lions," by Kahlil Gibran), verbs ("*seizes* a cocktail. . .*dumps* it down for courage and. . .*dances* out alone," by F. Scott Fitzgerald), or infinitives ("*to write* a book, *to be* in a movie, and *to get around* to recording the rock 'n' roll songs," by Joan Didion), as examples. A fourth category merely combines elements from the other three categories, as in the parallel participles and repetition of key words in this excerpt by Fitzgerald: "*Blinded by the* glare *of the* headlights and *confused by the* incessant groaning *of the* horns. . . ."[16]

There are two important requirements for writing successful parallel structures. First, the items placed in parallel to each other should be of the same part or parts of speech ("to write," "to be," and "to get around" are all infinitives); if this requirement is not met, the discordance is distracting ("to write," "being," and "to get around" are not parallel grammatically). One does not need to be a grammarian to match joined words and phrases properly; usually the visual form of the word is a reliable signal. Second, if parallel structures do not have the intended effect, their reason for being is lost. If, in striving for a word simply that "fits" grammatically or fills out a sequence of three or four (or whatever number), one opts for a word that has less than a suitable meaning, the effect can be that of a bad rhyme.

The last category of word choice to be discussed here is imagery, also known as figurative language or figures of speech. Since entire books have been written on the topic (and entire books have been devoted to the description and analysis of the imagery of various writers), little more than an introduction to the subject can be presented now. Imagery describes one thing by comparing it to another. In literal terms, the comparison is impossible, but the technique induces the audience to take characteristics of the second (the compared item) and impute them to the first item. Therefore, all of the imputed characteristics of the second item are instantaneously conveyed, without the need for specifying them in so many words. In addition, imagery causes the audience to "imagine" the second item, along with its more abstract and imputed characteristics, and a picture (even though it be induced) is worth the well-known thousand words. Take the example of "Richard the Lionhearted." All of the courage, strength, and stateliness of an animal is suddenly transferred to a man, while the vision of a lion hovers in the mind.

The example of "king of the beasts" imputes human characteristics to an animal, and the mental vision of that animal may have it wearing a crown. A brief description of certain types of figurative language, and "how" they work, is helpful as a background for creating such language.

In pure rhetorical device terminology, metaphors are called "tropes," which "always define a relationship between terms." While rhetoricians have identified a great many tropes, the four most important have been designated as the "master tropes." Metaphor, the most common, "states an equivalence between terms taken from separate domains."[17] An example is "George the Lion," as applied to a football player. The selection of the other domain (here, the animal world), as well as the item in that domain (lion), is less than casual. The two compared items should have both shared and unshared characteristics:

> If we say that George the man is like a lion we must also admit, no matter how much we might enjoy this noble characterization, that at the same time he is not like a lion at all. George might be large, powerful, and deadly, but where is his tail? A metaphor in a variety of ways places into juxtaposition two terms that are, or can be, thought of as both similar and dissimilar.

The similar items cannot be too numerous, however, or the effect of the items being simultaneously alike and different will be lost, as with "pail" and "bucket."[18]

While metaphor draws on separate domains, synecdoche and metonymy pull items out of the same domain. With synecdoche, "one term always includes or is included by the other as kind for type, part for whole." For example, "man" could stand for the component parts of a human being, such as hands, head, feet, torso; and "tree" could stand for limbs, trunk, and leaves. At the same time, "man" could also refer to American, Frenchman, Russian; and "tree" could represent oak, elm, or willow. These classification methods, by which a general term replaces others that are more general or more specific, are respectively called anatomical and taxonomic modes of classification. Because of the part-to-the-whole ratio, synecdoches often appear as exaggeration, as in "'I'm all sore' when one has a sore toe" and "'The car has broken down' when the cigarette lighter is out of order." Synecdoche is also the figure of speech used in terms like "the patter of little feet," which represents children.[19]

Metonymy is the replacement or juxtaposition of "contiguous terms that occupy a distinct and separate place within what is considered a single semantic or perceptual domain. "Homer," the agent, for example, replaces the *Iliad,* as act, in "you will read in Homer." The term "deep in his cups" uses "cups" to stand for the wine contained in them. This technique is explained as a means for expanding the abstraction. The use of Homer expands the idea to all of his works, not just the *Iliad* (although that may be the work under discussion). Similarly, "[b]y substituting 'The Fords stepped on it' for 'George and the boys won the race' we expand our reference to include the whole event: men in their machines; hard, exciting, and fast action."[20]

Irony, the fourth of the "master tropes," is best explained as an incongruity between meaning and actual words. This is achieved through the juxtaposition of concepts from the same or separate domains that are thought to be contradictory. While it usually involves concepts rather than only terms, the following meet the criteria for irony: "bright obscurity" and "sweet death."[21]

Attorneys who try to guide others in successful courtroom tactics often recommend the use of figurative language without ever using that term. They may say, "Use memorable words, not empty words." They may caution against mechanical repetition and provide a variety of ways to say the same thing: "He loves his work. He keeps busy. He burns the candle at both ends. He is burning himself out."[22] The last two examples are pure metaphor.

A few years ago an article came out in which a law professor recommends determining the sensory level of communication used by an audience (judge, client, opposing counsel) and then adopting and reflecting that same level, so as to improve communication. He theorizes that, since thinking is an extension of the sensory process, verbalized words will reflect the sense modality (visual, auditory, kinesthetic, or even neutral) that shapes the words. Thus, a visual speaker may "clearly get the picture," an auditory speaker may "hear what you are saying," a kinesthetic speaker may "get the point; it is not hard to grasp," and a neutral speaker may simply "understand." His insight suggests that people may respond more favorably to a certain type of imagery than others; notice how these examples might match different preferences: "soft as an evening sunset," "soft as a whisper," "soft as a kitten," and "soft as can be." His recommendation in speaking to a jury, whose individual preferences cannot be known, are to use only neutral terms, use terms of only one or two of the possibilities (such as auditory and visual), or use a variety of all of the terms.[23] If imagery is a component of more effective, more memorable speech, then it should be used; and if imagery appealing to all of the senses would appeal to more people than imagery limited to only one of the senses, the greater appeal would seem to determine the choice.

C. *The Rhetorical Connection*

Marie Hochmuth Nichols, one of the leading authorities on rhetoric and rhetorical criticism, traces the historical course of rhetoric to arrive at what should be the focus of modern speech criticism. She reminds us that the early orators placed great emphasis on history, which led to the political wisdom that was "considered absolutely essential to the deliberative orator and part of his training." At the same time, however, "early historians used speeches as the substance of history," although such speeches may have fairly represented past events or been entirely contrived. For the orator to recall and repeat with precision each of his speeches, as well as to induce their retention in the minds of his listeners, he would ease his task of memorization with certain stylistic devices, which would also make his speech more memorable to his audience. Apparently, a desire to perfect this skill and excel at the "flowers of rhetoric" would often surpass the inclination for historical accuracy.[24]

Nichols observes the sometimes inconsistent approaches taken by rhetoricians in analyzing speeches.

> Much of our difficulty comes, I think, from failing to reconcile two fundamentally different traditional conceptions of rhetoric, the Ciceronian tradition and the Renaissance tradition. The one argued that rhetoric concerned itself with five canons—inventions, arrangement, style, memory, and delivery; the other, stemming from Peter Ramus argued that rhetoric was essentially a matter of style and that invention and arrangement were parts of logic.

Notice that "style" forms a part of rhetoric in either definition. Nichols laments, however, that at that time (1966), rhetoricians were ignoring the analysis of style in their critiques of speeches:

> [C]ritics cannot shirk attention to language as they have done in the past. Just as literary critics have been forced to agree that in the last analysis attention must be focused on the art object if one is to evaluate it, so we may conclude that closer examination of

> the language of the human being in his moment of decision must be one means to our end. If rhetoricians are dealing with an art—and some of us tend to think we are—then the question is: How does creativeness manifest itself in the speech? the particular speech? How does it manifest itself in structure, in diction, in sentence movement?

She concludes that however the element is couched—style, language, or content—it is the function of the rhetorical critic to analyze it.[25]

In one sense, a methodology for rhetorical analysis drawn from Aristotle, Cicero, and Quintilian would be closest to the source of the science. But the brief historical sketch above demonstrates how changes in time, culture, and circumstances would cause a literal derivation of methodology from such sources to be less than appropriate for modern oral presentations. However, a modernization of classical rhetoric by George Campbell that appeared in 1776 is hailed as "a clarification of the thinking of a new generation of rhetoricians."[26] In Campbell's restatement appears not only the practically surviving elements of classical oratory but also rationale and descriptions that are dated only by his own writing style (reflecting an eloquence more suited to the eighteenth century). In short, Campbell clearly connects style and rhetoric; style is the means by which the speaker fulfills his rhetorical purpose.

Campbell begins his first chapter with a definition of eloquence translated from Quintilian: "That art or talent by which the discourse is adapted to its end."[27] And at the end of any discourse, he explains, is to convince the audience, whether conviction is the sole end or is meant to accompany some other end.[28] He makes the following distinction between grammar and style, which indicates style to be synonymous with eloquence:

> Now, the grammatical art hath its completion in syntax; the oratorical, as far as the body or expression is concerned, in style. Syntax regards only the composition of many words into one sentence; style, at the same time that it attends to this, regards further the composition of many sentences into one discourse. . . . the grammarian, with respect to what the two arts have in common, the structure of sentences, requires only purity; that is, that the words employed belong to the language, and that they be construed in the manner, and used in the signification, which custom hath rendered necessary for conveying the sense. The orator requires also beauty and strength. The highest aim of the former is the lowest aim of the latter; where grammar ends eloquence begins.[29]

Campbell offers his own synthesis of the classical rhetorical appeals of *logos, pathos,* and *ethos. Logos* is the appeal to logic, *pathos* to the emotions, and *ethos* to the desire to do whatever is just and right (ethical appeal is also thought to be generated by the speaker, such as when the audience likes and trusts him, which could be due to *his* apparent desire to do whatever is just and right). Campbell argues that the truth of a proposition can be demonstrated by conclusive arguments alone (logical appeal). However, for listeners to be convinced by an argument, they must understand, listen to, and recall it. Finally, even if they are convinced, the argument will not motivate them to act unless it is "felt." Thus, Campbell advises that an orator must first "excite some desire or passion in the hearers" and then "satisfy their judgment that there is a connexion between the action to which he would persuade them, and the gratification of the desire or passion which he excites. This is the analysis of persuasion."[30]

Insofar as making himself understood, Campbell warns that the speaker should make certain that his ideas are not beyond the grasp and language skills of his listeners. Certainly, in addition to actual types of argument used, this caution includes the stylistic concerns of language formality and level of vocabulary. In fact, simple arguments can be complicated by a confused style, just as complex arguments can be simplified by short sentences and small words. So as to induce the audience to be attentive, Campbell says that their "imagination must be engaged. . . .without some gratification in hearing, there will be no attention, at least of any continuance. Those qualities in ideas which principally gratify the fancy, are vivacity, beauty, sublimity, novelty." This topic, then, embraces imagery and vivid word choice. He then notes that, not only will such language lead to attentiveness, but it is also more likely to be recalled by the audience. Finally, it is through "eloquence" that the passions are enlisted. Arguing that persuasion combines appeals both to the intellect and the emotions, Campbell postulates the following as a result of an appeal only to the mind:[31]

> You have proved beyond contradiction, that acting thus is the sure way to procure such an object. I perceive that your reasoning is conclusive; but I am not affected by it. Why? I have no passion for the object. I am indifferent whether I procure it or not. You have demonstrated that such a step will mortify my enemy. I

> believe it; but I have no resentment, and will not trouble myself to give pain to another. Your arguments evince that it would gratify my vanity. But I prefer my ease. Thus passion is the mover to action, reason is the guide.

II. *RHETORICAL ANALYSIS OF EFFECTIVE ARGUMENTS*

With the very existence of rhetoric (meaning persuasion or identification, or attempts at persuasion or identification) simultaneously indicating the existence of an audience, rhetoric is concerned with effects on that audience.[32] The speaker has one or more goals that he seeks to meet by talking to his audience, and he believes that what he says, and how he says it, can help him attain his goals. He could be totally wrong in this belief. That is, it may be that his audience will react in a certain way, regardless of what he says. Some may be taken by his physical appearance and manner, and do his bidding without much thought. By the same token, he may remind others of a detested relative, and they may act precisely opposite to what he requests. Finally, he may unwittingly strike an emotional chord in others, with examples or phrasing, which could cause them to translate his message into one that is personally significant (or repugnant) to them.

But a speaker always prepares as if what he says and how he says it do matter. Even if the audience does his bidding, he can never *know* that it was because of his words and arguments, but the result lends credence to the effectiveness of his speech. It is in working backward from effect to supposed cause that speech critics have developed a methodology for analyzing speeches. Then, devising a "formula" for successful speeches, they are able to analyze a speech, not knowing how the specific audience reacted, and to indicate why the speech *should* have produced a favorable reaction.

The arguments analyzed below are complete or excerpted "speeches" from opening and closing statements in three cases. The first case was not a real case at all; it was a demonstration conducted by the Twenty-Eighth Annual Advocacy Institute of the Institute of Continuing Legal Education in Michigan. Seventeen practicing attorneys, law professors, a judge, and a sociologist/criminologist participated in the demonstration, in either the presentation or the evaluation phase. The opening and closing statements of two attorneys for the defendant are examined, in part because they show a bold response to a difficult problem. The success of this response is reflected in the comments of one of the evaluators.

The speeches next examined are the closing arguments for the guardian ad litem and the attorney for the plaintiff in the case of Karen Quinlan, presented to the Superior Court of New Jersey. While the court's opinion indicates limited success for the plaintiff at this stage, it is surely on the strength of precisely the same arguments that a different ruling resulted on appeal. Because the appellate argument does not take the form of a speech, but rather a question and answer session, counsel's argument below is selected for analysis.

The last speech selected for analysis is the prosecution's closing argument in the Sacco-Vanzetti case. Since the argument lasted approximately four hours (the total taken by the two defense counsel), only excerpts are analyzed. The prosecutor painstakingly reviewed the myriad pieces of evidence throughout his closing, providing the jury with a rational basis for their conviction of the defendants; but analysis reveals that the motivation to action was sought primarily through an awesome display of ethical appeal.

A. *The Case of Arthur Korn*

In the hypothetical fact situation, Arthur Korn was a 50-year-old family man and school teacher who, as a child, had failed to be evacuated from London during the bombings of World War II, which, in the words of his lawyer, constituted five years of "constant terror." Korn's father was killed at Dunkirk, which meant that he became the man of the house; and he and his mother moved to Indiana after the war. Korn became an English teacher, of average ability, but he had an excellent work attendance record. His physical and mental health were excellent until he attended a conference for teachers at the Welcome Inn at the Chicago O'Hare Airport, which had previously had problems with certain "undesirables." When he returned to his room one night, Korn went up in the elevator with a young man who followed him to his room, robbed him at knifepoint, and injured him. Although Korn recovered from the physical injury, he lost interest in teaching (and everything else) and developed headaches. His wife had to go to work to support the family, and Korn was diagnosed as having "a severe neurotic depression."

Korn's complaint was that the attack at the hotel triggered the mental disorder, the foundation for which had been set by his experiences during the war and the early loss of his father. Since the hotel knew about its problem with "undesirables," he argued that it failed to provide sufficient protection for its guests. In his opening statement, Korn's counsel noted that Korn was so disturbed that he was close to suicide.[33] Following is the opening statement by Tom Alexander, representing the Welcome Inn.[34]

May it please the Court.

[1] Ladies and gentlemen of the jury: As my opponent has told you, we all have ample discovery available. We all know what the evidence is going to show. As you might imagine, I've heard that speech before.

[2] We are here because we do not have liability in this case. I have decided, based on what I have seen in the evidence, to make no voluntary payment in this case. I believe that at the conclusion of this case you will reach the same decision, because the hotel did nothing wrong. Nothing the hotel did or failed to do caused the mugging or Mr. Korn's present plight as described by his lawyer.

[3] This incident happened as Mr. Korn entered a well-lighted lobby, ascended to his floor on a well-lighted elevator that worked properly, walked down the well-lighted corridor and opened his door with the key that was issued to him. The robber was admitted through the same door. He had no key. The robber could not have gained admittance to the room had it not been for the fact that Mr. Korn opened his door with his key.

[4] You will hear from the plaintiff about the evidence on which he wants you to base a verdict. When I present my evidence, you will also hear from the people who were there and the people who know about security in hotels—about the problems in hotels and how they deal with those problems. I believe that if you will examine the plaintiff's evidence in this case in the same light as it has been examined by the people who attended the depositions, you will reach the same conclusion they have reached: nothing the hotel did or failed to do caused the occurrence on which this suit is based.

[5] You will hear a lot of evidence designed solely to appeal to your sympathy, to give you the idea that this might be a good occasion to take some money from one party and give it to another party, without basing that decision on legal evidence and on instructions of law that His Honor will give you at the conclusion of the case.

[6] But, ladies and gentlemen, I ask you, as you swore to do when you entered the jury box, to study each witness the plaintiff calls with the purpose of determining how that witness will help

resolve the questions of negligence and proximate causation, as the court will define those terms, in favor of the plaintiff.

[7] I submit that you will not find any evidence that will help you with the major problem—the liability issue of the case. All that kind of evidence will come from the defense side, and it will be overwhelming.

[8] It is my duty as a lawyer to discuss every aspect of the case, even though I do not believe that there is any evidence of primary liability on the part of the hotel. Evidence will be brought before you to try to persuade you to jump the problems of liability and causation and to reach a verdict contrary to the evidence on those issues—the evidence concerning Mr. Korn's condition.

[9] After hearing the speech of my opponent, you may have reached at least a tentative conclusion that not only does he claim the hotel is responsible for the client being mugged, but the hotel is responsible for World War II and brainwashing. You will find that after this occurrence, Mr. Korn was not in the hands of attorneys; he was in the hands of a trusted family doctor who sought to find out if there was anything wrong with him as a result of this incident. Aside from a broken nose, which healed quickly, the family doctor, whom Mr. Korn and his family had gone to for years, told Mr. Korn that he could find nothing wrong with him. The family doctor sent him to a very capable, competent neurologist, one of the finest in the community. The neurologist also examined Mr. Korn thoroughly, testing him in every conceivable way. The neurologist then told him and his family doctor that there was nothing wrong with Mr. Korn.

[10] Not satisfied that something might not have been overlooked, they sent him to an orthopedist; that specialist examined his entire bone structure and reached the same result. Mr. Korn, however, was not satisfied with the opinion of his family doctor, his neurologist and his orthopedist, selected by his family doctor. He said, "You're all wrong; there is something wrong with me."

[11] Mr. Korn developed headaches. Of more significance was the fact that these headaches did not develop, as you might expect, the night of the incident, the day after the incident, or even a week after the incident. They occurred when Mr. Korn went back to teaching school. As he described it in his own words, and you will hear those words in this trial, "I could no longer take the rigors of teaching." Isn't that a fine statement for a man we had previously entrusted with the education of our children? You and I have been

exposed to teachers who did not regard teaching as rigorous, who did not regard it as an imposition on them to put up with the stress and strain of the classroom. Mr. Korn figured his own way out of this dilemma. The evidence will show that he was not only an unhappy teacher, but that he was a failure as a teacher as well. He lacked the respect of his students; he lacked the respect of his fellow teachers; and he lacked the respect of his superintendent. And he knew it.

[12] What did Mr. Korn do at this point? Like any man who is dissatisfied with his situation, he avoided it. At that time his actions were none of my business, except for the fact that I have children in that school—to that extent it was my business. It became my business when he said, "I wouldn't have taken to my bed, put my wife to work, refused to stir myself, had it not been for the fact that somebody robbed me." Even then, it wouldn't have been my business until he said that the robbery took place in the Welcome Inn. The Welcome Inn is my client, and then Mr. Korn's situation became my business.

[13] Up to this point it wasn't your business, either, except for the fact that you may also have children in that school. But it has recently become your business, because you now have the unshirkable duty of resolving this case.

[14] You cannot throw yourself in bed and stare at the ceiling and say, "I cannot withstand the rigors of deciding this case." You are going to have to decide it; and you are going to have to decide it based on proof.

[15] The big part of the case is going to be a wonderful citizen named Dr. Grass. Dr. Grass has decided, some two years after the fact, that all of Mr. Korn's problems—World War II, the bombing raids, the inadequacies, the nasty things his students said about him, the little things they wrote on the board that he didn't like but wouldn't do anything about—were of no consequence; he was getting along marvelously. Then he got mugged in the Welcome Inn, and that, ladies and gentlemen, ruined his life completely. Had it not been for that mugging, Mr. Korn would have resolved all his other problems.

[16] Although I have discovery available, I didn't really need much discovery to know what Dr. Grass was going to say.

[17] If I have a legal problem, I try to find myself a lawyer who is better than I am. In this case I didn't have a legal problem; I had the problem of what Dr. Grass was going to tell you in this case.

So I sought the best psychiatrist available—Dr. Edward Burton, a very distinguished man in this community. I asked him if Dr. Grass's assessment of Mr. Korn was valid. Dr. Burton said he would have to examine the gentleman and study his history, to determine the validity of this claim that the world fell in on Mr. Korn because of the mugger. Dr. Burton has done that, and he will be here to give you his evidence. It will be your duty as jurors to weigh that evidence in contrast to the evidence of Dr. Grass. You may ask how you can resolve the question if one psychiatrist says one thing and the other psychiatrist says another. That is the position Mr. Korn would take. The position you must take is that you must follow the court's charge and decide which of these witnesses is the better qualified, which of these witnesses is the more credible, which of these witnesses is telling us that which fits with our notion of logic and common sense. And you must decide which evidence to believe.

[18] There are two responsibilities you must meet: you must decide whether this hotel is responsible at all—whether there is any proof of wrongdoing by the hotel, proof that anything they did or failed to do caused the mugging; and you must decide whether the mugging caused Mr. Korn's present attitude about his work, about his family, and about himself.

[19] Ladies and gentlemen, you will hear the evidence, you have sworn to follow it. Thank you.

Alexander takes a bold position against the charges of Korn, attempting to demean them and any purported evidence. Although Korn is obviously disturbed in some way, Alexander wants to cut off any sympathy for whatever the affliction is, regardless of whether the hotel caused it. Alexander's entire presentation is one of strength—an expression of superiority of himself, his witness, and the jury, over opposing counsel, the plaintiff's expert, and the plaintiff. Representing a corporation is a challenge, since jurors have difficulty seeing the injustice of dipping into the pockets of an impersonal entity to compensate for the injuries to a real-person plaintiff. Therefore, counsel for corporations often bring an appealing corporate representative into the courtroom and try to personalize the client. Not Alexander. He places himself on trial, pitting himself against opposing counsel, tempting the jury to choose between his strength and the plaintiff's weakness.

In his opening paragraph, Alexander sets up the personal battle between himself and the other side with the use of "my opponent."

In another situation, he might personalize the situation, calling counsel by name, or characterize the dispute as one between the plaintiff and defendant. Then he quickly establishes his expertise and implies that his "opponent" has relied on cliche in his opening statement: "As you might imagine, I've heard that speech before." Almost immediately after giving the audience reason to trust his judgment, he provides his judgment, his *personal* judgment, of the case: "*I* have decided. . . to make no voluntary payment in this case." He is confident that the jury will agree, not because he simply believes the hotel was not liable, but because "the hotel *did nothing wrong*." He says that as if it were fact, not opinion.

The third paragraph contains only four sentences, one very short; but in it, Alexander relates that the hotel lobby, elevator, and hall were well-lit, the elevator worked properly, and the assailant had no access to a room key. He even implies that Korn was somehow responsible for the attack, in opening the door for the robber. The audience is reminded of the personal battle in the fourth paragraph, in the contrast of evidence from the plaintiff and "When *I* present *my* evidence."

In his opening statement, plaintiff's counsel went into detail about the hotel's problems with "undesirables" and its security measures. Alexander only generally addresses these, in paragraphs five through eight, repeatedly using terms like "evidence," "negligence," "liability," and "primary liability." At this point, he really does not expect the jury to understand what he is talking about. He initially characterizes the plaintiff's evidence as an "appeal to your sympathy," but he does not want to return to each of the points made by the plaintiff and hit them head on; to do so would reinforce those points in the jury's mind. Instead, he gives only the illusion of addressing them while actually sweeping them to the side. The use of abstract legal terms may make the jury think that he is confident of the legal implications of the evidence and does not feel it warrants detailed discussion at this point. To repeat: he does *not* want to discuss alleged shortcomings of the hotel here; he wants to talk about Korn, which he begins doing in the ninth paragraph.

Alexander begins this paragraph with another reference to his "opponent" and then likens the hotel's responsibility for Korn's attack to its responsibility for "World War II and brainwashing." Next, he ticks off the doctors ("trusted," "competent") who thoroughly examined Korn but found "nothing wrong" with him and contrasts their conclusion with Korn's, that there was "something wrong;" the juxtaposition of these phrases also contrasts the degree of expertise of the doctors with the lay assessment by Korn. While it cannot now be known how Alexander delivered these phrases, one can imagine certain ways that would have been effective. The first "nothing wrong" could have been drawn out, and said with the hands spread wide, open, empty. The second "nothing wrong" could have been said as if the words had come from the neurologist himself, with a negative shaking of the head while the words were spoken. Korn's "something wrong" could have then followed, with a question mark in the voice, a pause, and a puzzled look on the face following "something."

Immediately afterwards comes the manifestation of this "something," Korn's headaches, briefly stated, so as to minimize the importance of such an affliction. Then, to shift attention from the malady, Alexander quickly points out that they did not begin the night of the attack, the day after, or even the week after, but when Korn returned to teaching. Alexander then makes an ethical appeal by connecting Korn's comment on the "rigors of teaching" to a concern he appears to share with the jury about the quality of education of his and their children. Teachers generally have the respect of the community, and Korn's attorney sought to engender that respect for Korn in referring to his teaching in the opening statement. Alexander detracts from that respect by pointing out that Korn did not even like teaching and was not very good at it, based on the reactions of his students and fellow teachers. Thus, not only does Korn not deserve the respect that teachers would normally receive, but he is a menace to the profession by being there.

Alexander again makes an ethical appeal when he comments in the twelfth paragraph on how Korn handled his problem, by simply ceasing to go to school. That action made Korn Alexander's "business," since Alexander had "children in that school." In other words, if Korn's actions could affect the education of Alexander's children, then Alexander was not going to sit idly by and observe. (Of course, since the case is purely hypothetical, Alexander did not, in fact, have children in Korn's school; but his saying that he did certainly justified his display of indignation.) Alexander uses the term "my business" three more times, saying that his involvement grew more imminent when Korn decided to take to his bed and "refused to stir." But it was when this attitude of Korn's began to impact "my client" that it became "my business." Alexander has demonstrated his virtual disgust for Korn's reaction but has implied a live-and-let-live attitude so long as such a reaction does not affect those under Alexander's protection. When such an effect is threatened, he responds like a gladiator, and the respect that he earlier engendered for himself ("I've heard that speech before") suggests that he believes enough in his client, and is strong enough, to bear the brunt of any attack personally. The Welcome Inn is in an enviable position at this point, seeming most protected.

The "my business" becomes converted in the thirteenth paragraph to "your business," when Alexander implies that if Korn had not started all of this nonsense, the jury would be at their own jobs now instead of listening to one man's imagined maladies. But, now, because Korn *has* started all of this, the jurors cannot decide to adopt his attitude and lie in bed, rejecting "the rigors of deciding this case" (fourteenth paragraph). Indeed, Alexander indicates that he has far more faith in their stamina than Korn's.

The fifteenth paragraph is composed of four sarcastic sentences, in which Alexander seeks to discredit the plaintiff's expert, dismiss the expert's findings, relieve the Welcome Inn of responsibility, and indicate other causes of Korn's problems. Had Alexander set out to do each of those things without exaggeration or sarcasm, it would have taken far more than one sentence each.

Paragraph 16 both minimizes the seriousness of this case (i.e., the Welcome Inn has little to fear) while providing overall structure to the opening statement. Alexander began with opposing counsel's comment about the opportunity for discovery in the case; now he says that not much discovery was needed to determine the facts here. (Alexander could also be anticipating a later remark from opposing counsel about Alexander passing up the opportunity to depose the plaintiff's expert). What Dr. Grass was going to say, Alexander explains, did not require much discovery. Of course, this is an implication that Dr. Grass would say whatever the attorney who put him on wanted him to say. Instead, Alexander relates in paragraph 17 that he found (what he thinks was) a more respected expert, "a very distinguished man in the community," an implication that Dr. Grass is not such a man himself. Then Alexander tells the jurors what they should already know, that they must pick the witness that they most believe. Naturally, if Alexander's opinion carries any weight (and much of his entire speech has been designed to evoke credibility for himself), *his* expert will get the nod.

In paragraph 18, Alexander summarizes the jury's task into two parts: decide whether the hotel was responsible for the mugging, and determine whether the mugging is responsible for Korn's present "attitudes"; this reduction of chores should appeal to the jury. Paragraph 19, in its brevity, is almost Alexander's vote of confidence in the jury; it suggests that he believes that they think the same way he does, and if they have come to respect him, they should be flattered by the comparison.

The closing argument for the defendant in this demonstration was delivered by co-counsel to Alexander, John C. Shepherd. In the time between these two speeches, Korn testified, under the guidance of his able counsel. Even if everything Alexander said about Korn was true, the worst that could be said about Korn is that he was a weak man. Clever counsel could have caused that to be brought out as sensitivity and gentleness. In addition, speaking of human weakness in the abstract is different from faulting a real person for frailty when he is on the stand talking about his family, his childhood, and a physical attack that "absolutely amazed" him. Therefore, a tack like Alexander's *following* Korn's live testimony, might appear cruel and heartless. As indicated in his speech below, Shepherd's position is consistent with Alexander's, but more humane.[35]

May it please the Court. May it please you, Mr. Colson, ladies and gentlemen:

[1] We've come to the time of the trial when the lawyers again talk directly to you. We talked to you before, of course, when you were prospective jurors. After you took the oath to answer whatever questions might be put to you, we interrogated you, and you were the people who were selected by the Court and the lawyers to try this case. We talked to you in the opening statement, to try to outline for you what we anticipated some of the issues and the proofs might be.

[2] Of course, after you took an oath you were a different group from the one we had first talked to, because your oath made you jurors—officers of the Court, if you will. Now you are even more than that. Now you are people who have sat through this trial and heard all the evidence; and I certainly join with Mr. Colson in saying that you have been a very attentive jury. You've really listened to the evidence. Now, as officers of the Court, you're about to apply the law, which His Honor will read to you, to the facts in this case, and to bring in a judgment in this case based on these facts. You're about to determine what justice really is, in this particular lawsuit.

[3] Since you've been an attentive jury and have listened to the evidence carefully, many of you might feel that hearing from the lawyers at this point is unimportant. You took an oath to decide this case on the evidence and on His Honor's instructions, not on what the lawyers say.

[4] Many people share that feeling. Today this country, with mass communication and good education, is very different from the way it was when our jurisprudence was first established; then very few people had much education and they often needed the counsel and advice of lawyers. Because of these changes, many people feel that the final argument is no longer needed. But under our rules as they presently exist, it is the duty of counsel to address the jury for just a few minutes, as I am doing now.

[5] I say it is duty because, under our rules, the idea is that after the jury has heard all of the evidence, the lawyers are to try to assist them in connecting the evidence to the law which His Honor will read. With that in mind, I will spend just a few minutes visiting with you, so that you can carry out your sworn obligation.

[6] I want to be of some help, if I can. This time is not given to lawyers to stand up and harangue a jury into doing something that would not comport with justice. This time is not given to lawyers to create false issues, straw men, and use them to get a jury's emotions at a fever pitch. That isn't what this process is about.

[7] No; it's a time for some reflection, a time to look at the facts and the issues in the lawsuit.

[8] One thing we're not deciding here—surely no one can contend that we're trying to decide it—is whether under our flag injured people are entitled to come into court. Does raising that issue help anyone who is trying to decide this case? Certainly not. It creates an issue that doesn't even exist in this case.

[9] But, having brought it up, let me analyze that issue just a little. Of course you and I know that anyone who feels he has a cause of action ought to, and in our country is entitled to, hire a lawyer—as Arthur Korn did, in this instance, some years ago.

[10] But on the other hand, a defendant—you or I or anybody who is sued—also has the right to come into court, hear what the evidence is and be judged on that. And yes, you have that right, under our flag, even if you're a corporation. Even if you know that some lawyer is going to stand up here and keep talking about "gross" receipts of $3 million. If that figure has been mentioned once in this case, it's been mentioned a dozen times. Why? To be of some

assistance in getting at real issues? No. You're intelligent enough to know that as you sit in judgment here and look at the real facts of the case, and weigh the evidence as it relates to both the issues of the injury and the issue of what happened on that night, you're left with not a great deal of evidence to worry about.

[11] I want to mention one thing. When you get into your jury room, you're going to be visiting with one another and listening to one another, talking about what you've heard. If I say anything here that doesn't agree with your memory of this evidence, then disregard what I say. Your collective memory of this evidence is going to be good. I certainly wouldn't ever intentionally say anything that doesn't comport with the evidence.

[12] Let's take a look at it. I think now in all fairness we have to say that Arthur Korn is a sick man. He has a mental problem. He knows it. His lawyers know it. We all know it—much better this morning than we did at the beginning of this trial. We brought before you Dr. Burton. He is a college professor, an outstanding psychiatrist. Why did we choose him? We wanted you to have, when you went into that jury room, the very best available information on the subject. And he told you that Arthur Korn is a sick man, that he was sick before this accident; there can't be any dispute about it. He had certain built-in problems that perhaps he wasn't aware of. I don't think his lawyers knew about them before this April event. And then, in this hotel, he gave no appearance to anyone of being a man who needed any special protection. He came in and registered at the Welcome Inn. Now, had anybody known of the fragile condition of his mind at that time, his emotional instability, special arrangements might have been made. Had his wife known, she might have accompanied him on the trip. Certainly if there had been any way for the hotel to know that this man needed special care or attention, he would have gotten it.

[13] He checked into the hotel; he appeared to be a normal person. There was no reason to stop him, to interrogate him, to try to find out more about him. What am I getting at? There is no evidence that his assailant gave any signs of being a dangerous person. Any signs, I say, because wearing a leather jacket doesn't automatically mark a person as being a potential assailant. There was no indication and there is no evidence that this assailant should have been identified as such by my client.

[14] The plaintiff's lawyers, now, with hindsight, suggest that there could have been someone in the lobby to find out if this young

man had a key. Where is the evidence that he didn't have a key? His Honor is going to tell you in just a moment that you can't base a verdict on surmise, guesswork and conjecture.

[15] Why then is the suggestion made, in the final argument of this case, that you ought to use guesswork? To try to find that the person who committed this attack fit into any kind of a category, in the absence of evidence of that fact, would be to use just that—surmise and conjecture.

[16] During the trial, there was one time when His Honor and I had what appeared to be a difference of opinion on a question I asked. Your Honor, for any offense that I might have committed in that exchange, I apologize to the Court and certainly to my client. Somehow a connotation was drawn from the question I asked about how long Mr. Korn and the assailant were together. But the time element is such an important question when we're talking about preventing an attack.

[17] Let's examine the idea that if the hotel had had a television camera in the hall they could have prevented the attack. The evidence is, graphically, that the two men were together a very short time. What could the hotel have done in that split second, even if they had seen, in the monitor, the two men walk down the hall? This incident took place, Mr. Korn said, as soon as he turned around—he turned around, and that's when it happened. Now, in those short seconds, what could my client, Welcome Inn, have done to prevent that assault? Certainly the monitor wouldn't have prevented it. We can see that. Someone who checked to see whether this fellow had a key wouldn't have prevented it. There is no evidence here that the hotel, under these circumstances, could have done anything to avoid what later happened.

[18] I will not take a great deal of time to talk about the present circumstances of Mr. Korn, how he is not working and not teaching. He needs psychiatric help. I wish I could talk to him. I know one person who can and I know that surely he will. His lawyer, one of the most persuasive people in the community, will talk to him about seeing a psychiatrist. After his damage suit is over, his lawyer will see that he gets this treatment and returns to a happy life and occupation.

[19] But let's see what it is, instead, that he is talking about presently. He talks about how horrible the situation is and how permanent it is. He criticizes both doctors who came here because they won't guarantee positive results. He talks about what a dismal future

he has. And here, in his presence, his own lawyers talk about the possibility that he may commit suicide.

[20] I suggest to you that, although I don't represent the man, I've come to know a lot about him. I've come to know his medical record. Yes, he's going through a stormy period now, no question about it. But I believe you'll agree with me that he could have shortened this period if he had handled it in a different fashion. This man should have gone to a doctor instead of to the courthouse.

[21] I want to say this to you, Mr. Korn: I don't believe you're going to commit suicide. I'm convinced of that, as I read this record and as I know more about you. I've got faith in you. I think, now that this painful experience is over, that you are going to seek the kind of treatment that is available to you. You realize that it was only one kid who thought you were a bad teacher, that all the rest of them have great respect for you. You have that kind of confidence, and it's going to take you back to work. You're going to say to that adopted flag, "I came into court, I had a case, I had a great lawyer, he presented my case well."

[22] But the thing that has preserved the jury system in the United States is that jurors, even when they're bombarded with psychological arguments, big money, big corporate defendants, have listened as the judge read the instructions. They've heard, for example, as His Honor will tell you so clearly, that the burden is on the plaintiff to prove his case by a preponderance, or greater weight, of the credible evidence.

[23] The plaintiff's case is that the Welcome Inn could have prevented that young man from assaulting Arthur Korn. I suggest to you that there is no evidence to support that. When you bring in a verdict in favor of the defendant, you are not saying that you have no sympathy for Mr. Korn, because I know you do; we all do. But a verdict for the defendant in this case will allow you to say that when your turn came to serve as a juror, you had the courage to do the hard thing. You had the courage to follow the law and follow the evidence. Even though it meant a finding against a sick man, you had the courage to measure up to your responsibility, and you stood tall. You signed that verdict for the defendant.

Thank you.

The first seven paragraphs of Shepherd's argument appear to be only an extended introduction; since they comprise nearly one-third of his entire closing argument, it is initially curious that he devotes so much time to what attorneys usually compress into a single paragraph. One of the critics in this demonstration, however, Edward R. Stein, then a member of a law firm in Ann Arbor and a consultant for the Michigan Supreme Court,[36] suggests a convincing explanation for Shepherd's verbosity at this point. Plaintiff's counsel had just finished, as Stein notes, "on a very high note. This room was hushed." What Shepherd then did was talk "about nothing for five minutes. I've never before seen him talk about nothing, and sound like nothing, for so long. But we had to have that time to switch gears, and I assume he gave us a rest purposefully."[37] Stein's observation about the apparent effect of previous counsel's argument is one that could have been made only by someone in attendance; also, as a member of the audience, Stein is a credible critic of the effect of Shepherd's technique.

Shepherd's extended introduction, however, is noteworthy in two other respects. First, in being as general as it is, when plaintiff's counsel has just made a dramatic finish about the case at hand, it seeks to diminish the import of what has gone before. That is, if the defense has just been thrown a fireball, squarely over the plate from the perspective of the jurors, they might expect counsel to swing strong in a counterattack. But if, instead, defense counsel nonchalantly treats as a ball what has seemed to be a perfect strike, and there is no umpire to make a call, the jurors may think they have overestimated the effect of plaintiff's counsel's argument. Thus, Shepherd conveys that he has this juror responsibility introduction that he customarily gives and he sees no reason not to give it now; i.e., nothing that he has just heard moves him to do anything different this time.

A second aspect of Shepherd's introduction is that, even though the *content* borders on cliche, the way he delivers it is not. If Stein is right, then the jurors will not really be hearing Shepherd for the first couple of minutes; but if they do tune in before Shepherd has reached the meat of his argument, they should appreciate how he is saying what he is saying. An English professor at the University of Texas at Austin[38] is fond of telling his students of Milton that nobody reads *Paradise Lost* to find out what happens in the end; since it is basically the story of Adam and Eve, almost everyone knows what is going to happen. Instead, people read *Paradise Lost* to discover and to enjoy Milton's way of telling a familiar story.

In the first paragraph, Shepherd ostensibly takes the role of guide, which is frequently recommended so that the jury can know what to expect. He backs the jurors up to the time of their selection, trying to put their trial activities into a framework for them. The point here is that plaintiff's counsel essentially did the same thing in his argument. Shepherd is acting as if *he*, and not plaintiff's counsel, has the first argument. In other words, Shepherd conveys that, if this was said before, it was not said correctly; or, if it was said before, it did not sufficiently impress him so that he recalled it. In the next paragraph comes the reminder of the oath, again a traditional technique, but Shepherd uses that as a springboard, not an end in itself. He says that the oath has made the jurors "officers of the Court," a term he uses twice, being a subtle way of paying the jurors a high compliment. Attorneys also generally tell the jury that they have been attentive during the trial; Shepherd makes that statement but then follows it with another, which appears to be sincere: "You've really listened to the evidence." He uses the jurors' attentiveness as a transition to his next statement, why they are "hearing from the lawyers at the point." The answer is certainly not today the same as it was many years ago, when lawyers were much better educated than the masses. Today, he explains, jurors are as educated as attorneys and probably do not need any further explanation of the case. Again, he compliments the jury in a sincere and subtle way. In the fifth paragraph, he tells the jurors that he is talking to them not because he doubts their ability, but because it is his "duty" to do so, prior to their carrying out their sworn "obligation." The synonyms indicate that he feels he and the jury are on equal footing, verified by his describing his talking to them as "just a few minutes *visiting* with you."

He begins the sixth paragraph with an ethical appeal that, if said in an understated way, could seem genuine: "I want to be of some help, if I can." The qualification at the end—"if I can"—demonstrates a modesty that is consistent with his view of parity with the jury. This is not the time, he says, for a lawyer to create false issues or charge the jury emotionally. Notice how he has equated these items, and recall that plaintiff's counsel left the jury emotionally charged; Shepherd has implicitly dismissed his opponent's techniques and possible motives. This is, instead, a time "for some reflection."

Although the first seven paragraphs concern legal topic(s), the only terms that could be said to be used primarily in the legal field are "jurisprudence," which is used rarely even in the legal field, and "evidence," which is so commonly known that it may not even qualify as "legalese." Had Shepherd used legal terminology throughout, he would have defeated his purpose of being one with the jury; they would have realized that he was on a different plane, when it came to analyzing the issues in the case. Instead, he conveys that he thinks the jurors will look at the facts and issues and analyze them as he does.

In paragraph 8, Shepherd brings up what he says should not even be talked about (although he does talk about it), whether someone has a right to file suit for injuries. Actually, Alexander did broach this issue in his opening argument, implying that Korn dragged everyone into court with his allegation of liability. Apparently, Korn has appeared somewhat sympathetic in trial, and Alexander's approach would not be well received now. Thus, Shepherd talks about the other side of the coin; a defendant, even if a corporation, has a right to be heard on the evidence, too. And this means that, even though someone has a right to bring suit, he has no right to win just because he has brought suit; this is diplomatically expressed at the end of paragraph 21.

Shepherd then begins his review of the facts, but prefaces it in paragraph 11 with the caution that the jury disregard anything he might say that conflicts with the evidence. In paragraph 12, Shepherd both conveys sympathy for Korn and rationalizes Alexander's apparent callousness in his opening statement in implying that the extent of Korn's sickness emerged only during trial. Then Shepherd executes a fine play with the notion of appearance. He says that Korn had actually been sick all along "but gave no appearance to anyone of being a man who needed any special protection" (paragraph 12). He suggests that, had Korn appeared sick, the hotel might have taken special care of him. In the next paragraph, Shepherd refers to the assailant, who went up in the elevator with Korn. The assailant's appearance was also deceiving: "There is no evidence that his assailant gave any signs of being a dangerous person." The implication is that, if Korn could not recognize a thief by his appearance, why should the hotel have been able to do so? Also, Korn was as reliant on the thief's appearance (in not exiting the elevator or not leading the thief to his room) as the hotel was on Korn's appearance. In the next few paragraphs, Shepherd examines particular facts of the attack in light of the hotel's inability to have prevented the attack, whatever precautions might have been taken.

The ethical appeal advanced in paragraph 18 derives from Shepherd appearing to have genuine concern about Korn; his desire to help Korn himself ("I wish I could talk to him"), which dispels any idea of Shepherd being a hired gun for the corporation; and his respect for Korn's attorney ("one of the most persuasive people in the community"). Gone is the one-on-one battle that Alexander began to stage in the opening statement; apparently, developments during trial have evidently made that approach untenable. Instead, Shepherd is attempting to cast this dispute resolution as a civilized coming together of minds. He even shows no malice toward the attacker, referring to him as "this fellow" (paragraph 17) and "that young man" (paragraph 22) and refusing to believe he wore the badge of an assailant just because he wore a leather jacket (paragraph 13). A secondary effect of this neutral labeling of the assailant is that it minimizes in the jury's mind the violence and severity of the attack.

Regardless of what happens here, however, Shepherd is confident that Korn will recover, not only because his attorney will assist him, but because Shepherd is convinced that Korn has untapped potential. In a dramatic move that could succeed only if it did not appear intended for drama, Shepherd turns to Korn and says, "I've got faith in you." In this same paragraph (number 21), he also neatly prepares Korn for defeat in the courtroom, by telling Korn that he can be satisfied with having had his case presented as well as it could have been presented. Following that, Shepherd implies the basis for the jury deciding for the defendant, characterizing it as a stand against "psychological arguments" (paragraph 22) and a triumph of what is right ("measure up to your responsibility") over what is sympathetic ("finding against a sick man") (paragraph 23). In summary, the strength of Shepherd's argument is its ethical appeal, and he ultimately urges the jury to reach its decision because of ethics. He therefore tries to induce the jury to act as he makes them think he would. The clear consistency between Alexander's approach, which later had to be softened, and Shepherd's is apparent in Stein's analysis:

> He introduced. . . the kick-in-the-pants argument. "What Arthur Korn needs is a good kick in the pants. All this money isn't going to make him feel any better, if he's that sick. . . .What is he going to spend the money on if all he does is lie in bed all day?" I think John was getting at that when he was talking to Arthur Korn and saying, in effect, "Go ahead, Mr. Korn, you can do it, you can do it better." I think he wanted to give the jury a kick-in-the-pants attitude. In the courtroom it may be offensive to say, "This guy needs a good kick in the pants," but you certainly want one of the jurors to say it in the jury room.[39]

B. *In the Matter of Karen Quinlan*

In a seven-point Civil Action Complaint dated September 10, 1975, the plaintiff, Joseph Thomas Quinlan, sought from the Superior Court of New Jersey an adjudication that his daughter, Karen Ann, was mentally incompetent, and a granting to him of letters of guardianship "with the express power of authorizing the discontinuance of all extraordinary means of sustaining the vital processes of his daughter."[40] His attorney in this cause was Paul W. Armstrong. On September 15, 1975, Daniel R. Coburn, an attorney in New Jersey, was appointed guardian ad Litem of Karen Quinlan for the purposes of the filed action. Acting in response to an Order to Show Cause, Coburn filed an affidavit setting forth his position on the matter. In preparing his affidavit, he visited Karen in the hospital, reported her observable condition in detail to medical experts, and consulted other experts on the medical and legal signs and implications of "brain death." He concludes his affidavit in this way: "Without in any way intending to impugn the intentions or attitudes of any other party to this matter, it is my considered opinion as Karen's guardian and as an attorney-at-law of the State of New Jersey that such action [as 'mercy killing'] is totally without precedent in the law and at this point would constitute a homicide."[41]

When the court later ruled, it made Karen's father the guardian of her property, empowered to manage her business affairs. But it ruled that "it is a medical decision whether or not Karen should be removed from the respirator." Moreover, because of the "continued and magnified" anguish that Karen's father would not escape due to his conflict over the future care of his daughter, the court appointed Coburn to continue as guardian over her person.[42] In March 1976, the Supreme Court of New Jersey held that, upon the concurrence of Karen's family and guardian, her life support systems would be discontinued.[43]

When compared with the rulings of both the lower and the appellate courts, the closing arguments of Coburn and Armstrong reflect the respective outcomes, with the lower court seeming to adopt Coburn's position and the upper court, Armstrong's. (In the New Jersey Supreme Court, Armstrong was not allowed the opportunity to deliver a speech as such, but his position was nonetheless extracted with the usual question-and-answer technique.) What is remarkable about this case, and about these closing arguments, is that both sides had a noble end, and neither was seeking anything from the opposition. Also, the arguments were delivered to the court, not to members of a jury, who are thought to be more susceptible than the court to emotional arguments. Thus, although the topic was potentially fraught with emotion, it was not through this avenue that counsel could expect the best reception from their audience, who was as well aware as anyone of the need for a logical basis for the decision. Coburn's closing argument, which preceded Armstrong's before the court, is followed and analyzed below.[44]

Mr. Coburn. Judge Muir, Counsel, Mr. and Mrs. Quinlan, and the remainder of the Quinlan family:

[1] When I was chosen as guardian in this particular case, I stated on my opening that I felt like the little Dutch boy with 10 fingers and 20 holes in the dike. I had no idea where this case was going, much less what position I should take, or whether I would be right. I can state a couple of things that, as a result of this case, I have come to definite conclusions on.

[2] One is that for those people who happen to know me personally, I think it is safe to say that there is probably nothing in the world I cherish more than my own daughter. I doubt that I would ever see anyone who would have a stronger feeling. I feel Mr. Quinlan is in that position. Whatever the criteria will ever be for a father and a child, Mr. Quinlan should be that criteria.

[3] Last Friday, I happened to pick up the *Daily News* and I saw a picture of Mr. Quinlan going to the mailbox. I am not critical of any media or any other media, but it is incredible that Mr. Quinlan has survived this litigation—the entire thing—and that he has maintained the dignity that he has. It is incredible that the entire case has maintained some degree of dignity. Mr. Quinlan has subjected himself to something that I can't imagine any father or person would want to subject himself to. There are always lingering doubts.

[4] What are the motives? There is no doubt, in my opinion. There is nothing I am more certain of in life than Mr. Quinlan's motives. They are on the highest level, both from the religious point of view and the point of view of a father, which is probably at least in my opinion more important. I can't say anything about Mr. Quinlan. The only thing I can say for Mr. Quinlan is that he doesn't know what he will do if the request is not granted. I will suggest that, as I see it, the relief cannot be granted. That is my opinion.

[5] I hope that whoever, if someone else is selected to be guardian, whether it be myself or someone else, if Mr. Quinlan himself

is not selected guardian, I have my reservations about that because of his position in this case, that he cooperate with whoever the guardian is and whatever the guardian suggests. I am sure of it, and I know Mr. Quinlan said he would not want to do anything that would be contrary to God's will. Unfortunately, I think that God's will is that this case be started, that this case be concluded, and that something else be done for Karen.

[6] I am sure that every effort on Karen's behalf, from the human point of view, is fraught with the risk of death. Dr. Korein said just the tests themselves that will be necessary to determine to a great medical extent what is wrong with Karen may very well kill her. Whatever that may be, I have the utmost confidence in Mr. Quinlan, and that his faith which I respect as much as anything I can, will continue. I really don't think anything else, as to Mr. Quinlan's motives, should be even mentioned.

[7] As to Father Trapasso, I think it is just a wonderful thing that there are people like Father Trapasso in a situation like this. I don't think it was articulated as clearly as it could be, but I am sure part of Father Trapasso's opinion in this case is based on the fact that this case, this entire situation, has had a tremendous effect on the family. I am not talking about as far as finances, or anything else, but the emotional effect has been catastrophic. And one of the factors that had to be considered is what the Pope has said, and what the Catholic Church's teaching is, is the effect on the family. By trying a futile gesture, are we going to ruin what appears to be the remainder of a lovely family? I don't know if that is exactly what he meant, but that is how I interpret the statement.

[8] As to Karen's statements in this case when they occurred, I don't know about Mr. Armstrong, but it would seem that that was contrary to my position in the case to pose every legal obstacle that I could possibly muster to the relief sought in this case. I have absolutely no doubt that Karen Quinlan at some time in her life made statements to the effect that "I don't want to live as a vegetable," that she made statements to the effect of, "I don't want to be kept alive by gadgets," or "I don't want to be in a position where it is a waste of time." I have my serious doubts whether she ever used the phrase "extraordinary means of support," or whatever words she used. I don't understand exactly the recollection of the various members of the family in that regard: I don't know whether it is hoped that that is what she said, or whether at this point they are confident that that is what she said. I find it hard to believe that those are the exact

words which were used. I think the gist of her feeling would be sufficient, at least an expression of her intention.

[9] Unfortunately for the plaintiff, I don't think that the expression of intention has any validity in this Court. This is still a court of law. I feel that there is nothing that can be done, even in the event that Karen wished this. Perhaps the only way she can effectuate her right of self-determination was if she were in a position to sign herself out of the hospital and go to a motel and die, or go home and die. But she can't talk about that possibility, because it doesn't exist. In the event she regains full consciousness, which is highly unlikely, will she be able to ever make a determination to sign herself out of the hospital? The statements attributable to her unfortunately for the Quinlans can have very little weight in this Court.

[10] One thing that should be stated, I have been somewhat amazed during the entire trial at the approach taken by Mr. Armstrong. I know he is very devout in his position, and the word "devout" should be used, because it is a religious position. I think there are other things that may very well have been explored. I am confident that any approach taken in this case, medico-legal, religious, will not change the result one bit. I think the result is a certainty. I think that was a certainty the moment the physicians decided Karen Quinlan was not brain dead. It might have been different if she were brain dead. I would have taken a much different position. I say, as guardian speaking on her behalf, I could see no reason at all to sustain her life if she was dead, because according to the doctors if you are brain dead, you are dead. I am not sure exactly why Mr. Armstrong took that position, but certainly he has carried forth that position through all of the testimony.

[11] We have had references in this case to euthanasia. No one could be more eloquent than Mr. Porzio in his description of the background of situations like this, and I don't believe in coining phrases, and I don't think it is appropriate here, to say anything other than what we are asking for is religious enthanasia. It is as simple as that. It is not medical euthanasia; it is religious euthanasia. No one wants to use the phrase; that is what happened. Putting a religious label on it doesn't change it. There are no exceptions in the law, and there can't be any exceptions, no matter how valid the motives are. Whether it is in a religious framework, or any other framework, it can't be allowed.

[12] The significance of this case, as I see it, will not be in a legal sense. I think the decision will probably—despite requests that

Your Honor define brain death, or say what procedures should be employed should another case arise, or even in this case, I don't think anything of that sort should be done. It should be resolved strictly on the issues before us. Karen Quinlan is not brain dead. She is alive—absolutely—in the words of Dr. Plum.

[13] On that basis, we get to the constitutional argument. There is no argument possible that will allow the termination of life under the Constitution. The significance of the case is that it has raised the issue: the issue of life and death. It is all taboo. No one wants to speak about it. Today, if someone came before me and said, if my daughter and son said I don't want extraordinary means of life support, I would believe that that discussion took place, that those words were used, and they spoke in a religious framework as far as Karen Quinlan's Church; before this case, that was an impossibility. It could not have occurred. Doctors's didn't use that phrase, "extraordinary means of life support." They couldn't even agree on what it meant.

[14] The significance is in the first step. I don't think it is going to be a large step. At least someone has broached the question; and, as a lawyer, I see some advantage to be gained in that. I am not sure that it has not been outweighed by the effect it has had on the Quinlans, on the invasion of their privacy, which is an ironic thing when they are making an argument based on the right of privacy. Probably that right has been violated more times for them than anyone would hope.

[15] I use the word "hope." Obviously no one is going to come in here and say there is a means of recovery. I doubt that anyone will suggest that if Karen makes any recovery in this case at all that it would be to a 21-year-old woman. Certainly physically she can never recover. I think it was Dr. Plum who stated that her atrophied condition, her joints are arthritic, that she will always be, in the sense of physical appearance, grotesque; but that is not the criteria. You can't use a quality of life argument based on what someone looks like, any more than you can go back into Karen's background.

[16] I am saying this in all respect to the family, but it is a point that has to be made. There have been all sorts of discussions as to what caused this. It makes no difference at all whether this was caused from lead poisoning, from her job, from falling in her home, from a drug overdose; Karen is in this condition today. Medically, it might have some significance, but legally it has none.

[17] As to her lifestyle before this, it makes no difference whether she was the Virgin Mary, or Mary Magdalene. It is of no consequence at all. She is in that position. The case has to be decided on that basis. You can't talk about whether this has an effect on the family, in a financial sense, or it hasn't, because that is an artificial criteria.

[18] Karen is entitled to the same treatment as the wealthiest person in the world, or as the poorest person in the world. Everyone is entitled to that. As to the mass hysteria that may flow from this case, one thing we can say for the case of *In re Karen Quinlan* is that in the highest traditions of both the medical and legal proofs, we have had a hearing to determine this case. There aren't any quack doctors. We haven't a family that has an insurance policy with something to gain. There is no personal motive at all on the part of anyone here. None of the lawyers are going to profit from this case. They may profit in a financial sense; they may not. But certainly the price that has been paid by all of us is not worth whatever the rewards may be.

[19] It has been an experience that I hope I never have to go through again in my life as an attorney, because it is just not right for me, or for anyone, to be in a position of life and death. I think this belongs to the Legislature to decide, as Mr. Hyland said. I think once the criteria is established, then the Court and the doctors and the theologians can all apply that criteria. At this point, it can't be done. One of the advantages of the case is that Karen has managed to receive consultation and examination and treatments by perhaps the greatest neurologists in the world. Dr. Plum would not come to this court room if I offered him $5,000. He would not examine her if I offered him $5,000. Dr. Plum did this as a volunteer. Dr. Cook didn't want to be involved in this. They don't want to come to Court and be subjected to cross-examination by lawyers who are picayune. Dr. Loeser had nothing to gain. I am sure Dr. Korein came here as a volunteer. At least the doctors I have consulted, and Dr. Morse and Dr. Javed, have indicated to me that should the determination of this case be against Mr. Quinlan's request, and some other guardian be appointed, they would be willing to get up some sort of committee to screen the other things that are possible here, whether it is the test that Dr. Korein mentioned, or expert mental surgery, or anything else.

[20] It should be made clear that I had no burden to produce witnesses. I didn't have to have Dr. *X* come in and say there is hope,

and Dr. Y to say let's try this. That is not the purpose. Those doctors are available. I am sure a great many of their suggestions will not be applicable to this case because of the circumstances. But I could have paraded hundreds of doctors in here. I could have paraded thousands of people in here with retarded kids, people who are old and who don't want this to happen, people who have been declared dead, to come in here, and what would be accomplished? Nothing. Because this is not the forum for that. It is for the Legislature. This is a court of law, with a simple case. I could have produced no evidence at all on behalf of Karen Quinlan, and it would not have changed the result one single bit. The result is, again, going to be the same. She is not dead, and that is where the case falls.

[21] I would just like to state that the hope exists. No one is a miracle worker, but hope exists; and she is entitled to that right. As Mr. Porzio said, one out of a thousand, or one out of a million, at least that is hope. As it stands now, if nothing else is done for Karen Quinlan, the chances are none out of the million. She is going to die. There is no doubt about it. She is going to die, whether on or off the respirator, unless something is done. She is entitled to that chance. If she dies on an operating table during surgery, at least she had gone out fighting. She hasn't just died. That is why we are sitting here.

[22] We can produce witnesses probably for another three weeks, cross-examine, and that is three weeks less on her timetable, on her life. There is nothing to be accomplished by it. I hope that Your Honor's decision is as speedy as possible, in the event that it is a denial of the petitioner's request, so that something else can be tried.

[23] As to Dr. Korein, with his request, I am sure he said it in good faith. I hate to take it out of context. Dr. Korein has a request that clarification of the unwritten law be stated. I say there is a message to Dr. Korein, to Mr. Armstrong, to Mr. Crowley, and even to Mr. Quinlan with his religious beliefs, and that is: That in the Ten Commandments, the most important Commandment is, "Thou shalt not kill." That is the message that should be given to all of them.

Coburn's first sentence induces an instant liking for the man. Although his age and appearance are not known to us as readers, his affidavit, an excerpt of which is quoted above, shows him to be thorough, thoughtful, and professional. It is this high caliber of individual who begins by comparing himself to "the little Dutch boy." He also admits his initial wonder in his undertaking and is so restrained in expressing his opinions that one tends to trust the "couple of things that, as a result of this case, I have come to have definite conclusions on."

Coburn begins discussing the first of those things in the second paragraph: Quinlan's sincere conviction in what must have been the most difficult decision imaginable. Coburn exalts Quinlan's love for his daughter over even Coburn's love for his own daughter, saying that no one could love a child more than Quinlan loves his. In the third paragraph, Coburn observes how "incredible" it is that Quinlan, along with the entire case, has maintained the existing degree of dignity. He expresses amazement that Quinlan has held up so well, since "[t]here are always lingering doubts." This last statement, about doubt, seems on the surface to be an expression of empathy, but think of its implications for the audience. First, Coburn appears to have come to know Quinlan well, so well, that he almost seems to be speaking for Quinlan. Thus, when Coburn refers to "lingering doubts," the implication is that Quinlan himself may have them; and if *he* does, given his perspective, might not the court? Also, "lingering doubts" may well have been meant to linger in the mind of the court, particularly if its vocalization created an emphasis on the phrase and then a significant pause followed.

Coburn begins his fourth paragraph as if he is snapping his audience out of a lull left by the "lingering doubts"—"What are the motives?" effects an abrupt shift. Again, Coburn says that Quinlan's motives are "on the highest level," but he coins that with the report that Quinlan "doesn't know what he will do if the request is not granted." Subtly, Coburn seems to be suggesting that the relief is primarily for Quinlan. In the next paragraph (the fifth), he then states that Quinlan should not be appointed as guardian, implying that Quinlan's view of "God's will" might be different from someone else's. It is at this point that Coburn shifts his attention to Karen, whose name he has not yet mentioned.

Coburn says he believes God's will is that "something else be done for Karen," even though he is certain that every effort on her behalf "is fraught with the risk of death" (paragraph six). In the seventh paragraph, Coburn considers the opinion expressed by Father Trapasso and cautiously presumes to restate it ("I don't think it was articulated as clearly as it could be"), noting that the conclusion was apparently that a further, "futile gesture" would only threaten the surviving family. But once again, Coburn has delicately shown the emphasis not on Karen, but on others; in words to come, he shows the emphasis to be misplaced.

Family members have apparently testified that, before her affliction, Karen made statements to the effect that she would never want to be kept alive by artificial means. In paragraph eight, he questions the precision of the words imputed to her, "extraordinary means of support," seriously doubting that she could have by accident used the very words that would later be significant in court. He suggests that possibly her family only wished that she had used such words. However, as he notes in paragraph nine, even had Karen expressed such a desire, the law would not allow it to be carried out. Thus, he concludes, regretfully for the Quinlans, that the attribution of such statements to Karen have little legal significance.

In paragraph 10, Coburn once again says that he does not understand something, this time being the approach taken by Armstrong, which is supposedly a religious position. When Coburn does this, he casts doubt on the validity of the conclusion, report, or approach of another. When he questioned the Quinlan family's recollection of Karen's word choice, he suggested a more realistic explanation than remembrance, wishful thinking. With Armstrong's position, though, Coburn does not suggest a way to view it differently. Coburn simply cannot understand Armstrong's argument, since it boils down to whether Karen is brain dead, which the doctors have decided is not true. He says that, were she brain dead, he would have taken a "much different position."

In paragraph 11, Coburn confronts head on what others have apparently been afraid to say: "what we are asking for is religious euthanasia." But, he notes, attaching the term "religious" to the act does not make it legal, regardless of the motives, being an allusion to the apparently pure motives of Karen's father. Coburn conveys that there is not even room for argument on this question by saying simply, "it can't be allowed."

The previous paragraph is the only one in Coburn's argument that squarely addresses the law. In the next paragraph, he states flatly that it is not a legal question that is involved; it is a medical question. As will be seen, however, Armstrong argues that several constitutional guarantees are at issue here. But Coburn refuses to be drawn into a debate on that, and his dismissal of any legal issues could induce his audience to react in the same way. The medical question, he implies, is not a question at all, since it is proven that

Karen is not brain dead. His closing sentence of paragraph 12 appears almost as a revelation: "She is alive—absolutely—in the words of Dr. Plum." That one fact, he argues in paragraph 13, eradicates any constitutional argument, since under no condition does the Constitution allow the termination of life. But Coburn intuits that this case may draw the court's attention; therefore, he suggests a way to give it significance without deciding as the Quinlans want. Now, since this case has occurred, if someone were to be reported as saying that he did not want to be kept alive by "extraordinary means of life support," it would be believed. He implies that, since the term did not emerge before this case, then no one should seriously think that Karen used it around her family.

In paragraph 14, though, as quickly as he gives the case significance, he snatches it away again, for he cannot let the court think that it would be progressive to decide for the plaintiff. All this case has done is broach the "taboo" question of life and death; and while, theoretically, that is an interesting turn for the law, he doubts the value of that turn in comparison to its effect on the Quinlans, in the violation of their privacy. Coburn then notes the irony of their privacy claim for Karen, while their privacy "has been violated more times. . . than anyone would hope."

"Hope" does not make sense in the previous sentence—why would anyone hope that the Quinlans' right of privacy would be violated? Before one has time to question the word, however, Coburn uses it as a transition to Karen's fate, and hope is the underlying rationale for his argument in each of paragraphs 15 through 18. In paragraph 15, he says he knows that she could never resume life as she knew it, due to physical deformity, and transform this into a specious argument based on "what someone looks like." Also unimportant, from a legal standpoint, is what caused her condition (paragraph 16). She is not to be accorded this hope based on the kind of life she lived before or on the financial effect on the family (paragraph 17). In paragraph 18, in saying that Karen is entitled to the same treatment as anyone else, rich or poor, Coburn is saying she is entitled to the same benefit of the doubt that she may survive (hope).

And if his audience has forgotten that concept, Coburn provides a subtle reminder at the beginning of paragraph 19, in using "hope" again, but in a different way, to express the desire that he never again be in a position to decide life and death. This is also where he tells the court that what the plaintiff seeks is premature; unless the legislature sets out criteria first, "it can't be done." He further suggests that the courtroom is definitely not the forum to be setting these criteria either, for many experts, whose opinions would be necessary, do not want to be "subjected" to the examination of "picayune" lawyers. Once this proceeding is over, however, he says, he understands that several of the doctors that have been involved have indicated a willingness to form a committee to assist.

In paragraph 20 Coburn reminds the court that he had no obligation to put on evidence. However, he essentially puts witnesses on by proxy by telling the court he could have "paraded thousands of people in here" who, he implies, are in the same position or Karen or her parents. Such witnesses, of course, are either living or the parents of living children. The term "paraded" calls up the image of not only a great number, but also a festive, celebratory event, suggesting that all of those persons would be glad they were alive, regardless of their afflictions. But he did not do this, for this is a "simple case," reflected in his brief summary statement: "She is not dead, and that is where the case falls."

In paragraph 21, he states the "hope" issue clearly: "hope exists," whether Karen's chances are one in a thousand or one in a million. The result if nothing is done is stated in a short sentence, stark in its bluntness: "She is going to die." He reminds the court that Karen's time is running out; every day that the decision to do something more for her is delayed, she loses. He even requests that the court be speedy in its judgment, lest something happen to Karen in the interim (paragraph 22).

The final paragraph, with "Thou shalt not kill," contains a concession to the religious position taken by plaintiff and his counsel, and an appeal to the court of that nature (in case the judge is himself religious), but it also echoes the absence of any constitutional sanction of the termination of life that Coburn mentions in paragraph 13. Also, given that Coburn's affidavit is still before the court, and presumably a part of the evidence to be considered, the religious allusion calls up the conclusion there, expressed in secular terms, that a mercy killing of Karen "would constitute a homicide." And that is a legal determination that he feels is not open to debate.

Where Coburn would not argue law in detail and discuss relevant cases, Armstrong must. The thrust of his entire closing is summed up in two phrases near the end; throughout, he has sought to show the court that it can be guided by a "thirst for justice," not compassion, and he offers the assurance that "there is no murder here." His argument in full follows:[45]

Mr. Armstrong. If it please the Court, distinguished counsel, members of the Quinlan family:

[1] Dean Roscoe Pound, in the preface to his monumental work on jurisprudence points out that: "Justice is the great interest of man on earth. Of the three instrumentalities of social control by which that interest is made effective, namely, religion, morals, and law, the brunt of the labor in the world of today has fallen upon the law."

[2] Accepting that their daughter and sister, Karen Ann, now lies in a gradually deteriorating chronic vegetative state in the intensive care unit of St. Clare's Hospital; that there is a hopeless prospect of her cure through the art of medicine; counseled by their shared belief and the teachings of the Roman Catholic faith and supported by the love, faith and courage unique to a father and mother, sister and brother, the Quinlan family now turns for guidance to the law personified in this Honorable Court.

[3] Uncontroverted and expert medical testimony adduced during the course of this trial has revealed that Karen Ann Quinlan has sustained massive and irreparable brain damage, and that she now lies in a persistent or chronic vegetative state in the intensive care unit of St. Clare's Hospital where, through the use of a mechanical respirator, her deteriorating bodily functions are maintained.

[4] Let no one falsely state that the Quinlans' plea is based solely upon human compassion. Indeed, it is grounded under the most fundamental principles of common law and the United States Constitution.

[5] This Court clearly has the power to grant relief in this case, and at the same time to frame its decision in a manner that will protect the legitimate interests of all who appear before you today.

[6] The Chancery Court is the supreme guardian of all incompetents, and by an exercise of that venerable doctrine known as the doctrine of substituted judgment, it may exercise on behalf of an imcompetent any right which that unfortunate person could himself, if competent, exercise.

[7] It is submitted that Karen Ann Quinlan could lawfully take the action which is proposed to this Honorable Court, and that the Court may therefore in appropriate circumstances authorize such action on her behalf.

[8] Indeed, no competent adult is required by law to submit to medical treatment which offers no reasonable hope for relief or cure. Illustrative of this principle is the case of *J.F.K. Memorial v. Heston* which is, unfortunately, often relied upon for the opposite proposition. There, a blood transfusion was administered to an injured girl over the objection of her parents.

[9] It was in this case that the New Jersey Supreme Court had occasion to pen the dictum, "That it seems correct to say there is no constitutional right to choose to die." While granting the existence of such dicta, it must be pointed out that the relevant facts in *Heston* were quite different from those in the case at bar.

[10] In *Heston* the important fact to be borne in mind was that Miss Heston's ailment was completely curable, and curable by means of a technique which is practiced thousands of times every day in hospitals all over the world. On the other hand, uncontroverted evidence has shown that Karen's condition is medically hopeless.

[11] In the light of such evidence, another statement in *Heston* would provide sure guidance to this Court. While stating that refusal of treatment in Miss Heston's case would be tantamount to suicide, the Court realized that the situation would be, and I quote, "Arguably different when an individual, overtaken by illness, decides to let it run a fatal course."

[12] Indeed, as outlined in plaintiff's reply brief, the cases whose facts most closely parallel those before this Court all indicate that the refusal of treatment in medically hopeless situations is lawful and permissible. When it is realized that Karen could lawfully consent to the discontinuance of treatment, the Court must then consider whether such withdrawal would be appropriate. That is, as supreme guardian, the Court must ask itself whether the discontinuance of the treatment would serve Karen's best interests. In rendering this decision, the Court must address itself to Karen's physical, moral, spiritual, and material welfare.

[13] The testimony offered at this trial leads us to the conclusion that medicine must be the servant of man; and that technology must be the servant of medicine. The proper role of a physician is to promote the unified function of an organism.

[14] The testimony has also shown that both the treating physicians and the consulted medical experts know of no treatment which can offer any hope of improvement, or even arrest the deterioration of her body. Indeed, it has been testified that were she to have a

sudden hemorrhage, or require major surgical procedures, no doctor would take such measures.

[15] From such testimony, the use of the terms "physical best interests" assumes a new meaning. In such cases, further treatment can provide no medical benefit to the patient, and thus commanding its continuance will in no way further Karen's physical best interests. Surely the Court, charged with determining the best interests of Karen, cannot advance that her maintenance in this chronic vegetative state in any way serves her interests, let alone her best interest.

[16] Next, in determining Karen's moral best interests we ask the Court to take into account that complex of values and attitudes which recognize and give meaning to the term, "dignity of man." At present, Karen lies in St. Clare's Hospital, no more than 60 or 70 pounds of flesh and bone; a poor and tragic creature whose life is no more than a patterned series of the most primitive nervous reflexes, while in this court room it is seriously proposed, in the face of the most compelling contrary medical testimony, that her now disunified and unperceiving body be constrained to function against all its natural impulses.

[17] Could anything be more degrading to a human being—a human being who has come on this earth full of love and promise, who has known peace and joy, who has been the daughter of Joseph and Julia Quinlan? Can anything be more degrading, than to be offered up as a living sacrifice to the materialistic and misguided belief that death can somehow be cheated, if only we find the right combination of wires and gauges, transistors and tubes?

[18] Let her own prior expressions guide the way for those whom fate has charged with the decision.

[19] In conversation with those whom she held most dear, mother, sister and brother, confidante and friend, Karen's own words emerge to light the way. Evidence has shown that from a medical and religious point of view the use of the respirator and intensive care facilities in Karen's case is extraordinary, by reason of the unprecedented commitment of medical resources and personnel and the hopeless nature of Karen's condition.

[20] In addition the Court, acting as guardian, cannot fail to consider the tenets of the faith to which Karen belongs. That faith, which holds that life is good but not an absolute good, and that death is an evil but not an absolute evil, wisely teaches that man need not make use of extraordinary means to preserve earthly life. And, lastly,

the Court as guardian must realize expenditures and liabilities incurred on behalf of an incompetent should carry with them some reasonable hope of benefit.

[21] All the evidence indicates that Karen will receive no benefit from continuation of treatment and, therefore, neither she nor her estate nor indeed society should be charged with the burden that continued treatment would entail.

[22] For the foregoing reasons, then, it is clear that the Court would be acting properly as supreme guardian if it consented to the withdrawal of the extraordinary life support measures currently being administered to Karen Quinlan.

[23] It will be recalled, Your Honor, that Joseph Quinlan has made this unusual request within the framework of a guardianship petition. Within such a framework it is submitted that, should the Court not authorize the proposed withdrawal of treatment, Joseph Quinlan is nonetheless a fit person.

[24] Indeed, he is the fittest of persons to serve as guardian for his daughter. Testimony has shown him to be a loving father, interested only in the welfare of his family and children. Testimony, as well as his appearance before you today, has shown him to be a man of sound judgment and abundant good faith. Before taking any action, he has sought medical guidance, moral guidance, and guidance from this Court. He has stated that he would abide by whatever judgment the law should render, and would never take it upon himself to act in opposition to that judgment.

[25] Taking into account the good faith of Joseph Quinlan, and the natural bond existing between him and Karen, this Court, we feel, cannot deny him at least this small comfort: that he be recognized before the law as, what he is and always will be, the father and guardian of Karen Ann Quinlan.

[26] We now turn the Court's attention to the constitutional arguments advanced in support of the plaintiff's petition. Plaintiff contends that, while the determination of the constitutional issue is not necessary for the granting of the instant petition, failure to grant such would violate the constitutional rights of both Karen Ann Quinlan and her family.

[27] Plaintiff submits the State cannot, without demonstrating a contrary interest both compelling and secular, interfere with the free exercise of the Quinlans' religious beliefs, with their personal decisions, or with their sovereignty over their own bodies. The right to privacy includes individual and familial decisions to terminate

the futile use of extraordinary medical measures.

[28] The evidence has shown that Karen has expressed a desire not to be subjected to extraordinary medical treatment, and that the family as a group has decided that her wishes should be honored. The right of individuals to be sovereign over their own person was enunciated by the United States Supreme Court as early as 1891 in the case of *Union Pacific Railway Co. v. Botsford* and was extended to include familial autonomy in *Meyer v. Nebraska* and *Pierce v. Society of Sisters* in the early 1920s. It received its fullest exposition in the case of *Griswold v. Connecticut* which found support for the right to privacy in all the specific guarantees enumerated in the Bill of Rights as well as in the Ninth Amendment protection granted to unenumerated rights.

[29] This right has grown to include individual and familiar life-influencing decisions, and it cannot be denied that a family is legally competent to make the decisions implicit in the plaintiff's request.

[30] Further, the plaintiff sets forth that the free exercise clause of the First Amendment, as applied to the State's Fourteenth Amendment, protects the right of Karen Ann Quinlan and her family to discontinue the futile use of extraordinary medical measures. Plaintiff contends that this request is the product of a religiously based decision, made in accordance with the tenets of the religion to which he and his family belong.

[31] The evidence has shown that the Quinlan family, including Karen Ann Quinlan, are members and believe in the Roman Catholic faith which teaches that, as stated in the discourse of Pius XII admitted into evidence: Natural reason and Christian morals say that man, and whoever is entrusted with the task of taking care of his fellow man, has the right and the duty in case of serious illness to take the necessary treatment for the preservation of life and health. This duty that one has toward himself, toward God, toward the human community, and in most cases toward certain determined persons, derives from well-ordered charity, from submission to the Creator, from social justice, and even from strict justice, as well as from devotion toward one's family. But normally one is held to use only ordinary means, according to circumstances of persons, places, times, and culture. That is to say, means that do not involve any grave burden for oneself or another.

[32] A more strict obligation would be too burdensome for most men and would render the attainment of the higher, more impor-

tant good, too difficult. Life, health, and temporal activities are in fact subordinated to spiritual ends. On the other hand, one is not forbidden to take more than the strictly necessary steps to preserve life and health, as long as he does not fail in some more serious duty.

[33] Given this total subordination, it makes no difference that a given action is obligatory, or merely optional, so long as it is done or chosen within the framework of man's quest for spiritual good. If it is done within such a framework, it is, we submit, entitled to the protection offered by the free exercise clause of the First Amendment as applied to the states through the Fourteenth Amendment, and can be overcome only by a state interest no less compelling than that required to overcome a positive command.

[34] Moreover, the Quinlan family believes that in the quest of the highest spiritual good, familial decisions can have equal weight with individual decisions, especially with regard to an incompetent; and that medical advice can influence, but not determine, individual and familial decisions.

[35] As Pope Pius XII stated: "In ordinary cases one will grant that the anesthesiologist has the right to act in this manner, but he is not bound to do so unless this becomes the only way of fulfilling another certain moral duty." The rights and duties of the doctor are correlative to those of the patient. The doctor, in fact, has no separate or independent right where the patient is concerned. In general, he can take action only if the patient explicitly or implicitly, directly or indirectly, gives him permission. The technique of resuscitation, which concerns us here, does not contain anything immoral in itself. Therefore, the patient, if he were capable of making a personal decision, could lawfully use it and, consequently, give the doctor permission to use it. On the other hand, since these forms of treatment go beyond the ordinary means to which one is bound, it cannot be held that there is an obligation to use them, nor, consequently, that one is bound to give the doctor permission to use them.

[36] "The rights and duties of the family depend in general upon the presumed will of the unconscious patient if he is of age and *sui juris*. Where the proper and independent duty of the family is concerned, they are usually bound only to the use of ordinary means.

[37] "Consequently, if it appears that the attempt at resuscitation constitutes in reality such a burden for the family that one cannot in all conscience impose it upon them, they can lawfully insist that the doctor should discontinue these attempts, and the doctor

can lawfully comply. There is not involved here a case of direct disposal of the life of the patient, nor of euthanasia in any way: This would never be licit. Even when it causes the arrest of circulation, the interruption of attempts at resuscitation is never more than an indirect cause of the cessation of life, and one must apply in this case the principle of double effect and of *voluntarium in causa*."

[38] Here the State, in its case, has demonstrated no compelling interest in overcoming either the Quinlans' right of privacy, or their right to the free exercise of their religion.

[39] They have stated that such right may, in some circumstances, be overcome. And we agree with this, as a general proposition of law. But they have cited us to no law which requires that State interest prevail in the instant circumstances; nor have they cited us to any case whose relevant facts are similar to those before this Court.

[40] Their proofs in this regard have been limited to the vaguest of generalities which by no means reach the constitutional standard quoted by Mr. Justice Brennan in *Sherbert v. Verner*: "It is basic that no showing merely of a rational relationship to some colorable state interest in the regulation of a subject would suffice; in this highly sensitive constitutional area, only the gravest abuses, endangering paramount interests, give occasion for permissive limitation."

[41] Thus, in the absence of a demonstrated compelling State interest, it is respectfully submitted that the Court would err in not honoring the constitutionally based requests of the plaintiff.

[42] In addition, medical testimony presented in this case bears out plaintiff's contention that continuation of the treatment currently being administered to Karen would, if mandated by the Court, constitute cruel and unusual punishment of the type proscribed by the Eighth Amendment of the United States Constitution.

[43] We support the requests of Mr. Collester and Mr. Einhorn that guidance be given to the Prosecutor's Office and to St. Clare's Hospital, and we think that the guidance should be given to the physicians as well, with regard to the effect on all of them of the granting of plaintiff's request.

[44] The fact that the withdrawal of treatment is in the best interests of Karen leads to the conclusion that the Court should authorize consent to such withdrawal. The fact that such consent may be lawfully given is based on the determination that the doctors and the hospital have exercised sound medical judgment. That is, in the face of hopeless and irreversible coma, where life processes

are sustained only by extraordinary means, continued treatment serves no valid medical purpose; and that withdrawal of such extraordinary means would not constitute homicide since the causality implicit in such withdrawal is not predicated upon a breach of duty to Karen and is, therefore, not culpable.

[45] Such determinations of the rights of parties *inter sese* are the proper subject of a declaratory judgment, and may properly serve as a basis for enjoining both criminal prosecution and civil or administrative suits or proceedings.

[46] Thus it is, Your Honor, that we conclude our review of the sad and weighty issues that have brought us here before you in rare unanimity of spirit. The plea of all of us through this trial has been: Help us resolve these issues.

[47] The Quinlans' request, which initiated these proceedings, is clear: We love Karen, but we know that hope is gone. Let her return to her God, but let none who suffer by her illness suffer yet the more by her departure.

[48] This Court, moved not by compassion but by thirst for justice, can grant that request to the full. It can say not only: Karen, pass on in peace; it can say as well: Mr. Hyland, Mr. Collester, there is no murder here. Mr. Einhorn, your clients may accede to the request. They have done all the law can ask, and more.

[49] Dr. Morse and Dr. Javed, you have come to us for guidance. We give it to you now. Six long months of vigils over Karen's bed, six long months of loving conversation with Joe and Julia in their anguish, six long months of searching and of doubt, these will be counted nothing by us. Take counsel, once again among yourselves, far from crowded court rooms. We have seen enough to know that your decision will be true. Take your sister Karen, and if in your heart of hearts, counseled by your brother physicians and unfettered by fears that uncomprehending law will stay your hand, you determine that further ministrations would be no more than useless punishment, return her with our blessing to that state where her own body can heed, if it will, the gentle call that beckons her to lasting peace.

That Armstrong fairly ends on a plea to do justice shows the overall structure of his speech, for he begins with a quotation in which Pound notes that the law carries the primary burden for doing justice in the world. In his next sentence (which is also his next paragraph), Armstrong then says that the Quinlan family has turned to the law, "personified in this Honorable Court." There is no amount of transcribing effort that could make this second paragraph into more than one sentence; one dependent structure is piled atop another, awaiting the connection to the independent clause that ends (and allows the formation of) the sentence. Even in speech, it would be apparent that Armstrong was leading up to a conclusion (the personification clause); the intonation in his voice at the end of each dependent structure would have signaled that. This is a formalized way of writing and an even more formalized way of speaking, and the sentence ends with a formal designation of the court. Because of its difference, this technique may have been designed to get the audience's attention. It also, however, is reminiscent of a sermon.

Sermons often employ somewhat dramatic phrasing, along with formal language; both seem biblical and serious. Notice the formality of "gradually deteriorating chronic vegetative state," "hopeless prospect," and "the art of medicine." At the same time, observe that terms often used in a religious context also appear: "counseled," "belief," "teachings," "faith," and "guidance." Although Armstrong will later make an explicit argument based on the Quinlans' religious beliefs, he is not doing so now. However, he cloaks what he says is a matter of "the law" in a religious veil. Indeed, throughout the balance of his argument, when Armstrong is discussing the law in general, he often relies on unusual structure within sentences and formalized terms. But when he is discussing case law or making purely logical appeals, his language is unemotional and his sentences are less complicated.

Armstrong's third paragraph is again a single sentence and, again, could not be written as anything else; while it reveals much of the same information as the sentence before it, this later sentence is more factual and less inviting of an emotional response. It is therefore a suitable transition to the next sentence (paragraph four), which rebuts the notion that the Quinlan's plea is based only on compassion (but see the formality in "[l]et no one falsely state"). Instead, the Quinlans' argument is based in common law and the Constitution. This sentence, along with the next two (paragraphs five and six), are ostensibly bare bones factual statements with pure logical appeal. Armstrong, however, with nothing but additional adjectives, inserts ethical and emotional appeal into these three sentences: "the *most fundamental* principles," "Court *clearly* has the power," "protect the *legitimate* interests," "the *supreme* guardian," "the *venerable* doctrine," and "that *unfortunate* person."

In sharp contrast is paragraph seven, having *no* such terms. The term "lawfully" there is not an embellishment, nor is "appropriate"; both of those terms are necessary for the legal meaning Armstrong advances. "Honorable" is often used by attorneys before the reference to the court in which they are appearing. Thus, in his clearest statement of the law, he relies on only logical terminology. Next, in paragraph eight, which contains an example of case law, Armstrong is remarkably dry; two exceptions are in the unusual structure of the second sentence ("Illustrative of this principle is"), which people seldom use in speech, and the editorial comment, "unfortunately." The last sentence in that paragraph contains not one emotional or formal device. The first sentence in paragraph nine, however, contains the elaborate phrasing, "the New Jersey Supreme Court had occasion to pen the dictum." Was that only a slip in style, or did Armstrong intend to embellish the high court's action with his language and therefore tempt the present court to look more with favor on the dictum?

The language in paragraphs 10 and 11 could appear in a legal brief; it is straightforward and unembellished. Paragraph 12 is so logical and unemotional as to have been produced by another author; it serves as the introduction to the following discussion of Karen's "physical, moral, spiritual, and material welfare." In this context, surrounded by the kind of language that is here, "supreme guardian" loses its holy connotation and suggests only responsibility. The symmetry in the first sentence of paragraph 13 is fine enough to be plagiarized from a published author (though no such charge is made here): "that medicine must be the servant of man; and that technology must be the servant of medicine." Following that is a statement of apparent fact, as precisely designed as a prescription: "The proper role of a physician is to promote the unified function of an organism." Paragraphs 14 and 15, still discussing Karen's physical condition, could have been read from the unimpassioned statement of an attending physician.

Paragraph 16, however, begins to consider Karen's moral welfare, and the language is appropriately elevated to another level of formality and to metaphor: "a poor and tragic creature whose life is no more than a patterned series of the most primitive nervous reflexes," "a human being who has come onto this earth full of love and promise," "offered up as a living sacrifice," and "Karen's own words emerge to light the way."

Paragraph 20 is where Armstrong has the opportunity to talk about Karen's spiritual welfare. It is at first curious that he devotes no more than two sentences to this topic here, the only one of substance being a restrained summary of a tenet of her faith. He then shifts to her material welfare. It may be that Armstrong felt that to succumb to the opportunity to discuss religious basis here would be to cause the court to feel he was relying too heavily upon it, that his legal foundation was too weak. Instead, as we have seen, the religious persuasion can be effected through more subtle means.

Paragraph 22 summarizes the physical, moral, spiritual, and material welfare bases for the court's action. In paragraphs 23-25, Armstrong makes the case for Quinlan being Karen's guardian; these paragraphs show even less emotion than those of Coburn, when he was discussing Quinlan. Most of the remainder of Armstrong's argument consists of a logical, nondramatic presentation of constitutional issues. Paragraphs 26-29 concern the right of privacy. In paragraphs 30-37, Armstrong describes the constitutional protection afforded the Quinlans' decision because of its religious basis. The last three of these paragraphs are quotations from Pope Pius XII. Paragraphs 31-34, while they describe what the Quinlans believe, read as if they were a part of theology discussion, but not a moving sermon. Again, Armstrong has resisted the temptation to make emotional appeals while discussing religion; instead, he converts his discussions of religion into logical appeals. Paragraphs 38-41 demonstrate the absence of a compelling state interest. In paragraph 42, he notes violation of the Eighth Amendment if Karen is subjected to further medical treatment. Paragraphs 44-45 serve as a summary of the legal issues and proffered basis for the decision sought by the plaintiff. The last sentence in paragraph 44 demonstrates Armstrong's masterful use of adjectives. This time, however, his purpose is to pack the single sentence (complex though it is) with terms of legal significance: "hopeless and irreversible coma" (a criterion he has drawn from case law), "extraordinary means," and "no valid medical purpose." He then dispels the homicide issue with an observation that its elements are simply missing. In paragraph 45, he tells the court that what the plaintiff seeks is within the court's power.

The legal issues aside, Armstrong can return to the emotional and ethical appeals. In the part of his argument equivalent to a complainant's prayer in a petition. Armstrong constructs what is more akin to a religious prayer: "Help us resolve. . . these sad and weighty issues" (paragraph 46); "Let her return to God" (paragraph 47). Symmetry and language not unlike that often found in the Bible close paragraph 47: "let none who suffer by her illness suffer yet the more by her departure." In paragraph 48, Armstrong suggests how the court can answer all of those involved. Notice the reverence (like in a bestowed blessing) in the suggested response to Karen, "pass on in peace," but the practicality of the answer to those who fear legal transgression: "there is no murder here."

One can scarcely even read paragraph 49 without having an emotional response; its effect on the listeners must have been profound. Clearly, this is a eulogy, with all the markings of careful preparation. The thrice repeated "six long months" echoes like a death knell; referring to Karen's parents by their first names evokes the intimacy of a funeral. The directive, "[t]ake counsel. . . far from crowded courtrooms," is too formal to be uttered extemporaneously. The word choices and phrasing that follow not only convey a solemn formality and have religious connotations, but also are poetic in their memorableness: "your sister Karen," "in your heart of hearts," "your brother physicians," "unfettered," "stay your hand," "ministrations," "blessing," "heed," and "the gentle call that beckons her to lasting peace."

Given Armstrong's combination of *logos*, a rationale for the court to decide for the plaintiff, and *pathos*, motivation for the decision, one may wonder at the ruling of the lower court. The reason may have been as simple as a reluctance to make new law on that level. It may also have been that the emotional appeal, particularly in the closing of the argument, was so overwhelming, that the judge doubted his own ability to decide on the basis of legal issues alone.

C. *The Case of Sacco and Vanzetti*

The case of Sacco and Vanzetti has the tarnished distinction of being infamous. The two men were arrested on a streetcar in May 1920 and convicted a little over one year later for "a repulsive murder."[46] Their arrest drew no attention, and their conviction warranted "exactly seven and a half inches on an inside page" of the *New York Times*. However, in the six years between their conviction and execution, much of the public became convinced that Sacco and Vanzetti were guilty, not of murder, but of being foreigners in a country that was having "a red nightmare": "All the ardors of Hun-hating were therefore turned against the Reds, the Bolsheviks. Every foreigner was suspect."[47] They became heralded representatives of the emerging working class: "This story of two alien workers in America is an epic of all aliens and of all workers in America. . . .They demonstrated what grandeur there may be in simple, modest workers."[48]

The cause of these two men, who were subjected to what some have called "a frame-up implicit in the social structure. . . .a perfect example of the functioning of class justice,"[49] had a following that spanned social strata by the time of their deaths:

> Up to the last moment millions of men and women pleaded to a smiling governor for a reprieve; delegations of workers and professional men, outraged intellectuals, horror-stricken persons from every walk of life hammered in desperation upon the mind and heart of a smiling governor.[50]

And when those efforts failed, and the executions were over, the *New York Times* devoted five pages to the event.[51]

As history tells us, nothing appeared out of line with the trial until some time after its passing. Then, the charge was that something other than facts resulted in the conviction of Sacco and Vanzetti. Frederick G. Katzmann was the District Attorney who prosecuted the case and delivered the closing argument at the end of a six-week long trial. The bulk of this four-hour argument was devoted to a painstaking review of the evidence. That alone would seem to belie an attempt to ignore the facts; in other words, if the jury is bound to convict for other reasons, why bother with such a detailed factual analysis? What is perhaps more remarkable about Katzmann's argument, however, is the strong ethical appeal it reveals, causing him to appear to be anything but a hatchet man and anything but prejudiced against the defendants. In fact, his approach would make one think that his speech was coming at the *end* of the seven-year story of Sacco and Vanzetti, when strong public support had grown for the two men, instead of at the beginning, when they were unknown. The excerpts below demonstrate this.[52]

[1] May it please your Honor, Mr. Foreman and gentlemen of this jury, I congratulate you sincerely that the hour of your several deliverances is about at hand. I can conceive not only of no more important duty that may fall upon the shoulders of citizens of the county of Norfolk, but also no more trying duty than you have been performing for the past long six weeks. I congratulate your Honor, both these defendants and the Commonwealth, may I have the honor

to repeat, because of the quality of the service of you 12 men; and I know that I bespeak, as well, the thanks of the defense as I do of the Commonwealth in saying that sofar as 12 human beings could with the utmost devotion to duty perform a duty, from your very bearing in the court room it has been apparent that you were determined to do your duty and to do it to the utmost, and your countenances bespeak the intelligence which assures us that you will do it well.

[2] In congratulating you that the hour of your deliverance is at hand, I want also to congratulate my office, and self-congratulation plays a part in that, that as you are about to assume this momentous of duties, the burden is about to be lifted from our shoulders. For 14 months, gentlemen of the jury, our office has been weighed down with the responsibility that attached from a series and train of events over which we had no control, and God willing, had we been able to control it, would never have come to our office door.

[3] My brother has said that this is a rare opportunity for a district attorney. I say, to the contrary, gentlemen, that if I could have directed the train of events in South Braintree on April 15, 1920, I never would have had that opportunity. Heaven only knows how I have been borne down by it to the utter distraction of the routine work of the office for these long 14 months. You have had it for six weeks, gentlemen. Our office has had it for more than a year.

[4] And while I am speaking gentlemen in passing and before opening either upon the law or the facts in my argument, I want to congratulate both of these defendants upon the quality of the defense that they have had through the medium of two trained, skillful and experienced attorneys. They could not be more ably defended. Neither could they be defended with greater devotion to duty than have the gentlemen who have been representing them exercised and performed. But above that and above the fact that there are 12 good men from Norfolk County who are not going to be swayed either by prejudice of by fear, nor, worse than anything else, by emotion, that would make them fail in their duty, you 12 men, this trial has been presided over by a Justice of eminent person attainment.

[5] It is to be assumed, gentlemen of the jury, that a lawyer, a member of the bar, who is called to the high office of Justice of the Superior Court, will have, as a matter of course, learning commeasurate with that office, and that is pre-eminently true in the case of the learned justice who here presides. But there are some qualities,

gentlemen, that even a Justice of the Supreme Court cannot acquire, he cannot gain by experience, and those qualities must be born in him, and I refer above all to the quality of real human nature; a kindly heart and an inherent sense of justice that cannot be swerved from an impartial performance of duty to both parties to a case. And in that fact, perhaps more than any one fact, more than the presence of you men, more than the presence of able counsel, are the defendants to be congratulated that they have such Justice presiding over their destinies in a matter that has involved, as has been said over and over again, their very existence.

[6] May I say a word to you, gentlemen, about your duties to correct an unconsciously erroneous statement of the law given by my brother Moore. When you gentlemen retire to your jury to perform this most sacred of duties that may fall to the lot of 12 human beings, the matter is not to be decided save upon your consciences and upon the evidence. As he said, and well said, if there should come a division of opinion among you, our Supreme Court has laid down the law that while a juryman should never, never yield where he has a reasonable doubt conscientiously, that is not the whole rule of conduct that the Supreme Court has laid down for his guidance. It is further than that, and the Supreme Court has asked those who may find themselves in a well defined minority to give heed to the opinions of their fellows and to consider if they, the minority, possess such learning, such experience and such mental attainments that they must be right and the others wrong and to hearken to the voice and to the argument of the others and to consider well the fact that others and others in majority have a different opinion, whichever way that opinion may be.

[7] That, as I conceive it and as I understand the law is the true law of the conduct of jurors in their deliberations. And that rule never requires a juryman to give up a conscientious doubt, if that be his difference of opinion from his fellows, but he must look to his fellows, he must listen to them and he must consider if he personally, or if they—if he has fellows with him in the minority—are possessed of such superior wisdom that they are right and the others are wrong, and if they find that not the case, to yield when they so find that fact.

[8] I have listened to the arguments of learned counsel through a long morning, and I have wondered why it was that the tremendous force of personality and argument exhibited by both counsel has been directed almost entirely, gentlemen of the jury, to the

defense of the defendant Sacco and almost not an appreciable portion of either argument devoted to the defense of the defendant Vanzetti.

[9] Is it, gentlemen of the jury, that neither counsel who have argued to you have confidence in the alibi of the defendant Vanzetti, and that it is hopeless in their opinion, and that all their tremendous effort and intelligence must be directed to pulling out a verdict in favor of the defendant Sacco if they can, and that the alibi of the defendant Vanzetti does not satisfy these two gentlemen themselves? It may well be, gentlemen, but whatever the opinion of counsel, myself or the defendants' counsel, that is of no consequence to you. We are not allowed to express our personal opinions to you. It is not evidence. You are the men who are going to determine what the facts are; and I ask you to consider, in the light of what has transpired this very morning in this court room, if that is not a fact that you may well find.

[10] It is akin, gentlemen of the jury, to the opening made by other learned, skillful and experienced counsel. He never whispered a word to you, gentlemen, when he opened this case, as to where Vanzetti was on April 15th. And more than that, gentlemen, he never even suggested on the day that he opened this case for the defense, that they were prepared to admit that the defendants, Sacco and Vanzetti, were down in West Bridgewater at Simon Johnson's house on the night of May 5th, and if I forget everything else in my argument in what I conceive to be the orderly presentation of it, I hope I won't overlook that, gentlemen, because it is of tremendous probative force. The acts of counsel, gentlemen, bind the defendants themselves.

* * *

Mr. Jeremiah McAnarney. You made a statement a minute ago, that is you challenged me. You have said it too important a matter. You have said my questions with regard to Harry, the tailor, were addressed to this woman at a certain time, the questions in regard to Harry, the tailor, were asked on Monday. Mrs. Andrews testified the last of the week and the first of the week. Saturday she testified and Harry, the tailor, saw that in the paper Saturday, Morning, Harry, the tailor, came to me. Monday, morning in this court, by the records of this court, I examined Mrs. Andrews and asked her if she did not know Harry, the tailor, so long as it is important and as long as the truth is as I say it, I would like to have you acknowledge it.

[11] *Mr. Katzmann.* I always, Brother McAnarney, acknowledge the truth from any source.

Mr. Jeremiah McAnarney. Well, I would like it from me.

[12] *Mr. Katzmann.* Including you when you read from the record, sir.

Mr. Jeremiah McAnarney. Thank you.

[13] *Mr. Katzmann.* And if that is the record, I accept it. Whatever may be the fact as to when she testified, I said it was in cross-examination, and it was in cross-examination, and if it was after he was visited by Fay and by Kurlansky, when that part of my argument you should disregard, that it was before either one of them had seen them. I knew it was in cross-examination, because I took it from my own notes, and that is all I knew. Lola Andrews' testimony, gentlemen, still stand.

[14] And I call your attention, as I would have, of course, had I not been very kindly corrected by my brother, that Lola Andrews went over to the jail in February of this year and walked about the place, through the bakery and through the various rooms and wandered over of her own volition to an iron fence and looked down in a corridor and studied a man she saw down there for 15 minutes and she says that man is Sacco and that the defendant Sacco is the man who directed her into Rice & Hutchins factory.

* * *

[15] Now Gentlemen, I have tried you beyond what I ought. I trust you will overlook it in a public servant who is seeking to do his duty and to do no more. If I had my way I would not have trespassed upon your time or your strength at all, but I have been sworn here to perform a duty to the people of this district.

[16] It is my duty as a public prosecutor to see that the constitutional guarantee to you, to your fellows, and to your families and friends within this district is upheld, to the end that your lives and your property and your safety may be assured. If I fail in the prosecution of my duty to use every honorable, every reasonable effort to keep that guarantee under the constitution, then I am an inefficient public servant. My brother said this was a wonderful case for a district attorney. Gentlemen, this case means nothing whatever to me personally, I never laid an eye on these two defendants until the day of May 6th. I could have had no personal feeling. I possess none now whatever. I am struggling with all my humble ability to perform that duty impersonally against these defendants.

[17] If the Commonwealth has satisfied you beyond a reasonable doubt that they are guilty, the Commonwealth expects you to say so like men of honor and like men of courage. And the Commonwealth expects you to say they are not guilty if it has failed to satisfy you in accordance with the requirements of law.

[18] Make a decision, gentlemen, this case can never be more ably tried in the interests of these defendants than it has been in this trial. They have had their day in court, and the Commonwealth has had its day in court. Both parties desire a final decision on this accusation. In reaching that decision the Commonwealth asks of you that you sweep aside any consideration of personal pity, which I grant you must feel for these defendants, or for the wife and child of one of them.

[19] A jury must decide the facts judicially. The question of where the truth lies here is a cold proposition of fact that is to be decided without any regard to those who may be deprived of a husband and a father by your decision. If you were to bring about a miscarriage of justice—and I know you won't—because you would allow feelings of sympathy to sway you from a just verdict, you would have failed in the administration of the law, and indeed the law itself would have failed. You are now between the verdict the most important cog in the wheels and machinery of justice, and if you fail to function properly the whole machine and public justice stops and is not administered properly.

[20] Leave any consideration of sympathy for Mrs. Berardelli or sympathy for Mrs. Parmenter out of the case. Leave any sympathy for Mrs. Sacco or her boy out of this case. If her husband is guilty and the Commonwealth has proven it, he did not have sympathy for Mrs. Berardelli and Mrs. Parmenter, and he should have none extended to him.

[21] The question is one of fact, gentlemen, arrived at under the rules of law. It has been said to you that your decision will take away the lives of two men if it be that of guilty. Well, gentlemen, that is not so in one sense. You are not taking away the lives of the defendants by finding them guilty of a murder of which they are guilty. The law takes their lives away and not you. It is for you to say if they are guilty and you are done. You pronounce no sentence of death. Does the physician who is called in to a patient who is dying and who administers all the skill that he possesses to seek a recovery and if the malady with which the patient is afflicted is fatal and that patient dies, has the physician taken her life? You are

the consultants here, gentlemen, the twelve of you, and the parties come to you and ask you to find what the truth is on the two issues of guilt or innocence. Gentlemen of the jury, do your duty. Do it like men. Stand together you men of Norfolk.

Katzmann begins with the traditional compliment to the jury, couched in formal terms. In fact, his entire argument is characterized by formal style, which is probably mainly explained by its date of 1921, a time when lawyers were fewer in number and the profession was composed of more upper class members than today. Being less accessible to the general populace, the legal profession also undoubtedly had then more of a mystique than it does today, and Katzmann's language suggests that it was somewhat of a gentlemen's club. In using such formal language with the jurors, he conveys that he accepts them into the club. In the particular nature of his compliments, he reveals that he sees in them the signs of social class distinction: "your very *bearing* in the court room. . .and your *countenances* bespeak the *intelligence* which assurs [sic] us that you will do [your duty] well" (paragraph one). Especially if the jurors are not all members of the upper class, they could be flattered by Katzmann's assumption that they are. The first paragraph also contains biblical allusions or words and phrases with religious overtones ("bespeak," "deliverances"). Katzmann continues to use such language through his argument, but never with the apparent intent to create a particular emotional appeal based on religion. Instead, such words, seeming to characterize his way of speaking, convey that he is a righteous, God-fearing man.

In the second paragraph, Katzmann continues the compliment, but in a way that reflects favorably as well on the prosecution. Not only does he congratulate his office, but he notes that they have been working on the case for 14 months, which suggests their thoroughness. Also, in saying that his office is now passing the baton to the jurors, he implies that they have become an extension of the prosecution and its work. To dispel, however, any thoughts that he and his co-workers enjoyed having such an absorbing case, he adds that, had they had any control over it, it would "God willing. . . never have come to our office door" (notice how he has slipped in the reference to God).

Katzmann begins the third paragraph with a reference to opposing counsel, "[m]y brother." Not only does this term perpetuate the idea of a gentlemen's club, but it implies his "brotherly" affection even for his opponent. Defense counsel has pointed out that the case is a "rare opportunity" for Katzmann, who is obliged to say that, had he had control over matters, it would have been an opportunity he would have missed. At this point, Katzmann is faced with a choice of how to continue this point, which he should; he needs to say *why* he would have missed this opportunity if he could have. One option is to say that he would have preferred never to have learned of such a brutal crime and its grisly details, and never to have been faced with the prospect of sending two men, one a family man, to their deaths. But that is a part of his *job*; he cannot admit that he would prefer not to do the very things for which he was hired. Instead, he refers to that job, and says that, as "only *Heaven* knows," he has almost had to neglect his other work, just to attend to this case for the last fourteen months.

The compliment of opposing counsel in paragraph 4 could strike some as merely a matter of courtesy, increasing Katzmann's ethical appeal. However, it also has a logical basis. The defendants have had their case put forward as best it could be; the implication is that, if the jury nevertheless believe they are guilty, then they probably are. Katzmann slips in another compliment of the jury here, suggesting that he knows they will not be swayed by prejudice, fear, or, "worse than anything else," emotion, which could cause them to "fail in their duty." At the end of paragraph 4, he begins the compliment to the judge, which he continues into the fifth paragraph. There is a rational purpose here, as well: the jury should not think that the trial was conducted in any way that was prejudicial to the defendants.

In paragraphs 6 and 7, Katzmann completes the description of the Supreme Court's ruling in *Allen v. United States*, which evidently was slighted by defense counsel. Even in this ostensibly purely legal concern, Katzmann's language has religious overtones: "sacred," "fall to the lot," "give heed," "hearken to the voice." Thus, at the close of paragraph 5, Katzmann is talking about any in the minority listening to the arguments of those in the majority. He uses this as a transition to his next paragraph, where he says that while he was listening to defense counsel's "tremendous force of personality and argument," he observed a notable lack of attention to Vanzetti (paragraph 8). He asks whether that can be explained by defense counsel's realization that Vanzetti, in fact, had no satisfactory alibi. As quickly as he places this idea in the jury's mind, he attempts to retract it, saying that, even if that is the opinion of defense counsel, attorneys' opinions are not evidence (paragraph 9). But the idea, of course, nevertheless remains in the jury's mind. It is still there when Katzmann stays with the topic in the next paragraph, saying that, in his opening statement, defense counsel "never whispered a word" (a phrase full of delivery potential) as to Vanzetti's whereabouts on April 15th. He closes that paragraph with the statement that "acts of counsel. . . bind the defendants" (a conclusion difficult to reconcile with the warning that counsel's opinions are not evidence).

The next excerpt reveals Katzmann's adroit handling of a correction in his recollection of evidence. Counsel interrupts to state the evidence differently, and then asks that Katzmann acknowledge that version. Appearing utterly nonplussed, Katzmann ethically says to his "Brother" that he will always "acknowledge the truth from any source" (paragraph 11). Counsel seems a bit testy in reply, requesting a specific acknowledgment from him. Katzmann does not stoop to reply in kind, but graciously complies (paragraph 12), and as graciously refers to the correction in paragraph 14: "had I not been very kindly corrected by my brother."

In paragraph 15, Katzmann is beginning his conclusion of an argument that exceeded four hours. He apologizes to the jurors, but returns to the just-doing-my-job theme. It has only been the discharge of his duty as a "public servant" that has caused him to intrude upon their time at all. He reminds them that his job requires him to look after their property, lives, and safety. He uses his duty as the explanation for all of his efforts in this case, not any personal interest, as implied by the defense counsel in suggesting what an opportunity it was for him. Just as he assures the jury that he is acting totally without passion, in accordance with his duty (paragraph 16), he expects them to be unaffected by emotion and judge the defendants "in accordance with the requirements of the law." He even suggests that he feels pity for the defendants and the family of one of them, but says that the Commonwealth asks them (as it has asked him) to disregard that pity in coming to a verdict (paragraph 17). The machinery imagery in paragraph 19—"the most important cog in the wheels and machinery of justice"—suggests the ideal for which the jury should strive, without emotion. Now is not the time for sympathy for Sacco's family, Katzmann adds, for still another reason; if Sacco is guilty, then he himself was lacking in sympathy and does not now deserve it (paragraph 20). (The argument goes slightly awry, however, since, if the sympathy is directed to Sacco's *family*, why should *his* acts deprive *them* of sympathy now?)

Katzmann's conclusion (paragraph 21) reflects none of the religious language used in his opening remarks and, perhaps, for a calculated reason. Ultimately, religion exists because of death, being a means of explaining death. In this last paragraph, Katzmann does not want the jury to connect their decision with the death of the defendants, lest they fear and shirk the weight of such a heavy burden. Instead, he likens their chore to that of a physician, who merely diagnoses a fatal disease and is not responsible for its consequences. And in the same breath that Katzmann relieves them of the responsibility of taking life, he points them to a lesser duty, the one he himself has discharged, of weighing the evidence unemotionally; that is the manly thing to do.

D. *Conclusion*

In the introduction of this book the suggestion appears that modern uses of rhetoric may differ from those of the classical rhetoricians simply in the purity of the motivation. However, as we have seen, no matter how high the motive, speeches of the classical rhetoricians were often so far from the truth as to confound historians.[53] In addition, although Aristotle emphasized "natural reason," the concepts of *ethos* and *pathos*, and their uses, derive from classical rhetoric; and to the extent that they can "divert issues from truth and justice, rhetoric can and does overwhelm 'natural reason.'" Therefore, the concern may be less over deceptive, diversionary, and misleading appeals or arguments, which may be tolerable under the circumstances, than over "*intolerable* fallacious and sham argumentation."[54]

> Certain types of deceptions, certain types of misleading implications, and certain types of diversionary tactics have been acceptable and tolerable to audiences. What Aristotle misses is the *grounds* for this acceptance of deceptive strategems in the rhetoric of advocacy. What is missing is the connection between deceptive strategems and the cooperative principles of discourse.
>
> . . . .
>
> Thus, what is missing in Aristotle is the recognition that a rhetoric of advocacy needs to start with conventional norms and that these norms vary in different social and cultural contexts and discourse situations. What is legitimate in the way people deceive one another in a rhetoric of persuasion depends upon the sorts of cooperative and deceptive langauge games people play with

one another. And, to put the last stone in place, rhetorical strategies *are* language games.[55]

III. *THE USE OF DEMONSTRATIVE EVIDENCE*

Conclusions reported or reached in earlier chapters almost dictate the advisability of demonstrative evidence:

- Vividness increases recall ("Theory: Primacy vs. Recency").
- In post-trial deliberations, mock jurors enhance the effect of demonstrative evidence (an artificial leg, in "Presentation of Evidence and Arguments").
- Arguments that are associated with vivid testimony (the guacamole dip spilled on a white shag carpet) are better recalled than arguments associated with pallid testimony ("The Juror as a Unique Subject").
- Jurors form their own stories of "what happened" ("The Juror as a Unique Subject").
- Trial work calls for performance ("Drama").
- Jurors are very much affected by what they see in the courtroom (the account of Juror Number Four in "Analysis of the Jury during Trial").
- Vivid words in questions are often incorporated into jurors' recollections of answers ("Testimony Style").

The effect of vividness has a psychological basis, which in turn explains the success of trial techniques involving story and picture theory. This rationale is the focus of the initial section below. While "demonstrative evidence" often conjures up images of elaborate (and expensive) dog-and-pony shows, an attorney can rely on a variety of methods to create the pictures he wants in the jurors' minds, as indicated in the next section.

A. *Story Theory*

"Lawyers and jurors share the common heritage of learning from stories. It began in childhood."[56] Probably all of us can recall being told or read the standard children's stories; the reader, for each of us, also undoubtedly emphasized certain words, adopted what he or she thought was the voice of each character, and made faces to emulate the emotions in the words. All of this was done to make the stories interesting to us; a significant side effect is that it also caused us to recall the stories, years after their telling. On perhaps a more respected level, recall that classical historians were indebted to the rhetoricians for incorporating accounts of history into their speeches. Since the speeches were oral, and the rhetoricians both needed to recall them and needed to give their audience reason to recall them, they relied upon narrative, story-like accounts. Unfortunately, for purposes either of recall or impression on the audience, some of the accounts strayed from the truth.[57] In addition, poetry in its earliest, ancient forms, took the form of oral epics, which virtually told the story of a person's life and adventures.

Thus, organizing data into an account with a beginning, middle, and end has long been a technique for recall. The explanation for its success could be as simple as its being a reflection of human life, which has a marked beginning and end, with that in between being the middle. Knowing that people organize data this way is a first step to impressing upon them which data they should organize that way. Ideally, counsel simply tells the jury what the facts are and where they should go in the sequence, and the jury obediently places them accordingly. The reality is that the jury may not "see" the same facts counsel does; those facts may be missed altogether or replaced by a fabrication of the jurors. Post-trial interviews with jurors and debriefings of mirror jurors demonstrate that they retain little information from the evidence, confuse important points, and often entirely miss what the trial attorney thought to be critical points.[58]

The jury should certainly not be blamed for counsel's lack of clarity, although it is important to note that what may seem perfectly clear to others at the counsel table may still be lost on the jury. And lack of attention is rarely induced by the jurors themselves:

> What we perceive is not a photographic record or an audio transcript of all that we have heard; rather, it is a selectively organized personal construct. Ideally, jurors would like to be able to remember all that they see and hear. However, selective attention to stimuli results in the elimination of some information and a reorganization (and perhaps distortion) of the information that is retained. It is, therefore, important to understand how stimulus factors can be controlled so that the key issues in an attorney's theory of the case will be among the cognitions formed and remembered. Frequency, movement, repetition, and change will all add to the probability that a stimulus will be retained. The intensity with which a statement is made and the extent to which

> it can be made to stand out against an undifferentiated background are equally critical.[59]

Thus, what counsel seek to do is cause the jury to see and hear the story *they* are telling, not the one the jury may think facts like those in the present case might show, not the one the jury saw on television the night before, not the one that some of the jurors may have experienced themselves, and certainly not the one the opposition is telling. Many of the opening statements you have heard conform to one pattern or another of the story method, as in these examples: "Ladies and Gentlemen of the jury, this is the familiar story of a romantic triangle"; ". . .although this may sound like the familiar story of a romantic triangle"; ". . .the prosecution would have you believe this is the familiar story of a romantic triangle"; ". . .this is unlike any story of a romantic triangle that you have ever heard." In each instance, counsel is telling the jury that either, yes, they may rely on everything they have ever heard about romantic triangles, or, no, they should forget everything they have heard before, because this is a brand new story.

The childhood story-reading experience makes us susceptible to the hint of the beginning of a story. But instead of saying, "once upon a time," counsel uses a

> thematic start, which rivet's the jury's attention. . .followed by a narrative of the evidence that supports the theme. . . .
>
> Members of the jury: The case you will hear and decide involves the refusal of an insurance company to live up to its promise. . . .
>
> Members of the jury: This case is not about contracts, it's about arson.[60]

The same recommendation is made for closing argument:

> Jurors love a story. . . .
>
> Do not mimic the prosecution. Do not argue, "The informant in this case received some inducements to give favorable testimony for the prosecution"; instead, say, "The informant made a deal with the prosecution. He would sell his soul to avoid going to the slammer."[61]

Counsel must be concerned not only with the jury's inattention but also with their "autistic or idiosyncratic perception," which refers to the tendency of people to "limit or adjust perception to fit their own needs and values, and. . .to personalize, or even distort, testimony to make it correspond to their own frames of reference."[62] In other words, it is simpler for people to place what they see or hear into their own frames of reference instead of expanding those frames, and this is what generally happens when testimony is vague or ambiguous and short in duration. "The antidotes are apparent: clarity and amplification are essential to the presentation of your case in chief." Thus, it is recommended that counsel "repeat key facts during the trial, even if it is cumulative to 'fix' those facts in the jurors' memories."[63]

The effect of the technique of repetition of key facts is twofold. First, it continues to place before the jury the facts that are important to the client's position in the case, which should be a deterrent to each juror assigning weight to the facts based only on his or her judgment and experience. Second, it helps to create the story counsel wants to be formed in the jury's mind. Jurors *will* form stories, and they will use the facts in the case (or their own, unaided interpretation of them) to do so. If counsel can impress upon jurors which facts are important, these are the facts the jurors will use. Stories told to children also rely upon repeated data, and while, to adults, unrepeated details of even the most familiar stories fade (who exactly killed the wolf in "Little Red Riding Hood"? what was Goldilocks doing in the middle of the woods? where did the wolf come from in "The Three Little Pigs"?), some things will never be forgotten: "What big ears/eyes/teeth you have, Grandma," "Who's been sleeping in my bed/eating my porridge?" and "I'll huff and I'll puff 'til I blow your house down."

In addition, repeated facts can be couched in such a way as to advance the client's position each time. Take, for example, this fact situation. A shopkeeper has living quarters above his store in a gang-infested section of the Bronx. One night, he hears hooligans trying to break into his store. Then, he hears them in his house, coming up the stairs to the room where his younger sister sleeps. He rushes out of his own room, waving a gun, and chases them out of the front of his store. Once on the street, they taunt him from a distance, throwing rocks and sticks at him. The only light between him and them is a flickering street light. Then, from their general direction, a figure starts toward him. The person speaks, but the shopkeeper cannot hear over the taunts of the hooligans; he cannot see well because of the inconsistent light. He tells the figure to stop; when it does not, he fires, shooting a policeman. The words "flickering street light" should ideally come first from the client, in his testimony. Whenever he thereafter refers to the lighting problem, counsel should ask, "And this was because of the flickering street light?" In addition, whenever other witnesses testify, counsel should also attempt to draw a confirmation of the light conditions: "And you saw this because you were standing right under the flickering street light?"

The term theme "impact" words or "buzz" words can be used to refer to the key issues in any case that jurors will focus on and to which they can relate.[64] Every case must have a simple and concise theme and the corresponding theme "impact" words or "buzz" words which must be reported numerous times in opening statement, through numerous witnesses, and in closing argument. Good "impact" words and repetition are the keys. The repetition of these "impact" words provides a constant guiding of the jury to interpret the testimony and evidence in light of them. (Remember that the best argument and theme is a simple one. Also, jurors are interested in what motivates people. The motives of the client and witnesses should be explained to the jury and these motives must be consistent with the theme of the case.)[65] For example, assume an automobile accident case in which a driver committed an act of negligence and the plaintiff is alleging the defendant failed to keep a proper lookout. The defendant was on route to his employment at the time of the accident. This could be the case of the preoccupied driver. In a medical malpractice case, the comments of the mirror jurors revealed their concern with the parents' not questioning the physicians and nurses if the baby were "truly" sick.[66] Therefore, the defense should have focused on the theme that the parents were uncaring.

Thus, while some attorneys advise the chronological approach in opening statement, in part because it allows for a vivid description of evolving action and possibly a dramatic building to a climax (both of which should hold the jury's attention), it may be better to construct the *voir dire* and opening statement around the theme "impact" words or "buzz" words. Of course, when jurors piece together their own versions of what happened, they will undoubtedly use chronological order, but the "impact" words voiced in the *voir dire* and opening statement and repeated throughout trial, should induce them to look at the facts based on those theme "impact" words or "buzz" words.

A simple concise theme echoes the advice of others to simplify the case as much as possible for the jury, whether the means are expressed as "clarity and amplification" or KISS (keep it simple, stupid). "Demonstrative evidence is the tool or technique available to use at trial which permits you to emphasize, dramatize and explain your case in a more effective fashion."[67]

B. *Ways to Use Demonstrative Evidence*

In the chapter on *voir dire*, means of "reading" prospective jurors were suggested for a variety of litigation budgets and included a range of techniques from statistical surveys and psychologists at the counsel table to gut reactions of weathered attorneys. Similarly, the rules of evidence are being found capable of accommodating more and more elaborate (and costly) renditions and summaries of the facts and testimony. As we will see, however, *more* is not always *better*, and there are successful no-cost and low-cost ways to "emphasize, dramatize and explain your case" more effectively.

First, counsel should never overlook the demonstrative ability of words alone. Dombroff defines demonstrative evidence as evidence that "has, in some form or fashion, been processed." He then notes five broad purposes sought through the use of demonstrative evidence: educating an audience, explaining something to an audience, persuading an audience, dissuading an audience, or reinforcing something that the audience already believes.[68] Taking nothing away from Dombroff's purposes, those are also reasons for speaking to an audience. Dombroff's suggestion is that words themselves are enhanced through a visual medium. That is certainly true when reference is made to objects, animals, or people. If an audience is told to think of a mountain, no two people will visualize the same mountain. But if they are told to think of a steep mountain, high in the Alps, their visual images will be closer, and one might inquire of the relevance of any differences in their images now (such a mountain, for example, could have been the site of a skiing accident). On the other hand, probably no number of words could convey the hour-by-hour difficulties faced by a quadriplegic in simply getting through the day; if a juror had a relative or knew someone in that condition, he or she would understand, but probably not otherwise.

As indicated in the chapter on style, however, words can go a long way in conveying visual images. Also, a sensitive description of selected incidents in the day of a quadriplegic could be sufficiently representative of his or her plight to have the emotional and logical appeal of a film. The "Picture Theory of Trial Advocacy" refers to the creation of a picture in the courtroom without using demonstrative evidence.[69] This definition is consistent with Dombroff's in assuming that language alone is unenhanced evidence. However, when one realizes the choices available in language, then it may really be that there may be a "demonstrative language," drab and denotative language enhanced with imagery and connotative word choices. For the shorter trials, "large exhibits and elaborate presentations" may seem inappropriate, "too polished. . . too much."

> With or without exhibits, lasting pictures can be created by words alone. . . .
>
> Anything from a single word to an entire story creates vivid pictures in the jury's mind. Choice of a single word can shape the course of an entire trial, and a careful choice of words throughout trial can make your theory of the case come alive.
>
> Color, consistency, contrast, and closing are the touchstones that make it easier to create pictures in the courtroom with words alone.

One example comes from the trial of Claus von Bulow, when his attorney was attempting to establish that von Bulow's maid had planted evidence indicating that he had murdered his wife:

Q: I take it, it was *Maria, the maid,* who told you about the events that transpired on the 27th of December, 1975, is that right?

A: That's correct.

Q: And it was also, in February of the next year, *Maria, the maid,* who brought the black bag to your attention at the (von Bulow) residence of 960 Fifth Avenue, is that right?

A: In was early in the year, January or February, that's correct.

Q: But it was *Maria, the maid,* who brought the black bag to your attention, is that right?

A: That's correct.

Q: And later on that year, it was *Maria, the maid,* who brought the bag to your attention for the second time, is that right?

A: That's correct.

Q: And subsequently, around Thanksgiving of 1980, it was again *Maria, the maid,* who brought the bag to your attention, is that correct?

A: That's correct.

The repetition of the phrase, along with its alliteration, causes it to be memorable.[70]

Although "Maria, the maid" is colorful in a way, what the authors actually had in mind with "color" was the use of vivid language, as in "What did you think after you *heard* your arm *crack*, and you *saw* your *skin tear*?" "Maria, the maid" is more an example of consistency, which, in this instance, "resemble[s] a child's chant with its simplicity and teasing." Contrast refers to the thing that is rarely done or seen, and in its scarceness or unusualness stands out in relief against everything else—such as establishing that a witness has a high IQ and then defeating his professed motive for testifying as being moral responsibility by demonstrating that he is guilty of legal and moral transgressions himself. Closing refers to the final argument, which allows "high drama." "When the lawyer talks with pictures that are created by analogies, then the story is complete. Stories are real and tangible, and that makes them memorable."[71]

A second evidence enhancement technique requires only two props: a blackboard and chalk. Not only is this method desirable when the client's budget prohibits a full-blown presentation, but, as a contrast to the bells and whistles of the opposition, it can be alarmingly effective: "There is nothing mysterious about [a blackboard]. It has no 'high tech' odor that suggests the presentation is slick or canned." Moreover, we have associations with the blackboard that are almost contemporaneous with our being read stories: "people have been trained to read the blackboard (some even to copy laboriously from it)." And those who write on a blackboard cannot escape comparison with teachers, to whom we have all been taught to attend.[72]

Certain caveats accompany the recommendation of using a blackboard. First, only a few words should be printed on it, and they should be printed instead of written.[73] If the witness is counsel's own, the gift of the testimony will probably be known beforehand. Therefore, counsel should already know which pre-selected key facts or psychological anchors will apply to the witness's testimony, and these can guide the selection of words for the blackboard. Second, the attorney should do the writing on the blackboard while the witness testifies; asking the witness to do both could cause his oral testimony and his writing on the board to suffer. Third, before passing the witness on direct examination, the attorney should erase the blackboard: "Chances are your opponent will think of something creative to do with what you have left, and you will not enjoy it."

If the information on the blackboard seems especially useful and could rise to admission as an exhibit, a Polaroid picture could be taken of it, and the picture could later be offered into evidence.[74]

A slightly more elaborate use of demonstrative evidence turns the spoken word literally into visual evidence through the photographing of key questions and answers and then their enlargement onto poster board. Only if it is suspected that a trial witness will recant or be unable to explain previously transcribed testimony can the posters be prepared before trial. Moreover, if cross-examination comes the day after direct, the enlarged testimony will probably be more effective, since the jury should recall the subject matter if not the specific testimony of the witness that is later questioned. Of course, if testimony is to be enlarged for the next day, the court reporter must be alerted to the possible need of running transcripts when counsel so indicates, and a photographer, aware of the potential need, can be available to prepare, enlarge, and mount the photograph overnight.[75]

If the mere enlargement of words onto poster board seems an inadequate way to attract the jury's attention, recall the last time you sat on a bus or subway and, after completing your study of the faces and clothes of those around you, you turned to the advertisements and graffiti and began to read them as if they held some special message. After they have become accustomed to their surroundings, jurors welcome the introduction of any new stimulus. Although it is a particularly extreme example, given the length of the trial, Kennebeck's account of his service on the jury in the Black Panthers trial provides an inkling of what jurors must often feel:

> Week after week, day after day, the same defendants in their places. . . same scenario. There were hours of tedium. Some of us would almost nod off now and then, but since every point of testimony and evidence got a thorough going-over by both sides, none of us missed anything important.[76]

Perhaps the most vivid and dramatic of the demonstrative evidence techniques involve video tape. The point is made in the chapter on drama that jurors' expectations are primarily drawn from the depictions of trials and lawyers that they see on television. The underlying rationale for this is twofold. First, people as a whole spend a great deal of time watching television. Second, they find what they see to be credible (it is not necessarily that television possesses some inherent believability; it is simply that since people spend so much more time with it than they do in the courtroom, they are more likely to rely on televised depictions as their basis of reality). It would therefore follow that evidence presented through the same medium would be comfortably received by the jury and may carry with it a certain credibility.[77]

Without video tape, the only alternative to a live witness is a deposition transcript, and the only alternative to designating the page and line references and having the court reporter include them without a reading at all is a reading by counsel or co-counsel, in a simulation of the actual question and answer session. Of course, this allows no opportunity for the fact finder to assess the demeanor of the witness or even to visualize him or her. Many video-taped depositions show only the witness, in a seated position, answering questions. If one side or the other hopes to use a taped deposition of an expert in court, the standard mode may not be that interesting or persuasive.

> There is no more reason to fix the camera on the witness only than there would be if the witness were testifying live in court. A live witness is allowed to move about, to show exhibits, and to illustrate on a shadow box, or positive X-ray. . . . Any device that presents the testimony in a more vivid and imaginative manner is an improvement to the communication process.[78]

Films and movies are especially helpful in personal injury cases, when the plaintiffs are often vastly improved in appearance by the time of trial. "The 'cameo' film taken at significant periods during the victim's treatment conveys to the jury a picture of the intangible aspects of 'suffering' that cannot be effectively presented in any other manner." The suggestion is earlier made that, while possible, it would take the talents of a wordsmith to convey the suffering of a paraplegic or quadriplegic with only oral skills. For that reason alone, "day in the life" movies may be justified. However, there may be even a sounder reason. It is only in relatively recent history that quadriplegics have survived their afflictions; formerly, when injury occurred high on the spinal column, resulting in paralysis from the neck down, the victim usually did not live or did not live long. However, with advanced medical techniques and procedures,

> the number of living people with such injuries has increased dramatically. . . .

> The legal profession must keep pace with the medical profession in the proper handling of severely disabled cases. It is not true that the serious injury case presents itself.

A certain backlash, however, is possible with "day in the life" movies. If the film presents the plaintiff as being so injured that he or she is virtually a lost cause, the jury may wonder what good any money recovery will do. Also, the jury could resent blatant attempts to play on their emotions.[79]

Dombroff warns of overkill in another respect. Not only might the budget not allow for elaborate presentation, but if it seems out of proportion for the case at hand, the jury may believe that it is meant to compensate for shortcomings in the plaintiff's or defendant's case.[80] In addition, the contrast element earlier discussed should not be forgotten. If the testimony of every witness is summarized on poster board, that becomes the norm. Then, where is the relief necessary to make one stimulus different from any other?

One solution is to vary the types of demonstrative evidence. Such types includes photographs, both enlarged, for placement on an easel, and normal-sized, for passing among the jurors; charts, diagrams, and graphs; maps, some of which are magnetized and can therefore allow for traffic simulation with model cars; and models.[81] One solution for organizing a great number of pieces of demonstrative evidence is color coding (probably for counsel's sake as much as the jury's):

> For example, if witnesses A, B, and C testify about a number of subjects and it is particularly important to tie together their testimony about one subject, perhaps construction costs, you can use the same color band for the heading or outline of each witness's exhibit on this subject. Thus, when your engineering witnesses testify about construction costs, the relevant exhibit may be a chart or a board with a distinctive green band. When your accounting witnesses testify about construction costs, their relevant chart or board exhibit also has a green band. And when your safety expert testifies about that same subject, his exhibit is similarly identified. When you do your final argument, you bring out the green color coded exhibits from each witness, put them side by side, and argue how this testimony all meshes together to support the overall proposition.[82]

Color coding could also indicate which exhibits go with which witness.

While demonstrative evidence is most often used to provide a contemporaneous explanation of generated testimony, it can also have its place in opening statements and closing arguments. If one of the purposes in using such evidence, however, is to gain the jury's attention, that purpose is probably wasted in the opening statement. At that point, the jurors have not had time to lose interest; they are still studying their new environment, learning its rules, and becoming familiar with the personalities of those before them. However, two aspects of human behavior examined in earlier chapters suggest the wisdom of using a blackboard to chart the course of counsel's case. Placed in a new situation, we seek guidance; in particular, jurors look to counsel as to an instructor in a new course. Knowing that jurors expect counsel to fill this role, counsel could satisfy their expectations by going to the blackboard and emulating the teacher that they want him to be. Second, there is a finite number of information items that can be mentally retained without their being grouped into categories, organized by chronology or some other method, or related to items already familiar. If counsel assaults the jury with too many of these items, they will simply not be recalled. Thus, the story that he hopes to develop in his opening statement will be missing critical elements. He can use the blackboard to assist the jury with organizing and groupings.

In closing argument, "[t]he most significant disadvantage in using demonstrative evidence. . .is also its greatest strength, i.e., visual impact. A closing argument is the last opportunity to address the jury before they retire to decide the fate of your client. Anything which detracts from the accomplishment of that task is to be avoided."[83] On the other hand, when there is a great deal of evidence to be reviewed (as in the Sacco-Vanzetti case, as indicated in the previous chapter), fact- or issue-coded exhibits of various witnesses could lead to an orderly (and accurate) summary of the evidence.

Whether used in opening statement or closing argument, perhaps the prime requirement of demonstrative evidence is that it not detract from counsel himself and what he is saying. That means that any handling of demonstrative evidence must be smooth. The following is an actual example of how paper alone can lead to one's undoing. Skilled counsel, while cross-examining an appraiser, asked him to identify certain appraisals he had made, along with letter updates and client correspondence asking for the updates. Counsel would plop a document onto the frame of the witness box and ask a question about it. Then, he would ask a question that called for the witness to compare one appraisal with another or to match up a letter update with its request. To facilitate his finding the documents more readily, the witness spread them out around him, balanced on the frame of the witness box (counsel actually engineered this move). Soon, the witness box (and the witness) was literally surrounded with paper. When counsel would ask a question, the witness would turn to scan the various documents around him. Seeming impatient, counsel would repeat the question, which caused the witness to move less carefully. Documents began to fall to the floor, and the witness repeatedly bent down to retrieve them, trying all the while to answer counsel's questions, which meant that words often floated up from an empty witness box, behind which the witness was gathering documents. The sight was ludicrous, and the witness appeared inept. When questioned after trial about this technique, counsel admitted that it was exactly that; he said he wanted the witness to look like a little bird in his nest, fairly buried in the paper that flapped about with his every move.

In conclusion, the importance of demonstrative evidence has been increasingly recognized by successful trial lawyers, as exemplified by a quote from west Texas attorney, R. Temple Dickson:

> The jury is the beginning and end of a successful trial. Close battles will invariably go to the side that has done its job in developing insight into the jury's attitude. In short, work done in pursuit of understanding the jurors and increasing their comprehension and retention of the evidence is as important as developing the facts of the case. Demonstrative aids are a powerful tool. Demonstrative aids allow the jury to not only hear the evidence, but to see and read it for themselves. Jurors are also accustomed to being taught in school with a blackboard, charts, diagrams, and various forms of visual displays.[84]

NOTES

1. *See* "Analysis of the Jury during Trial," section II of Chapter 4.

2. Charrow, *Linguistic Theory and the Study of Legal and Bureaucratic Language, Exceptional Language and Linguistics* 82 (L. Oblet & L. Menn ed. 1982).

3. *Id.* at 87–89.

4. Young & Sullivan, *Why Write? A Reconsideration, Essays on Classical Rhetoric and Modern Discourse* 215, 216–19 (R. Connors, L. Ede, & A. Lunsford ed. 1984).

5. *Id.* at 223.

6. Reynolds, *Trial Tactics*, Litigation, Spring 1982, at 14, 17.

7. Young & Sullivan, *supra* n.4, at 225.

8. Touhy, *Effective Final Argument for the Plaintiff*, Litigation, Spring 1982, at 41, 44, quoting from a closing argument of Philip H. Corboy.

9. Shakespeare, *King Henry V*, line 96.

10. Touhy, *supra* n.8, at 43, also quoting Corboy.

11. Crawford, *Opening Statement for the Defense in Criminal Cases*, Litigation, Spring 1982, at 27, 29.

12. Chaika, *Language, The Social Mirror* 34–35 (1982).

13. *Id.*

14. Glickman, *Persuasion in Litigation*, Litigation, Spring 1982, at 30, 33.

15. *Id.* at 33.

16. Graves, *Symmetrical Form and the Rhetoric of the Sentence, Essays on Classical Rhetoric and Modern Discourse* 170, 174–78 (R. Connors, L. Ede, & A. Lunsford ed. 1984).

17. Sapir, *The Anatomy of Metaphor, The Social Use of Metaphor* 3, 3–4 (J. Sapir & J. Crocker ed. 1977).

18. *Id.* at 3–6.

19. *Id.* at 4, 13–15.

20. *Id.* at 4, 21.

21. *Id.* at 4.

22. Glickman, *supra* n.14, at 33.

23. Barkai, *Based Language in Legal Communication*, The Practical Law., Jan. 1981, at 39, 44–46, 54–55.

24. Nichols, *Rhetoric and Criticism* 20, 30 (1963).

25. *Id.* at 70–78.

26. Potter, *Foreword* to G. Campbell, *The Philosophy of Rhetoric* (L. Bitzer ed. 1963).

27. Campbell, *The Philosophy of Rhetoric* 1 (L. Bitzer ed. 1963).

28. *Id.* at 33.

29. *Id.* at 35.

30. *Id.* at 71–72, 78.

31. *Id.* at 72–78.

32. For a discussion of tho relationship among identification, rhetoric, and persuasion, *see* "The Expert Attorney," section I in Chapter 1.

33. *Persuasion: The Key to Success in Trial* 25–30, 91 (G. Holmes ed. 1978) (hereafter cited as "Persuasion").

34. Reprinted by permission from *Persuasion: The Key to Success in Trial*, edited by Grace W. Holmes (The Institute of Continuing Legal Education, Ann Arbor, Michigan, 1978), at 31–34.

35. Reprinted by permission from *Persuasion: The Key to Success in Trial*, edited by Grace W. Holmes (The Institute of Continuing Legal Education, Ann Arbor, Michigan, 1978), at 322–26.

36. *Id.* at xi–xii.

37. Reprinted by permission from *Persuasion: The Key to Success in Trial*, edited by Grace W. Holmes (The Institute of Continuing Legal Education, Ann Arbor, Michigan, 1978), at 335.

38. Val LeClercq is the English professor.

39. Reprinted by permission from *Persuasion: The Key to Success in Trial*, edited by Grace W. Holmes (The Institute of Continuing Legal Education, Ann Arbor, Michigan, 1978), at 336.

40. I *In the Matter of Karen Quinlan* 2–3 (2d ed. 1982).

41. *Id.* at 24.

42. *Id.* at 568.

43. II *In the Matter of Karen Quinlan* (2d ed. 1982).

44. I *In the Matter of Karen Quinlan* 528–32 (2d ed. 1982).

45. *Id.* at 532–39.

46. Lyons, *The Life and Death of Sacco and Vanzetti* 7 (1927).

47. *Id.* at 36, 39.

48. *Id.* at 9.

49. *Id.* at 53.

50. *Id.* at 8.

51. *Id.* at 7.

52. II *The Sacco-Vanzetti Case* 2179–82, 2221–22, 2236–37 (1969) (transcript).

53. Nichols, *supra* n.24, at 20, 30.

54. Yoos, *Rational Appeal and the Ethics of Advocacy, Essays on Classical Rhetoric and Modern Discourse* 82, 83 (R. Connors, L. Ede, & A. Lunsford ed. 1984).

55. *Id.* at 96–97.

56. Ordover, *Persuasion and the Opening Statement*, Litigation, Winter 1986, at 12.

57. Nichols, *supra* n.24, at 20, 30.

58. Author's observation and research as a jury and trial consultant on retention and information-processing.

59. Vinson, *Litigation: An Introduction to the Application of Behavioral Science*, 15 Conn. L. Rev. 767, 769 (1983).

60. Ordover, *supra* n.56, at 12.

61. Cleary, *The Final Argument in a Criminal Case*, Practical Law., Sept. 1, 1981, at 39, 47.

62. Colley, *Friendly Persuasion*, Trial, Aug. 1981, at 42, 45.

63. *Id.*

64. Lecture by author, Dynamics of Jury Selection Seminar, Naples, Florida (Sept. 30, 1983).

65. Lee, *Closing Argument in a Criminal Case*, Trial, October 1986, at 104.

66. *Phillip J. Birchfield et ux. v. Texarkana Memorial Hosp., et al.*, in Bowie County, Texas, 1984.

67. Dombroff, *Dombroff on Demonstrative Evidence* 3 (1983).

68. *Id.* at 2–3.

69. Axam & Altman, *The Picture Theory of Trial Advocacy*, Litigation, Winter 1981, at 8.

70. *Id.*

71. *Id.* at 9–11, 67.

72. McElhaney, *The Blackboard*, Litigation, Winter 1986, at 53, 54.

73. *Id.* at 69.

74. *Id.* at 70.

75. Singer, *Testimony as Demonstrative Evidence*, Litigation, Summer 1977, at 19–20.

76. Kennebeck, *Juror Number Four* 109 (1973).

77. Perlman, *Seeing Is Believing, Making Proof More Meaningful*, Trial, June 1981, at 34.

78. *Id.* at 36.

79. *Id.* at 37.

80. Dombroff, *supra* n.67, at 6.

81. *Id.* at 208–209.

82. Siemer, *Tangible Evidence, How to Use Exhibits at Trial* 12–13 (1984).

83. Dombroff, *supra* n.67, at 209.

84. Interview with R. Temple Dickson (Oct. 22, 1984) (after his $1.6 million verdict in Nolan County, Texas in *Jowers v. Atchinson, T. & S.F. Ry.*, presently on appeal).

CHAPTER 7
WHY A JURY AND TRIAL CONSULTANT CAN BE USEFUL TO AN ATTORNEY

SYNOPSIS

CHAPTER 7
WHY A JURY AND TRIAL CONSULTANT CAN BE USEFUL TO AN ATTORNEY*

In the proper case, the use of expert assistance in jury selection and evaluation can spell the difference between winning and losing. The selection of the appropriate jurors, conditioned to accept the evidence, and monitored during the trial by a shadow or mirror jury, can result in a favorable jury verdict. The purpose of this article is to emphasize the opportunities that are afforded by *voir dire*, and to acquiant the trial lawyer with the techniques and procedures that are available to help him achieve a jury victory. Not every case in a law office requires the spotlighted focus that is provided by expert trial assistance in jury selection; but many law offices have a case where the liability issues are close, the damages may be significant, and with the proper preparation, a successful jury verdict could result.

Jury duty is the only remaining involuntary service in the country. However, a jury is a captive audience in *physical presence only*, not in attention, logic, or in waiting to hear all evidence before reaching a decision. The majority of jurors make up their minds about the verdict early in the litigation proceeding. Kalvin and Zeisel[1] determined that eighty percent of the jurors have made a decision by the conclusion of the opening statement. My studies of full *voir dire* examination, as it is still permitted by several states, has lead me to conclude that approximately seventy percent of jurors have decided the case by the conclusion of the *voir dire* and, more importantly, rarely change their minds. The fact that jurors make decisions early in the trial does not, of course, mean that those jurors will not change their opinions; however, human beings usually are reluctant to modify an initial impression. Psychological research has shown that initial impressions have a tendency to persist, even in the face of later contrary evidence.

Each juror evaluates what transpires in the courtroom on the basis of his or her life experiences and predispositions. The decision is based on the individual juror's previously possessed biases, opinions, and prejudices. The degree to which a litigator can tap into these preconditions during *voir dire* or opening statement is determinative of the outcome of the case.

---

*Reprinted from *Trial Diplomacy Journal*, Vol. 10, No. 1, with the permission of Professional Education Systems, Inc., 200 Spring Street, P.O. Box 1428, Eau Claire, WI 54702.

Every lawyer has heard that one can win or lose his case during jury selection; but, many do not realize why or how this happens. Seasoned litigators acknowledge that jury selection is the most vital component of the trial proceedings. In fact, once the last person on the jury is selected, I believe the outcome of the trial is essentially determined. Each juror evaluates the litigation proceeding in vastly different ways as a direct function of his or her life experiences, feelings, habits, intuitions and resulting biases, prejudices, and opinions.

In the past, juries were selected by hunches, educated guesses, and intuition. In the early 1970's attorneys initiated the use of psychological techniques in an effort to assist in jury selection in criminal trials. Later, these psychological and behavioral science techniques were successfully employed in civil trials involving personal injury, products liability, child custody, and antitrust suits. The trial attorney should be familiar with the psychological techniques that are available to supplement his or her intuitive approach, or personal formula for selecting a jury, as well as other aspects of the trial.

Clarence Darrow, in the 1930's, recognized the importance of jury selection and stated:

> In this undertaking, everything pertaining to the prospective juror needs to be questioned and weighed; his nationality, his business, religion, politics, social standing, family ties, friends, habits of life and thought; the books and newspapers he likes and reads, and many more matters that combine to make a man.[2]

By the intelligent utilization of psychological techniques, an advantage can be obtained over the opposing counsel. Experience has lead me to agree with Broeder's research[3] that indicates that most trial attorneys are "grossly ineffective, not only in weeding out 'unfavorable' jurors but even in eliciting the data which would have shown particular jurors as very likely to prove 'unfavorable.'"

Experienced counsel generally believe that a strictly intuitive approach to jury selection is unreliable and illogical:

> Most of the trial bar are willing to acknowledge that the approach of jury selection has been anything but scientific. It smacks of a modern alchemy full of jargon, superstition, and mystification, but little real knowledge. All too often, it constitutes babbling an obligato of cliches in an ingratiating attempt to establish warm contact with the jurors. This 'kamikaze' approach to choosing

> jurors uses some instinct and a little intuition with a dash of voodoo thrown in.[4]

The present state of the art is that jury selection does not have to be entirely educated guesswork and hunches. The attorney's personal formula may be enhanced by the application of knowledge from the fields of psychology, sociology and statistics. Many experts believe that the psychological and sociological techniques that are in use today complement the experienced trial attorney's already well-developed approach to jury selection.

In the usual *voir dire* proceedings that take place today there is little chance for the attorney to obtain the most favorable jury possible. The hit-or-miss jury selection strategy that occurs in most courtrooms rarely results in the best jury. The typical *voir dire* fails to uncover or to identify prejudicial jurors. To expect a prospective juror to speak openly and candidly in the courtroom environment is unrealistic. Most jury panel members distort their answers in an effort to please the authority figure (the Judge) and their fellow jurors. In fact, I have found that approximately one out of every three panel members will lie or misstate the truth on *voir dire*. Also, the Court may impose time limitations and other constraints on the examination which can have an intimidating effect. The courtroom environment encourages mimic responses of those jurors who verbalize first, as opposed to honest, open and revealing responses.

Unique and novel applications of psychology, sociology, and statistics are being employed in jury selection by successful litigators. These methods of jury selection are based on a correlation between jurors' attitudes and jurors' verdicts.[5]

The Justice Department studied several unsuccessful political trials in 1970 and explained the Government's defeat in the following manner:

> [The cases] were tried before juries at least partially composed of people willing to be convinced of government misconduct or willing to believe the exculpatory motives alleged by the defense. The defense sought, and was able to evoke the sense that the Government used the legal system to legitimize or [endorse] unpopular policies or decisions.[6]

Jury selection is the key to a successful outcome. Insight into the attitudes of the people who will decide the case is extremely valuable. In certain instances, the difference in jury verdicts depends on who is the best Jury Selector. Rudimentary rules of thumb, such as "don't take anyone whose profession begins with a 'p' in civil defense" and "don't take a Lutheran in criminal defense" are questionable generalizations which have been replaced by an analysis of prospective jurors' attitudes and demeanor. It has been found that the more analytical we become, the more success we will have.

The discussions which follow concern the more innovative procedures that have been used by jury consultant experts under the direction of the trial attorney in order to obtain the best possible result for the client. A case wherein effective use may be made of some, or all, of these procedures does not necessarily have to be a high profile or notorious one. It is sufficient that the case needs to be won and that the litigation can afford some, or all, of the approaches, from jury selection to final verdict. When the stakes are high (that is, your client faces imprisonment or death), nothing should be overlooked that could be helpful. In a civil case where the client could be exposed to the award of significant damages against him, or where a substantial recovery could be obtained for him, some or all of these procedures can aid in that endeavor. In a case where winning is a *must*, then the use of these techniques is a must!

The following systematic techniques are available to the attorney who practices his profession in the courtroom:

1. Assessment of community attitudes through research and juror profiles.
2. Background information of prospective jurors, including residential observation (drive-by photographs of their homes reveal a lot).
3. Juror personal history questionnaire (see what they state that has been important in their lives).
4. Design *voir dire* questions that do more than simply measure the incourtroom communication skill of a prospective juror (uncover the built-in prejudices by open-ended questions).
5. Focus group
6. Trial simulation
   a. Mini or mock trial
   b. Shadow or mirror jury

Even before the case is filed, it is possible to obtain information that could help select a community which would provide the most favorable prospective jurors. This can be accomplished by the community attitudinal survey. Also, the survey results can be utilized in any type of litigation to determine a profile of the 'ideal' juror and 'least desirable' juror.

I. *ASSESSMENT OF COMMUNITY ATTITUDES AND JUROR PROFILES*

Community attitudes can be assessed by a survey that is conducted under the direction of the jury (and trial) consultant, typically a Ph.D. in psychology. Questions are designed to elicit specific attitudes. For example, if the litigation involves a manufacturer's liability, questions concerning the community's familiarity, or acceptance of the product, can be presented to the community from which the jury is to be selected. The survey typically is conducted by telephone and the interviewees, who are selected by random or stratified sample, are called by a market resarch team.

The community survey is conducted with questions designed by the jury consultant to determine what attitudes, biases, sentiments, and feelings exist in the community where the case is going to be tried. Obviously, this is important in cases that are notorious, but it is just as important in cases which contain issues or parties where community feelings are unknown. That is, what kind of person in the community will respond favorably to a suit in which a bank, a school board, or a church is involved? What type of person could be expected to appreciate a suit involving psychological injuries, as opposed to a suit involving injuries which are capable of being demonstrated by x rays and photographs? The main object of this data is to allow the jury expert to develop the profile of the 'ideal' juror who could be expected to respond favorably to the evidence presented to the jury, and the profile of the 'least desirable' juror. This 'ideal juror' and 'least desirable' juror most likely will never be encountered. However, since the 'ideal juror' and 'least desirable' juror profiles are derived from categorization of interviewees' responses, this offers a device for ranking the prospective jurors on the suggested variables such as age, education, occupation, length of time in the county and other statistically significant factors. Those jurors who possess more of the preferred characteristics of the 'ideal' juror will rank highest on the scale and those with fewer of the preferred demographics will be eliminated first.

The community attitudinal survey has many uses. It may be utilized to support a motion for a change of venue. It can also uncover attitudes of prospective jurors regarding the fault or culpability of the defendants. The survey also will identify the attitudes of participants toward punitive damages and the amount of damages the community would most likely award.

In summary, one of the functions of the community attitudinal survey can be to develop a mathematical equation and classification procedure to more accurately predict the prospective juror's opinion, with associated statistical probability of such opinion. This mathematical function is based on demographic characteristics of those residents who are eligible for jury service in the community where the trial is to take place. The derived model will serve as an aid to the attorneys in verification of their choices for jurors. The data analysis will indicate commonly held community attitudes and opinions about the plaintiff or defendant and issues in the case. This analysis will provide the trial team with a general understanding or profile of the community and allows an evaluation of the juror that is most likely to appear at trial. It also makes it possible to get an idea about how the jurors will receive the case.

Completion of the research objectives requires a systematic collection of opinions and demographic characteristics of prospective jurors. Subjects are interviewed by a telephone survey. The sample is unbiased in that all individuals who are eligible respondents have an equal chance of being interviewed. Potential interviewees are usually selected by the generation of random telephone numbers. (In some jurisdictions it may be desirable to use other sampling techniques such as stratified sampling.) In order to qualify as a respondent for the community attitudinal analysis, an individual must be over eighteen years of age and eligible for jury duty.

The critical step is to determine what it is that the lawyer desires to be measured and what questions to ask. Generally, the questionnaire samples attitudes toward the relevant facts, issues, parties, and correlates basic demographic information (for example, age, occupation, education and marital status).

The community attitudinal survey was conducted in the celebrated murder trials of a Texas multi-millionaire in the 1970's to determine the profile of the 'ideal' juror and the 'least desirable' juror. A juror profile model was developed through appropriate statistical analytical methods. Independent or predictor variables (such as age, occupation, marital status, education and length of residency in the county) were identified. The independent variables were indicators of the socialization of an individual that contributed to the attitudes held by that prospective juror. The survey also sought to answer relevant question such as:

1. What were the community's attitudes in general about the facts of the case and related issues?
2. What were the attitudes which were likely to predispose a prospective juror to be less than neutral to the accused citizen who was a very wealthy businessman?
3. Would the background or demographic characteristics classify those members of the community who were predisposed negatively to the issues or the client?
4. Would the community be likely to accept or reject a theory of defense such as prosecution solely because of the wealth of the accused?
5. How best could the lead counsel communicate with the local jurors?
6. Was it even possible to select 12 persons who had not prejudged the accused citizen because of extensive media coverage of the event and the daily fanning of the flames of prejudice?
7. What areas of inquiry are the most critical for the *voir dire* examination? For example, church affiliation was determined to not be as significant as the frequency of church attendance.

Of course, the courtroom environment contributes to the juror's decision-making process. Interactions in the courtroom, nonverbal communication, group dynamics and other behavioral variables play a major role in the selection of the jury. Some jurors will decide the outcome of the case based solely on feelings about counsel or the perceived credibility of the client or dislike of the opponent. These important determinants cannot be measured statistically; therefore, they must be discovered and evaluated in the courtroom. The more varied the information that the litigator has at his disposal, the better he can predict a prospective juror's likely response. Jurors think and respond in a manner that is complementary with their backgrounds and life experiences.

While no quantitative analyses can exactly predict the prospective juror's decision, nevertheless, one common principle is important. The quantitative analyses will use correlations between known characteristics and attitudes to determine how a prospective jury member is *most likely* to resond in a specific situation. Of course, the profile is not intended to replace the attorney's judgment but only to augment his information and to verify his subjective impression, or cause him to hesitate in his decision. The profile can increase his confidence and peace of mind in his decision on those persons on whom the attorney cannot "really" decide.

The community attitudinal concept also was used successfully in a personal injury case in Dallas, Texas, and provides an illustration of the various uses of this type of analysis in civil litigation. The author assisted the attorneys who represented the injured plaintiff. Dallas County, Texas, is known for its historically conservative jury awards in civil litigation and its "1500" year sentences in criminal cases. The attorneys wanted to know how to overcome the conservative attitudes of Dallas County jurors regarding monetary awards. The plaintiff had been injured in an amusement ride accident at the State Fair of Texas in October, 1983. Lead counsel was especially interested in determining the approximate amount of punitive damages likely to be awarded by a jury. The author considered several procedures which might give the answer to this question. A survey of the community from which the potential jurors would be selected was determined to be the best procedure. A random sample from the community was selected and questions that were carefully designed were used. Interviewees were asked about their knowledge of the facts of the case, their attitude about punishment damages, and basic demographic or background information. We were also interested in determining what effect a previous accident (1979 Swiss Skyride accident at the State Fair of Texas) had on the Dallas community and what effect, if any, this occurrence would have on the jury's ability to award punitive damages for the injuries sustained in a second accident at the State Fair of Texas. Profiles of the 'ideal' juror and 'least desirable' juror were derived with the associated predictor variables such as age, sex, occupation and education. The attorney then could use this information in association with additional information obtained by *voir dire* and pre-trial investigation to assist him in his selections for the jury. The average amount of punitive damages most likely to be awarded (i.e., "probable verdict") by a Dallas County jury was determined. The survy data was consistent with the trial team's experience in jury selection and case evaluation. It identified the severe punishment attitude of Dallas County jurors. The results of the community attitudinal analysis which showed how severely a Dallas County juror would punish a defendant for defective equipment that caused death or injury were presented in a settlement brochure to the defendant insurance representatives at a settlement conference. In the event the case did not settle, this tool would also provide the plaintiff with an advantage at the trial. The derived mathematical function would classify prospective jurors into "pro" or "con" groups. This methodology would be used by the trial team to determine those jurors who were favorably predisposed to the awarding of punitive damages. The derived statistics were persuasive in the multi-million dollar settlement of this case.

The community attitude assessment and derivation of juror profiles can assist the trial attorney in his or her choices for the jury. This effective technique does not, of course, guarantee the desired decision. The results should be conceptualized as an additional source of information to be evaluated by the litigator. This information should be augmented by obtaining all other possible information about the prospective jury panel.

II. *BACKGROUND INFORMATION*

An attempt should be made to obtain all available background information about potential jurors without, of course, contacting them in any way. Instead, information should be obtained from readily available public records, such as automobile license registrations, property records, credit services, litigation records, voter registration lists and police accident reports. City directories also provide a useful source of information. A large area map may be obtained and each juror's home should be indicated on it. This should identify the socio-economic strata of each prospective juror. A private investigator or member of the trial team should talk with representatives of the community in order to obtain information about reputation, civic and social memberships, personal experiences and family history. In a small town or rural community local counsel may prove an invaluable aid regarding particular idiosyncrasies of the prospective jurors and other personal knowledge of the community residents. Additionally, local counsel may have maintained information concerning a juror's past behavior in other litigation. This information should be evaluated with the *caveat* that the local attorney's relationship with the community and its members may prejudice his opinions. A community network model of organizations, members and gathering places with resulting "probable contact" with parties and witnesses may be constructed. A photograph of the prospective juror's home (and business) and neighborhood is very helpful. These drive-by photographs or residential observations will reveal, for example, probable property value, neatness and up-keep of lawns and homes, neighborhood area, type of cars, recreational vehicles and recreational items, burglar bars and bumper stickers which reflect important attitudes. Several years ago, I was involved in a case concerning an injury to a small child. Drive-by photographs and residential observations were taken. Those prospective jurors with the popular bumper sticker "Have you hugged a kid today?" were of particular interest. Similarly, in a criminal case, I was not particularly interested in those prospective jurors with "Crime Watch" decals on their windows and large iron security fences. This is additional information that should be processed by the jury selection expert and trial attorney in their assessment of the desirability of a particular juror. The trial attorney may gain an advantage here because opposing counsel may not have collected such information. At the risk of being obvious, pretrial investigation of prospective jurors does not involve direct contact with potential jurors or their family members and is limited only by the amount of money one is willing to spend in this effort.

III. *JUROR PERSONAL HISTORY QUESTIONNAIRE*

Most jurisdictions require prospective jury members to complete a juror Information Card or Juror Qualification Card. These ask for only very limited background information such as age, occupation, marital status, number of children, and involvement with other lawsuits. I recommend that an additional juror questionnaire of personal history be utilized. This questionnaire is typically three to five pages in length and asks detailed basic background questions and questions about attitudes which are relevant to the case. Opposing counsel must be given the opportunity to add or delete questions. The Court will usually allow this questionnaire to be completed on the day of trial unless opposing counsel objects. The Court often has been concerned with the mechanics of copying the completed questionnaires and distributing them quickly. I have found it helpful to have staff members present to assist in copying and assembling the questionnaires. This questionnaire allows for more information to be obtained about a prospective juror. This may assist the trial attorney in effectively and intelligently using his preemptory challenges. I design an extensive questionnaire to be completed by the prospective jurors in both civil and criminal litigation. Initially, I tested the detailed questionnaire as an effective tool for jury selection in 1976. Prospective jurors received a copy of this questionnaire in the mail to be completed in advance of the jury selection in the *United States v. John DeLorean* in 1984.

IV. *DESIGN* VOIR DIRE *QUESTIONS THAT DO MORE THAN MEASURE THE IN-COURT COMMUNICATION SKILL OF A PROSPECTIVE JUROR*

The examiner on *voir dire* should prepare the questions carefully, because *voir dire* may be the most important aspect of the case, and the winning party usually has properly prepared his strategy and questioning for use during jury selection. Impartiality is a state of mind which lawyers say they are looking for in jurors, but in reality impartiality does not exist. Biases and predispositions will determine the outcome of the trial and techniques from the fields of psychology and sociology can provide an advantage to the innovative trial attorney. The jury consultant can assist the litigator in preparing *voir dire* questions that are designed to disclose juror attitudes and backgrounds, while relaxing the jurors and establishing credibility. The questions must condition and educate the prospective jurors about the theory of the case. It is critical that a trial theme be established early in the case and reinforced frequently throughout the litigation. This theme has to begin during *voir dire* and the use of favorable catch phrases or psychological hooks is recommended. Research indicates that the theme that is presented first is more likely to be believed and that a well-prepared average attorney will prevail over a non-prepared more gifted attorney. This preparation must be demonstrated to the jury immediately, however. The jury's attention is greatest during the initial phase of a trial; accordingly, the skillful attorney will get his message on critical issues across at this time.

The jury's first impressions of the courtroom participants are lasting and most difficult to change. My research and investigations indicate that jurors are favorably impressed by the attorney who memorizes the panel members' names. Such personalization creates in the minds of the majority of prospective jurors an image of an attorney who is intelligent, extremely interested in the case and well-prepared. The lawyer who wants to succeed at trial should make the effort to commit the names of the jury panel to memory and to call each prospective juror by his name. Jurorors will award verdicts to lawyers who are able to establish a rapport with them that persuades them to conclude that the lawyer is sincere, honest, knowledgeable about the law and well prepared.

In a civil trial the attorney for the plaintiff must get the attention and arouse the interest of the jury immediately on *voir dire.* Jurors who are assigned to a trial court in most metropolitan areas are herded and shuffled and are already feeling "put down" by the time they appear for trial. Most of the panel would rather be somewhere else; they believe their time is too valuable to waste at the courthouse. Thorough organization, a central theme, candor, and brevity often can help to accomplish the desired result on *voir dire.*

An effective *voir dire* should include open-ended questions which often begin with the phrase "How do you. . .?" and "What are the. . .?" The difference in obtaining a one-word meaningless response to an inquiry such as "The plaintiff in this case is asking for one million dollars. Do you believe anyone can be so injured that she should be awarded that sum?" versus a revealing explanation which is required by the question: "How do you feel about awarding a sum as large as one million dollars?" is readily apparent. An important follow up question can be "How did you feel when I asked you that question?" Since most jurors are unfamiliar with the courtroom environment, the anxiety and tension they feel must be dissipated. Otherwise, the juror will not self-disclose his true feeling and opinions during *voir dire* examination.

Experienced trial attorneys and jury consultants agree on several basic premises:

1. Jurors should be similar to the client or be able to identify with the client and this similarity or identification must be realized and brought home to the jury on *voir dire.*
2. The trial attorney must not make a statement during *voir dire* that he cannot substantiate during the trial.
3. The trial attorney must expose any and all negative aspects of his position at this time. He then has an opportunity to deal with the negative issues in his case with the jury and to learn from them how they will react to this evidence.
4. During the *voir dire* the trial lawyer must discuss the critical issues in the lawsuits and they should be kept simple and as few as possible. Catch phrases or psychological hooks should be repeated during all aspects of trial.

An excellent question to ask in *any* type of litigation is a potential juror's position on capital punishment. Research on personality and capital punishment indicates that an individual who is in favor of the death penalty is more likely to convict in *any* type of criminal case. Interestingly, a profile of the pro-death penalty person and his behavior in civil litigation has been researched with the conclusion that this type of juror is more inclined to punish the negligent tortfeasor for wrongdoing, but is reluctant to reward a slightly negligent plaintiff.

The jury and trial consultant can assist the attorney in the evaluation of verbal, nonverbal, and group behavior. The silent messages of the individual jurors are noted and evaluated. There is a tendency on the part of some persons to misstate the truth during *voir dire* examination. This may be the result of peer pressure, or a desire to be seated on the jury, or the lack of recognition of a prejudice. The choice of words and the immediacy of the response by the prospective juror are keys to the truthfulness of his answers. The prospective juror's response to the plaintiff's attorney is compared with his manner of responding to defendant's attorney and to the Court. Basic background questioning provides a response baseline. His manner of baseline responding is compared to his responses on critical or case-related inquiries. The maintenance of eye contact is noted, as are such responses as fear or anxiety. Unfinished sentences, deep breathing, and disjointed thoughts may indicate anxiety. Inappropriate laughter often indicates a need for approval. It is important to note the posture and walking style of each prospective juror as he enters the courtroom, since this is one measure of confidence of a person. It is most important to interpret the overall gestalt of the prospective juror and not to rely on one gesture or one response to imply a certain personality type. Observing and interpreting verbal and nonverbal communication provides the trial team with additional valuable information about a prospective juror.

Research has been conducted on the group dynamics or group behavior during jury deliberations. Any group will break down into subgroups and from each subgroup a leader will emerge. This subgroup formation is an important variable to consider in jury selection. The trial attorney should consider the balance of dominant, passive, and flexible personalities that is desired on the jury. In a twelve-person jury, the decision will actually be made by three or four persuaders. The remaining members on the jury will simply go along with the persuaders. The successful advocate will direct the trial to these dominant persuaders. As a general premise, these three or four influential and dominant persons are the more highly educated ones and who rank higher on the socio-economical scale than do the other jurors.

V. FOCUS GROUP

A focus group is a relatively new concept in the litigation field that can be used to great advantage. It has rapidly gained acceptance among trial attorneys as a powerful technique for evaluating litigation issues. The focus group is defined as a question and answer session about the issues of the litigation matter.

The trial team can make economical use of a focus group when the budget does not permit in-depth or other research. The expense of this critical issues study is considerably less than other techniques of systematic jury research. The focus or deliberation group is composed of three to ten persons. Ideally, these participants will be similar in characteristics to jurors to be chosen from a particular community. The group is presented important facts, issues, and attitudes of the case for discussion. The jury expert leads the group discussion and the trial team may hear the discussions via closed circuit television. This discussion may last several hours or several days. The procedure can be repeated with several different groups of participants in order to ensure reliability and validity. Leading a deliberation group effectively requires considerable skill, because the leader must invoke the participants' true feelings, reactions, impressions and biases.

In reality, the concept of a focus group has been present forever. It involves talking with people and encouraging them to share ideas, feelings, and opinions. This concept of group opinions has been employed in marketing research for approximately twenty-five years. A product is evaluated by a potential buyer's participation in a focus group to determine how he really feels about the product, idea, or need for such a product. Therefore, it only makes good sense that a litigator should seek to evaluate his case prior to a jury's verdict.

No witnesses are presented to the participants in the focus group. The basic issues and strategies are presented to the group for evaluation and discussion. The leader guides the group in dealing with specific facts. From my experience in conducting deliberation groups, I have identified the following consistent trends among the participants, regardless of where the study is conducted:

1. Over eighty percent of the participants believe that citizens accused of a crime are probably guilty. However, these people believe they can be fair and impartial jurors. Approximately three-fourths of this group will also state that it is not possible that

the citizen accused of a crime could be not guilty, while still maintaining that they can be fair and impartial.

2. Over ninety percent of the participants believe that if the citizen who is accused does not testify, it is because he is guilty.
3. Over eighty percent of the participants have difficulty in awarding damages for injuries which do not have a demonstrable physical effect.
4. Over seventy percent of the participants initially expect the defense's expert witnesses to be more credible than the plaintiff's.

In summary, the participants in the focus group must be directed by the jury expert in order to obtain maximum benefits because this informed leadership is required in order to uncover latent feelings and to generate original thoughts. This setting permits discovery of how people really view life and its issues. For example, the focus group may be asked "What would you have to hear to decide the citizen accused is not guilty?" and "How large an award do you think this injury is worth?" Under proper guidance the discussion can unveil the reaction of the participants to a great many issues in a short period of time. This procedure will give the trial attorney insight into the issues and problem areas the real jury will discuss in reaching a verdict:

VI. *TRIAL SIMULATION*

A. *Mock or Mini Trial*

A more elaborate technique for evaluating litigation issues and obtaining feedback about issues, witnesses, and the trial attorney is the "mock" or "mini" trial. Mock trials were first employed in the early 1980's in preparation for trial and for improvement of trial presentation. The mock trial involves the simulation of an actual trial with opening statements, witnesses, evidence, closing argument, jury deliberation and verdict. *Voir dire* is optional. Twelve persons who are representative of the people who are most likely to appear on the jury are employed as mock jurors. The litigation matter is presented to the mock jurors in a condensed fashion. The opponent's witnesses are role played as is opposing counsel. The opponent's opening statement, final argument, and questioning of key witnesses are anticipated and presented to the jury. Critical demonstrative evidence may be presented for evaluation.

Attorneys typically do not practice the theory of the case and the strategy. This innovative concept allows the lawyer to determine how the mock jurors react to his theory of the case, certain witnesses' testimony and the litigator himself. This "test" run of the case also affords the opportunity to gain insight into the group dynamics of jury deliberation. Lawyers have typically practiced opening statements, final arguments, examination of witnesses and some cross-examinations. The mock trial now allows practice of most of a trial on a "test" audience. A dress rehearsal of the case can determine the effectiveness of a particular strategy, opening and closing arguments, and expert witnesses, as well as the effectiveness of the attorney. It can also be helpful in determining the profile of the 'ideal' and 'least desirable' juror. The attorney may want to include a videotape of this mock jury's deliberation in a settlement brochure which could be presented to the insurance company. The attorney and trial team observe the mock jury as it deals with the issues and the witnesses presented. This prevents the attorney from urging or defending a case in which he has no conception of how jurors will react to the fact of his case.

I recommend that the entire proceedings of the mock trial be videotaped. Then the tapes can be coded for important points and discussion in order to quickly refer back to parts of the mock trial. Most importantly, the attorneys can hear and see the mock jury discuss the issues and reach their verdict by a one way mirror. After the mock jury has worked through the issues to a verdict, including damages awarded, they are debriefed by the jury consultant. The attorney may discuss the witnesses and issues with the mock panel if he so desires. A transcription of the deliberation phase of the mock jury should be made. This will identify the thought processes of the jurors as well as questions to be answered for the actual jury. The trial attorney may be surprised at the reasons attributed to the group's decision and the effect of dominant or persuasive personalities on the group process. Useful information and insight into the strengths and weaknesses of the case is obtained from this informal discussion.

The mock or mini trial is an excellent diagnostic mechanism to uncover the strengths and weaknesses of the case. It paints in broad strokes the picture the actual jury will receive at trial time. I have found the mock trial to be invaluable for testing trial strategy and for preparation.

B. *Mirror or Shadow Jury*

A powerful litigation tool with startling accuracy is the simulated jury used during the courtroom trial. This is commonly referred to as a "mirror" or "shadow" jury. The shadow jury observes the courtroom proceedings from the same perspective as the actual jury. The shadow jury is impaneled by selecting twelve (or six) persons from an initial panel of about twenty who most nearly match the actual jury in demographic characteristics and attitudes. Of course, no two people will match exactly on all factors such as education, occupation, marital history and attitudes. However, the goal of the trial consultant is to check the progress of the trial and to obtain observations from the shadow jury at a point when the attorney still has control over the courtroom proceedings and the opportunity to correct misimpressions and to answer questions.

This innovative concept allows the trial attorney to receive daily evaluations of the reactions of the jury to the evidence and witnesses. The courtroom trial is virtually the only professional endeavor that does not have monitoring and the necessary adjusting as a result of this monitoring. For example, the theater would not begin a play without a dress rehearsal nor would a surgeon operate without monitoring the vital signs of the patient. The mirror or shadow jury was designed to help an attorney to monitor his progress and to obtain feedback at a time when corrections are still possible.

The mirror jurors are employed to work in the same manner as the actual jurors. They must observe the trial each day, hearing and seeing only the evidence that the actual jury does. They discuss the case only with the jury expert who meets with them each day. The mirror jurors soon assume psychologically the same position as the real jurors.

The trial consultant analyses the information, both positive and negative, and interprets it for the trial attorney. Important aspects of the case will be revealed, such as:

a. The level or degree of comprehension and understanding of the evidence;
b. A determination of the attorney's effectiveness and the strengths and weaknesses of the case;
c. Acceptance, evaluation and understanding of expert technical testimony;
d. What the primary deciding factors of the case are;

e. Most importantly, how the case and lawyer are being received.

In addition to the advantage of daily feedback, both positive and negative, the shadow jury can be polled each day on the liability issue and amount of damages to be awarded. This information can be helpful in knowing whether to accept a settlement offer or, if you represent the defense, to make a settlement offer.

A six-person shadow jury that I recently conducted in a month-long medical malpractice case gave very important information to the trial team. The key qualities of the actual jury were identified and people were selected who matched those qualities, including the demographic characteristics. This group of selected persons and I sat in the courtroom daily. We did not sit together so as not to be obvious. (Opposing counsel may attempt to let the actual jury know of the existence and purpose of the shadow jury; therefore, it is recommended that a Motion in Limine be urged in order to prevent the actual jury from being prejudiced against the party using this method.) Our small in-court 'jury' was debriefed each evening as to their retention, reaction and feelings as to the witnesses, attorneys, demonstrative evidence, and the case generally.

The debriefing revealed important information as to the attitudes carried by the jury in this medical malpractice litigation. Our group revealed that they were concerned that the defendant doctors would lose their licenses and the right to practice medicine if they were found liable for medical negligence. It became apparent that the burden of proof in medical malpractice litigation is significantly altered by the juror's traditional and respectful attitude toward the medical profession. The proof required by the jury, before a verdict against the doctors is possible, approaches the criminal burden of "beyond a reasonable doubt." After it was discovered that the jury felt so protective toward the defendant doctors and hospital, these concepts were repeatedly diffused throughout the trial.

The feedback from the mirror jury pointed out that after several days of technical medical testimony, they were mostly confused and largely failed to comprehend this information. For example, they were confused by the technical testimony of the medical expert witneses as to whether or not excessive oxygen to new born infants caused blindness. The lead counsel changed his trial strategy when he learned that our monitoring group, when they were confused, simply substituted their common sense for the technical and conflicting testimony of the experts. Our 'jury' group thought that an expert witness lost credibility when it learned that he was of foreign birth, had been educated abroad, or was an academician or "teaching" doctor and not a treating one. It became necessary to clarify these points at the trial the next day by presenting additional testimony. The shadow jury wanted to have all these matters explained, regardless of how seemingly unimportant they may appear to the trial attorney. It was through our discussions with the shadow jury that we learned that there existed a need for additional evidence in order to convince this group of the negligence of the defendant hospital and doctors.

The lack of understanding of the expert technical testimony concerning the mechanism of 'too much' oxygen causing blindness in newborn infants that was discovered in our debriefing session, was used as a guide for extensive questioning of the expert medical rebuttal witness in order to remove any doubt concerning the defendants' being responsible for the blindness of the baby.

The proposed change was examined by our group for comprehension of terminology and responses. This resulted in our compiling a list of problems or questions raised during the deliberations. These difficult areas which had been identified were addressed in final argument in such a way that the actual jury's confusion was eliminated or reduced.

In summary, the trial team was heavily influenced by comments from these shadow jurors and structured the presentation of the case and argument around their attitudes and beliefs. The shadow jury returned its verdict within two hundred thousand dollars of the multimillion dollar award made by the actual twelve-man jury that heard the case.

The interaction with our shadow jury reaffirmed the premise that people enter the jury box with preconceived prejudices, feelings, passions, and beliefs which affect the way they see and hear the evidence. The juror selectively perceives the evidence to support his feelings about the litigation. In fact, the "pigeon-hole" theory of perception is a typical jury phenomenon. This means that a person who has reached an early decision will focus on certain facts and selectively accept those facts which support his already held opinion and, consequently, reject all contrary evidence no matter how persuasive.

Our six-person jury formed subgroups within itself. This subgroup formation is an important factor in the decision-making process. Three subgroups typically emerge:

1. those who are pro-plaintiff;
2. those who are pro-defendant; and
3. those who decline to verbalize an opinion.

Each group will have a strong leader. These groups exert influence on each other and the members of the group are able to learn the other viewpoints prior to the deliberation phase by verbal and non-verbal communication. It is important to identify the subgroup structure in the actual jury. Some clues to this discovery is who goes to lunch together, talks together at recesses, or who rides to the courthouse together. Jurors, like people everywhere, tend to associate with fellows who are of a similar perceived opinion.

The use of the shadow group during trial considerably reduces the unpredictability of results. Through this technique a measuring stick is provided that can provide a reading as to how the evidence was received and what impact it had on the jury. My personal experience has shown me that many times the shadow jury will reach the same conclusion as does the actual trial jury, even as to the amount of damages. In fact, the mirror jury has been identical on the liability issues and within 10% of the amount awarded by the actual jury in all proceedings in which I have participated.

VII. *GENERAL COMMENTS*

It is my observation that in a trial nothing is too trivial or unimportant to be overlooked. Even the manner of the dress by the client, witnesses, and attorney should be considered. All the participants in the courtroom are closely watched by the jurors. The manner in which one is dressed makes a statement to the jury. Dress is a medium of communication that conveys information about who a person is and is not. Observers use clothing to categorize people on variables as a social status, occupation, ethnicity, sex-role identification, honesty, believability, and perceived credibility. To insure success, an attorney should know what statements are being made by his client, his witnesses, and himself.

A videotape rehearsal can be used to show the attorney, client and witnesses how they will be perceived at trial, and specific problem areas can be identified and dealt with. For instance, most witnesses look at the attorney who is questioning them rather than at the jury. A videotape rehearsal demonstrates this and the witness can change his courtroom behavior so that he can make eye contact with the jury as he gives his testimony.

The jury expert can also assist the litigation team with demonstrative evidence. Research indicates that jurors recall only about 40% of what they have heard after a span of three hours and only 10% of what they have heard after a time lapse of one day. Advertising has recognized this human limitation for years. For example, commercials on television average thirty seconds because the average attention span is twenty to thirty seconds and the research indicates that persons must observe an object for approximately twenty-five seconds for retention. The use of demonstrative evidence can increase retention to slightly less than 75% after a time interval of three hours and an increase to 60% retention following a day of testimony.

One of the questions most frequently asked at seminars is "what type of person do I want on a damage suit jury or a criminal case?" Stereotypes are too dangerous to rely on exclusively. The decision-making process is so complex that it cannot be reduced to workable broad generalizations. Too many variables and interactions have to be considered. However, a good rule in jury selection is to find out *who* the prospective jurors are and *what* they think about themselves. A basic concept of human behavior is that if one thinks negatively about himself, he is unlikely to think positively of your client. The prospective juror should be content with his station in life, regardless of what it may be. Also, given the limitation of generalizations, one can state that the best predictors are usually occupation, age, education, frequency of church attendance and religion, and sex. For example, those in detailed occupations, such as electrical engineering, are more inclined to focus on the logic of the case and not the emotional component. The younger jurors are more inclined to see the litigation in terms of right or wrong. Attractive people, whether client or attorney, will do better in litigation than unattractive people. However, this basic statement is confounded with sex. An attractive male fares better in all situations; but, an attractive female may be disliked by less attractive female jurors and may threaten the male jurors.

Again, there is little evidence to support stereotypes in the courtroom. Such stereotypes are usually just common sense deductions and idiosyncratic experience. The "identify" or "similarity" theory does have some support in the literature. The attorney would like those jurors who are empathetic to his client and can identify with, or are similar to, the client and his facts.

The use of systematic jury selection techniques can assist the trial attorney in obtaining a successful verdict. There is no logical reason why the attorney should leave something as critical as jury selection to chance. The use of these techniques reduces chance and complements the attorney's intuitive approach or personal formula for success. Trial attorneys around the country who have used the methods discussed here consistently acknowledge their helpfulness and effectiveness.

NOTES

1. *The American Jury,* 1966, pages 352–372.
2. Younger, "Unlawful Peremptory Challenges," *Litigation,* Fall 1980, p. 23.
3. "*Voir Dire* Examination: An Empirical Study," 385 Cal. L. Rev. 503, 505 (1965).
4. Fahringer, "In the Valley of the Blind: A Primer on Jury Selection in a Criminal Case," *Trial Diplomacy Journal* Vol III No 2 (1980).
5. *Trial Diplomacy Journal* Jury Study, Vol V No 1 and No 2.
6. "Study Says Attitudes of Jurors Hurt U.S. in Its 'Political Trials,'" *N.Y. Times,* April 19, 1975, p. 15.

INDEX